Improving the Performance of Wireless LANs

A Practical Guide

CHAPMAN & HALL/CRC
COMPUTER and INFORMATION SCIENCE SERIES

Series Editor: Sartaj Sahni

PUBLISHED TITLES

ADVERSARIAL REASONING: COMPUTATIONAL APPROACHES TO READING THE OPPONENT'S MIND
Alexander Kott and William M. McEneaney

DELAUNAY MESH GENERATION
Siu-Wing Cheng, Tamal Krishna Dey, and Jonathan Richard Shewchuk

DISTRIBUTED SENSOR NETWORKS, SECOND EDITION
S. Sitharama Iyengar and Richard R. Brooks

DISTRIBUTED SYSTEMS: AN ALGORITHMIC APPROACH
Sukumar Ghosh

ENERGY-AWARE MEMORY MANAGEMENT FOR EMBEDDED MULTIMEDIA SYSTEMS: A COMPUTER-AIDED DESIGN APPROACH
Florin Balasa and Dhiraj K. Pradhan

ENERGY EFFICIENT HARDWARE-SOFTWARE CO-SYNTHESIS USING RECONFIGURABLE HARDWARE
Jingzhao Ou and Viktor K. Prasanna

FUNDAMENTALS OF NATURAL COMPUTING: BASIC CONCEPTS, ALGORITHMS, AND APPLICATIONS
Leandro Nunes de Castro

HANDBOOK OF ALGORITHMS FOR WIRELESS NETWORKING AND MOBILE COMPUTING
Azzedine Boukerche

HANDBOOK OF APPROXIMATION ALGORITHMS AND METAHEURISTICS
Teofilo F. Gonzalez

HANDBOOK OF BIOINSPIRED ALGORITHMS AND APPLICATIONS
Stephan Olariu and Albert Y. Zomaya

HANDBOOK OF COMPUTATIONAL MOLECULAR BIOLOGY
Srinivas Aluru

HANDBOOK OF DATA STRUCTURES AND APPLICATIONS
Dinesh P. Mehta and Sartaj Sahni

HANDBOOK OF DYNAMIC SYSTEM MODELING
Paul A. Fishwick

HANDBOOK OF ENERGY-AWARE AND GREEN COMPUTING
Ishfaq Ahmad and Sanjay Ranka

HANDBOOK OF PARALLEL COMPUTING: MODELS, ALGORITHMS AND APPLICATIONS
Sanguthevar Rajasekaran and John Reif

HANDBOOK OF REAL-TIME AND EMBEDDED SYSTEMS
Insup Lee, Joseph Y-T. Leung, and Sang H. Son

PUBLISHED TITLES CONTINUED

Improving the Performance of Wireless LANs

A Practical Guide

Nurul Sarkar

CRC Press
Taylor & Francis Group
Boca Raton London New York

CRC Press is an imprint of the
Taylor & Francis Group, an **informa** business

A CHAPMAN & HALL BOOK

CRC Press
Taylor & Francis Group
6000 Broken Sound Parkway NW, Suite 300
Boca Raton, FL 33487-2742

© 2014 by Taylor & Francis Group, LLC
CRC Press is an imprint of Taylor & Francis Group, an Informa business

No claim to original U.S. Government works

Printed on acid-free paper
Version Date: 20130729

International Standard Book Number-13: 978-1-4665-6063-5 (Hardback)

Library of Congress Cataloging-in-Publication Data

Sarkar, Nurul.
    Improving the performance of wireless LANs : a practical guide / author, Nurul Sarkar.
        pages cm -- (Chapman & Hall/CRC computer and information science series)
    Includes bibliographical references and index.
    ISBN 978-1-4665-6063-5 (alk. paper)
    1. Wireless LANs. 2. Network performance (Telecommunication) I. Title.

TK5105.78.S27 2014
004.6'8--dc23   2013028432

Visit the Taylor & Francis Web site at
http://www.taylorandfrancis.com

and the CRC Press Web site at
http://www.crcpress.com

To my parents, my wife, Laila A. Sarkar,
and my son, Hamidul I. Sarkar

Contents

SECTION III CONCLUDING REMARKS

Foreword

I T HAS BEEN MORE than a decade since wireless local area networks (WLANs) based on the IEEE 802.11 standard family have become commercialized. Inexpensive WLAN access points have found their way into almost every household and enterprise, and WLAN devices are embedded in the chips of laptops, tablets, mobile phones, printers, and many other household and commercial appliances. The networking capability of the WLAN has made it one of the most successful technologies of the 21st century, and its use has become almost irreplaceable with any other communications technology.

The ease of use in WLAN and seamless mobility among applications are the most important features of it. In comparison with advanced cellular data technologies like 3G universal mobile telecommunications system (UMTS) and long term evolution (LTE), WLAN still provides great speed and ease of use, making it a great companion for data communications in indoor and even outdoor environments. The early problems of the WLAN, including security and data rate, have been gradually resolved to a degree that people now comfortably use its services without such worries. With all the advances in WLAN standards, still it relies on a good-wired backbone, whether in the form of an asymmetric digital subscriber line (ADSL), wired LAN, or other technologies.

The performance of the WLAN is, however, very dependent on traffic conditions and environmental factors. The WLAN may work perfectly when a few users share a limited inward Internet access, but its performance would rapidly degrade if there were too many users trying to share a single access point. Some of the parameters affecting the WLAN performance go back to the legacy Transmission Control Protocol/Internet Protocol (TCP/IP) model, while other parameters come from the way the IEEE 802.11 standards manage the physical and medium access control (MAC) layers of the WLAN.

In this book, Dr. Nurul Sarkar has tried to explore the performance issues of the WLAN in a very practical and efficient way. Starting with the explanation of the WLAN features and standards, the author has provided a complete guideline to the design and deployment of the WLAN system. The second part of the book provides a very useful study on propagation and MAC performance issues affecting the WLAN with some real experimental data. Each chapter of the book is accompanied by some mini-projects, making the book ideal for being used in classrooms by the students.

Dr. Sarkar has contributed a milestone to the theory and practice of WLAN systems with the publication of this book. Specifically, this book has marked the latest information and future research direction for an important technology of this century.

Besides addressing the fundamentals of the WLAN systems, which have been the subject of previous books, this book provides additional practical information, including site measurements, environmental effects on WLAN performance, protocol redesign for routing and MAC, and traffic distribution. The book also provides some useful guidelines to planning and deployment of a good WLAN system in different residential and commercial buildings, and concludes with recent and future development of the WLAN for emerging applications. To summarize, this book stands at the forefront of current literature in the field of WLAN technology.

Abbas Jamalipour, PhD, Fellow IEEE, Fellow IEICE, Fellow IEAust
Professor of Ubiquitous Mobile Networking
School of Electrical and Information Engineering
University of Sydney, NSW
Australia

Preface

THERE HAS BEEN TREMENDOUS growth in the deployment of IEEE 802.11-based wireless local area networks (WLANs) in recent years. This growth is as a result of flexibility, low cost, simplicity, and user mobility offered by the technology. Such networks are being deployed widely in homes, offices, schools, shops, hotels, warehouses, factories, and almost anywhere that people live and work. Despite the potential benefits of WLANs, one of the challenges faced by network researchers and engineers of WLANs is to increase capacity (per user) and quality of service (QoS) of a typical WLAN with a medium to large number of users. Another challenge is to provide a better QoS to all active users in harsh propagation environments, such as obstructed office buildings, noise, or interfering signals.

It is well known that the traditional 802.11 WLANs do not perform well with respect to actual data rate and response time under medium to high traffic loads. For example, network performance drops significantly when multiple users access the Internet concurrently. A good knowledge and understanding of WLAN performance is required for efficient design and deployment of such systems.

While there are numerous literature and textbooks on wireless networks, very few of them actually quantify the key performance-limiting factors and describe the methods of improving WLAN performance. This book bridges the gap by providing practical guidelines for improving wireless network performance. This book provides both theoretical background and empirical results for the design and deployment of indoor WLAN systems. The key factors influencing WLAN performance are identified and measured. This book describes various techniques for improving WLAN performance and provides guidelines for optimum system design and deployment.

I believe this book is unique and is a useful resource to students, teachers, and network researchers, designers, and planners at the university, polytechnic, and private training institutions.

This book has the following salient features:

- Provides comprehensive coverage in a single text on WLAN performance for students (both senior undergraduate and postgraduate) and network researchers from industry and academia

- Offers students, faculties, researchers, engineers, network designers, and planners both theoretical background and practical knowledge of design, modeling, and performance evaluation of WLANs

- Presents empirical study through radio propagation measurements and simulations for various network design scenarios

- Provides an overview of the latest emerging network technologies, such as next-generation Wi-Fi (802.11ac), very high throughput Wi-Fi (802.11ad), wireless mesh networking (802.11s), emergency QoS (802.11u), and vehicle-to-vehicle communications (802.11p)

- Enhances teaching and learning, and research capability in the area of WLAN performance at all levels

- Presents highly technical subject matter without complex mathematical formulas by using a balance of text and figures

- Begins each chapter with a set of learning outcomes (what the learner would be able to achieve after reading each chapter) and provides chapter summary as well as review questions at the end, including additional reading list

- Provides numerous illustrations, practical examples, mini-projects, and an extensive glossary and a list of acronyms

ORGANIZATION AND OUTLINE

The book is organized into three sections:

Section I: "Theoretical Background." Section I consists of Chapters 1 through 6 and provides an introduction and background information for WLAN design and performance improvement. Chapter 1 provides a rationale for the book. Chapter 2 highlights WLAN architecture, 802.11 physical layer (PHY) and medium access control (MAC) layer characteristics, and performance-limiting factors. The radio propagation environment, wireless MAC and routing protocols, and cross-layer design (CLD) optimization all play an important role in determining the performance of a typical WLAN. I have therefore dedicated separate chapters to deal with each of these WLAN performance-limiting factors: Chapter 3 for radio propagation characteristics, Chapter 4 for wireless MAC protocols, Chapter 5 for wireless routing protocols, and Chapter 6 for CLD optimization.

Section II: "Empirical Study." Section II consists of Chapters 7 through 14 and provides a detailed coverage of the various methods for improving WLAN performance and the related issues supported by empirical results. While there are many factors that cause WLAN performance to drop, wireless access methods (network protocols) and places (environments) where wireless networks are being used are the most significant. Other factors, such as audio and video traffic, routing protocols, radio signal blockage by walls and floors, antenna type, and signal interference also influence WLAN performance. The key factors influencing the performance of a typical 802.11-based WLAN, such as propagation environment, wireless protocols, access point (AP) configuration, routing protocols, CLD optimization, and traffic type and their distributions, are thoroughly investigated and reported in this section. A study on the effect of antenna type, and signal interference on WLAN performance is beyond the scope of the book.

The effect of radio propagation environments on WLAN performance is reported in Chapter 7. Chapter 8 presents propagation measurement results for the performance study of 802.11g in an obstructed office space. Chapter 9 reports on a class of wireless MAC protocol called buffer unit multiple access (BUMA), which was developed by modifying an 802.11 protocol. The effect of AP configuration and placement is investigated in Chapter 10. The effect of routing protocols on WLAN performance is examined in Chapter 11. Chapter 12 reports on improving WLAN performance by CLD optimization. The effect of traffic distribution on WLAN performance is investigated in Chapter 13. Chapter 14 examines the combined effect of signal strength and traffic type on WLAN performance.

Section III: "Concluding Remarks." Section III consists of Chapters 15 and 16 and provides an overview of system implications and recent developments in WLANs. Chapter 15 summarizes the key findings from Chapters 7 to 14 and provides implications for WLAN design and deployment from a system planning point of view. Finally, Chapter 16 introduces some recent developments and emerging technologies in WLANs, such as 802.11n, 802.11ac, 802.11ad, 802.11u emergency QoS, 802.11p V2V communication, 802.11s mesh networking, 802.22 cognitive radio networks, green communication and networking, and 802.11i secure WLAN.

TARGET AUDIENCE FOR THIS BOOK

This book is written for both an academic and a professional audience. The book would be a useful resource (handbook) for students, faculties, and network researchers, engineers, developers, and planners who are interested in getting into the most recent advances in wireless network design, modeling, and performance evaluation. As a textbook, it can be used in a second course on wireless communication and networking with a prerequisite course on introductory networking or data communications. It should also be useful to practitioners in the wireless networking and telecommunication industry.

HOW TO USE THIS BOOK

The theoretical foundation, new ideas, and empirical results presented enable the book to be used by teachers, students, and practitioners as a practical handbook for enhancing teaching and learning of WLAN design, planning, deployment, and performance evaluation. Students can also benefit from the learning aids, such as learning outcomes, list of suggested readings, summaries, key terms, figures and illustrations, review questions, and mini-projects, that are provided in each chapter.

Some of the possible courses for which this book can be used include those on advanced computer networks, high-performance networks, wireless communication networks, and network performance evaluation. There is enough material in the book for a one-semester or one-quarter course for 12 or 13 weeks of lectures. Individuals would benefit by revisiting the chapters on wireless MAC and routing protocol in Section I before studying Section II. However, advanced students may skip Section I and study Section II straightaway.

Professionals working as network engineers, research scientists, and network administrators will also find this book a valuable reference to the most recent advances in WLANs in general and performance issues in particular. *Network engineers* can use this book as a reference handbook. They can skip Section I and read Chapter 15 ("Implications for System Planning and Deployment") from Section III before reading the relevant chapters from Section II. In fact, Chapter 15 is written for network engineers and practitioners highlighting the implications for network design and performance evaluation. *Network practitioners* can skip Section I and read relevant chapters from Section II; for example, Chapters 7, 8, and 10 for propagation measurements results and Chapters 9, 11, and 12 for network modeling and simulation experiments.

LEARNING AIDS

The book provides the following learning aids:

- **Learning outcomes:** Each chapter begins with a list of learning outcomes that preview the chapter's main ideas and highlights the key concepts and skills that students can achieve by completing the chapter. Learning outcomes also assist teachers in preparing a lesson plan for a particular topic.

- **Figures and illustrations:** The key concepts in wireless networking and communications are illustrated using diagrams and screenshots throughout the book. These illustrations help students to develop a better understanding of the key wireless networking concept.

- **Further reading:** A list of readings at the end of each chapter provides learners with valuable resources for independent exploration on specific topics of interest. These lists are particularly useful for network researchers and professionals.

- **Summary:** Each chapter provides a brief summary of the contents presented in the chapter. This helps learners to preview key ideas in the chapter before moving on to the next chapter.

- **Key terms:** Each chapter provides a set of key terms and abbreviations. Both students and teachers can benefit by using the listing of key terms to recall key wireless networking and communication concepts before and after reading the chapter.

- **Glossary:** A glossary of wireless networking terms is provided at the end of the book. Both students and teachers may benefit by using the glossary to brush up on the key concepts of wireless communication and networking terms, perhaps before reading the chapter.

- **Review questions:** Each chapter provides a set of end-of-chapter review questions linked to the learning objectives, allowing the teachers to evaluate their teaching effectiveness. Answers to most of the review questions can be found in the relevant chapter(s), and hence students are encouraged to revisit the relevant sections of the chapter to answer the questions. By answering the review questions, students can develop a deeper understanding of many key wireless networking concepts and tools. Teachers and instructors can use the review questions to test their teaching effectiveness and to initiate class discussion.

- **Mini-projects:** For each chapter, a list of problems or performance evaluation experiments is provided for advanced students to explore wireless networking and communication concepts and to gain a deeper understanding of the topics and solutions described in the chapter. The practical activities in the form of small projects can be carried out using tools such as ns-2, Omnet, OPNET, and other credible simulators. OPNET IT Guru (a smaller version of OPNET commercial network simulator), which can be downloaded at no cost, could also be used to conduct some of the mini-projects. Some advanced mini-projects are quite challenging and can be given to students as whole semester projects.

Acknowledgments

I THANK THE AUTHORITY OF Auckland University of Technology for giving me support in many different ways to complete this work. I also thank two reviewers for their constructive feedback to improve the overall quality of work, especially review questions and mini-projects. I am pleased to acknowledge the help of my former postgraduate students Eric Lo, for conducting radio propagation measurements contributing to Chapter 8, and Wilford Lol, for conducting MANET simulation experiments for Chapter 11. My thanks go to the entire production team at Taylor & Francis Group for their ongoing support. Last and most importantly, I thank my wife, Laila Sarkar, for her patience, love, and encouragement throughout this project.

Nurul I. Sarkar

About the Author

NURUL I. SARKAR IS an associate professor in the School of Computer and Mathematical Sciences at Auckland University of Technology (AUT), New Zealand. He is regularly invited to give keynote talks on his field of specialization at various national and international forums. He has more than 18 years of teaching experience in universities at both the undergraduate and postgraduate levels and has taught a range of subjects, including computer networking, data communications, wireless networking, computer hardware, and e-commerce. He holds a PhD in electrical and electronic engineering (field of study: wireless networks) from the University of Auckland. *Tools for Teaching Computer Networking and Hardware Concepts*, his first edited book, was published by IGI Global in 2006 and has received commendation worldwide.

Dr. Sarkar leads the Network and Security Research Group at AUT. He has published more than 120 articles in refereed international journal and conference proceedings, including *IEEE Transactions on Education, Elsevier Journal of Network and Computer Applications, International Journal of Wireless and Mobile Networks, International Journal of Advanced Pervasive and Ubiquitous Computing, International Journal of Business Data Communications and Networking, Journal of Selected Areas in Telecommunications, International Journal of Wireless Networks and Broadband Technologies, Measurement Science and*

Technology, International Journal of Web-Based Learning and Teaching Technologies, International Journal of Electrical Engineering Education, International Journal of Technology Diffusion, International Journal of ICT Education, and *SIGCSE Bulletin.* He has had several externally funded research grants, including a TEC collaborative research grant of nearly $650K, TechNZ (FRST) grant, BuildIT grant, and University of Auckland grant.

Dr. Sarkar was the recipient of AUT's Design and Creative Technologies Faculty Research Awards 2012 and the co-recipient of the 2009 IJICTE editor's award for most outstanding paper for a research article on mini-project-based learning as an effective tool for teaching advanced computer networks to graduate students. He was also the co-recipient of the 2006 IRMA International Conference Best Paper Award for a fundamental paper on the modeling and simulation of wireless networks. His research interests are in multidisciplinary areas, including wireless network architecture, wireless MAC and routing protocols, multiple QoS supporting emergency traffic in WLANs and WiMAX, voice over IP (VoIP) and video over WLANs, wireless mesh networks, cognitive radio networks, network security, and tools to enhance methods for teaching and learning computer networking and hardware concepts.

Dr. Sarkar is a member of various professional organizations and societies, including IEEE Communications Society (ComSoc) and Australasian Association for Engineering Education. He served as chairman of the IEEE joint New Zealand North and South ComSoc Chapter, which won the "Best Chapter Achievement Award" in 2012. He was a guest editor for *AP Journal of Networks* and is an associate editor for *International Journal of Wireless Networks and Broadband Technologies,* and member of various international editorial review boards. He served as associate technical editor for the *IEEE Communications Magazine* (2005–2010), and TPC co-chair for IEEE ICC 2014, APCC 2012, IEEE TENCON 2010, and ATNAC 2010. Dr. Sarkar serves on the technical program committees of various leading networking conferences (e.g., IEEE Globecom, ICC, WCNC, PIMRC, UbiCoNet, ISCC, ATNAC, APCC, and ACM SIGCSE) as well as track and session chairs for several national and international forums. Dr. Sarkar is a senior member of IEEE and fellow of ITU-UUM.

Acronyms

802.11	IEEE 802.11
ACK	Acknowledgment
AODV	Ad hoc on-demand distance vector
AP	Access point
ARF	Automatic rate fallback
ARQ	Automatic request
BEB	Binary exponential backoff
BER	Bit error rate
BPSK	Binary phase-shift keying
BS	Base station
BSS	Basic service set
BTMA	Busy tone multiple access
BUMA	Buffer unit multiple access
CBD	Central business district
CBR	Constant bit rate
C-BUMA	Channel-aware BUMA
CCK	Complementary code keying
CDF	Cumulative distribution function
CDMA	Code division multiple access
CFP	Contention-free period

CLD	Cross-layer design
C-PRMA	Centralized packet reservation multiple access
CSI	Channel status information
CSMA	Carrier sense multiple access
CSMA/CA	Carrier sense multiple access with collision avoidance
CSMA/CD	Carrier sense multiple access with collision detection
CTS	Clear to send
CW	Contention window size
dB	Decibel
dBm	dB-milliwatts
DBTMA	Dual busy tone multiple access
DCF	Distributed coordination function (IEEE 802.11)
DCS	Distributed cycle stealing
DIDD	Double increment double decrement
DIFS	DCF interframe space
DLL	Data link layer
DS	Data sending
DS-CDMA	Direct sequence code division multiple access
DSDV	Destination sequence distance vector
DSR	Dynamic source routing
DSSS	Direct sequence spread spectrum
EDCA	Enhanced distributed channel access
ERP	Extended rate physical
ESS	Extended service set

ETSI	European Telecommunications Standards Institute
FAMA	Floor acquisition multiple access
FCR	Fast collision resolution
FDD	Frequency division duplexing
FDMA	Frequency division multiple access
FER	Frame error rate
FHSS	Frequency-hopping spread spectrum
FTP	File transfer protocol
FZP	Fresnel zone plate
GAMA-PS	Group allocation multiple access with packet sensing
HR/DSSS	High-rate DSSS
HSDPA	High-speed downlink packet access
HTTP	Hypertext transfer protocol
IBSS	Independent BSS
ICT	Information and communication technology
IP	Internet protocol
IPv4	Internet protocol version 4
IPv6	Internet protocol version 6
IPM	Industrial plant monitoring
IR	Infrared
ISM	Industrial, scientific, and medical
ISO	International Standards Organization
ITS	Intelligent transport systems
ITU	International Telecommunication Union
LLC	Logical link control

LMR	Label-based multipath routing
LOS	Line of sight
LTE	Long term evolution
MAC	Medium access control
MACA	Multiple access with collision avoidance
MACAW	Multiple access with collision avoidance for wireless LANs
MAN	Metropolitan area network
MANET	Mobile ad hoc network
MB	Megabyte
Mb	Megabit
MDT	Mean deviation of throughput
MILD	Multiplicative increase and linear decrease
MP3	MPEG audio layer 3
MPDU	MAC protocol data unit
MPEG	Moving Picture Experts Group
MPLS	Multiprotocol label switching
MPR	Multipoint rely
MS	Mobile station
MSDU	MAC segment data unit
MT	Mobile terminal (mobile station)
MTU	Maximum transmission unit
NAV	Network allocation vector
OFDM	Orthogonal frequency division multiplexing
OFDMA	Orthogonal frequency division multiple access
OSI	Open systems interconnection

OTCL	Object-oriented TCL
PAN	Personal area network
PBCC	Packet binary convolution coding
PCF	Point coordination function
PDA	Personal digital assistant
PDF	Probability density function
PER	Packet error rate
PG	Path gain
PHY	Physical layer
PMD	Physical medium dependent
PPDU	PHY protocol data unit
PPP	Point-to-point protocol
PRMA	Packet reservation multiple access
PRNG	Pseudorandom number generator
PSTN	Public switched telephone network
PUMA	Priority unavoidable multiple access
QoS	Quality of service
QPSK	Quadrature phase-shift keying
RAMA	Resource auction multiple access
RF	Radio frequency
RFID	Radio frequency identification
RIP	Routing Information Protocol
RM	Real media
RMS	Root mean square
RMVB	Real media variable bit rate
RREP	Route reply

RREQ	Route request
RRTS	Request for RTS
RSS	Received signal strength
RSVP	Resource reservation protocol
RTP	Real-time transport protocol
RTS	Request to send
RTSP	Real-time streaming protocol
Rx	Receiver
SINR	Signal-to-interference-and-noise ratio
SIP	Session initiation protocol
SIR	Signal-to-interference ratio
SNR	Signal-to-noise ratio
SSID	Service set identifier
TCL	Tool command language
TCP	Transmission control protocol
TDD	Time division duplexing
TDMA	Time division multiple access
TDMA/DR	TDMA with dynamic reservation
TORA	Temporally ordered routing algorithm
TTL	Time to live
Tx	Transmitter
UDP	User datagram protocol
UMTS	Universal mobile telecommunications system
U-NII	Unlicensed national information infrastructure
UTP	Unshielded twisted pair
VANET	Vehicular ad hoc network

VoIP	Voice over IP
WAN	Wide area network
WAP	Wireless access point
WCD	Wireless collision detection
W-CDMA	Wideband CDMA
WCL	Wireless connection lost
WDS	Wireless distribution system
WEP	Wired equivalent privacy
Wi-Fi	Wireless fidelity (IEEE 802.11)
WiMAX	Worldwide interoperability for microwave access
WLAN	Wireless local area network
WMV	Windows media video format
WPAN	Wireless personal area network
WRP	Wireless routing protocol
WVF	Windows video format
WWW	World Wide Web
ZRP	Zone routing protocol

I

Theoretical Background

Introduction

LEARNING OUTCOMES

After reading and completing this chapter, you will be able to:

- Discuss the evolution of wireless local area networks (WLANs)

- Discuss the development of IEEE 802.11 standards

- Discuss the potential benefits of using WLANs

- Discuss the performance issues of WLANs

- Discuss commonly used performance investigation methodology for WLANs

INTRODUCTION AND BENEFITS OF WLANS

There has been tremendous growth in the deployment of IEEE 802.11 (802.11) wireless local area networks (WLANs) in recent years. This growth is due to the flexibility, low cost, simplicity in operation, well-defined standards (e.g., 802.11a/b/g/n), and user mobility offered by the technology. The potential deployment areas of WLANs are hospitals [1, 2], where quick access to patient database information is critical; high-growth companies where frequent office shifting or temporary facilities are required; dynamic work environments such as manufacturing sites where wired infrastructure facilities are not available and the need for communication and file sharing is high; and in difficult wiring environments, such as older buildings [3, 4].

Furthermore, WLANs are currently being used as an attractive alternative, or complement, to wired LANs in many educational and commercial organizations worldwide [5–9]. For instance, New Zealand universities have reduced their need to outfit additional computer laboratories by setting up WLANs in the library and other study areas where students can connect their notebooks for accessing Intranet as well as the Internet [10, 11]. Nonetheless, the application of WLANs is not confined only to substituting for wired networks; it also enables communication schemes that are not available in wired networks. With the proliferation of mobile computers and handheld devices, such as personal digital assistants (PDAs), iPhones, and cellular phones, WLANs are becoming increasingly important as a means of data exchange, for example, Wi-Fi Internet services in Auckland City, London, Paris, and the New York metropolitan area [12–14], Wi-Fi in smartphones [15], Wi-Fi for vehicular ad hoc networks (VANETs) [16], and large-scale Wi-Fi networks deployed in urban areas [17].

Wireless technology will continue to evolve at a rapid pace in the future. Further developments of this technology involve bandwidth increase (i.e., high throughput) and reliability. In anticipation of the availability of increased bandwidth, various network-based business and multimedia applications are also being developed. Prasad and Prasad [18] discuss some applications, such as teleconferencing, telesurveillance, and video-on-demand operating on wireless network backbones. The potential benefits of WLANs are highlighted below [19]:

- **Mobility:** WLANs can provide users with real-time information within the organization without the restrictions inherent with physical cable connections.

- **Flexibility and simplicity:** The WLAN installation does not involve the tedious work of pulling cables through walls and ceilings. WLANs allow access from places unreachable by network cables.

- **Cost:** Overall the installation cost of WLAN is lower than that of wired LAN. The discrepancy is even higher in dynamic environments requiring frequent moves and changes.

- **Scalability:** WLANs can be configured relatively easily because there are no physical network cables required.

WLAN STANDARDS

The Institute of Electrical and Electronic Engineers (IEEE) released the 802.11 standard for WLAN in 1997. The specification requires a data transfer rate of 1 and 2 Mbps while retaining compatibility with existing LAN hardware and software infrastructure. The standard defines protocols for the medium access control (MAC) layer and physical transmission in the unlicensed 2.4-GHz radio band. After successful implementation by commercial companies such as Lucent Technologies, an amendment was made for better performance in the same year. The resulting standard was IEEE 802.11b, which specifies higher data transfer rates of 5.5 and 11 Mbps.

The 802.11b standard differs from the 802.11 in the MAC layer even though it retains compatibility with its predecessor. The physical layer (PHY) is left unchanged. The 802.11b standard was approved in 1999, and during that year the term *wireless fidelity*, or *Wi-Fi*, was introduced. The 802.11b has proven to be very successful in the commercial domain, and the majority of Wi-Fi devices still support the 802.11b standard.

In parallel with 802.11b, another variant of the original 802.11 was also made. This variant is referred to as 802.11a, which differs from both 802.11 and 802.11b by using the 5-GHz band rather than 2.4-GHz band. The 5-GHz radio band is unlicensed in the United States, but not in many other countries, especially in Europe. The 802.11a standard provides up to 54 Mbps, which is much faster than both 802.11 and 802.11b. However, the use of different radio frequencies denies compatibility between 802.11a and 802.11/802.11b. Nevertheless, 802.11a was found satisfactory and approved in 1999.

To resolve the incompatibility problem between the standards, an amendment to 802.11a was approved in 2003. The new standard is referred to as 802.11g, which operates in the 2.4-GHz radio band while retaining the 54-Mbps data transfer rate of 802.11a. There are other standards in the 802.11 family, such as 802.11n, 802.11u, and 802.11ad (discussed in Chapter 16), as summarized in Table 1.1.

MOTIVATION FOR WLAN PERFORMANCE STUDY

Despite these potential benefits of WLANs, one of the challenges faced by engineers and designers of WLANs is to increase throughput per user of a typical WLAN with a medium to large number of users. The quality of service (QoS) requirement for WLAN applications involves one or more

TABLE 1.1   IEEE 802.11 Standards Family

Standard	Description	Status
802.11	WLAN; up to 2 Mbps; 2.4 GHz	Approved June 1997
802.11a	WLAN; up to 54 Mbps; 5 GHz	Approved September 1999
802.11b	WLAN; up to 11 Mbps; 2.4 GHz	Approved September 1999
802.11g	WLAN; up to 54 Mbps; 2.4 GHz	Approved June 2003
802.11f	Inter-AP Protocol (IAPP)	Approved 2003
802.11h	Use of the 5-GHz band in Europe	Approved 2003
802.11i	New encryption standards	Approved November 2004
802.11e	New coordination functions for QoS	Approved November 2005
802.11n	MIMO physical layer	Approved October 2009
802.11u	Emergency QoS	Approved February 2011
802.11ad	Very high throughput Wi-Fi	Approved December 2012
802.11ac	Next-generation WLAN draft	Drafted in December 2012; final in 2014

Source: IEEE 802.11-2007, *IEEE Standard for Information Technology—Telecommunications and Information Exchange between Systems—Local and Metropolitan Area Networks—Specific Requirements—Part 11: Wireless Medium Access Control (MAC) and Physical Layer (PHY) Specifications (revision of IEEE 802.11-1999)*, New York: IEEE, 2007.

aspects, such as throughput, packet delay, and packet drop ratio and fairness (i.e., equality in channel access). Another challenge is to provide a QoS to all active stations on the network in the presence of noise or interfering signals.

Table 1.2 shows that the throughput of 802.11 WLANs operating under normal channel conditions deteriorate significantly as traffic loads increase [20, 21]. To maximize the performance promised by these technologies, the key performance-limiting factors need to be identified and quantified and careful system design and deployment are necessary.

To achieve these objectives, the key performance-limiting factors of WLANs, such as MAC protocols, radio propagation environments, routing protocols, and the traffic type and their arrival distributions, have been quantified. A new wireless MAC protocol was developed as an extension to the original 802.11 that not only eliminates the possibility of "wasting" bandwidth in the backoff state, but also significantly improves system performance. The effect of radio propagation environments on WLAN performance was examined through various propagation measurement scenarios in an obstructed office block, computer laboratory, and a suburban residential house. By integrating radio propagation modeling (i.e., the PHY) and a MAC protocol, a robust cross-layer

TABLE 1.2   An Example of Effective Data Rates (Throughput) Offered by 802.11 WLANs

Technology	Maximum Data Rate (Mbps)	Operating Conditions	Effective Data Rate (Throughput) per User		
			Low Traffic (2 active users)	Medium Traffic (5 active users)	High Traffic (10 active users)
802.11a	54	Perfect	17 Mbps	7 Mbps	3 Mbps
(OFDM)		Normal	11 Mbps	5 Mbps	2 Mbps
802.11b	11	Perfect	5 Mbps	2 Mbps	1 Mbps
(DSSS)		Normal	3 Mbps	1 Mbps	500 kbps
802.11g	54	Perfect	17 Mbps	7 Mbps	3 Mbps
(CCK, OFDM)		Normal	11 Mbps	5 Mbps	2 Mbps

Source: J. Fitzgerald and A. Dennis, *Business Data Communications and Networking*, 10th ed., New York: John Wiley & Sons, 2009.

design framework that offers better delay-throughput performance was developed. The effect of access point (AP) configuration and placement was examined by propagation measurements. The impact of routing protocols on the performance of a typical 802.11 network has been investigated by extensive simulation. The effect of packet arrival distributions and transport protocols on system performance has been explored by simulation studies. The combined effect of signal strength and traffic type on WLAN performance has been analyzed. By comparing system performances, the effectiveness of the key performance-limiting factors on WLAN performance was also investigated.

METHODOLOGY ADOPTED FOR WLAN PERFORMANCE STUDY

A main objective of this book is to identify and measure the key factors influencing WLAN performance. To achieve this objective, computer simulations and radio propagation measurements in real environments have been used to estimate system performance. Real hardware to measure WLAN performance and generalization of the research findings by simulation have been used in preference to the complex theoretical modeling of indoor radio propagation and system implementation. However, analytical modeling (i.e., mathematical approach) is only an approximation and always produces discrepancies with real systems. It is therefore essential to verify the results of such analytical models with either propagation measurements in a real environment or by computer simulation [22–24].

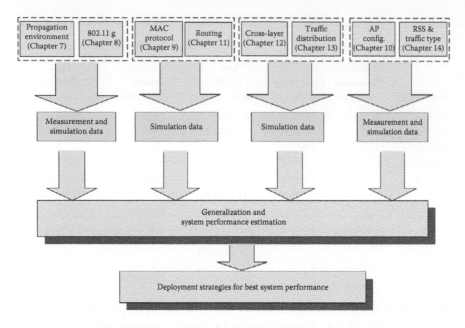

FIGURE 1.1   Block diagram of the adopted methodology.

Figure 1.1 outlines the methodology adopted in this book. A measurement-based performance estimation approach was used to quantify the influence of the propagation environment on system performance (Chapter 7), performance of 802.11g in an obstructed office space (Chapter 8), the effect of an AP configuration and placement on WLAN performance (Chapter 10), and the combined effect of signal strength and traffic type on WLAN performance (Chapter 14). This measurement-based methodology has also been employed by many leading network researchers for propagation studies [25–29] and real-time traffic characterization [30–33]. The advantage of this measurement approach is that the influence of radio propagation is included implicitly, and therefore it provides an unbiased representation of the environment and facilitates trustworthy performance estimation.

Both the network simulator 2 (ns-2) [33] and OPNET Modeler [34], object-oriented discrete-event network simulation packages, were used extensively as primary tools for the performance study of 802.11 WLANs, including the performance evaluation of a new wireless MAC protocol (Chapter 9), the effect of routing protocols (Chapter 11), cross-layer WLAN design optimization (Chapter 12), and to quantify the impact of traffic arrival distribution on WLAN performance (Chapter 13). Simulations were also used for generalization of the propagation measurement results reported in Chapters 8 and 14.

Ns-2 was chosen because it is used extensively in the academic community (ns-2 is also free). In a recent study on empirical validation of ns-2 wireless models using simulation, emulation, and real networks, Ivanov et al. [35] reported that WLAN topologies are accurately represented in ns-2, once the simulation parameters are accurately tuned. Another motivation of using ns-2 is that one can compare the proposed approach with the other protocols on a single common and prevalidated platform for simulations. Ns-2 version 2.31 was the most recent version of the network simulation package at the time of this work. We also use OPNET Modeler (a commercial network simulation package), which was available under OPNET University Program. Hence, OPNET-based modeling is also included in this book to verify ns-2 results and to generalize propagation measurement results.

CONTRIBUTION AND STRUCTURE OF THIS BOOK

The overall structure of this book is shown in Figure 1.2. Improving the performance of WLANs requires a basic understanding of WLANs, radio propagation characteristics, wireless MAC and routing protocols, and cross-layer design optimization for WLANs. Therefore, it is important to develop a good theoretical foundation for these areas before considering improving system performance. Chapters 2 to 6 provide foundation and background material for the book.

Chapter 2 provides an introduction to WLANs highlighting the architecture, similarities and differences with cellular networks, and performance issues. WLAN performance-limiting factors are identified and described. In particular, 802.11 PHY characteristics and location-dependent effects (such as capture effect and hidden and exposed station problems) are discussed, which are fundamental issues in the design and deployment of such systems. The 802.11 MAC schemes, including distributed coordination function (DCF) and point coordination function (PCF), are described in detail. The shortcomings of 802.11 are also highlighted in this chapter.

Chapter 3 provides an introduction to radio propagation characteristics relevant to the design and performance study of WLANs. In particular, the radio propagation mechanism, signal interference, multipath propagation, signal attenuation, received signal strength, signal-to-noise ratio (SNR), and bit error rate (BER) are also discussed.

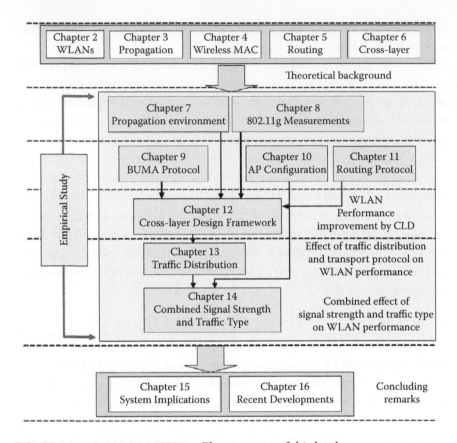

FIGURE 1.2 (SEE COLOR INSERT.)   The structure of this book.

Chapter 4 addresses the issues and challenges in the design of wireless MAC protocols. Wireless MAC protocols are a key factor influencing the performance of WLANs. The effect of radio propagation environments on the performance of wireless MAC protocols is discussed. To provide a review of literature on wireless MAC protocols, previous related research in the design and performance improvements of wireless MAC protocols is also surveyed in this chapter.

Chapter 5 reviews routing protocols for WLANs. The properties and design issues of routing protocols are discussed. The commonly used mobile ad hoc network (MANET) routing approaches are reviewed. The performance issues of routing protocols are discussed. A new proposal for an improved MANET routing protocol is also presented.

The cross-layer design (CLD) optimization plays an important role in improving the performance of WLANs. Chapter 6 provides an overview for CLD optimization for WLANs. The strengths and weaknesses of CLD approaches are discussed. A review of recent literature on CLD approaches is also presented.

The empirical (practical) part of this book is presented through Chapters 7 to 14, which are primarily concerned with quantifying the key factors influencing WLAN performance. To quantify the influence of these key performance-limiting factors, both simulation and measurement-based approaches were adopted.

In Chapter 7, the impact of radio propagation environments on WLAN performance in an obstructed office space, basement parking lot, computer laboratory, and suburban residential house environment is investigated. It is observed that line-of-sight (LOS) blockage by walls and partitions has a dramatic effect on the transmission time as well as link throughput of Wi-Fi networks in an obstructed office building and a typical wood-framed suburban residential house. The effects of transmitting and receiving antennas' orientation, office partitions, single wall separations, floors, LOS path in a basement, microwave interference, and LOS blockage by office walls on WLAN performance are investigated and reported. The primary objective of this propagation study was to obtain some insights into Wi-Fi computer links in obstructed office spaces and suburban residential house environments. The measured data collected during indoor propagation studies form a comprehensive database of a range of environments and deployment scenarios that could be used directly in conjunction with computer simulations to estimate indoor WLAN performance.

Chapter 8 reports on the performance of 802.11g in an obstructed office space. Both propagation measurements and simulation are used for system evaluation.

Chapter 9 reports on the design of a new wireless MAC protocol called the buffer unit multiple access (BUMA) protocol, developed as a modification of 802.11 DCF that overcomes the shortcomings of 802.11 networks. BUMA's performance is evaluated by the ns-2 simulator. In this chapter, BUMA is described and simulation results are presented to verify that the protocol's performance is better than that of the traditional 802.11 DCF protocols.

The impact of AP configuration and placement on WLAN performance is investigated by radio propagation measurements and is reported in Chapter 10. Various methods of AP configuration are described. The practical implications are also discussed in this chapter.

The routing protocols play an important role in determining the performance of a typical 802.11 MANET. The effect of MANET routing protocols on WLAN performance is investigated by extensive simulation experiments and is reported in Chapter 11. The performances of four typical MANET routing protocols are compared, which include one proactive routing protocol, Optimized Link State Routing (OLSR), and three on-demand routing protocols, Ad Hoc On-Demand Distance Vector (AODV), Dynamic Source Routing (DSR), and Temporally Ordered Routing Algorithm (TORA).

Chapter 12 proposes a joint PHY-MAC CLD framework for estimating as well as improving WLAN performance. The proposed framework is based on a cross-layer MAC protocol called the channel-aware buffer unit multiple access (C-BUMA). C-BUMA is a minor modification of the BUMA, integrating PHY characteristics with the MAC sublayer. In this chapter, C-BUMA is described and two algorithms (channel prediction and MAC protocol modeling) are presented for implementation of the proposed CLD framework. The implementation of BER in ns-2.31 to study the impact of BER on a typical 802.11 network is also reported in this chapter.

Chapter 13 examines the effect of traffic arrival distributions and transport protocols (e.g., Transmission Control Protocol [TCP] and User Datagram Protocol [UDP]) on WLAN performance. In the investigation, exponential, Pareto ON-OFF, Poisson, and constant bit rate (CBR) models are used. It is observed that the packet arrival distributions at the stations have a significant effect on system performance.

Chapter 14 investigates the combined effect of signal strength and traffic type (e.g., voice and video) on WLAN performance through propagation measurements as well as using simulation study. It is observed that the received signal strength (RSS) has a significant effect on the playback delay of voice and video streaming in ad hoc and infrastructure networks. The relative performance of voice and video traffic for different RSS values is quantified and the optimum deployment strategies are identified.

Chapters 15 and 16 provide concluding remarks for the book. In Chapter 15, the major findings from Chapters 7 to 14 are presented from the perspective of system planning and deployment. This relates the key factors influencing WLAN performance discussed to the design and deployment of a real system. The WLAN design issues, challenges, and deployment strategies are outlined and recommendations are made for various system design scenarios. A number of possible future developments of networking research are also presented.

Chapter 16 highlights recent advancement and standardization in wireless networks, such as multiple-input multiple-output (MIMO) 802.11n, next-generation Wi-Fi (802.11ac), very high throughput Wi-Fi (802.11ad), emergency QoS (802.11u), vehicle-to-vehicle communications (802.11p), cognitive radio networks (802.22), wireless mesh networking (802.11s), green communication and networking, and secure WLAN protocol (802.11i). As the demand for indoor WLAN increases, further research is needed to develop smart algorithms for improving WLAN performance.

FURTHER READING

For more details about subjects discussed in this chapter, we recommend the following books and references. The items in [] refer to the reference list at the end of the book.

Books

[36] Chapter 4—*Wireless Personal and Local Area Networks* by Sikora

[37] Chapter 16—*Computer Networks and Internets with Internet Applications* by Comer

Research Papers

[38]

[39]

SUMMARY

This chapter provided an introduction to the book. It highlighted the potential benefits of using WLANs. The 802.11 standardization for WLANs is discussed. The motivation for WLAN performance study is also discussed. A research methodology for investigations in this book was chosen by adapting previous research [24, 25]. This methodology involves the performance estimation as well as improvement of WLANs. Both measurement-based and simulation approaches were adopted for their accuracy and flexibility in estimating WLAN performance. Finally, the main contribution and structure of this book are discussed. More details about WLAN that provide the background material for the book are presented in Chapter 2.

KEY TERMS

Access point (AP) configuration
Bandwidth
Carrier sense multiple access with collision
  avoidance (CSMA/CA)
Complementary code keying (CCK)
Direct sequence spread spectrum (DSSS)
Effective data rate
IEEE 802.11a/b/g
Medium access control (MAC)
Network performance

Orthogonal frequency division
  multiplexing (OFDM)
Physical layer (PHY)
Performance-limiting factors
Quality of service (QoS)
Traffic type
Throughput
Vehicular ad hoc network (VANET)
Wireless fidelity (Wi-Fi)

REVIEW QUESTIONS

1. Identify and discuss three main differences between a WLAN and a wired LAN. You answer must be nonarguable, i.e., no one can argue about the quality of your answer.

2. WLANs have been standardized by IEEE 802.11 working group. Discuss the evolution of IEEE 802.11 standards for WLANs.

3. The international standards bodies or working groups developed standards for WLAN protocols. List and describe three main benefits of having international standards bodies in network and telecommunications.

4. WLANs provide many benefits and are being deployed worldwide. List and describe three potential benefits of using WLANs.

5. While WLANs provide many benefits, they are not as good as wired LANs for some applications and practical scenarios. List and describe three disadvantages of using WLANs.

6. Network researchers are facing real challenges in improving the performance of a typical WLAN. List and describe two potential performance issues/challenges in WLAN design.

MINI-PROJECTS

The following mini-projects aim to provide a deeper understanding of the topics covered in this chapter through a review of the literature. More mini-projects have been presented in Section 2 of this book to emphasize hands-on practical learning experience.

1. Network researchers have been facing real challenges in improving the performance of WLANs in recent years. To gain insight into the performance of WLANs, it is useful to be able to review the literature on various issues and challenges related to WLAN performance. Conduct an in-depth literature review on WLAN performance issues and challenges.

2. Both customers and suppliers can benefit from WLAN standardization. This mini-project aims to enhance the knowledge and understanding of the WLAN standardization process and its potential benefits. Conduct an in-depth literature survey on WLAN standardization.

Wireless Local Area Networks

LEARNING OUTCOMES

After reading and completing this chapter, you will be able to:

- Describe the architecture of a typical WLAN

- Discuss the difference between a WLAN and a cellular network

- Identify and discuss the key factors influencing WLAN performance

- Describe IEEE 802.11 physical layer characteristics

- Discuss the impact of capture effect and hidden and exposed nodes on WLAN performance

- Compare and contrast 802.11 distributed coordination function (DCF) and point coordination function (PCF) access mechanisms

INTRODUCTION

In Chapter 1, the motivations for the performance study as well as improvement of WLANs were outlined. A primary objective of this book is to identify as well as quantify the key factors influencing WLAN performance. To achieve this objective, a general understanding of WLANs is required. This chapter aims to provide an introduction to various key concepts of WLANs that are necessary for the design, deployment, and performance evaluation of such systems.

The commonly used architecture of a typical WLAN focusing on both ad hoc and infrastructure networks is presented. The similarities and differences between WLAN and cellular networks are then highlighted. The key performance-limiting factors of WLANs, which are important issues for network design and performance improvement, are discussed, followed by the description of the physical layer (PHY) characteristic of 802.11 WLANs.

The "Location-Dependent Effects" section describes location-dependent effects in WLANs, including capture effect and hidden and exposed station problems. The impact of these effects on WLAN performance is also discussed in this section. In the "IEEE 802.11 Medium Access Control Methods" section, the medium access control (MAC) protocols implemented in 802.11, namely, DCF and PCF, are described. The shortcomings of 802.11 are highlighted in the "Shortcomings of 802.11" section. The "WLAN Performance Estimation Approaches" section outlines WLAN performance estimation approaches adopted in this book.

WLAN ARCHITECTURE

There are two commonly used network architectures for the design of WLANs: (1) ad hoc network and (2) infrastructure network. An ad hoc network (Figure 2.1) is a type of wireless network architecture that has neither a fixed infrastructure nor wireless access points (APs) (i.e., no centralized control system). In ad hoc networks, each mobile terminal (MT) acts as router to communicate with other stations. Such a network can exist on a temporary basis for sharing network resources among the MTs, and is also referred to as an independent basic service set (IBSS). An IBSS

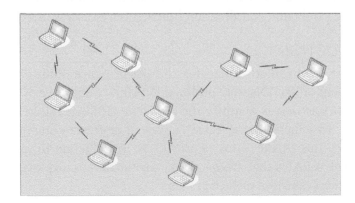

FIGURE 2.1 A typical wireless ad hoc network with nine MTs.

can still work perfectly even when a station leaves the network. Typical applications of ad hoc networks include battlefields and disaster areas, such as flooding, hurricanes, fires, and earthquakes, where wired backbone networks are not available.

An ad hoc network can be categorized as single hop or multi hop. In single-hop ad hoc networks, stations can communicate directly to their neighboring stations (one hop) within the transmitting range of an MT. In the multihop ad hoc networks, the source station can communicate to the destination station through one or more intermediate stations, and therefore a multihop ad hoc network can have hundreds of MTs. However, there are several issues and challenges in the design of multihop ad hoc networks, including routing, topology maintenance, location management, and end-to-end packet delay, highlighted by many network researchers and designers [40–44].

Figure 2.2 shows a typical infrastructure-based WLAN with two APs, called AP1 and AP2, which are linked to the wired backbone through an Ethernet switch. An AP is a centralized device that coordinates data transmission among the wireless stations in the network. Therefore, stations communicate only with an AP, and the AP then passes the content of the transmission to the intended receiver. Besides the functions that common wireless stations have, an AP also works as a bridge between wireless and wired networks.

Figure 2.2 shows four wireless stations within the same radio coverage area, communicating with the associated AP1, forming a basic service

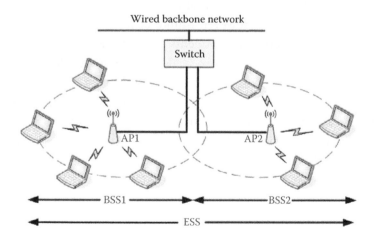

FIGURE 2.2 (SEE COLOR INSERT.)   An infrastructure network with two BSSs.

set 1 (BSS1). Similarly, three stations communicate with AP2 and form a second basic service set 2 (BSS2). The wired backbone network connects BSS1 and BSS2 through AP1 and AP2, respectively, and a switch to form a single network called an extended service set (ESS). The ESS has its own identifier, the ESSID, which is the name of that network used to distinguish it from other networks. In an ESS system, an MT may move from one AP to another and still continue to communicate with other stations.

WLAN architectures have a significant effect on the design of wireless MAC protocols. Recent research into wireless MAC protocol design issues and challenges is outlined in Chapter 4. The performance comparison of 802.11 ad hoc and infrastructure networks is presented in Chapter 9.

WLAN VERSUS CELLULAR NETWORKS

A general understanding of the similarities and differences between WLAN and cellular networks is required for efficient design and deployment of WLAN systems. WLANs are deployed to serve the needs of local users (i.e., limited distance coverage) rather than highly mobile users. They are typically used in buildings to provide high-speed wireless access to campus and corporate networks, or in residences and small business to allow multiple users access to the same Internet connection. Other WLAN coverage areas include public hotspots in some city neighborhoods. In contrast, a cellular network covers a much wider area on a regional, nationwide, or even global scale, which is particularly useful for highly mobile users for both voice and nonvoice services. Therefore, the deployment of cellular networks requires a huge capital investment and careful system planning. However, unlike cellular systems, WLANs are not very complex, and their components (e.g., wireless cards and APs) are fairly simple and inexpensive. Both CDMA systems and 802.11b WLAN use direct sequence spread spectrum (DSSS) technology for data modulation. While the architecture of an infrastructure WLAN is very similar to that of a cellular network (e.g., mobile terminals access the network through fixed base stations in both cases), technical aspects such as MAC protocols, interference handling, and network performance issues are different. WLANs use traditional carrier sense multiple access with collision avoidance (CSMA/CA)-based MAC protocols for channel access, whereas the MAC protocols for cellular networks are based on frequency division multiple access (FDMA), time division multiple access (TDMA), and code division multiple access (CDMA).

In WLANs, radio signal interference is unpredictable, and it is up to the wireless MAC protocols to mitigate the effect of interference on system performance. For example, 802.11 DCF retransmits the corrupted packets (i.e., interfering packets) to maintain wireless communication at the cost of longer packet delays. In cellular networks, interference is limited and can be identified by the system. For example, if a CDMA signal is interfering with another signal, it can be identified by that 1.23 MHz wide profile.

Cellular networks operate on licensed frequency spectra, and therefore it is unlikely that other transmitting devices will affect their system performance. In contrast, WLANs operate on unlicensed frequency spectra (e.g., industrial, scientific, and medical [ISM] bands), and therefore other devices (e.g., Bluetooth devices) operating in the same ISM band can affect their system performance. The impact of interference on WLAN performance is further discussed in Chapter 3. Another difference is that WLANs have faster data transmission rates than cellular networks.

WLAN PERFORMANCE-LIMITING FACTORS

The performance of a typical WLAN depends on various factors, including radio propagation characteristics and environments (i.e., PHY layer), MAC protocols (i.e., data link layer), and traffic type and their distribution (i.e., upper protocol layers). The PHY layer characteristics that influence WLAN performance include signal strength, noise, and interference, bit error rate (BER), concurrent transmission due to hidden station problems and retransmission, antenna deployment, and modulation schemes. The data link layer characteristics, such as MAC protocols, packet length, and the contention window length, also affect WLAN performance. WLAN performance also depends on upper protocol layer characteristics such as traffic type (i.e., voice and video) and their distribution. Figure 2.3 outlines the key performance-limiting factors of WLANs.

The received signal quality measurement parameters, such as received signal strength (RSS), signal-to-noise ratio (SNR), signal-to-interference ratio (SIR), and BER, are also fundamental issues in the characterization of wireless channels. They also have a significant impact on WLAN performance. These parameters are briefly described in Chapter 3. The location-dependent effects due to hidden and exposed station problems degrade WLAN performance. For example, WLAN performance degrades significantly due to hidden and exposed station problems, resulting in packet losses. These effects are discussed in the "Location-Dependent Effects" section.

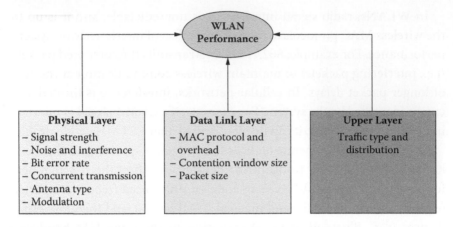

FIGURE 2.3   WLAN performance-limiting factors.

In wireless communication networks, both the transmitting and receiving antennas play a vital role in determining the radio signal propagation in wireless channels. The key antenna design parameters, such as radiation pattern, beamwidth, gain, and polarization, have significant impact on WLAN performance [23, 25]. Wireless system performance also depends on the type of modulation method being used for data encoding. The effect of modulation on throughput performance of 802.11a/b is highlighted in the "IEEE 802.11 Physical Layer" section. However, the impact of antenna parameters and modulation methods on WLAN performance is beyond the scope of this book.

A wireless MAC protocol has a significant effect on the performance of a typical WLAN. This effect is investigated in Chapter 9 along with performance evaluation of a new MAC protocol. To gain insight into the performance of wireless MAC protocols, it is important to have a basic understanding of 802.11 MAC methods. An overview of 802.11 MAC is presented in the "IEEE 802.11 Medium Access Control Methods" section. The performance of a typical WLAN also depends on traffic type and its arrival distributions. The effect of traffic arrival distributions and the combined effect of RSS and traffic type on system performance are examined in Chapters 13 and 14, respectively.

IEEE 802.11 PHYSICAL LAYER

The 802.11 PHY has two sublayers: physical layer convergence procedure (PLCP) and physical medium dependent (PMD) [45]. The PLCP converts MAC frames into transmitting frames, and PMD defines data transmission between wireless stations and medium. The 802.11 PHY layer can operate in any one of the following modes: (1) DSSS operating in the ISM band (2.4 to 2.4835 GHz), (2) frequency-hopping spread spectrum (FHSS), and (3) industrial plant monitoring (IPM) (300 to 428 GHz). They all support 1 and 2 Mbps rates based on binary phase-shift keying (BPSK) and quadrature phase-shift keying (QPSK), respectively. More details about 802.11 technology can be found in [39].

The 802.11b PHY [46] is an extension of the original DSSS PHY layer. It also operates in the ISM band, and provides 5.5 and 11 Mbps rates in addition to 1 and 2. Both are encoded using DSSS based on an 11-bit Barker chipping sequence that results in a signal spread over a wider bandwidth at reduced radio frequency (RF) power. Each channel occupies 22 MHz of bandwidth, allowing three nonoverlapping channels in the 2.4-GHz band. To provide the high data rates of 5.5 and 11 Mbps, 802.11b uses a complementary code keying (CCK) modulation method. The data rate information is carried in the header of 802.11b frames (transmitted at 1 Mbps), so that the receiving station knows what clocking rate to use for the payload portion of the frame as it arrives.

Loss, fading, noise, and interference affect the received signal quality of wireless channels, and hence impact on the overall system performance. Moreover, packets corruption increases at higher transmission rates. To overcome these problems, most 802.11b products dynamically adjust the data transmission rate based on an estimate of the channel error rate [47]. The automatic rate fallback of 802.11b is discussed in the "Automatic Rate Fallback" section.

IEEE 802.11g has the same maximum data rate of 54 Mbps as 802.11a; however, it has two different operation modes. In the 802.11g-only mode, all stations in the WLAN are 802.11g stations, so that they can operate in a way that is more efficient but not compatible with 802.11b. In the 802.11b-compatible mode, some stations in the WLAN can be 802.11b stations. The main motivation for using 802.11g over 802.11a is that 802.11g is compatible with 802.11b, while 802.11a is not.

The 802.11g network PHY layer has three compulsory and two optional components. The compulsory components are extended rate physical (ERP)–DSSS, ERP-CCK, and ERP–orthogonal frequency division multiplexing (OFDM). The two optional components are ERP–packet binary convolution coding (PBCC) and DSSS-OFDM [48]. Both ERP-DSSS and ERP-CCK are backward compatible with the 802.11b standard, and

TABLE 2.1   IEEE 802.11a Data Rates Corresponding to
Modulation and Coding Rates

Data Rate (Mbps)	Modulation	Code Rate	Bytes per Symbol
6	BPSK	½	3
9	BPSK	¾	4.5
12	QPSK	½	6
18	QPSK	¾	9
24	16-QAM	½	12
36	16-QAM	¾	18
48	64-QAM	⅔	24
54	64-QAM	¾	27

Source: IEEE, *Part II: Wireless LAN Medium Access Control (MAC) and Physical Layer (PHY) Specifications: High-Speed Physical Layer in the 5 GHz Band*, IEEE 802.11a WG/D5.0, New York: IEEE, 1999.

ERP-OFDM is a core component of 802.11g. IEEE 802.11g uses OFDM to provide high data rates in the ISM band.

ERP-PBCC is an optional feature in 802.11g to provide 22 and 33 Mbps. DSSS-OFDM uses DSSS as header for the encoding packet and OFDM for payload encoding. DSSS-OFDM provides backward compatibility with 802.11b. IEEE 802.11g uses CCK for 5.5 and 11 Mbps, and DSSS for 1 and 2 Mbps to provide backward compatibility with 802.11b. More details about the 802.11g PHY layer can be found in [48].

The 802.11a network uses the same MAC protocol as 802.11b, but with a different set of parameters. In 802.11a, the PHY preamble and the contention time slot are shorter and the maximum data rate is larger. However, the 802.11a network PHY [49] is based on OFDM and provides eight PHY layer data rates from 6 to 54 Mbps (Table 2.1, column 1) by employing different modulation and coding schemes in the 5-GHz Unlicensed National Information Infrastructure (U-NII) band. Table 2.1 shows that typical WLAN performance can be improved by adopting an appropriate modulation method. The transmission overheads of 802.11a can be found in Appendix C.

Automatic Rate Fallback

The different modulation techniques used for different data rates of 802.11 can be characterized by more robust communication at the lower data rate. For instance, a typical WLAN can achieve a larger transmission range at

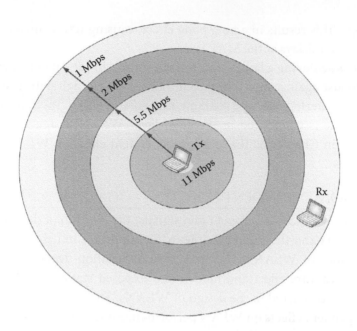

FIGURE 2.4 (SEE COLOR INSERT.)   Data rate and coverage area in 802.11b.

lower data rates (e.g., 1 Mbps) compared to higher data rates (11 Mbps). Figure 2.4 shows the four cell regions with respect to the four data rates of 802.11b. The data rate versus transmission ranges of 802.11b according to path loss models can be found in Appendix C.

Stations moving around the cell would be able to transmit at higher data rates in the inner regions of the cell. The 802.11 standard does not specify how the appropriate rate can be selected. The automatic rate fallback (ARF) algorithm is used to achieve the highest data rate at each moment [50]. The ARF algorithm falls back to a lower data rate when a station moves to outer regions or encounters high interference, and upgrades to a higher rate when it moves back into the inner region or channel conditions improve. The change in data rate is stepwise, e.g., the ARF algorithm will change the data rate from 1 to 2 Mbps but not skip to 5.5 or 11 Mbps.

Referring to Figure 2.4, during the course of data transmission the ARF might select 11 Mbps. As a result, some or all of the packets might be lost as the receiver might be beyond the coverage area. Consequently, the ARF algorithm will decrease the data rate to 5.5 Mbps. After successful packet transmissions, it will again select the higher data rate (11 Mbps), which will again cause retransmissions and the lowering of the data rate to

5.5 Mbps. This results in a ping-pong effect, causing retransmissions and severe packet delays at the MAC layer.

Besides achieving a larger transmission range, lower data rates are also more robust against interfering conditions such as high path loss, high noise and interference, and extreme multipath effects. The rate adaptation scheme is considered in the cross-layer WLAN design framework discussed in Chapter 6. The location-dependent effect on WLAN is discussed next.

LOCATION-DEPENDENT EFFECTS

Due to the broadcast nature of radio signals, the location of the transmitting antenna and the receiving antenna is important in determining the performance of WLANs. There are various location-dependent effects, including capture effect and hidden and exposed station problems that need to be considered in the design of WLANs. The impact of these location-dependent effects on WLAN performance is discussed next.

Capture Effect

The capture effect is most likely to occur if two or more stations transmit concurrently to a destination station [51]. As a result of concurrent transmissions, packets may collide at the destination station, resulting in packet retransmissions that severely affect WLAN performance. The signal strengths at the receiving station depend on various factors, including distance between the transmitting and receiving antennas, transmitting antenna power, background noise of the propagation environment, and radio signal interference. The receiving station will pick up data only from a station with the strongest signal. This aspect of capture effect is beneficial; however, it introduces network unfairness.

The performance of DCF under capture effect is analyzed in [52]. The impact of capture effect on the performance of the CSMA/CA protocol under the Rayleigh fading channel is investigated in [53].

Figure 2.5 illustrates the basic concept of the capture effect. Assuming the participating stations A, B, and C have identical transmitting power and are operating in LOS conditions, if stations A and C transmit packets to station B, station B will likely receive packets from C. This is because C has a stronger signal being closer to station B than station A. A signal collision may occur in the absence of capture effect. However, using a sophisticated power controller system at the transmitter can reduce

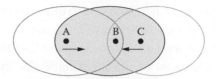

FIGURE 2.5   Illustrating the basic concept of capture effect.

the capture effect. More details about capture effect can be found in the wireless networking literature [52, 53].

Hidden and Exposed Station Problems

The diagram in Figure 2.6 illustrates the basic concept of both the hidden and exposed station problems. When a wireless station is in the range of a receiver but not in the range of a transmitter, it can lead to an increased number of collisions. Such a station is referred to as a hidden station. The hidden station problem [54, 56] can be either a hidden sender problem or hidden receiver problem. The hidden sender problem occurs if a station transmits a packet to a destination station that is currently receiving a packet from another station. In Figure 2.6, station M transmits a packet to station N. Station O, a hidden sender, also has a packet to be sent to station N, but it does not hear the ongoing transmission from station M. In this scenario, a collision will occur if station O transmits a packet to station N.

The hidden sender problem can be avoided by using handshaking, such as request-to-send/clear-to-send (RTS-CTS) control packets before transmission. In Figure 2.6, station M transmits a packet to station N, and station N broadcasts a message before or while it starts receiving a packet from station M. While handshaking may be used to avoid collisions, it can also cause a hidden receiver problem. For example, station N uses handshaking to inform all other stations that it is receiving a packet. Station O hears the handshaking and defers packet transmission. Now station P has a packet for transmission to station O. Since station P is far away from

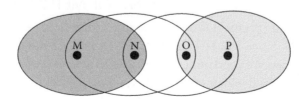

FIGURE 2.6   Illustrating the basic concept of hidden and exposed station problems.

station N, it does not hear handshaking from station N, and therefore station P transmits a packet to station O. Station O receives the packet successfully, but cannot send an acknowledge (ACK) to station P because sending an ACK would cause a collision at station N. In this scenario, station O is a hidden receiver. The hidden receiver problem can be reduced by using an out-of-band signaling mechanism as proposed in dual busy tone multiple access (DBTMA) [56]. A detailed analysis of the hidden station effect on WLAN performance can be found in [57, 58]. The impact of hidden station problems on 802.11 WLANs was investigated in [59–65].

Like hidden station problems, the exposed station problem has both exposed sender and receiver problems [54]. The exposed sender problem may occur if a station's packet transmission is exposed by an ongoing transmission. For example, in Figure 2.6, station O transmits a packet to station P, and station N can hear this transmission because it is within the transmission range of O. Station N has a packet for station M, but cannot initiate the transmission because this would cause a collision. In this case station N is an exposed sender. Using receiver-initiated handshaking can reduce the exposed sender problem.

The exposed receiver problem can occur when two stations transmit simultaneously, e.g., when station O transmits a packet to station P, and station M also transmits to station N. The transmission from station O may collide with the transmission from station M even though the transmission from station O is not intended for station N. In this case, station N is an exposed receiver. The exposed receiver problem is a difficult one to avoid in WLANs completely. A special class of MAC protocol called a multichannel MAC protocol avoids the exposed receiver problem by using several orthogonal frequencies for packet transmission [66, 67]. In this book, however, the impact of the hidden and exposed station problems on WLAN performance is not investigated. The 802.11 MAC methods are described next.

IEEE 802.11 MEDIUM ACCESS CONTROL METHODS

The wireless MAC protocol is one of the most important components of a typical WLAN. Since 802.11 WLANs are widely used in both home and office environments, a good understanding of MAC methods is required for efficient design and deployment of such systems. The 802.11 [39, 46] MAC contains two sublayers: (1) DCF and (2) PCF, shown in Figure 2.7. DCF is a mandatory contention-based access protocol, whereas PCF is an optional contention-free polling-based access protocol. DCF has been widely

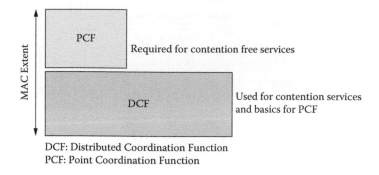

DCF: Distributed Coordination Function
PCF: Point Coordination Function

FIGURE 2.7   IEEE 802.11 MAC architecture.

deployed because of its simplicity in operation and robustness. This proto-col is further considered in Chapter 9 in the performance study of 802.11 WLANs. The DCF and PCF channel access mechanisms are described in the "IEEE 802.11 DCF" and "IEEE 802.11 PCF" sections, respectively.

IEEE 802.11 DCF

In the DCF, wireless stations communicate on a network using a conten-tion-based channel access method known as CSMA/CA. DCF defines two mechanisms for packet transmission: (1) basic access mode with two-way handshaking (DATA-ACK-DATA …) and (2) four-way handshaking (RTS-CTS-DATA-ACK-RTS-CTS …). This section describes the DCF four-way handshaking access method since the basic two-way handshak-ing mechanism follows the same principle, except the RTS and CTS con-trol packets.

The principle of operation of the DCF four-way handshake is illustrated in Figure 2.8. In the four-way handshaking mechanism, a station mon-itors the channel until an idle period equal to a DCF interframe space (DIFS) is detected. If the channel is found to be busy, the station defers (and continues listening to the channel) until the channel becomes idle for at least one DIFS. Then the station begins its backoff time to avoid col-lisions. After a successful backoff time the station transmits a packet. To avoid channel capture, a station must wait a random backoff time between two consecutive new packet transmissions, even if the medium is sensed idle in the DIFS. In the backoff time, the time axis is slotted and a station is allowed to transmit only at the beginning of each time slot. The collision avoidance technique adopted in 802.11 is based on a binary exponential backoff (BEB) scheme, which is implemented in each station by means

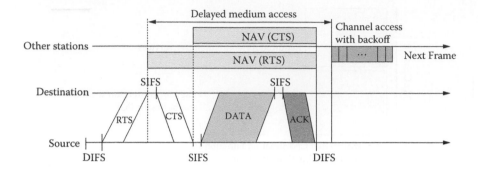

FIGURE 2.8   DCF RTS-CTS method (four-way handshaking). (From J. F. Kurose and K. W. Ross, *Computer Networking: A Top-Down Approach*, 4th ed., New York: Addison Wesley, 2008.)

of a parameter known as the backoff counter. The backoff time is used to initialize the backoff counter. This counter is decreased only when the medium is idle and is frozen when activity is sensed. The backoff counter is periodically decremented by one slot time each time the medium sensed is idle for a period longer than one DIFS. A station transmits a packet when its backoff counter reaches zero. The random backoff time can be computed as follows [39, 46]:

$$Backoff\ time\ (BT) = Random\ () \times aSlotTime \qquad (2.1)$$

where *Random* () is an integer randomly chosen from a uniform distribution over the interval $[0, CW - 1]$, where CW is the contention window size. *aSlotTime* (default value is 20 μs in 802.11) is set equal to the time needed by a station to detect the packet transmission from any other stations.

At the first transmission attempt CW is set to CW_{min} (minimum contention window size), and it is doubled ($2^m \times CW_{min}$, where m is the maximum retransmission count for a given packet) at each retransmission up to the maximum value of CW_{max}. After a successful transmission, the contention window is reset to CW_{min}. In the 802.11 DSSS specification, $CW_{min} = 31$ and $CW_{min} = 1,023$. A detailed description of the backoff algorithm can be found in [38, 39, 68].

The RTS-CTS mechanism is optional in DCF and is used to mitigate long data packet collisions. Before transmitting a data packet, a station transmits a short RTS packet, and the destination station replies to it after a time period equal to the short interframe space (SIFS) with a CTS packet. The transmitting station is allowed to transmit its actual data packet only if the CTS packet is received correctly. Other stations that overhear either an RTS or a CTS, or both, set their network allocation vector (NAV) to the value carried by the duration field (i.e., length of the data frame to be transmitted) of the RTS-CTS packet. The NAV is a value that indicates to a station the remaining time before the wireless medium becomes available. Any other station that hears either RTS or CTS packets can use the data packet length information to update its NAV containing the information of the period for which the channel will remain busy. Thus, any hidden station can defer its transmission suitably to avoid collisions. Since transmitting RTS and CTS packets increases the overhead, there is a trade-off between such overhead and the overhead incurred due to collisions between large-sized packets in the basic access mode. The RTS threshold that determines the appropriate use of the RTS-CTS mechanism is defined in the 802.11 protocol [39]. More details about basic DCF and RTS-CTS can be found in [69, 70]. DCF is further considered in Chapter 9 for performance comparison purposes.

IEEE 802.11 PCF

Real-time multimedia traffic, such as voice and video, requires bounded end-to-end delay unlike non-real-time data traffic. DCF (described in the "IEEE 802.11 DCF" section) is not suitable for supporting real-time traffic because it does not provide any service differentiation (i.e., all packets are treated equally whether real time or non-real time). To overcome this service differentiation problem, the IEEE 802 committee defined an optional access method, PCF.

PCF is a centralized, polling-based access mechanism that requires the presence of an AP that acts as point coordinator (PC). This PC initiates and controls the contention-free period in which PCF is used. The PC first senses the channel for the PCF interframe space (PIFS) period and then starts a contention-free (CF) period by broadcasting a beacon frame. All stations, upon receiving the beacon, will set a value equal to duration time contained in the duration field of the beacon's control header within their NAV. The length of the CF period depends on the coordination result from the neighboring PCs; the maximum value is the same as the super-frame. But, if there is more than one PC using the same radio frequency, which may conflict with other PCs, then the length of the CF is smaller than the super-frame. PCF would be especially well suited for real-time traffic for quality of service (QoS); however, PCF is not implemented in current 802.11 products. The 802.11 committee developed a new standard called

802.11e [71, 72], which is an extension of DCF and provides a distributed access mechanism for service differentiation. More details about PCF can be found in the computer networking literature [39, 46, 73–75].

SHORTCOMINGS OF 802.11

Although 802.11 has been standardized and is gaining widespread popularity as a channel access protocol for WLANs, the protocol has several potential limitations. One of the limitations of the 802.11 protocols is the low bandwidth utilization under medium to high traffic loads, and consequently, it achieves low throughput, high packet delay, and a high packet drop ratio. Another deficiency of the 802.11 protocol is poor fairness in sharing a channel bandwidth among the active stations [76]. Another fundamental problem of the 802.11 protocol is high transmission overheads (headers, backoff time, interframe spaces, and acknowledgments) [20, 77, 78]. The proposed buffer unit multiple access (BUMA) protocol described in Chapter 9 overcomes these shortcomings of 802.11. The overhead of DCF is also analyzed in Chapter 9.

WLAN PERFORMANCE ESTIMATION APPROACHES

The performance of a typical WLAN system can be measured with respect to mean throughput and packet delay. This section describes methods for WLAN performance estimation adopted in this book. Since this book focuses on performance improvement of WLANs, it is necessary to adopt a methodology that is able to quantify the effectiveness of such performance estimation in real systems.

In the estimation of WLAN performance, both propagation measurements and simulations were used. A measurement-based approach was adopted because it inherently includes the interactions between the real hardware and the environment. It also provides an unbiased representation of the radio channel without any assumptions on how signals propagate in the environment. Although this measurement-based approach is time- and labor-intensive, it can be significantly reduced by automating the measurement system and process as highlighted in [25]. While simple statistical propagation models offer quick estimates of how signals propagate in an indoor environment, they do not capture all the variables/parameters of real systems. Similarly, the development of analytical models for the performance evaluation of 802.11 WLANs for station N ≥ 2 is very difficult because of capturing the dynamic behaviors of multiple stations. Therefore, many leading network researchers have used computer simulation for performance studies of computer and telecommunication networks [44, 79–84]. In addition, the analytical results are only based on simplistic network models and only meaningful asymptotically. For a realistic wireless network where various parameters affect network performance, the asymptotic scaling law does not really reflect the actual network behaviors. As a consequence, a measurement-based approach is selected for estimating the RSS in this book. While propagation measurements can be used for formulating an opinion about the deployment of WLANs in an indoor environment, they have limitations when it comes to generalization of the research findings. To overcome this generalization problem, computer simulation was also adopted. Simulation methods were also used to analyze the performance of wireless MAC protocols, investigate the impact of traffic arrival distributions on WLAN performance, and optimize cross-layer design. Instead of evaluating the accuracies of various propagation models as in [85], both measurement- and simulation-based performance estimation approaches were used in this book. The development of an accurate propagation modeling method is beyond the scope of this book.

FURTHER READING

For more details about subjects discussed in this chapter, we recommend the following books and references. The items in [] refer to the reference list at the end of the book.

Books

[36] Chapters 4 and 9—*Wireless Personal and Local Area Networks* by Sikora

[37] Chapter 16—*Computer Networks and Internets with Internet Applications* by Comer

Research Papers

[38]

[39]

[68]

[86]

SUMMARY

In this chapter, the fundamentals of WLANs were outlined and essential background information on the design and deployment of such systems was provided. In particular, the architecture of a typical WLAN, including wireless ad hoc and infrastructure networks, has been described. The similarities and differences between WLAN and cellular networks were highlighted. The factors influencing WLAN performance have been identified and described. The impact of radio signal interference on WLAN performance was also outlined. The details of the 802.11 PHY characteristics affecting WLAN performance that are fundamental in the design and deployment of WLAN systems were discussed, and the MAC protocols implemented in the 802.11 WLANs, including DCF and PCF, were described in detail.

The design issues of wireless MAC protocols are discussed in Chapter 4. A research methodology for investigations in this book was chosen by adapting previous research [24, 25]. This methodology involves the performance estimation of WLANs. Both measurement-based and simulation approaches were adopted for their accuracy and flexibility in estimating WLAN performance. The radio propagation characteristics are described in Chapter 3.

KEY TERMS

Access point (AP)
Acknowledgment (ACK)
Automatic rate fallback (ARF)
Backoff
Binary phase-shift keying (BPSK)
Bit error rate (BER)
Capture effect
Centralized
Clear to send (CTS)
Code division multiple access (CDMA)
CSMA/CA
Distributed coordination function (DCF)
Exposed station
Extended service set (ESS)
Frequency division multiple access (FDMA)

Hidden station
Independent basic service set (IBSS)
Medium access control (MAC)
Mobile terminal (MT)
Network allocation vector (NAV)
Physical layer PLCP
Point coordination function (PCF)
Polling-based access mechanism
Quadrature amplitude modulation (QAM)
Quadrature phase-shift keying (QPSK)
Received signal strength (RSS)
Request to send (RTS)
Signal collision
Signal-to-interference ratio (SIR)
Signal-to-noise ratio (SNR)

REVIEW QUESTIONS

1. WLANs are being deployed almost everywhere in which people live and work. List and describe two commonly used architectures of a typical WLAN.

2. Although there are some similarities between a WLAN and a cellular network, they are very different. List and describe three differences between a WLAN and a cellular network.

3. There are various factors that influence the performance of WLANs. Identify and describe four main performance-limiting factors of WLANs.

4. While link layer protocols may affect the performance of 802.11 networks, it is useful to be able to understand the PHY characteristics of 802.11, especially for network design and evaluation. Discuss the physical layer characteristics of 802.11 networks.

5. Discuss (with a diagram) the basic concept of capture effect. Discuss the impact of capture effect on WLAN performance.

6. Using a diagram, discuss the difference between hidden node and exposed node problems in wireless networks. Discuss the impact of hidden and exposed nodes on WLAN performance.

7. DCF and PCF are commonly used channel access mechanisms in 802.11 networks. Compare and contrast DCF and PCF access methods of 802.11.

MINI-PROJECTS

The mini-projects aim to provide deeper understanding of the topics covered in this chapter. More mini-projects are presented in the subsequent chapters to emphasize hands-on practical activities, including propagation measurements and simulations experiments.

1. Infrastructure-based WLANs can be found in many places, including university campuses, hospitals, and small businesses worldwide. The purpose of this project is to develop a good knowledge and understanding of WLAN design and applications. Conduct

an in-depth literature review on infrastructure-based WLANs focusing on design architecture, protocol, channel assignment, and applications.

2. WLANs are being deployed in large organizations worldwide. It is useful to be able to gather more information about the usage of WLANs in large organizations. Conduct a survey (using a questionnaire) on WLAN deployment in large organizations.

CHAPTER 3

Radio Propagation Characteristics

LEARNING OUTCOMES

After reading and completing this chapter, you will be able to:

- Describe various mechanisms of radio propagation

- Discuss the effect of interference on WLAN performance

- Describe the effect of multipath propagation on WLAN performance

- Discuss the effect of signal attenuation on system performance

- Define received signal strength (RSS), signal-to-noise ratio (SNR), signal-to-interference ratio (SIR), and bit error rate (BER)

INTRODUCTION

In Chapter 2, WLAN architecture, location-dependent effects, and 802.11 physical and medium access control (MAC) protocols were outlined. One of the main objectives of this book is to quantify the key performance-limiting factors of WLANs. To achieve this goal, a general understanding of radio propagation characteristics is required. This chapter aims to provide background material for the book, especially for Chapter 7. An overview of radio propagation mechanisms is presented. The effect of the radio propagation environment on WLAN performance is reviewed. The performance of a typical WLAN can be affected by signal interference, attenuation, and multipath propagation effect. An overview of signal interference, multipath propagation, and attenuation is presented in the "Signal Interference," "Multipath Propagation," and "Attenuation" sections, respectively. The "Signal Quality: RSS, SNR, SIR, and BER" section describes the impact of received signal strength, signal-to-noise ratio, signal-to-interference ratio, and bit error rate on WLAN performance.

RADIO PROPAGATION MECHANISMS

There are three basic mechanisms of radio propagation in wireless and mobile communications. These are reflection, diffraction, and scattering. These mechanisms are briefly described below.

- **Reflection:** It occurs when a propagating electromagnetic wave impinges on an object that has very large dimensions compared to the wavelength of the propagating wave. For example, reflections occur from the surface of the earth, from tall buildings and walls.

- **Diffraction:** This occurs when a radio signal path between a transmitter and a receiver is obstructed by a surface of the tall buildings or similar objects. In other words, waves bend by the surface of the obstacle.

- **Scattering:** This occurs when objects are smaller than the wavelength of the propagating wave. For example, when a radio signal propagates through street signs or lampposts, the incoming signal is scattered into several weaker outgoing signals.

Received power (or its reciprocal, path loss) is generally the most important parameter predicted by large-scale propagation models based on the physics of reflection, scattering, and diffraction. Small-scale fading and multipath propagation may also be described by the physics of these three basic propagation mechanisms. More details about propagation mechanisms can be found in wireless communication textbooks [87].

RADIO PROPAGATION ENVIRONMENT: A REVIEW OF LITERATURE

The power received at a mobile receiver in an indoor environment is primarily influenced by the characteristics of the surrounding propagation environment [27, 28]. For proper deployment of Wi-Fi networks in a multistory building, it is essential that the features that influence the propagation characteristics of the building are identified.

A wireless channel is affected by the distance between a transmitter and a receiver (i.e., path loss), propagation characteristics of radio signals in certain environments (e.g., obstructed office environment), obstacles due to office walls and corners (i.e., shadowing and multipath fading [88]), and the presence of other devices operating in the same frequencies (e.g., 2.4 GHz cordless phones). To handle the problems of signal path loss and multipath fading, and to provide a better SIR at the destination station, radio propagation modeling is required. Path loss models for both line-of-sight (LOS) and non-LOS conditions are highlighted below.

Analytical models for predicting path loss between a transmitter (Tx) and a receiver (Rx) for LOS and non-LOS conditions are given by Equations (3.1) and (3.2), respectively [27]:

$$\bar{L}(d) = L_{FS}(d_0) + 10n\log_{10}\frac{d}{d_0} \tag{3.1}$$

$$\bar{L}(d) = L_{FS}(d_0) + 10n\log_{10}(d) + \sum_i KoiLoi \tag{3.2}$$

where $\bar{L}(d)$ is the average path loss value (in decibels) at distance d between Tx and Rx, $L_{FS}(d_0)$ is the free-space path loss at a reference distance d_0 and n and is the path loss exponent that characterizes how fast path loss increases with increase of Tx-Rx separation. Koi is defined as the number of penetrated obstructions of type i, Loi is the attenuation of the i th type of obstruction, and i is the number of different obstructions.

As shown in Equation (3.2), the model for estimating path loss for the non-LOS condition includes additional path loss from the obstructions between the Tx and Rx.

A radio propagation environment is one of the important factors that influence the throughput performance of Wi-Fi networks. A detailed discussion of wireless communications, and of radio propagation in general, can be found in [27, 89]. Many previous studies in the area of indoor WLAN have focused on the engineering approach of measuring radio links, e.g., propagation modeling and measurements such as path loss, received signal strength, and attenuation. In this section we review a selected set of literature that is indicative of the types of approaches used for radio propagation measurements. No attempt is made to be complete, but key characteristics of propagation are highlighted.

Seidel and Rappaport [28] investigated path loss prediction models for indoor wireless communication in multifloored buildings. Punnoose et al. [90] conducted various experiments in a controlled laboratory environment to investigate the interference between Bluetooth and IEEE 802.11b direct sequence spread spectrum (DSSS) devices. Schafer et al. [91] reported radio wave propagation measurements and simulation experiments in hospital settings. The attenuation of single walls and rooms was also investigated and reported.

Moraitis and Constantinou [92] investigated several characteristics of radio propagation through indoor channels between fixed terminals: (1) path loss measurements for both LOS and non-LOS cases, (2) fading statistics in a physically stationary environment, and (3) a detailed investigation of the people movement effect on the temporal fading envelope.

Pena et al. [93] investigated the attenuation and the equivalent permittivity and conductivity of brick and concrete walls for the 900-MHz band using ray-tracing modeling. Sarkar and Sowerby [94] investigated the performance of Wi-Fi link throughput in an obstructed office environment. Using 802.11b cards, they examined the impact of LOS blockage by office walls and partitions on Wi-Fi link throughput.

A study was conducted by Messier et al. [95] at Worcester Polytechnic Institute to investigate the influence of various factors on the performance of WLANs. One of the aims of the study was to find a correlation between received signal power and throughput. Anderson and Rappaport [96] conducted wideband multipath measurements at 2.5 and 60 GHz for indoor wireless communication. Yang [97] examined the effects of radiated radio frequency (RF) interference on wireless communication systems. Two specific examples are investigated, including a dongle for a wireless mouth and a PCMCIA card for a laptop computer.

The above review of literature reveals that the effect of propagation environments on Wi-Fi link throughput is an unexplored area in the field of wireless networks. More research work is required in the field of propagation environments to improve the performance of WLANs. The radio propagation measurement approach was used for system performance evaluation in this book.

SIGNAL INTERFERENCE

Signal interference degrades WLAN performance by increasing BER as well as retransmission rates. For example, signal leaking from a microwave oven operating in the industrial, scientific, and medical (ISM) band interferes with WLANs by corrupting packets [98, 99]. Similarly, Bluetooth devices operate in the ISM band, causing coexistence interference, and hence degrade WLAN performance [100, 101]. Jo and Jayant [102] pointed out that the WLAN throughput degrades significantly if Bluetooth and WLAN devices coexist within a 2-m radius. However, the packet loss due to Bluetooth interference can be mitigated by decreasing WLAN transmitter power [101].

Although the 802.11 standard defined 14 channels, only 3 nonoverlapping channels (1, 6, and 11) are being used in practice. Two or more access points (APs) configured with the same channel or adjacent channels result in co-channel interference. Park et al. [103] reported that link throughput of 802.11b drops to 2 Mbps as a result of co-channel interference. To mitigate the effects of co-channel interference, robust modulation methods can be used (e.g., orthogonal code sets, complementary code keying [CCK]) [104]. Channel impairments such as loss, fading, noise, and interference are highlighted in the "Attenuation" section. This book does not investigate the impact of interference on WLAN performance, as other network researchers have investigated it extensively [47, 105–108].

MULTIPATH PROPAGATION

Signal reflection or diffraction may lead to multipath propagation, which is very common in indoor wireless environments. The radio signal would reflect from objects during transmission (e.g., wall, ceiling, and office partitions). The multipath causes signal fading, and therefore the receiver would not get sufficient signal power for communications effectively [109].

Signal fading is caused by interference between two or more versions of the transmitted signal that arrive at the receiver at slightly different times. These waves, called *multipath waves*, combine at the receiver antenna to give a resultant signal that can vary widely in amplitude and phase, depending on the distribution of the intensity and relative propagation time of the waves and the bandwidth of the transmitted signal.

ATTENUATION

When two wireless mobile stations communicate, the signal power drops due to signal attenuation. As a result of signal attenuation, the received signal may not have sufficient strength for effective communication, and therefore the system performance degrades significantly. Furthermore, metal door and structural concrete walls have a more significant impact on signal attenuation than other constructional materials in an indoor environment [110]. Table 3.1 lists the commonly used building materials and the corresponding attenuation.

SIGNAL QUALITY: RSS, SNR, SIR, AND BER

The state of radio signal (e.g., good or bad) plays an important role in determining the overall performance of WLANs. The commonly used terms related to signal quality, such as RSS, SNR, SIR, and BER, are briefly described below.

Received Signal Strength

Most network analysis tools and vendors' client management utilities provide a representation of signal strength. The commonly used units for RSS measurements are milliwatts (mW), dB-milliwatts (dBm), received signal strength indicator (RSSI), and a percentage measurement. These units are related to each other, and it is possible to convert from one unit to another. For example, the relationship between dBm and mW is given by [111]

$$dBm = 10 \log_{10}(mW) \tag{3.3}$$

or

$$mW = 10^{dBm/10} \tag{3.4}$$

TABLE 3.1   Signal Attenuation for Various Constructional Material

Material	Attenuation (dB)
Plasterboard	3–5
Glass wall with metal frame	6
Cinderblock wall	4–6
Window	3
Metal door	6–10
Structural concrete wall	6–15

RSS is defined in 802.11 as RSSI; it is intended to be used as a relative value within the chipset. RSSI is not associated with any particular mW scale and is not required to be of any particular accuracy or precision. Therefore, the signal strength numbers reported by an 802.11 card are not consistent between vendors. In this book, however, dBm is used for RSS measurement.

Signal-to-Noise Ratio

The performance of any physical (PHY) layer implementation can be well understood by observing its packet loss rate as a function of the received SNR. The SNR is a relative measure of the strength of the received signal and noise powers (in this case noise refers to thermal noise internal to the chipset). The SNR is typically measured in decibels (dB) and is given by

$$SNR_{dB} = 10\log_{10}\frac{S}{N} \qquad (3.5)$$

where S and N are the received signal and noise powers, respectively.

More details about noise and its classification can be found in the computer and data communications literature [73, 112]. Typically, the larger the SNR, the better the chance of any packet being received error-free. The actual performance of packet loss rate as a function of SNR depends on system implementation. For instance, Steger et al. [113] conducted various controlled laboratory tests under hardware-emulated channel conditions and found that the 802.11b-compliant cards from different manufacturers actually perform differently in identical channel conditions. However, in this book both RSS and SNR measurements are used for system performance evaluation (Chapters 7, 8, 10, and 14). In the investigation, no external sources of interference, including co-channel interference, are considered.

Signal-to-Interference Ratio

SIR refers to the strength of the signal relative to the ambient RF energy in the environment. Because of the difficulty in measuring background noise and interference, the SIR measurement approach was not considered in this book. However, a powerful spectrum analyzer may be required to measure SIR.

Bit Error Rate

BER is the ratio of the number of error bits received to the number of total bits sent during a fixed period. The performance of a typical WLAN is strongly affected by BER. Increasing BER would result in lower throughput, high packet delay, and a high packet drop ratio [114]. The effect of channel BER on system performance is investigated in Chapter 12.

FURTHER READING

For more details about subjects discussed in this chapter, we recommend the following books and references. The items in [] refer to the reference list at the end of the book.

Books

[27] Chapter 5—*Wireless Communications: Principles and Practice* by Rappaport

[87] Chapter 3—*Introduction to Wireless and Mobile Systems* by Agrawal and Zeng

Research Papers

[28]

[115]

SUMMARY

In this chapter, the radio propagation characteristics are revisited. It provided some essential background material information for Chapter 7. In particular, radio propagation mechanisms, multipath, attenuation, and signal interference are discussed. The key concepts of received RSS, SNR, SIR, and BER are defined, and their impact on system performance is discussed. The design issues of wireless MAC protocols are discussed in Chapter 4.

KEY TERMS

Automatic rate fallback (ARF)	Path loss
DCF interframe space (DIFS)	Point coordination function (PCF)
Direct sequence spread spectrum (DSSS)	Radio propagation
Distributed coordination function (DCF)	Rayleigh fading channel
Extended service set (ESS)	Short interframe space (SIFS)
EEE 802.11	Signal collision
Independent basic service set (IBSS)	Wireless local area network (WLAN)

REVIEW QUESTIONS

1. A general understanding of the methods of radio propagation mechanisms is required for deeper understanding of WLAN design and deployment. Identify and describe three methods of radio propagation.

2. Radio signal interference plays an important role in determining the performance of WLANs. Discuss the effect of radio signal interference on the performance of a typical 802.11 network.

3. In indoor WLAN systems, multipath propagation can seriously affect the performance of WLANs. Explain how multipath propagation can affect the performance of a typical 802.11 network.

4. Signal attenuation is one of the factors affecting WLAN performance. Discuss the effect of signal attenuation on the performance of a typical 802.11 network.

5. Define the following terms: received signal strength, signal-to-noise ratio, signal-to-interference ratio, and bit error rate.

6. Discuss the relationship between RSS and data rate in the following propagation environments: (a) open space and (b) obstructed office block.

MINI-PROJECTS

The following mini-projects aim to provide deeper understanding of the topics covered in this chapter through literature review. More mini-projects have been presented in Section II of this book to emphasize hands-on practical learning experience.

1. The purpose of this project is to develop a good knowledge and understanding of radio propagation characteristics and methods. Conduct an in-depth literature review on various methods of radio propagation. (Hint: Identify the methods, categorize them, and discuss the strengths and weaknesses, and issues and challenge.)

2. Radio signal interference can severely affect the performance of WLANs. The purpose of this project is to develop sound knowledge and understanding of signal interference and its impact on system performance. Conduct an in-depth literature review on methods of minimizing signal interference. (Hint: Identify the methods of minimization, categorize them, and discuss the strengths and weaknesses, and issues and challenges.)

3. Multipath propagation severely affects the performance of WLANs, especially in obstructed office block. Conduct an in-depth literature review on multipath propagation. (Hint: Focus on the methods of mitigating multipath effects, and discuss their strengths and weaknesses, and overall issues and challenges.)

Wireless Medium Access Control Protocols

LEARNING OUTCOMES

After reading and completing this chapter, you will be able to:

- Identify the leading researchers and their contribution in the design of wireless medium access control (MAC) protocols

- Review some representative wireless MAC protocols

- Discuss the issues and challenges in the design of wireless MAC protocols

- Describe commonly used network performance metrics

- Discuss the impact of radio propagation on MAC protocol design

- Discuss the effect of network performance on MAC protocol design

INTRODUCTION

The fundamentals of radio propagation mechanisms were discussed in Chapter 3. They provided essential background information underpinning the key performance-limiting factors of WLANs. One of the objectives of this book is to quantify the effect of MAC protocols on the performance of a typical WLAN. To this end, a basic understanding of the issues in the design of wireless MAC protocols is required. This chapter provides that information.

In the "Wireless MAC Protocols: A Review of the Literature" section, a review of the literature considering the design and performance improvement of wireless MAC protocols is presented. The leading network researchers and their main contributions are also highlighted in this section. The "MAC Protocol Performance Issues" section discusses various performance issues of wireless MAC protocols. Two important design issues of wireless MAC protocols are discussed in the "Design Issues for Wireless MAC Protocols" section: radio propagation environments, and network performance and service requirements. The influences of the radio propagation environments and network performance on the design of wireless MAC protocols are discussed in the "Influence of Radio Propagation on MAC Protocol Design" and "Effect of Network Performance on MAC Protocol Design" sections, respectively. Finally, the chapter is summarized in the last section.

WIRELESS MAC PROTOCOLS: A REVIEW OF THE LITERATURE

A good MAC protocol for WLANs should provide an efficient mechanism for sharing a limited wireless channel bandwidth, together with simplicity of operation, high bandwidth utilization, and fairness in serving all stations. Ideally, low mean packet delay, high throughput, low packet drop ratio, and a good degree of fairness when traffic is high are desired; however, the 802.11 MAC protocols do not provide all the quality of service (QoS) provisions simultaneously. Therefore, a variety of MAC protocols have been developed to suit different circumstances where various trade-off factors were considered [63, 116–124]. A good overview of wireless MAC protocols focusing on MAC classification can be found in [125]. In this book, the investigation on the performance improvement of WLANs is therefore concentrated on modifying a MAC protocol as reported in Chapter 9. In this section, a review of the literature on wireless MAC protocols focuses on: (1) MAC protocol classification, (2) contention versus contention-free, and (3) representative MAC protocols.

Wireless MAC Protocol Classification

Wireless MAC protocols can be classified in different ways. For example, Chandra et al. [126] have classified wireless MAC protocols into three categories based on the commonly used WLAN topology: (1) ad hoc, (2) infrastructure, and (3) hybrid (combined ad hoc and infrastructure).

MAC protocols designed for wireless ad hoc networks are quite different from those designed for infrastructure-based networks. Most MAC protocols for ad hoc networks use either handshaking or busy tone signals to avoid packet collisions, and therefore ad hoc MAC protocols can further be classified into busy tone and collision avoidance. In both classes of ad hoc MAC protocols, sending special signals or packets can reduce collisions. Examples of ad hoc MAC protocols include busy tone multiple access (BTMA) [56, 127], wireless collision detection (WCD) [128], multiple access with collision avoidance (MACA) [61], multiple access with collision avoidance for wireless networks (MACAW) [63], and floor acquisition multiple access (FAMA) [129].

In infrastructure-based MAC protocols, the base station (BS), a centralized controller, coordinates transmission among the mobile terminals (MTs). The infrastructure network allows a highly optimized MAC. MAC protocols for infrastructure networks can be categorized into random access, guaranteed access, and hybrid access. The random access protocols achieve high efficiency and maintain simplicity in operation. The guaranteed access protocols eliminate collisions by using polling techniques. The hybrid access protocols can further be classified into two groups: random reservation and demand assignment. The random reservation protocols require and reserve the bandwidth in a free fashion, whereas the protocols with demand assignment transmit a request and wait for a BS to assign a bandwidth. Examples of infrastructure-based MAC protocols include resource auction multiple access (RAMA) [130], packet reservation multiple access (PRMA) [131], and time division multiple access with dynamic reservation (TDMA/DR) [132].

The performance of ad hoc MAC protocols is slightly lower than that of infrastructure MAC protocols. This performance degradation is due to propagation delays caused by handshaking (i.e., control packets) for collision avoidance. The hybrid MAC protocols are designed for networks based on an ad hoc centralized topology. This type of network is viewed as an ad hoc network (one that can be easily set up in any place without a BS), with a centralized administrator usually being a mobile BS. The Bluetooth personal area network is an example of a hybrid MAC protocol [133].

Contention-Based versus Contention-Free MAC Protocol

In addition to the wireless MAC protocol classification outlined earlier, the existing MAC protocols can be divided into two main categories: (1) contention based and (2) contention-free. A contention-based protocol requires a station to compete for access to a common channel each time it sends a packet. Carrier sense multiple access (CSMA) protocols are good examples of basic contention-based MAC protocols [134]. In the CSMA protocols, a station senses the channel before it transmits a packet and defers transmission unless the channel is idle. This generally prevents a station from transmitting simultaneously with other stations within its transmission range. While CSMA protocols are a significant improvement over the ALOHA protocol [135], they do not perform well when traffic is high. Another example of a contention-based protocol is distributed coordination function (DCF) based on CSMA with collision avoidance (CSMA/CA) [39, 46]. This protocol is basically a listen-before-talk scheme. DCF is described in detail in the "IEEE 802.11 DCF" section in Chapter 2.

While contention-based protocols have unique characteristics, such as random access, simplicity in operation, and ease of implementation, they have network instability problems, especially when traffic is high. To overcome these instability problems, various contention-free protocols have been developed, including fixed assignment (in time or frequency), polling, token passing, or dynamic reservation. Fixed-assignment protocols are typically based on TDMA [136], where each station can transmit data at the beginning of its allocated time slot without collisions. The main limitation of TDMA is the wastage of channel bandwidth, particularly for bursty traffic.

The slot assignment strategy is also somewhat complex in mobile networks. While polling schemes reduce the time wastage of TDMA, they still incur polling delays at all stations. Token passing schemes have similar problems because the token must be circulated to all stations in the ring irrespective of whether the stations have packets for transmission or not. 802.11's point coordination function (PCF) ("IEEE 802.11 PCF" section in Chapter 2) is another example of a polling-based MAC protocol [39]. To overcome the problems of fixed assignments, polling and token passing various dynamic reservation-based protocols have been developed where stations reserve the channel for transmissions [61, 63, 129, 130, 137].

Representative MAC Protocols

In the last 30 years, numerous MAC protocols have been developed for WLANs. Table 4.1 lists the leading network researchers and their main contributions in the design and performance improvement of MAC protocols for WLANs. The year when these wireless protocols were developed or published in the computer networking literature is shown in column 3. Column 4 highlights the mechanisms that were used in the design and improvement of selected MAC protocols for WLANs.

TABLE 4.1 Leading Researchers and Their Contributions in the Design of Wireless MAC Protocols

Researcher	Contribution	Year	Description/Key Concept
Karn, P.	MACA [61]	1990	Avoiding collisions by using control packets RTS and CTS
Bharghavan, V.	MACAW [63]	1994	Improving the efficiency of MACA by using a better backoff algorithm
Bianchi, G., et al.	Adaptive contention window [138] C-PRMA [131]	1996 1997	Introducing an adaptive contention window size and a centralized packet reservation multiple access protocol
Garcia-Luna-Aceves, J. J., et al.	FAMA [129] GAMA-PS [139]	1995 1998	Obtaining control of the channel before transmission; channel is divided into a sequence of cycles for group transmission
Conti, M., et al.	SDP [38] Dynamic 802.11 [140] 802.11+ [141]	2001 2000 2000	Introducing a simple Dynamic 802.11 protocol, adaptive backoff algorithm, and dynamic tuning of 802.11
Nicopolitidis, P., et al.	TRAP [142]	2002	Introducing a TDMA-based polling scheme
Natkaniec, M., and Pach, A. R.	PUMA [123] DIDD backoff [143]	2002 2000	Proposing a new backoff mechanism called double increment double decrement (DIDD)
Bensaou, B., et al.	Collision-free [144] Fair MAC [145] DFWMAC [146, 147]	2004 2003 2001	Proposing a collision-free MAC, topology-blind fair MAC, and 802.11 DFWMAC protocols
Kwon, Y., et al.	FCR [116]	2003	Achieving fast collision resolution by increasing contention window size
You, T., et al.	CSMA/IC [59] CSMA/CP [64]	2003 2003	Assigning unique ID to each packet to prevent collision in the control channel
Jagadeesan, S., et al.	ICSMA [148]	2003	Reducing exposed station problems by using two data channels
Xiao, Y.	Improvement to 802.11 DCF [77]	2004	Achieving better system performance by concatenation and piggybacking
Peng, J., et al.	Collision detection MAC [149]	2007	Introducing collision detection by using pulses in an out-of-band control channel
Minooei, H., and Nojumi, H.	New backoff method [150]	2007	Introducing a new backoff algorithm to improve the performance of 802.11

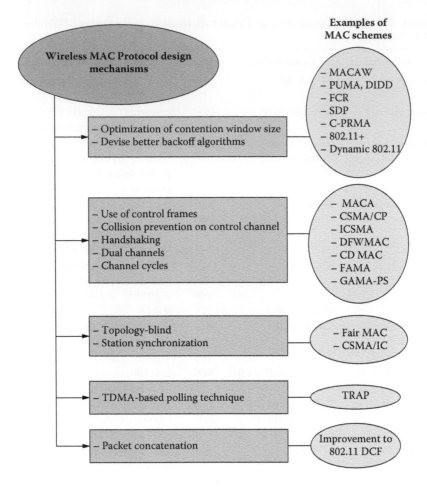

FIGURE 4.1 Mechanisms used in the design of representative wireless MAC protocols.

These mechanisms were grouped into five main categories (Figure 4.1). A brief description of each of the main contributions in the design of the wireless MAC protocols listed in Table 4.1 is given below.

Multiple Access with Collision Avoidance Protocol
Karn [61] proposed the MAC protocol called MACA to address the hidden station problems. This scheme is based on the protocol used in Apple LocalTalk networks, and uses request to send (RTS) and clear to send (CTS) control packets to explicitly indicate the intention of placing data onto the channel. Most of the hidden station problems are solved by this RTS-CTS approach, and data packet collisions are avoided. If the sending

station does not hear a CTS in response from the receiving station, it will eventually time out, assuming a collision occurred, and then schedule the packet for retransmission. MACA uses the binary exponential backoff algorithm to select this retransmission time.

Multiple Access with Collision Avoidance for Wireless Networks Protocol

Bharghavan et al. [63] developed the MAC protocol for WLANs called MACAW to improve the efficiency of MACA [61] by adding a retransmission mechanism to the MAC sublayer. Besides using RTS-CTS, three other control packets are introduced: (1) data sending (DS), (2) acknowledgment (ACK), and (3) request for RTS (RRTS). In the MACAW, an RTS-CTS handshake and subsequent data transmission is followed by an explicit ACK. Before sending a data packet, a station sends a short 30-byte DS frame, and it uses the RTS-CTS-DS-DATA-ACK message exchange to transmit a data packet. When the sender does not receive the ACK within a time-out period, it assumes that the data were corrupted and considers retransmission. Whenever a station receives an RTS to which it cannot respond (due to deferral), it then contends during the next contention period and sends an RRTS to the sender of the RTS. The motivation for designing MACAW was also to improve the fairness of MACA. This fairness improvement is mainly due to the selection of a better backoff algorithm called multiplicative increase linear decrease (MILD), and some additional control packets in the system.

Centralized Packet Reservation Multiple Access (C-PRMA) Protocol

Bianchi et al. developed a MAC protocol for WLANs, C-PRMA [131]. In [138, 151], an algorithm for adaptive contention window size is proposed for 802.11 WLANs. The key concept is to dynamically select the optimum backoff window size based on an estimate of the number of contending stations. This optimization is performed through the measurement of channel activity by each station. They showed that by using this adaptive contention window size, instead of binary exponential backoff (BEB), the performance of 802.11 could be significantly improved, especially at high loads and large user numbers.

Floor Acquisition Multiple Access and Group Allocation
Multiple Access with Packet Sensing (GAMA-PS) Protocols

Garcia-Luna-Aceves et al. [129, 139] developed a number of MAC protocols for WLANs, including FAMA [129] and GAMA-PS [139] protocols. FAMA combines the advantages of CSMA and MACA. In FAMA, each station senses the channel for a given waiting period before transmitting control packets to avoid collisions (of control packets). The key idea is to acquire control of the channel (floor) before transmission. Also, following a data transmission, a waiting period is enforced on all the neighbors of the transmitter-receiver pair to ensure collision-free delivery of the ACK frame. GAMA-PS is designed for spread spectrum WLANs that cannot provide accurate carrier sensing or time slotting. In GAMA-PS, the transmission channel is divided into a sequence of cycles; each cycle begins with a contention period and ends with a group transmission period. GAMA-PS uses a form of dynamic reservation where a station can make a channel reservation by sending an RTS using a packet sensing strategy (i.e., a station backs off only when a packet is corrupted, not after detecting a carrier). After receiving an RTS packet, the destination station responds with a CTS packet. This RTS-CTS exchange occurs during a contention period. Once a station successfully completes an RTS-CTS exchange, it is allocated its own transmission period, and the station maintains ownership of this transmission period as long as it has data for transmission.

Simple Dynamic Protocol (SDP), Dynamic 802.11 and 802.11+

In a series of papers Conti et al. [38, 140, 141] proposed a MAC protocol for WLANs called SDP. Its performance is investigated in [38]. SDP is a backoff-tuning algorithm that only requires simple load estimates. More specifically, SDP only requires an estimate of the average time the channel is idle and the average time the channel is busy due to collisions. These two quantities can be estimated directly from the carrier sensing mechanism implemented in each station of 802.11 networks. In [140], an extension of the original 802.11 called Dynamic 802.11 is presented. This dynamic protocol is based on a distributed backoff-tuning algorithm that is used to tune the size of the backoff window at runtime. Each station executes this backoff-tuning algorithm independently. In [141], another enhancement of 802.11, called 802.11+, is presented. In the 802.11+, the channel contention window size is computed at runtime through a distributed algorithm that estimates the window size corresponding to the theoretical limit.

Priority Unavoidable Multiple Access (PUMA) Protocol
Natkaniec and Pach developed the MAC protocol called PUMA [123] to improve 802.11 WLAN performance. The concept is to introduce a priority scheme for time-bounded services. Both a special jam signal and an additional timer are required to support isochronous transmission. Network performance improvement is achieved using double increment double decrement (DIDD), a new backoff algorithm [143].

TDMA-Based Randomly Addressed Polling (TRAP) Protocol
Nicopolitidis et al. [142] developed a MAC scheme for WLANs called TRAP, an extension of the RAP protocol [152]. TRAP employs a variable-length TDMA-based contention stage with the length based on the number of active stations. At the beginning of each polling cycle, all active MTs register their intention with the BS by transmitting a short pulse. The BS uses the aggregate received pulse to estimate the number of active stations. Based on this estimate, the BS then schedules the contention stage to have an adequate number of time slots, P, for the active stations registering their intention for transmission. The BS sends a READY message containing P. Each MT computes a random value (address) in the interval $[0, ..., P-1]$, and transmits its registration request in the respective time slot. The BS then polls each station according to the received random addresses. If two or more MTs select the same random address, their random address transmissions collide and are not received at the BS. Thus, the random addresses received correctly at the BS are always distinct, with each number identifying a single active MT. If the BS successfully receives a packet from an MT, it sends an ACK before polling the next MT.

Fast Collision Resolution (FCR)
Kwon et al. [116] proposed an efficient distributed contention-based MAC algorithm called FCR, which attempts to resolve the collisions quickly by increasing the sizes of the contention windows of both the colliding and deferring stations. In this scheme, all active stations will redistribute their backoff timers to avoid possible future collisions.

Interleaved Carrier Sense Multiple Access (ICSMA) Protocol
Jagadeesan et al. [148] proposed a MAC protocol suitable for wireless ad hoc networks known as ICSMA. This protocol uses two data channels (say, channels 1 and 2) of equal bandwidth, and the handshaking process is distributed between the two channels. In this scheme, a station is allowed

to transmit by using either channel, depending on availability. For example, a source station may send an RTS packet to a destination station over channel 1, and the destination station responds with CTS on channel 2. Similarly, if a station sends a data packet on channel 1, then the receiver can acknowledge over channel 2. ICSMA uses the same binary exponential backoff mechanism as DCF, including waiting times such as DIFS and PIFS. The ICSMA performs better than the 802.11 protocol with exposed stations with respect to throughput, mean packet delay, and fairness.

Collision-Free MAC, Fair MAC, and 802.11 Distributed Foundation Wireless MAC (DFWMAC)

Bensaou et al. [144–147] developed a number of MAC protocols for WLANs. In [144], a class of collision-free MAC scheduling algorithms, namely, linear increase and random scheme, has been proposed. These algorithms provide a transmission code mapping method to guarantee collision-free transmissions. An improvement in the long-term fairness of DCF was shown. The performance of the topology-blind, fair MAC is investigated in [145]. DFWMAC is a CSMA/CA protocol that provides both a mandatory basic access method and an optional RTS-CTS access method. In DFWMAC, four packets, namely, RTS-CTS-DATA-ACK, are used for data transmission between two stations. The 802.11 DFWMAC [146, 147] is a fairness extension of the basic DFWMAC. Fairness is achieved by using an improved backoff algorithm where each station adjusts its contention window according to the estimated share it obtained.

Carrier Sense Multiple Access with ID Countdown (CSMA/IC) and Carrier Sense Multiple Access with Collision Prevention (CSMA/CP) Protocols

You et al. [59, 64] proposed two MAC methods for improving 802.11 WLAN performance: CSMA/IC [59] and CSMA/CP [64]. In CSMA/IC, the transmission radius is fixed to a certain unified value and the sensing radius is at least twice the transmission radius. By proper station synchronization, only two stations can compete for a medium at a time, and the station with the packet that has the larger unique ID has priority. By exchanging synchronizing packets, CSMA/IC can be 100% collision-free even in random access environments. In CSMA/CP, the wireless channel is partitioned into a control channel and one to several data channels. The key concept in achieving 100% collision-free transmission is to prevent collisions in the control channel.

Concatenation and Piggybacking Mechanisms

Xiao [77] investigated concatenation and piggybacking mechanisms in reducing the overhead of 802.11, thus improving system performance. One mechanism is to concatenate multiple frames into a single transmission provided frames are available and have the same source and destination addresses.

In the piggyback mechanism, a station is allowed to piggyback a data frame to the ACK if it has data to send.

Collision Detection (CD) MAC Protocol

Peng et al. [149] proposed a MAC protocol capable of collision detection in the wireless environment. The proposed protocol uses two channels, data and control, where a station is allowed to transmit simultaneously on both channels. The control channel has a much smaller bandwidth than the data channel and is used for exploring channel condition and medium reservation. The data channel is used for transmitting user payload and ACKs. The basic idea is to use out-of-band contention pulses that have pauses of random lengths to enable two transmitting stations to detect each other. Pulses are relayed by intended data frame receivers; therefore, hidden stations would be able to detect each other if they transmit at the same time. In addition, CTS pulses are used in the proposed protocol to assist collision detection and reduce control frames in the data channel.

New Backoff Algorithm

Minooei and Nojumi [150] proposed a new backoff algorithm to improve 802.11 performance in congested networks. The proposed backoff method is different from BEB used in 802.11 in two aspects: (1) it reduces contention among active stations when the WLAN is not in a saturated status, thus improving the throughput; and (2) it decrements the backoff counter by one instead of resetting CW to CW_{min}.

An extensive literature review reveals that much work has been done on developing better backoff algorithms to improve WLAN performance. A method of improving WLAN performance by modifying the 802.11 MAC protocol based on the concept of packet concatenation is considered and reported in Chapter 9.

MAC PROTOCOL PERFORMANCE ISSUES

Various performance issues, such as packet delay, throughput, fairness, packet drop ratio, stability, scalability, power consumption, radio propagation environment, and service differentiation, are important considerations in the design of MAC protocols for WLANs.

Mean packet delay, throughput, fairness, and packet drop ratio are commonly used metrics for measuring WLAN performance and are used in Chapters 7 to 14. A good knowledge and understanding of these performance metrics is required for design and deployment of WLANs. A brief description of each of the performance metrics is given below:

- **Packet delay:** This parameter is defined as the time it takes for a packet to travel across the network from the source to the destination, and is usually measured in fractions of seconds or time slots. A packet traveling to a station experiences several types of delay, including queuing delay, channel access delay (contention time), and transmission time. It is useful to know the mean and maximum packet delay for a particular application. The delay requirements usually depend on the content being transmitted over the network. For example, real-time voice and video are more delay sensitive than data traffic. More details about packet delay performance of 802.11 can be found in [153].

- **Throughput:** Throughput can be measured in various ways. For example, it is the mean rate of successful message delivery over a communication channel. It can also be defined as a fraction of the total channel capacity that is used for data transmission. Throughput is the actual data rate (as opposed to theoretical data rate) that a channel can support. Commonly used units for throughput measurement are bits per second (bps), packets/second, packets/slot, and channel utilization (in %). The goal of a good MAC protocol is to maximize throughput and minimize channel access delay. The throughput performance of 802.11 has been analyzed extensively in networking literature [140, 151, 154–156].

- **Fairness:** There are various fairness metrics: throughput fairness, delay fairness, or a combination. Throughput fairness is defined as the spread or variation of an individual station's throughput from the networkwide mean throughput. Therefore, a wireless MAC protocol is said to be 100% fair if the throughput fairness is zero. Throughput fairness is further considered in Chapters 9 and 12. Delay fairness can be achieved by ensuring that the delay is equal for all packets regardless of their origin. MAC protocol fairness issues have been addressed in wireless networking literature [147, 157–159]. Generally speaking, a high fairness is desirable.

- **Packet drop ratio:** Packet drop ratio is directly related to packet collision rate (i.e., high packet collisions at the destination stations result in a high packet drop ratio). This metric determines the capability of a MAC protocol in delivering packets successfully to the destination stations. A MAC protocol with a low packet drop ratio is desirable.

- **Stability:** For proper operation, a network should be stable at all times. Normally, a network can become unstable when traffic is high. The challenge is to design a MAC protocol that can offer stability when traffic is high.

- **Scalability:** A scalable network would be able to cope with an increase in the number of stations. One way of achieving scalability is to upgrade networking devices, such as switches and routers. The challenge is to design a MAC protocol that can support future growth.

- **Power consumption:** Due to size and weight constrictions of mobile devices, battery power is usually very limited; therefore, it is important to design a MAC protocol that consumes little power. Various schemes for power saving have been investigated in [160–162].

- **Radio propagation environments:** The wireless channel is generally time varying, space varying, frequency varying, and polarization varying, dependent on the locations of the transmitting and receiving antennas, as well on the particular indoor environment. Radio propagation environments have a significant effect on the performance of a typical WLAN [94, 163]. The challenge is to design a MAC protocol that can operate even in a harsh propagation environment. The influence of radio propagation on MAC protocol design is discussed in the "Influence of Radio Propagation on MAC Protocol Design" section. The effect of radio propagation environments on WLAN performance is further investigated in Chapter 7.

- **Service differentiation:** Because of the increasing popularity of multimedia services, such as voice over IP (VoIP) and streaming video, wireless and mobile networks are expected to support real-time multimedia traffic. One of the requirements for QoS of this real-time traffic is low latency. The challenge is to design a MAC protocol that can satisfy these latency requirements [164, 165].

DESIGN ISSUES FOR WIRELESS MAC PROTOCOLS

This section discusses the impact of the radio propagation characteristics and network performance on the design of wireless MAC protocols.

Influence of Radio Propagation on MAC Protocol Design

Wireless channels have several unique characteristics that make the design of a MAC protocol for them more challenging than designing a MAC protocol for wired networks. This section outlines various issues related to wireless propagation characteristics and their impact on MAC protocol design.

In wireless environments, it is often difficult to transmit and receive data simultaneously since the received signal power is weaker than the transmitted signal power. Time-varying channel conditions such as radio signal reflection, diffraction, and scattering are also problematic in wireless environments. Due to the propagation characteristics of radio signals in certain environments, several copies of the same transmitted signal may arrive at the receiving station at different times, from different directions, and at various strengths. This phenomenon is called multipath [27]. To overcome multipath effects and to provide a better signal-to-interference-and-noise ratio (SINR) at the destination station, radio propagation characterization is required. Although multipath propagation does not directly influence the design of a MAC protocol, it does affect the duration of synchronization and propagation delay.

Signal fading is another challenging issue in radio propagation. It occurs when the received signal strength (RSS) drops below a certain level. Due to signal fading, some parts of the packet transmission may be missed, and in the worst-case scenario, the entire connection can be lost. To cope with this signal fading in WLANs, control packets are transmitted between the BS and MTs to estimate the RSS of the transmission. A handover of the MT is likely to occur when the RSS of the current BS is weaker than the RSS of the neighboring BS [27, 166].

Because there are more sources of interference between the transmitter and the receiver, errors are more likely in a wireless environment than in a wired environment. In wired LANs, bit error rates (BERs) are usually less than 10^{-6}, and are mainly due to random noise. In WLANs, BERs are usually around 10^{-3} [167]. These errors usually occur in bursts; however, longer bursts can occur due to signal fading. It is possible that an entire packet can be lost due to a burst of errors. Many strategies are used to minimize the effect of burst errors. By reducing packet length, the probability of an error occurring in a packet can be decreased. Forward error correction is a technique used to detect and correct burst errors [168]. Packet retransmission and acknowledgment are also used to ensure a packet is delivered to its destination.

Radio signals in the high-frequency bands are directional. Therefore, the locations of the transmitting and receiving antennas are an important consideration in a wireless environment. There are three location-dependent effects: capture, hidden station, and exposed station. These effects need to be considered in designing MAC protocols for WLANs. A detailed description of these location-dependent effects was provided in Chapter 2 ("Location-Dependent Effects" section). Infrastructure-based WLANs can avoid problems of both hidden and exposed stations by using hand-shaking control packets before transmission. The impacts of the radio propagation environments and the channel BER on WLAN performance are investigated in Chapters 7 and 12, respectively.

Effect of Network Performance on MAC Protocol Design

A station access to a common channel is one of the challenging issues in network design. Without proper access control, two or more stations may transmit simultaneously, resulting in packet collisions and delay. To address this problem, a variety of MAC protocols have been developed and described in the wireless networking literature [64, 126, 157, 169]. A review of the literature on the design of wireless MAC protocols, including various representative MAC schemes, was presented in the "Wireless MAC Protocols: A Review of the Literature" section. The performance of a typical WLAN depends largely on how effectively a MAC protocol coordinates the signal transmissions among the active stations since that determines how efficiently the limited bandwidth of the wireless channel is shared. Although 802.11 has been standardized and is gaining widespread popularity as a channel access protocol for WLANs, the protocol has performance limitations with respect to low bandwidth utilization under medium to high traffic loads. This performance limitation results in low throughput and high packet delay.

The service differentiation and fairness issues of 802.11 have been discussed in [154, 159, 164, 170]. The 802.11e task group is proceeding to build the QoS enhancements of the 802.11 network [71]. Although various innovative MAC protocols have been developed and described in the computer networking literature, very few protocols satisfy all the QoS provisions while retaining simplicity of implementation in real WLANs. A new MAC protocol called buffer unit multiple access (BUMA), developed as a minor modification of DCF, can be used to overcome the limitations of 802.11 mentioned above. The channel-aware BUMA (C-BUMA) protocol is used in cross-layer WLAN design optimization (Chapter 12). BUMA is described in Chapter 9.

FURTHER READING

For more details about subjects discussed in this chapter, we recommend the following books and references. The items in [] refer to the reference list at the end of the book.

Books

> [171] Chapter 5—*Computer Networking: A Top-Down Approach* by Kurose and Ross

> [172] Chapter 4—*Computer Networks* by Tanenbaum and Wetherall

Research Papers

> [38]

> [39]

> [68]

SUMMARY

In this chapter, a review of the literature in the design and performance improvement of wireless MAC protocols was presented. Wireless MAC protocols can be classified into three main categories based on network topology. These are ad hoc, infrastructure, and hybrid. The MAC protocols designed for ad hoc networks are very different from those designed for infrastructure networks. Most of the MAC protocols for ad hoc networks use only handshaking and busy tones to avoid collisions. The MAC protocols for infrastructure networks use a BS as a central controller for allocating channel bandwidth among the active stations. The leading network researchers and their main contributions in the design of wireless MAC protocols were identified and discussed. The design principles of wireless MAC protocols are different from those of wired network protocols. Factors affecting WLAN performance need to be considered in the design of MAC protocols. These factors can be divided into two categories. The first are those associated with the wireless channel used for packet transmissions. The second category involves network performance and service requirements. These factors and their impact on the design of wireless MAC protocols were discussed. Performance enhancement mechanisms for 802.11 WLANs are further discussed in Chapter 9. Wireless routing protocols are discussed in Chapter 5.

KEY TERMS

Ad hoc network
Backoff algorithm
Binary exponential backup (BEB)
Contention window
Carrier sense multiple access (CSMA)
Carrier sense multiple access collision avoidance (CSMA/CA)
Carrier sense multiple access with collision prevention (CSMA/CP)
Carrier sense multiple access with ID countdown (CSMA/IC)
Clear to send (CTS)
Fairness
Fast collision resolution (FCR)
Floor acquisition multiple access (FAMA)
IEEE 802.11
Medium access control (MAC)
Multiple access with collision avoidance (MACA)

Multiple access with collision avoidance for wireless networks (MACAW)
Multiplicative increase and linear decrease (MILD)
Packet delay
Packet drop ratio
Packet reservation multiple access (PRMA)
Priority unavoidable multiple access (PUMA)
Quality of service (QoS)
Request to send (RTS)
Signal-to-noise ratio (SINR)
TDMA-based randomly addressed polling (TRAP)
Time division multiple access (TDMA)
Throughput
Wireless local area network (WLAN)

REVIEW QUESTIONS

1. Many network researchers have developed wireless MAC protocols and have contributed to the networking literature. Write down the name of five leading researchers in the design of wireless MAC protocols.

2. Various wireless MAC protocols have been proposed and reported in the networking literature. Identify and describe five representative wireless MAC protocols.

3. MACA is one of the earlier MAC protocols proposed for WLANs. Describe the principle of operation of the MACA protocol.

4. Discuss the difference between MACA and MACAW protocols.

5. Discuss the difference between RAMA and PRMA protocols.

6. The performance of a typical WLAN can be measured using appropriate network performance metrics. List and describe three important network performance metrics.

7. Network researchers are facing challenges in the design of new wireless MAC protocols. Discuss two important issues or challenges in the design of wireless MAC protocols.

8. Discuss the effect of radio propagation environments on wireless MAC design.

9. Discuss the effect of the upper protocol layer on the design of wireless MAC protocols.

MINI-PROJECTS

The following mini-projects aim to provide a deeper understanding of the topics covered in this chapter, mainly through literature review. More mini-projects have been presented in the subsequent chapters to provide hands-on practical experience.

1. Wireless MAC protocols play an important role in determining the performance of WLANs. Conduct an in-depth literature review on wireless MAC protocols to extend the work presented in the "Wireless MAC Protocols: A Review of the Literature" section.

2. Conduct an in-depth literature review on design issues and challenges for wireless MAC protocols to extend the work presented in the "Design Issues for Wireless MAC Protocols" section.

CHAPTER 5

Wireless Routing Protocols

LEARNING OUTCOMES

After reading and completing this chapter, you will be able to:

- Discuss the issues and challenges in the design of mobile ad hoc network (MANET) routing protocols

- Review routing protocols for MANETs

- Classify and describe various routing approaches for MANETs

- Compare and contrast traditional routing protocols for MANETs

- Discuss the impact of routing protocols on WLAN performance

INTRODUCTION

In Chapter 4, the wireless MAC protocol design issues and challenges were discussed. The main motivation of this book is to quantify the key issues/factors influencing WLAN performance. To achieve this objective, a general understanding of routing protocols for WLANs is required. This chapter aims to provide an introduction to routing protocols for WLANs that are necessary for design and performance evaluation of such systems.

We first discuss the properties and then design issues of routing protocols for MANETs. The various routing approaches are then described. We then compare the performance of various MANET routing protocols. Finally, we propose an improved routing protocol for MANETs.

PROPERTIES OF ROUTING PROTOCOLS

The performance of a routing protocol is determined by its properties. Typical examples of properties of routing protocols include free loop, distributed operation, routing computation and maintenance, demand-based operation, multiple routes, and power conservation. Routing protocols should be distributed in operation and not be dependent on a centralized node, as centralized operations are not scalable. Because nodes can enter or leave a network, a distributed routing operation is more fault tolerant than a centralized routing operation. Routing protocols should also guarantee that routes supplied are free loop and are free from stale routes that consume bandwidth and processing power. Efficient routing computation and maintenance is another property of routing protocols. Nodes are required to have access to the route as quickly as possible within a minimum desired setup connection time. Each routing protocol (or a group of protocols) computes and maintains the route differently.

Proactive routing protocols store complete topological information to minimize the control overhead, but they consume network resources such as battery life, bandwidth, and processing power. To avoid and reduce reactions to topological changes and congestion, multiple routes are used. Participating nodes keep a valid record and at least two stable routes so that in an event where one route is not available, the other route is executed, saving both bandwidth and processing power to be consumed by broadcast control information messages [173].

Power conservation is a desirable property of a routing protocol, as nodes such as laptops and personal digital assistants (PDAs) have very limited resources; therefore, an optimal use of scarce resources such as bandwidth, processing power, memory, and battery life is vital. Collisions of packets may occur when packets are transferred from source to destination; a minimum packet collision is a good property required for a routing protocol. This property will minimize the collision as much as possible during broadcast messages, contributing to a reduction of data loss and prevention of stale route occurrences.

DESIGN ISSUES OF ROUTING PROTOCOLS

There are a number of challenging issues that need to be considered when designing MANET routing protocols. These issues include unreliable wireless environment, dynamic topology, node mobility, limited network capacity, variable link quality, energy-constrained nodes, interference, and hidden and exposed node problems. The power efficiency and hidden and exposed node problems are vital to consider when designing a routing protocol.

Distributed state in unreliable environment: The status and condition of the environmental challenges is an important role to a routing protocol's performance. The distribution of resources in any unreliable environment becomes a challenge to enable communication; therefore, routing protocols should consider the best utilization of resources such as bandwidth, processing power, and battery life.

Dynamic topology: The MANET network topology changes dynamically as a result of node mobility, causing sessions of transferring packets to suffer from interference, leading to frequent path breaks. The interference occurs when an intermediate or destination node in a route disappears from the network range. When a link breaks, it is important that a routing protocol efficiently learn new available paths and build a new topology so that reliable connections are established. The network load causes overheads and degrades overall network performance. The network mobility management is important and needs to be considered when designing MANET routing protocols.

Limited network capacity: MANETs have limited channel bandwidth and data rates lower than those of wired networks. This raised an important issue for a routing protocol to use the bandwidth optimally. As a result of limited bandwidth of routing protocols, less topology information can be stored. Although complete information about network topology is required for an efficient routing protocol, in the case of MANET routing protocols, this topology information will cause an increase in node control messages and overheads, which wastes channel bandwidth. Control messages are sent over the network, enabling nodes to establish connections before data packets are transferred. An efficient routing protocol is required for a balanced usage of the limited channel bandwidth.

Resource constraint: The processing power and battery life are essential to nodes in MANETs. Increasing processing power consumes more battery life. Nodes in a MANET are portable, and hence processing power and battery life are limited. When overheads occur, more processing and battery life are used to resolve the situation. Therefore, it is important to design a routing protocol that efficiently transfers data within the limited life span of battery life using less processing power.

Interference and collision: As a result of concurrent transmissions, collisions occur when each node does not know about other node transmissions. The exposed terminal problem contributes to the inability of a node that has been blocked due to the transmission of nearby nodes; thus, the radio reusability spectrum is affected. Transmission cannot occur when spectrum is occupied; therefore, it is important to avoid collision by proper handshaking before transmission.

MANET ROUTING APPROACHES

MANET routing protocols have distinguishing characteristics in the way they exchange information and establish communications. The routing protocols can be classified into three broad categories: flat, hierarchical, and geographical. The flat routing is further classified into two main categories: table driven and source-initiated on-demand routing [174].

On-demand (also called reactive) routing protocols determine routes only when a node has a data packet to send. A node with a packet to send is referred to as a source node. If the route to the destination is not known, the source node initiates a search (i.e., route discovery) to find possible routes to the destination. The optimized route is then used and maintained, establishing connection and communication until such a route is no longer required or becomes invalid [175]. Dynamic Source Routing (DSR), Ad Hoc On-Demand Distance Vector (AODV), and Temporally Ordered Routing Algorithm (TORA) are examples of on-demand routing protocols.

Table-driven (also called proactive) routing protocols attempt to maintain consistent and up-to-date information of all possible routes to destinations at all times regardless of whether the routes are needed or not. To support this consistency, the protocol broadcasts messages to gather update information and all possible connectivity through the network [175]. Proactive protocols require each node to maintain more than one table to store routing information regardless of the need for such route information [176]. Proactive protocols share common features, such as background information exchange, regardless of the communication request strategy employed [174]. Examples of table-driven routing protocols include Fisheye State Routing (FSR), Optimized Link State Routing (OLSR), Destination Sequenced Distance Vector (DSDV), and Topology Broadcast Based on Reverse Path Forwarding (TBRPF).

Optimized Link State Routing

The OLSR protocol is an optimized pure state link algorithm. It is designed to reduce retransmission duplication with a proactive nature where the routes are always available when needed. It uses hop-by-hop forwarding packets [177, 178]. To accommodate this, the nodes exchange topological information periodically using multipoint rely (MPR) nodes. MPR is a distinctive feature over other protocols. Other features of OLSR include neighboring sensing, and hello and topological control (TC) messages. In OLSR, MPR-selected nodes are the only nodes that forward control traffic, hence reducing the size of the control messages from flooding the network, and therefore minimizing the overheads [179]. MPRs periodically advertise their link state information to each other's nodes. MPR also forms a route from a given source to a destination. A hello message is periodically broadcast by each node for link sensing, neighbor detection, and the MPR selection process. A neighboring detection is a process where two nodes link, sense, and consider each other as a neighbor only if a link is established symmetrically. A link can be considered bi- or unidirectional. A hello message sent by a node contains its own address and all the addresses for its neighbors. Each node can obtain topological information up to 2 hops from a hello message. The MPR selection process uses 1- and 1-hop symmetrical information to recalculate the MPR set. MPR recalculation occurs when a change in a 1- or 2-hop neighborhood's topology has been detected. When receiving the update information, each node recalculates and updates the route to each known destination [180]. A TC message is used to broadcast topological information throughout the network; however, only MPR nodes are used to forward the TC messages to nodes in its routing table.

Figure 5.1 illustrates the principle of operation of the OLSR routing algorithm. It begins by checking if any route to the destination is available in the routing table. If the route to the destination is not available, the source node initiates a broadcast for all possible routes. Should there be a route available, the link is established using a hello message and the sender is ready to send the packet. Once the destination is reached, transmission begins. If failure occurs, the TC message is sent to update topological changes in MPR nodes.

Dynamic Source Routing

DSR is a reactive routing protocol that uses the arithmetic of source node routing, where the source node determines the route that a data packet

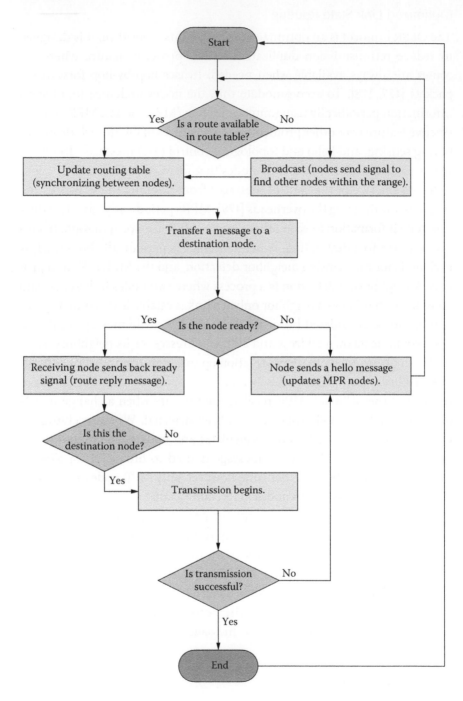

FIGURE 5.1   OLSR routing algorithm.

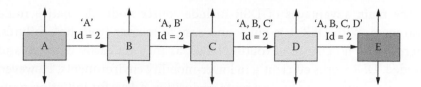

FIGURE 5.2   DSR route discovery process.

should follow to the destination. DSR works in a self-configuring and self-organizing manner for route discovery and route maintenance. Unlike proactive protocols, DSR does not require periodic table update. However, when a node wants to send a message to a destination, it uses route cache to verify the availability of a route and initiate a route request, if such a route to the destination is not available in its route cache [181].

A *route discovery* consists of route request and route reply processes. A route request (RREQ) message is broadcast over the network to find all possible routes to the destination. A route request header contains source, destination, and the hop counts it takes to reach the destination, as shown in Figure 5.2. Each receiving node checks to see whether it knows the route to the destination. If it does have a record from a route request sent recently, it discards the request and forwards the request along its links. However, if it does not have a record, it stores to its own address and forwards the request along the outing links. In receiving the route request packet the destination node responds by sending a route reply (RREP) packet to the source node that carries the route incorporated in the route request packet. A route being established is stored in the route cache where the source node explicitly lists these routes in the data packets header. This scheme allows a multihop route to the destination.

A RREP message is generated when the RREQ message reaches the destination, or a node that has an expired route. If the node generating the route reply message is the destination node, it places the record of nodes in the route request into a route reply that has the source, destination, and source route information [182].

Route maintenance is executed when it receives a route error message (RERR) generated from a node that has transmission problems. Receiving an error packet, the node that generated the error packet is removed from the route cache and all route cache-containing hops to this node. In addition to route maintenance, acknowledge packets are also used for verification of correctness in route links.

The main advantages of DSR include source node alternative route awareness. With DSR it is quick and easy to recover from link failures. There is also no chance of routing loops, as they are easily detected and avoided. DSR works efficiently in lower-mobility environments. However, it has disadvantages of having route acquisition delays for initiating route discovery. This may not be acceptable in high-mobility environments [175]. Aggressive flooding is problematic in DSR and is an important factor to consider because it decreases the ability to maintain overhead in mobile environments. Furthermore, a larger header is required to store information in a large network that requires extra bandwidth and processing power for its computation.

Figure 5.3 shows a flowchart of the DSR algorithm. If a node has a packet to send, the algorithm checks for a valid route to the destination in its route cache. If the route is not available, a route request is initiated and broadcast over the network. However, if the route to the destination is available in the route cache, it is then established and the node sends a packet to the receiving node. If the receiving node is ready, transmission begins and terminates if transmission is successful. If a failure occurred, a route RERR is sent that triggers route maintenance, which enables the source node to look for possible alternative routes.

Ad Hoc On-Demand Distance Vector

AODV provides a good compromise between proactive and reactive routing protocols. It uses a distributed approach in which a source node is not required to maintain a complete sequence of intermediate nodes to reach the destination [176]. It is also an improvement from DSR by addressing the issue of high messaging overhead and large header packets in maintaining routing tables at nodes, so that packets do not have to store much routing information in the headers. AODV uses a routing table in each node and keeps one to two fresh routes. AODV possesses the good features of DSDV, including hop-by-hop routing, periodic beacon messaging, and sequence numbering. A periodic beacon message is used to identify neighboring nodes. The sequence numbering guarantees loop-free routing and a fresh route to the destination. AODV has the advantage of minimizing the routing table size and broadcast process as routes are created on demand [183]. The route discovery and route maintenance mechanisms of AODV are similar to those of DSR.

In *route discovery*, if a node wants to send a packet to a destination, it initiates RREQ throughout the network. A RREQ message contains

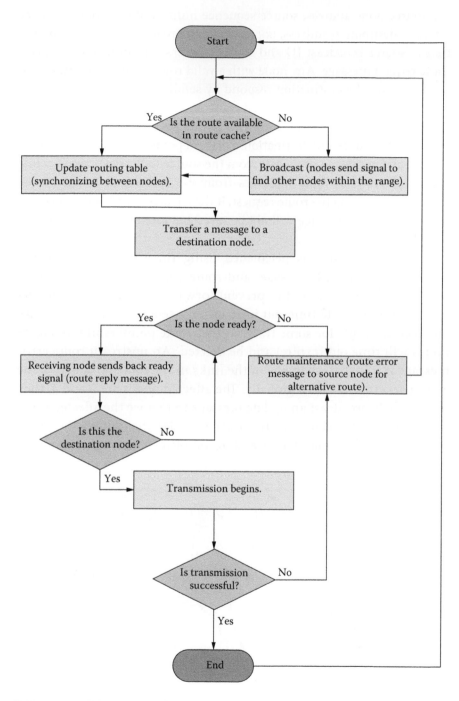

FIGURE 5.3   DSR routing algorithm.

the source node address, source sequence number, destination sequence number, destination address, hop count, and broadcast ID. The combination of source broadcast ID and source address is to uniquely identify a route request message. Any node with a valid route to the destination also needs to have the destination respond by sending a route reply message. A link failure or invalid or expired route will trigger route maintenance. During route discovery there are two pointers set at intermediate nodes between the source and destination. Forward pointers are set for the route request and packets to propagate from the source to the destination, while back pointers relay reply messages from the destination to the source (Figure 5.4). During the route request, if the route is found in the table list, the route request message will not be saved but forwarded to other nodes [175, 184].

Route maintenance is performed using three different messages: hello message, RERR message, and route time-out message. A periodic hello message is used to prevent forward and backward pointers from expiring. Route time-out messages are sent if there is no activity on a certain route for some time, so that route pointers in immediate nodes will time out (expire) and be deleted. An upstream route error message is initiated when one of the links in the route fails; hence, the error packet is broadcast globally. The affected nodes are 3 and 4; they immediately broadcast an update message to remove the affected route from their route cache and from other nodes that stored the failed route [185]. Route maintenance is accomplished through the use of

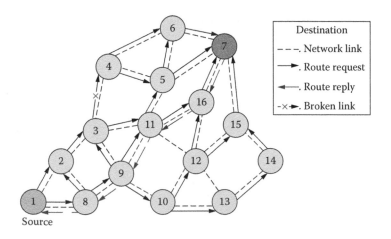

FIGURE 5.4 (SEE COLOR INSERT.)   AODV routing mechanism.

error packets and acknowledgment; when the link is broken (transmission error), an error message is sent to other nodes. The nodes with the error routes are erased from route tables. When a link failure occurs, the route repair is executed using local and global route repair. A local route repair is where the intermediate nodes try to repair the route at first, but if there are no available routes in intermediate nodes, the message is then sent to the source, where the source initiates a global route repair [186].

Without source routing, AODV relies on routing table entries to propagate an RREP back to the source node, and subsequently to route data packets to the destination [187]. The advantages of AODV are loop-free routing, optional multicast, reduced control overhead, and a quick response to link breakage. However, disadvantages include packet delays caused by the route discovery process and the bidirectional connection needed to detect a unidirectional link.

AODV faces large delays during route construction. Link failures can also initiate another route discovery, therefore creating extra delays and consuming more bandwidth, especially when the size of the network increases [178]. Immediate nodes can lead to inconsistent routes if the sequence number is very old and has a higher but not the latest destination sequence number, thereby having stale entries [188].

Figure 5.5 shows the flowchart of the AODV algorithm. The algorithm checks if a route to the destination exists in the route table. It establishes a connection and proceeds to transmission. If an error occurs, a local route is initiated among the intermediate nodes. If a route to the destination does not exist in the intermediate nodes, a global route repair is trigged, enabling the sender to initiate a broadcast for possible routes to the destination.

Temporally Ordered Routing Algorithm

TORA is a distributed routing protocol that uses a reversal algorithm. It is designed for routes initiated by source nodes or, rather, on demand. TORA is unique by maintaining multiple routes to a destination, establishing a route quickly and minimizing overhead by not reacting during topological changes until all possible routes are lost. The protocol then initiates a route discovery when all routes to the destination are lost [176, 189]. As a distance vector routing approach, TORA still maintains state on a per-destination basis. However, the shortest-route paths are considered less important; therefore, preference is given to longer routes to avoid

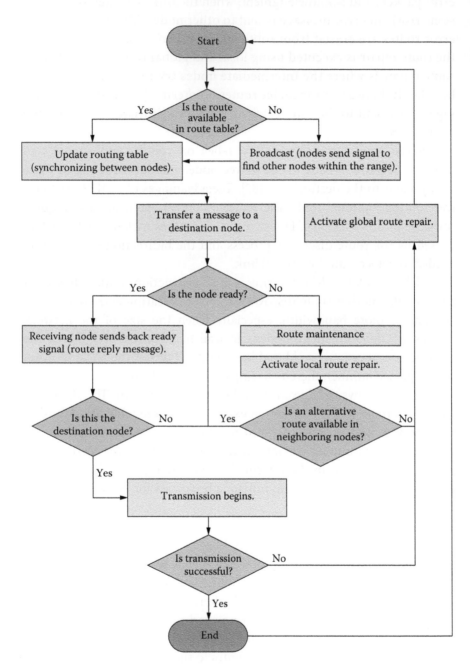

FIGURE 5.5   AODV routing algorithm.

overhead in trying to rediscover new routes [187, 1990]. Additionally, the metric used in establishing a routing structure does not represent a distance. In TORA the destination-oriented nature of the routing structure supports a mixture of reactive and proactive routing per destination base. During reactive operations, the source node initiates the establishment of a route to the destination on demand. This form of operation is advantageous in high dynamic networks, with relatively thin traffic patterns, as it may not be necessary or desirable to maintain routes between every source-destination pair at all times. Likewise, selecting a proactive operation resembles a traditional table-driven approach, hence allowing the route to proactively be maintained to destinations for which routing is frequently and consistently required [190]. TORA, however, does not work well in low-mobility networks.

TORA consists of three basic functions: route creation, route maintenance, and route erasure. During route creation and maintenance, nodes use a height metric to establish a directed acyclic graph (DAG) rooted at the destination. The links are then assigned an upstream or downstream direction, based on the relative height metric of neighboring nodes. During mobility the DAG route is usually broken; therefore, route maintenance is initiated to reestablish a DAG. Reestablishment of the route occurs an infinite number of times, which means its directed portions return to a destination within an infinite time. Once a network partition is detected, all links in that portion of the network, those that become partitioned from the destination, are marked as undirected to enable erasure of invalid routes [187, 188]. Timing is an important factor, as the metric height depends on logical time of link failure. TORA assumes that all nodes have a synchronized clock system. Each node runs a separate copy of the algorithm for each destination; thus, when a node requires a route, it broadcasts to all the nodes in the network. All query packets contain the destination address for the required route. Each node maintains just 1-hop local topology information and has detection partition capabilities. Another unique property differentiating it from other routing protocols is that it has limiting control packets to a smaller region during the reconfiguration process initiated by a link failure [181].

Figure 5.6 illustrates the principle of operation of the TORA routing protocol. Node 1 sends a route request and creates a route. A possible DAG is created using nodes 2 and 3. In the event of a failure, the node moves to the next level of reference, to find possible routes to the destination before deleting the route and changing the topology. When broadcast in

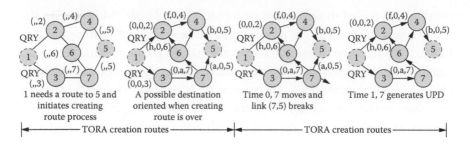

1 needs a route to 5 and initiates creating route process

A possible destination oriented when creating route is over

Time 0, 7 moves and link (7,5) breaks

Time 1, 7 generates UPD

|← TORA creation routes →|← TORA creation routes →|

FIGURE 5.6 TORA routing mechanism. (From S. R. Chaudhry et al., A Performance Comparison of Multi on Demand Routing in Wireless Ad Hoc Networks, presented at the IEEE International Conference on Wireless and Mobile Computing, Networking and Communications (WiMob '05), 2005, pp. 1–8; T. Larsson and N. Hedman, Routing Protocols in Wireless Ad-Hoc Networks: A Simulation Study, thesis, Lulea University of Technology, 1998.)

the event of a failure, it activates the cycle and starts again by generating a reference level and forming a possible DAG.

TORA works better than other on-demand routing protocols in high-mobility networks. However, the main challenges occur in the concurrent detection of partitions and subsequent detection of routes, resulting in temporary oscillation and transient loops. Hence, local reconfiguration of paths resulted in a lesser and nonoptimal route. This makes TORA very sensitive to link failures.

Figure 5.7 shows the flowchart of the TORA algorithm. The enabling communication has three basic functions: route creation (broadcast), route maintenance, and route erasure. The algorithm first checks if a route is available to the destination. A broadcast message is initiated if there is no route available. A topology is generated and the height of nodes to the destination is calculated. If there is a failure, route maintenance is trigged and undergoes various checks to resolve the connection. If a possibility is not found, the route is erased and a broadcast message is initiated to regenerate topology. Should the route exist and be without failure, the connection is established and transmission is executed.

COMPARISON OF ROUTING PROTOCOLS

The main function of MANET routing protocols is to establish and enable transfer of data packets from a source to a destination node. Each routing protocol reacts differently to enable connections and maintain the route. The three on-demand protocols (DSR, AODV, and TORA) share some common properties, while each has its own

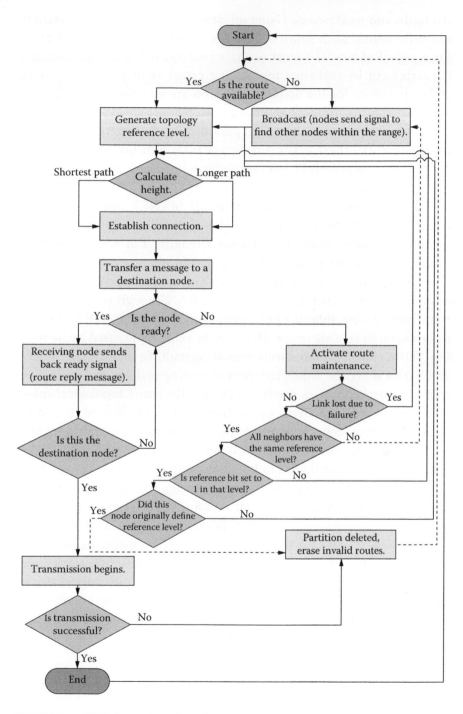

FIGURE 5.7 TORA routing algorithm.

strengths and weaknesses. Using on-demand routing, one is certain to use valid routes. Each route is stored in a route cache, or a route table, for a period of time. In most reactive routing, the route maintenance is carried out by real-time monitoring rather than periodic updates, and only entries for the active destination are monitored. OLSR is the proactive routing protocol and has routes that are always available to a destination. Updates are executed periodically or triggered by changes in the network. There exists a common feature in both proactive and reactive routing protocols, but they differ significantly when it comes to performance [184].

Table 5.1 compares the four traditional MANET routing protocols (e.g., OLSR, DSR, AODV, and TORA) based on route computation, routing updates, loop freedom, and their strengths and weaknesses. The routing protocols share similarities in loop freedom and routing metric properties. AODV uses not only the shortest path but also the freshest route in its routing metric. AODV and TORA, although reactive in their route computation, inherit a proactive routing approach as OLSR to store information in routing tables. DSR, on the other hand, used cache routing. TORA and DSR share similarities using multiple routes. DSR, AODV, and TORA share the same properties of routing updates. Being reactive, routing updates occur as needed; therefore, the entire topological information is not required. Being a proactive protocol, OLSR needs the entire topology information; therefore, route tables require periodical update. Updating information and route maintenance is dealt with quite differently. OLSR uses a neighbor's link state to update and maintain its routes. TORA uses the node height following a waterfall model to determine the optimal route to a destination. Both DSR and AODV use the route error message to trigger maintenance and updating of routes. In DSR the route error message is sent back to the source before route maintenance is triggered; however, in AODV, a local route repair is sent to find alternatives to the destination, and if this fails, a global route error message is sent to the source node, which initiates the route maintenance by broadcasting through the network. These differences demonstrate the advantages and disadvantages in their behaviors toward routing performance.

PERFORMANCE OF ROUTING PROTOCOLS

In this section we highlight the issues of routing performance and propose an improved routing protocol for MANETs by modifying the existing ones.

TABLE 5.1   MANET Routing Protocol Comparison

Parameter	OLSR	DSR	AODV	TORA
Route computation	Table driven	On demand	On demand	On demand/ proactive
Routing structure	Flat	Flat	Flat	Flat
Routes maintained	Route table	Route cache	Route table	Route table
Multiple route possibilities	No	Yes	No	Yes (DAG)
Source routing	No	Yes	No	No
Method	Flooding	Broadcast	Broadcast/ flooding	Broadcast
Stored information	Entire topology	Routes to desired destination	Next hop for desired destination	Neighbor heights
Routing updates	Periodically	As needed (event driven)	As needed (event driven)	As needed (event driven)
Hello messages	Hello message used to find information about link status and host neighbors; from MPR nodes to all the nodes	No hello message	Small size, used as a supplement for neighbor detection	Label-based multipath routing (LMR) messages to query about neighbors and heights
Update information and route maintenance	Neighbor's link state	Route error	Route error	Node's height
Multicast capability	No	No	Yes	No
Routing metric	Shortest path	Shortest path	Freshest and shortest path	Shortest path
Loop-free	Yes	Yes, source route	Yes, sequence number	Yes
Mechanism of routing	One hop	Source routing	Next hop	Heights
Loop freedom maintenance	Sequence number	Source route	Sequence number	DAG query update

(Continued)

TABLE 5.1   MANET Routing Protocol Comparison (Continued)

Parameter	OLSR	DSR	AODV	TORA
Advantages	Reduced number of broadcasts	Promiscuous overhearing and multiple routes	Adaptable to highly dynamic topologies	Multiple routes
Disadvantage	Overlapping MPR sets	Scalability problems due to flooding, source routing, and large delays	Large delays, scalability problem, hello messages	Temporary routing loops, causing large delays

Performance Issues

The performance of a routing protocol is an important issue in providing optimal quality of service (QoS). QoS should be considered for all data traffic requesting communication in MANETs. Other factors affecting the performance of routing protocols include node mobility, increase of node sizes, and traffic loads.

Quality of service: Maintaining QoS in an ad hoc protocol is a very challenging task, especially to support real-time applications in mobile networks. Providing optimum performance requires a QoS routing protocol and a resource reservation scheme. Real-time traffic requires reservation of bandwidth, a low delay, and a high-reliability routing protocol [191]. Best-effort routing protocols are considered to be both proactive and reactive. The low-mobility proactive routing protocols such as OLSR can provide good quality of service. In a high-mobility environment, reactive protocols such as DSR, AODV, and TORA provide a better QoS performance rate. The investigation of AODV, DSR, and DSDV [192] shows that in real-time traffic the use of AODV is preferred over the use of DSDV and DSR. QoS consists of managing the characteristics and lowering the constraints that existed between a source and a destination, enabling a guaranteed connection for communication [186]. Providing QoS to most data and real-time application traffic is quantified in terms of time-outs and delay avoidance and utilization of the limited resources.

Node mobility: The speed of a node in MANET plays an important role toward the performance of routing protocols. Mobility of nodes has a direct impact on pause time; it is a time for which a data packet stays in a node waiting for a destination, before moving to another destination. Pause time is also used to measure the performance of mobile nodes in MANET [179]. The research in [177] shows that more packet drops are due to unreliable routes when node speed increases in both DSR and AODV. In a low-speed network environment DSR performance is constantly good provided that routes maintained in route cache are valid and useful and without breakage. In a high-speed network AODV performed better than DSR. Since DSR relies on cache routes, high-mobility routes become stale. This can lead to an increased number of packet drops. The optimized proactive protocol OLSR is also found to be superior over both DSR and AODV due to its mechanism of early detection of link failures [177, 193]. Furthermore, DSR has a lower delay than AODV with a longer pause time [194].

The performance results in [195] confirm that AODV is reliable in a high-speed environment and gets better throughput; however, the reliability of TORA is worse. DSR performs poorly in high-mobility environments since it exploits caching aggressively to maintain multiple routes to the destination, suggesting that the use of DSR should focus on networks with less mobility [188]. Yet in earlier studies [189, 196], AODV was found to perform poorly in high mobility due to the picking up of stale routes, and hence having a higher packet drop than DSR and TORA. The multiple routes, DAG property, and multicast environment in TORA provide sustainable performance in higher-mobility environments [183].

The effects of varying mobility on the four routing protocols are significantly different. Mobility imposes stress on routing protocols, especially in the event of route failure, and subsequent route rediscovery, which decreases data packet transmission. Traffic patterns, if not implemented or dealt with by routing protocols, will degrade the performance in mobility networks [197, 198]. The increase of speed not only increases the delay, but also increases the medium of access delay. If nodes move at a lower speed, routes can be sustained for a longer period. High mobility also suggests that rather than looking for the shortest routing path, a more optimized path should be considered and used to reduce overhead [199].

Network size: The network size or the number of nodes in a network plays an important role toward the overall performance of a routing protocol. AODV is considered to have performed poorly in a small-sized network, due to the flooding of routing packets. In smaller networks DSR outperformed TORA and AODV. TORA, on the other hand, performed poorly in small networks compared to other routing protocols. In OLSR, the overhead also increases as the number of nodes increases, therefore resulting in an increase in routing table size and the number of broadcast messages. As network size increases, the average delay also increases [179]. Most proactive protocols do well in small networks; however, OLSR also performed well in large networks [193]. The underlying reason has to do with the way routes are requested and maintained in OLSR. However, Zaballos et al. [183] recommended that OLSR should not be used in either networks with a large number of nodes or a mobility environment. This is due to a high probability of not maintaining a route quickly, therefore increasing convergence time, and the constant searching for possible destination increases control traffic.

Another study [177] on the effect of network size on routing protocols stresses that for a large network size, nodes may communicate with each other if path lengths are kept constant. The routing loads always increase when a network becomes denser. DSR performs better than AODV in regards to delay in network when nodes are between 10 and 20, while AODV has a better delay than DSR in a 30-source node network [196]. Layuan et al. [195] further confirm that AODV has a smaller throughput in a network with a size less than 30 than DSR. TORA has a greater drop in throughput for a network size smaller than 50 than a network of a size greater than 50 nodes. To keep the speed constant while nodes increase, DSR shows a larger throughput than AODV [188].

Traffic pattern has an impact on varying network size; therefore, considering traffic pattern in an increasing network is of great importance since the cost to pay for a bad route caching decision is high in larger networks for route rediscovery [197]. In a mobile environment, and in a large-sized network, the probability of finding a node for reroute discovery also increases [198]. The performance comparison in [200] supports the literature by identifying OLSR and DSR as recommended routing protocols for small networks, OLSR and

AODV as protocols for medium networks, and TORA and OLSR for large networks. TORA and AODV have efficient performance, while OLSR has degraded performance in large networks and when mobility increases.

The performance for all four routing protocols becomes less constant when network size increases. With a large density, more and more nodes will try to access the common medium; therefore, this increases collision rates, resulting in packet loss and a decreasing throughput [199]. Routing protocols with efficient performance must have a mechanism to cater for mobility and be able to rediscover a route in a way that reduces or keeps the overhead constant.

Data traffic load: The performance of routing protocols depends on data traffic loads. Traffic load is determined by the packet length of a type of data. The routing protocols react differently to traffic loads. Perkins et al. [201] conclude that data traffic loads do have a different impact on routing performance as the network size varies. DSR outperformed other reactive protocols when the traffic load was low, and OLSR performance was better at all traffic loads. When considering routing overhead, routing load increases tremendously when traffic load increases. The increase in traffic load results in establishing more routes to be sorted; hence, this will increase the overhead, yet Mbarushimana and Shahrabi [177] demonstrate that OLSR has the lowest delay compared to DSR and AODV. The increase in data traffic also increases bandwidth usage. The consumed bandwidth for delivered packets is the same as those use to traverse through the network. Additionally, bandwidth is also required for data packets that are dropped. Routing protocols with unicast slows down packet transmission; therefore, DSR with unicast suffers more than AODV [202]. The increase in the traffic volume affects the performance of all routing protocols; the worst affected is DSR, being primarily composed of unicast packets, while AODV has a high fraction of overheads due to its multicast mechanism [197].

A Proposal for Improving MANET Routing Performance

Finding an optimal routing protocol for all situations may not seem viable, as it requires vast and substantial research into the behavior of routing algorithms. In this research extensive and simulation experiments have been conducted to find the most suitable and reliable routing algorithms for a given situation. The node mobility, density, and loads are the drivers for the performance of a routing protocol. In a dynamic changing topology both TORA and AODV, in most cases, performed well, while in less stressful situations OLSR and DSR performed better.

Since our focus was on node mobility, we intended to modify both TORA and AODV. TORA performs well in large networks and a high-mobility environment. When mobility is low, TORA's packet delays increase, and hence we look at ways to reduce the delays in a large network when medium node mobility exists.

AODV also performs in the same manner as TORA; however, the increase in mobility does not increase throughput in medium-sized networks compared to small networks. AODV is better than TORA in the sense that delay is lower; however, as mobility increases, link failures occur frequently, causing high overheads, which therefore increases delays in medium networks. Another reason for increased delay in AODV is that the protocol maintains a routing table and uses the shortest and freshest route available at high node mobility. The shortest routes may not be viable when nodes are moving at a high speed. This results in more broadcast messages initiated, causing increased overhead and delays impacting system performance.

We propose an improved MANET routing protocol by combining advantages of both AODV and TORA. The question may arise: In what ways can AODV's overhead be defeated? The answer is to look at ways to keep the routes from constantly breaking by considering route lifetime, multiple paths, and density of nodes.

Using multiple paths will allow the AODV algorithm to trigger the source node to use the next possible shortest path to the destination when alternative routes in a local route repair are not found in neighboring nodes. Instead of initiating a broadcast message to update the routing table, the alternative path should be triggered when there are no possible routes in the neighboring nodes routing tables during a local route repair. The risk here is that it may end up waiting too long for a response; therefore, more messages are sent, overloading the network. The advantage here is that the network may not be that overloaded compared to initiating broadcast messages for route updates when there is a link failure, or there are no alternative routes found in neighboring nodes.

The use of route lifetime will allow predetermination of the next available route when the current route is reaching its expiry date. Hence, the probability of getting link failures and stale routes is lowered. The downside of a route lifetime is that a route may still be valid for some longer period than predicted. However, to be on the safe side, rather than to trigger unwanted broadcast messages and overloading the network, the next shortest possible route should be used.

As the number of nodes increases, some routes are used more frequently than others. Due to limited resources in MANETs, the density of nodes plays an important role in distributing the load over the network. When one route's density becomes very high, the alternative shortest route is used. However, the stale routes and longer paths in alternative routes may occur. The main advantage is balancing the load so that the shortest and freshest route is not overloaded and becomes expired sooner than its expected lifetime.

Figure 5.8 shows the flowchart of the proposed improved routing protocol called Priority AODV (P-AODV). It uses the alternative shortest path. The paths are considered after the topology is generated. A timer is set to keep track of a route lifetime; the timer is also influenced by the speed of the node to calculate the expiry time. Priority used paths are those with the shortest path and freshest route to a destination. If a route expires or is used heavily, the alternative route is trigged. Both routes should be capable of establishing connections to send data packets from a source to a destination node. When a route failure occurs, local route repair is initiated. If no possible routes are available in neighboring nodes, the alternative shortest route is triggered; however, if the alternative route has been used, the global route repair is then initiated. This research only specifies the proposed algorithm in a flowchart. The P-AODV can be implemented in a credible network simulator such as OPNET or ns-2 for performance evaluation.

FURTHER READING

For more details about subjects discussed in this chapter, we recommend the following books and references. The items in [] refer to the reference list at the end of the book.

Books

[171] Chapter 5—*Computer Networking: A Top-Down Approach* by Kurose and Ross

[172] Chapter 4—*Computer Networks* by Tanenbaum and Wetherall

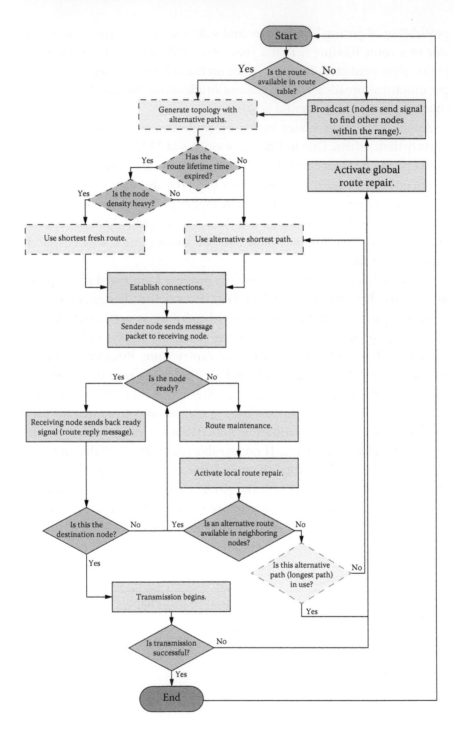

FIGURE 5.8 Proposed P-AODV algorithm.

Research Papers

[173]

[203]

SUMMARY

In this chapter, the fundamentals of MANET routing protocols were outlined and essential background information on the design and performance evaluation of such systems was provided. In particular, the properties, design issues, and approaches of routing protocols were described. The node mobility is one of the key factors affecting the performance of routing protocols. The network size and traffic load also play a vital role in the overall system performance. In the presence of node mobility, routing protocols have mixed reactions. The chapter concludes by discussing the issues on MANET routing protocols. A proposal for an improved routing protocol is also presented. The cross-layer design strategy for WLANs is discussed in Chapter 6.

KEY TERMS

Ad Hoc On-Demand Distance Vector (AODV)	Multipoint rely (MPR)
Collision	Network capacity
Dynamic source routing (DSR)	On demand
Exposed station	Optimized Link State Routing (OLSR)
Exposed terminal	Personal digital assistants (PDAs)
FSR	Temporally ordered routing algorithm (TORA)
IEEE 802.11	Throughput
Interference	Topology
MANET	WLAN

REVIEW QUESTIONS

1. MANET is one of the important communication systems for mobile devices, including wireless laptops, iPads, tablets, and other mobile devices. Due to its inherent characteristics, the MANET protocols need to be carefully designed and implemented for better system performance. Identify and describe two important issues/challenges in the design of a MANET routing protocol.

2. There are various MANET routing protocols that have been proposed over the last 20 years. List and describe four traditional routing protocols for MANETs.

3. MANET routing protocols have some unique characteristics/properties. Identify and describe two important properties of MANET routing protocols.

4. AODV is one of the widely used routing protocols in MANETs. List and describe two advantages and two disadvantages of AODV.

5. To select a best routing protocol, it is useful to be able to compare various existing MANET routing protocols. Compare and contrast AODV, OLSR, and DSR routing protocols.

6. Discuss the impact of routing protocol on the performance of a typical 801.11 network.

MINI-PROJECTS

The following mini-projects aim to provide a deeper understanding of MANET routing protocols through a review of the literature. More mini-projects are presented in the subsequent chapters to emphasize hands-on practical learning experience.

1. The purpose of this project is to develop sound knowledge and understanding of MANET routing protocols. Conduct an in-depth literature review on MANET routing protocols. (Hint: Read 15 to 20 recent relevant journal/conference papers, categorize various MANET routing protocols, discuss their strengths and weaknesses, and design issues and challenges.)

2. Write a report on the strengths and weaknesses of traditional MANET routing protocols. Discuss why a new routing protocol is needed for MANETs.

3. The purpose of this project is to explore your knowledge and understanding of MANET routing protocols. Develop an algorithm (e.g., pseudocode or flowchart) for an improved routing protocol for MANETs.

Cross-Layer Design for WLANs

LEARNING OUTCOMES

After reading and completing this chapter, you will be able to:

- Review previous work on cross-layer design (CLD) optimization for WLANs

- Discuss the motivation for using CLD optimization

- Discuss the strengths and weaknesses of CLD methods

- Categorize CLD methods based on open systems interconnection (OSI) layering approaches

INTRODUCTION

Research on CLD optimization in WLANs has recently attracted significant interest. It is concerned with sharing information between various protocol layers, as specified in the International Standards Organization/ Open Systems Interconnection (ISO/OSI) reference model. Traditionally, network protocol architectures follow a strict layering approach to ensure interoperability, fast deployment, and system implementation. However, lack of coordination between protocol layers limits the network performance of such architectures. To overcome network performance problems, the CLD framework (i.e., the integration of two or more protocol layers) has been proposed by many network researchers [204–206]. This is an area of great international interest because network engineers are challenged continually to extract greater performance from a very limited number of wireless channels. This chapter provides background information on CLD optimization for WLANs. The motivation for CLD in WLANs is outlined in the "Motivation for CLD" section. The various approaches in achieving CLD are described in the "Various Approaches to CLD" section. The strengths and weaknesses of CLD methods are discussed in the "Strengths and Weaknesses of CLD Approaches" section. The "CLD Optimization: A Review of the Literature" section reviews relevant literature on CLD optimization focusing on the techniques used to improve WLAN performance.

DEFINITION OF CLD

CLD can be defined in several ways. In traditional layered architecture (e.g., OSI), direct communication between nonadjacent layers (e.g., linking between link layer and application layer) is not permitted, and communication between adjacent layers is limited to procedure calls and responses. In CLD approaches, communication protocols can be designed by avoiding the rules of the reference layered communication architecture, for example, by allowing direct communication between protocols at nonadjacent layers or sharing variables between layers. Such violation of a layered architecture is called the CLD. Another definition could be designing protocols at different layers independently by imposing some conditions on the processing at other layers.

A CLD approach can be realized in several ways: (1) creating new interfaces for explicit notification from a lower to higher layer and vice versa, (2) merging of adjacent layers (e.g., physical [PHY] and medium access control [MAC] layers), (3) design coupling without creating new interfaces, and (4) vertical optimization across layers. These CLD approaches are discussed in the "Various Approaches to CLD" section. More details about CLD for WLANs can also be found in wireless networking literature [50, 207].

MOTIVATION FOR CLD

As a novel idea for network design, CLD appeared nearly a decade ago for improving the performance of wireless networks. In recent years, it has become recognized that performance gains can be achieved by active cooperation with two or more layers to have better cross-layer communication. For example, data link layer protocols can be adjusted to suit the changing conditions of the PHY layer to get better system performance [204, 205].

Wireless links create various problems for protocol design that cannot be handled well in layered protocol architectures. For example, a Transmission Control Protocol (TCP) sender assumes that a packet error on a wireless link is a result of network congestion rather than bit error rate (BER). Wireless media also offer new modalities of communication that layered architectures do not support. For example, the PHY layer can be made capable of receiving multiple packets concurrently. The stations can also make use of the broadcast nature of the wireless channel to cooperate with one another in involved ways. Making use of such novel modes of communication in protocol design requires violating the layered approach. Research has shown that conventional layered protocol architectures do not provide optimal performance, especially for multimedia applications in WLANs. A promising approach to overcome these performance issues that has received a lot of attention in recent years is the notion of CLD [208, 209].

VARIOUS APPROACHES TO CLD

While CLD can be achieved in various ways, we discuss only the following four methods of achieving CLD optimization for WLANs:

- **New interfaces between layers:** This is achieved by designing new interfaces between the layers. These interfaces are used for information sharing between the layers at runtime. The direction of information flow along the new interfaces could be upward (from a lower to a higher layer), downward (from a higher to a lower layer), and back and forth (i.e., iterative flow between two layers). In CLD, if a higher-layer protocol requires information from the lower layer(s), a new interface will be created at runtime for information exchange between the lower and higher layers. An example of the CLD approach using upward information flow could be channel-adaptive modulation or link layer schemes [50]. The key idea is to adapt the parameters of the transmission (e.g., modulation) in response to the channel condition, which is made available to the MAC sublayer by an interface from the PHY.

  In the case of downward information flow, CLD proposals rely on setting up parameters on the lower layer of the OSI protocol stack at runtime using a direct interface from the higher layer. For example, a voice over Internet Protocol (VoIP) run at the application layer can inform the data link layer about the delay requirements so that the link layer can schedule packets with higher priority to meet the delay requirements. In the case of back-and-forth information flow, two layers perform different tasks concurrently and can collaborate with each other at runtime. Joint scheduling and power control would be an example of the back-and-forth information flow CLD approach.

- **Merging of adjacent layers:** In this design approach, two or more adjacent layers are combined together to form one super-layer in the protocol stack. In this approach there is no need to create a new interface in the protocol stack. A joint PHY-MAC layer optimization is a good example of merging adjacent layers in the CLD approach [210].

- **Design coupling without new interfaces:** This approach involves coupling two or more protocol layers (nonadjacent layers) at design time without creating any new interfaces for information sharing at runtime. A joint optimization of rate adaptation in the PHY and data link layers and quality adaptation in the application layer proposed by Lee and Chung [211] is an example of design coupling in the CLD approach.

- **Methods based on optimization theory:** This CLD method refers to adjusting parameters that span multiple layers in the protocol stack. It is useful to be able to jointly optimize parameters from all layers. Different vertical compositions of an optimization problem can be mapped to different layering schemes in a communication network. This approach provides a unifying, top-down approach to design protocol stacks [212].

STRENGTHS AND WEAKNESSES OF CLD APPROACHES

It has been well argued in the literature that the network performance can be improved significantly using CLD approaches for WLANs [50, 213] and other networks such as vehicular ad hoc networks (VANETs) [214], mesh networks [215, 216], and wireless sensor networks [217]. For instance, the packet losses in the MAC layer or channel condition in the PHY layer can be passed on to the transport layer so that the TCP would be able to differentiate congestion from packet losses. This CLD approach of TCP redesign would greatly improve the system performance.

In spite of several strengths, CLD is not always the "silver bullet" that removes all limitations. It has weaknesses and limitations that must be considered. High on this list is design complexity when it comes to practical implementations. Lack of standardization is another limitation of CLD methods. CLD standardization is required for compatibility, interoperability, and to be independent of single solutions. The system stability would be another issue in CLD approaches because they violate/avoid traditional strict layering network architecture.

CLD OPTIMIZATION: A REVIEW OF THE LITERATURE

In this section we review a selected set of the literature that is indicative of the range of approaches used for CLD optimization to improve WLAN performance. Table 6.1 lists the leading network researchers and their main contributions to CLD optimization in WLANs. A brief description of each of the main contributions is given below.

Cross-Layer Design: A Survey and Taxonomy

Foukalas et al. [218] survey existing CLD applications and summarize the key properties in a comprehensive taxonomy of CLD approaches. In particular, they present the architectures and models proposed so far for CLD in wireless mobile networks and identify key functional entities in cross-layer management procedures. The cross-layer signaling mechanisms are categorized. The technical challenges for the implementation of these CLD proposals are identified and possible solutions are discussed.

TCP Path Recovery Notification (TCP-PRN)

Lee et al. [219] proposed a cross-layer approach for TCP optimization over wireless and mobile networks. In particular, they proposed a TCP path recovery notification (TCP-PRN) mechanism to improve the performance of TCP. The main idea is to recover as quickly as possible the adverse impact of the temporal link disconnection due to a handoff. To alleviate the effect of such packet losses during the disconnection, TCP-PRN notifies its TCP sender by sending a special ACK indicating which packets are lost due to this temporal link disconnection. The TCP sender then immediately attempts to retransmit those lost packets and restores the reduced congestion window and slow start threshold, if a false retransmission time-out occurs.

TABLE 6.1   Leading Researchers and Their Contributions in CLD Optimization

Researcher	Contribution	Year	Description/Key Concept
Foukalas, F., et al.	CLD survey and taxonomy [218]	2008	Surveying CLD applications and summarizing their key properties
Lee, M., et al.	TCP-PRN [219]	2008	Proposing a TCP path recovery notification (TCP-PRN) mechanism to prevent performance degradation during a handoff
Cheng, P., et al.	Best video quality using CLD [220]	2008	Proposing a CLD for real-time video traffic in CDMA wireless mesh networks
Khan, S., et al.	Rate adaptation solution [50]	2008	Proposing a cross-layer rate adaptation solution for 802.11 networks
Lee, S., and Chung, K.	Joint quality and rate adaptation [211]	2008	Introducing joint quality and rate adaptation for wireless video streaming
Yuan, Y., et al.	OC-MAC [221]	2007	Introducing a cooperative MAC protocol in wireless ad hoc networks based on CLD
Xia, Q., et al.	WFS-ARC [222]	2007	Proposing a weighted fair scheduling adaptive rate control (WFS-ARC) for WLAN performance improvement
Ge, W., et al.	Rate optimization for multicast [223]	2007	Proposing a CLD approach to provide efficient multicast communications
Choudhury, S., and Gibson, J. D.	Payload length and rate adaptation [224]	2007	Proposing a CLD to optimize single-user throughput by selecting data rate and payload as a function of channel conditions
Moltchanov, D., et al.	Cross-layer evaluation framework [225]	2006	Proposing a cross-layer wireless channel modeling for data link and IP layer performance evaluation
Dunn, J., et al.	Rate-proportional 802.11 fairness [226]	2006	Proposing a cross-layer scheme for rate-proportional 802.11 fairness
Pham, P. P., et al.	Rayleigh channel predictability [227]	2005	Proposing a CLD employing the predictability of Rayleigh channels to improve ad hoc network performance
Madueno, M., and Vidal, J.	Joint PHY-MAC layer design [210]	2005	Investigating a joint PHY-MAC layer design to improve ad hoc network performance

Best Video Quality Using CLD

Cheng et al. [220] proposed a CLD framework for obtaining the best video quality in CDMA wireless mesh networks. In the framework, source coding, power control, automatic request (ARQ) control, and delay partitioning functionalities in different layers are jointly optimized. The key idea is to maximize the decoded video quality by minimizing the weighted end-to-end distortion sum under strict end-to-end delay constraints. The video quality is improved by adjusting source coding rates, end-to-end delay distributions, and stations' transmit power.

Rate Adaptation Solution

Khan et al. [50] proposed a CLD framework for rate adaptation in 802.11 networks. Unlike other approaches for rate adaptation of applications' demands, timing constraints of the underlying protocols were not considered [211, 222, 224]. In the proposed solution, the rate is adapted to the changing channel state, application preferences, and underlying MAC sublayer timing constraints. The proposed design is based on a cross-layer framework involving two-way (application layer with rate adaptation algorithm) communications. It also incorporates a frame loss differentiation mechanism for assessing channel variations while performing rate adaptation.

Joint Quality and Rate Adaptation

Lee and Chung [211] proposed a CLD for video streaming over WLANs. The proposed CLD is based on the joint optimization of rate adaptation in the PHY and data link layers and quality adaptation in the application layer. This CLD is basically the combination of two earlier proposals: rate adaptation [50] and video quality [220] described above. The rate adaptation method adjusts the data transmission rate based on the measured signal strengths at the transmitting antenna and informs the quality adaptation scheme about the rate limits. The quality adaptation method then utilizes this information to adjust the quality of the video stream. It is shown that the proposed CLD improves wireless link utilization and quality of video stream simultaneously.

Opportunistic Cooperative MAC (OC-MAC)

Yuan et al. [221] proposed an OC-MAC protocol based on cross-layer information utilization. The idea is to determine the best relay station between source and destination based on instantaneous channel measurements. After determining the relay station, the destination station decides whether or not to use it for data transmission. OC-MAC uses relay stations for data transmission only if it can improve system performance. OC-MAC performed better (in terms of packet delay and throughput) than distributed coordination function (DCF).

Weighted Fair Scheduling Adaptive Rate Control (WFS-ARC) Framework

Xia et al. [222] proposed a CLD framework that integrated weighted fair scheduling (WFS) and adaptive rate control (ARC) to improve WLAN performance. In the framework, the PHY layer knowledge is shared with the MAC and logical link control (LLC) sublayers to provide efficient resource allocation. The WFS-ARC adjusts the data rate parameters at the MAC layer, based on the available channel state information at the receiver provided by the PHY layer. A weighted fair scheduler at the LLC schedules the packet transmission to satisfy the fairness constraints. Unlike other CLD approaches where the rate adaptation is performed at the transmitter, WFS-ARC rate adaptation is performed at the receiver [211, 224].

Rate Optimization for Multicast Communications

Ge et al. [223] proposed a CLD scheme to provide reliable and efficient multicast wireless communications. In the scheme, the transport layer erasure coding (used to enhance the reliability of multicast communications) is combined with the MAC layer multicast policy. Rate optimization of network models with single-input single-output (SISO) and multiple-input multiple-output (MIMO) links are analyzed.

Rate Adaptation and Payload Length

Choudhury and Gibson [224] proposed a CLD to optimize single-user throughput by selecting the transmitted bit rate and payload length as a function of channel conditions for both additive white noise and Nakagami-m fading channels. Payload length is used as an optimization parameter, and the proposed CLD jointly optimizes payload length and data rate for a given channel condition.

Cross-Layer Performance Evaluation Framework

Moltchanov et al. [225] proposed a cross-layer performance evaluation framework for wireless channels at data link and IP layers. An efficient wireless channel model for bit error processing is proposed first, and then the bit error model is extended to the IP layer using cross-layer mappings. The resulting IP packet error process model preserves bit error processing and captures specific peculiarities of protocols at the PHY and data link layers.

Rate-Proportional 802.11 Fairness

It is well known that 802.11 networks are unfair because they attempt to enforce channel access fairness by giving each station an equal probability of accessing a wireless medium for each transmission. Consequently, low-bit-rate stations occupy the medium for a far greater proportion of the time than high-bit-rate stations. To overcome this unfairness problem, Dunn et al. [226] proposed a CLD scheme that provides rate-proportional fairness to the 802.11 networks. The idea is to adjust the message length at the IP layer to reduce the number of bytes per packet sent by low-bit-rate stations while allowing higher-bit-rate stations to send full-length packets.

Rayleigh Channel Predictability

Pham et al. [227] proposed a CLD approach that employs the predictability of Rayleigh fading channels to improve the performance of ad hoc networks. The key idea is to share channel status information (CSI) with the upper layers. Having CSI before packet transmissions, the upper layers know whether the channel is good enough to guarantee a successful transmission. This approach was shown to improve network throughput and reduces packet losses.

Joint PHY-MAC Layer Design

Madueno and Vidal [210] proposed a joint PHY-MAC layer design of the broadcast protocol in ad hoc networks. The key idea is retransmission combining, which is adopted from the network-assisted diversity multiple access (NDMA) scheme [228] proposed for resolving collisions over the random access channels of cellular systems. The benefits of retransmission combining for broadcasting in ad hoc networking are investigated in [210].

In addition to the above proposals, earlier works on CLD include the following. Shakkottai et al. [229] discussed the issues of cross-layering where the PHY and MAC layer knowledge is shared with higher protocol layers to allocate network resources and applications over the Internet. Conti et al. [230] proposed a CLD architecture called MobileMan to optimize the performance of mobile ad hoc networks. Performance is improved by increasing local interaction among protocols and decreasing remote communications. Dirani et al. [231] investigated cross-layer modeling

TABLE 6.2   Categories of CLD Approaches Reviewed

Cross-Layer	Example of CLD Proposals/Approaches
PHY-MAC	Rayleigh channel predictability
	Rate adaptation and payload length
	Opportunistic cooperative MAC (OC-MAC)
PHY-MAC-LLC	Weighted fair scheduling adaptive rate control (WFS-ARC)
PHY-data link-application	Joint quality and rate adaptation
PHY-application	Rate adaptation solution
PHY-data link-IP	Rate-proportional IEEE 802.11 fairness
	Cross-layer performance evaluation
PHY-transport	TCP path recovery notification (TCP-PRN)
MAC-transport	Rate optimization and transport layer

for the capacity of WLANs using three different types of packet scheduling: CDMA with opportunistic scheduling used in Universal Mobile Telecommunications System/high-speed downlink packet access (UMTS/HSDPA), carrier sense multiple access with collision avoidance (CSMA/CA) in the 802.11 networks, and orthogonal frequency division multiple access (OFDMA) as in 802.16 WiMax.

The CLD approaches reviewed in this section are grouped into seven main categories, shown in Table 6.2.

The proposed CLD described in Chapter 12 adopted the idea of sharing wireless channel states with a MAC protocol for optimum packet transmissions. It is a joint PHY-MAC layer design, drawing ideas from the open literature, i.e., Rayleigh channel predictability [227]. Figure 6.1 illustrates the key concept of the proposed CLD framework. The channel-aware MAC protocol is one of the key elements of the proposed CLD.

FURTHER READING

For more details about subjects discussed in this chapter, we recommend the following books and references. The items in [] refer to the reference list at the end of the book.

Books

[172] Chapter 4—*Computer Networks* by Tanenbaum and Wetherall

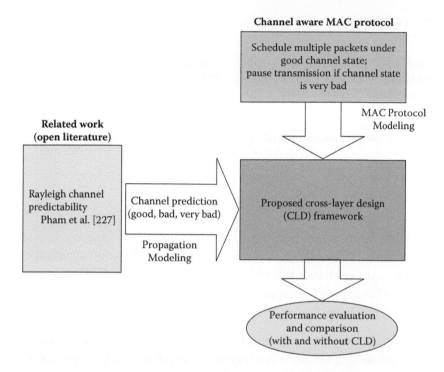

FIGURE 6.1   Developing the proposed CLD framework for WLANs.

Research Papers

   [50]

   [208]

   [216]

   [229]

SUMMARY

In this chapter, an introduction to CLD for WLANs was presented. A CLD method can be used to improve the performance of a typical WLAN. The definition, motivation, and various approaches to CLD optimization were presented. The strengths and weaknesses of CLD methods were highlighted. A review of literature on CLD optimization was also presented. The key researchers and their main contributions in CLD optimization were identified and discussed. The effect of propagation environment on WLAN performance is investigated in Chapter 7.

KEY TERMS

Carrier sense multiple access with collision avoidance (CSMA/CA)

Channel status information (CSI)

Cooperative MAC

Cross-layer design (CLD)

Distributed coordination function (DCF)

Link layer

Multicast communication

PHY-MAC optimization

Physical layer (PHY)

Point coordination function (PCF)

Rate adaptation

Weighted fair scheduling

Wireless local area network (WLAN)

REVIEW QUESTIONS

1. CLD approaches have been gaining popularity among network researchers in recent years. This is because CLD optimization can be used to enhance WLAN performance. However, CLD approaches may have some limitations. Discuss the strengths and weaknesses of CLD methods.

2. Explain why CLD optimization is needed in wireless network protocol design. (Hint: What happens if there is no CLD optimization in WLANs?)

3. Various network researchers have developed network protocols using CLD optimization. Name three key researchers and their main contributions in CLD optimization for WLANs.

4. CLD optimization can be achieved in various ways. Describe the three methods of achieving CLD optimization in WLANs.

MINI-PROJECTS

The following mini-projects aim to provide a deeper understanding of the topics covered in this chapter mainly through literature review. More mini-projects have been presented in the subsequent chapters to emphasize hands-on practical learning experience.

1. CLD optimization is a useful method for improving WLAN performance. In this exercise you will have an opportunity to conduct an in-depth literature review on CLD optimization for WLANs. Read 15 to 20 recent relevant journal/conference papers and summarize your research findings. Identify the key researchers and their main contributions on CLD optimization; use Table 6.3 to record your findings.

TABLE 6.3   Leading Researchers and Their Contributions in CLD Optimization for WLANs

Researcher	Contribution	Year	Description/Key Concept

2. Write a review report on the strengths and weaknesses of CLD approaches for WLANs. (Hint: Explain why we need a robust CLD framework for WLANs.)

II

Empirical Study

Effect of Radio Propagation Environments on WLAN Performance

LEARNING OUTCOMES

After reading and completing this chapter, you will be able to:

- Conduct propagation measurements to study the performance of indoor WLANs

- Discuss the effect of transmitter-receiver orientation on 802.11 link throughput

- Discuss the effect of office wall partitions on WLAN throughput

- Discuss the effect of line-of-sight (LOS) blockage on WLAN performance

- Discuss the effect of floors and single-wall separation on 802.11 link throughput

- Discuss the effect of microwave oven interference on 802.11 networks

INTRODUCTION

In Chapter 3, the radio propagation characteristics and the related issues were discussed, which provided background information for this chapter. An empirical study on the effect of radio propagation environments on WLAN performance is required for better understanding of the key factors influencing WLAN performance. This chapter reports on a propagation measurement campaign that was carried out using a pair of wireless laptops and access points (APs) in office and residential house environments. Using a series of simple experiments, the effect of radio propagation environments on transmission time as well as link throughput between a pair of Wi-Fi computers is studied. Details of the indoor environments used in the propagation study are presented in the "The Environments Used" section. The "Measurement Procedure and Resources Used" section describes the measurement procedure and resources used. Details of the experiments and some representative measurement results are presented in the "Measurement Results" section. The "Measurement Accuracy and Validation" section discusses measurement accuracy and the validation of the propagation measurement results. A brief summary concludes the chapter.

THE ENVIRONMENTS USED

Three different indoor environments were used in the propagation study; they will be referred to as Environments A, B, and C. Environments A and B are situated at the Auckland University of Technology (AUT) city campus, and Environment C is situated in Avondale, an Auckland suburb.

Environment A: Duthie Whyte Building

Environment A is located on the first floor and in the basement of AUT's Duthie Whyte (WY) building within the School of Computing and Mathematical Sciences office block, shown in Figure 7.1. The building is a typical multistory, reinforced concrete structure with floor dimensions of approximately 39 × 20 m. The first floor ceiling is suspended and contains metal components, which could influence radio wave propagation. The exterior of the building essentially consists of glass windows and the floors are concrete slabs. There are no buildings immediately adjacent to the WY building; however, there are nearby buildings of similar height to the north and west.

Figure 7.2 shows the floor plan of the first floor of Environment A. The offices are partitioned with a mixture of timber and plasterboard. The

FIGURE 7.1 (SEE COLOR INSERT.)   External view of Environment A.

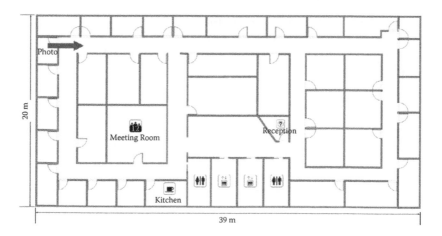

FIGURE 7.2   Floor plan for the first floor of Environment A. The arrow indicates internal photo angle.

FIGURE 7.3 (SEE COLOR INSERT.)   Internal view of Environment A office space. Offices are on both sides of the corridor.

office partition frames are metallic. Figure 7.3 shows the internal corridor with offices to the left and right. The angle from which the photo was taken is shown in Figure 7.2. The offices contain metallic furniture, filing cabinets, and whiteboards that can also influence radio propagation.

The floor plan and internal view for the basement parking lot of Environment A are shown in Figures 7.4 and 7.5, respectively.

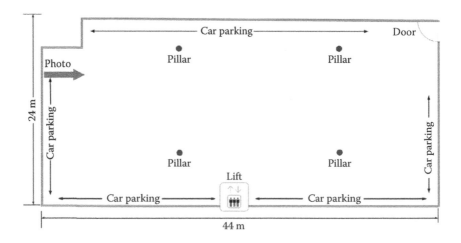

FIGURE 7.4   Floor plan for the basement of Environment A. The arrow indicates internal photo angle.

FIGURE 7.5 (SEE COLOR INSERT.)   Internal view of Environment A basement parking lot.

Environment B: AUT Tower

Environment B is part of the floor area located on the second floor of the AUT tower building. The AUT tower (Figure 7.6) has a similar construction to the WY building in Environment A. The floor plan and an internal view for the computer laboratory of Environment B are shown in Figures 7.7 and 7.8, respectively. The angle from which the photo was taken is indicated in Figure 7.7.

Environment C: Suburban House

Environment C (Figure 7.9) is a typical three-bedroom, single-level suburban house with a floor area of 133 m². The house is timber framed with plasterboard walls. The exterior of the house essentially consists of metal tiles, glass windows, brick walls, and a wooden door. There are three single-level houses around this house of similar size. A large tree is located on a neighboring property. The floor plan (Figure 7.10) shows the internal layout of Environment C. Figure 7.11 shows an internal view of Environment C. The angle from which the photo was taken is indicated in Figure 7.10.

MEASUREMENT PROCEDURE AND RESOURCES USED

The setup for Wi-Fi computer links consisted of a pair of 802.11b direct sequence spread spectrum (DSSS) laptops with identical configuration (Intel

FIGURE 7.6 (SEE COLOR INSERT.)   External view of Environment B (AUT tower).

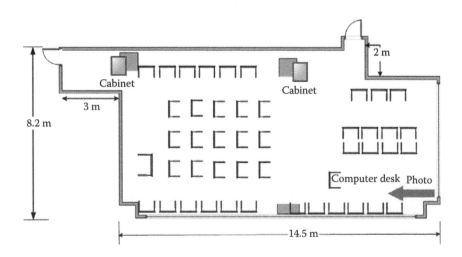

FIGURE 7.7   The layout of Environment B. The arrow indicates internal photo angle.

FIGURE 7.8 (SEE COLOR INSERT.) The open plan computer laboratory in Environment B.

FIGURE 7.9 (SEE COLOR INSERT.) External view of Environment C (suburban residential house).

Celeron 2.4 GHz, 512 MB RAM, 30 GB hard disk, MS Windows XP). The wireless AP was a D-Link DWL-2100AP [233]. The 802.11b wireless adapters used in the experiment were D-Link DWL-650 (11 Mbps) PCMCIA cards (omnidirectional) with a power output of 14 dBm [234]. One of the laptops was set as the transmitter (Tx) and the other as the receiver (Rx). During the experiment both were positioned at the lap height (45 cm) of a seated person

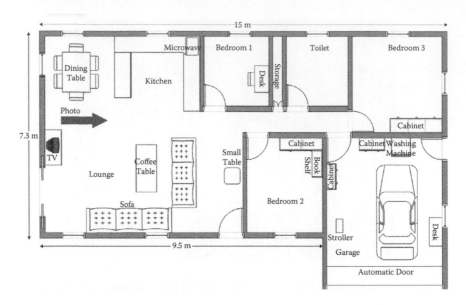

FIGURE 7.10   The layout of Environment C. The arrow indicates internal photo angle.

FIGURE 7.11   Internal view of Environment C. Bedroom 3 is situated at the end of the corridor.

by placing the laptops on chairs. A text file of 133.9 MB was sent using the "Send Files" feature of the Colligo TM Workgroup (peer-to-peer) to obtain the transmission time [235], unless otherwise specified. WirelessMon [236] was used to measure received signal strength (RSS). The RSS measurement using WirelessMon was found to be reliable within a ±10% margin, as outlined in [237]. Link throughput is the main performance metric used in this study. The throughput (Mbps) was computed by dividing the file size (Mb) by the total transmission time (seconds).

MEASUREMENT RESULTS

Environment A

Table 7.1 lists the eight experiments that were conducted to study the impact on WLAN performance of radio propagation in Environment A.

Experiment 1: Effect of Tx-Rx Orientation

In this experiment the effect of Tx-Rx orientation on the file transmission time as well as link throughput of the 802.11b WLAN in an ad hoc mode is investigated. Table 7.2 defines the four Tx-Rx orientations that were used in the experiment. This experiment was conducted in the Environment A office space. The layout of the measurement locations is shown in Figure 7.12.

The Tx was kept fixed at the leftmost end of the long narrow corridor (length 35 m), while the Rx was moved to various positions ranging from 1 to 35 m away from the Tx, which covers the entire length of the corridor. For each observation, the file transmission time (in seconds) was recorded and the link throughput (in Mbps) was calculated. The results are shown in Figure 7.13. The Tx-Rx orientations were found to have no impact on throughput from 1 to 35 m. The omnidirectional antennas used

TABLE 7.1   Experiments Carried Out in Environment A

Experiment	Description/Investigation
1	Effect of Tx-Rx orientation
2	Effect of LOS condition in the basement
3	Effect of LOS blockage
4	Effect of office wall partitions
5	Effect of floors
6	Effect of single-wall separation
7	Effect of microwave oven interference

TABLE 7.2   Four Orientations of Tx-Rx

Tx-Rx Orientation	Definition
Tx→; Rx→	The Tx and Rx antennas are facing the same direction (Rx antenna is pointing away from Tx).
←Tx; ←Rx	The Tx and Rx antennas are facing the same direction (Tx antenna is pointing away from Rx).
Tx→; ←Rx	The Tx and Rx antennas are facing each other.
←Tx; Rx→	The Tx and Rx antennas are facing away from each other.

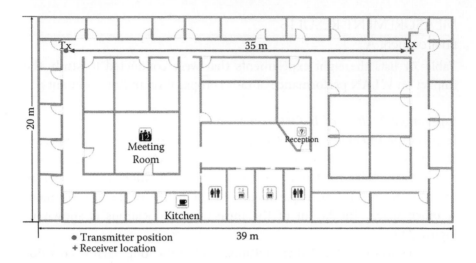

FIGURE 7.12 Floor plan of Environment A office space indicating the measurement locations for the effect of Tx-Rx orientation on the link throughput experiment.

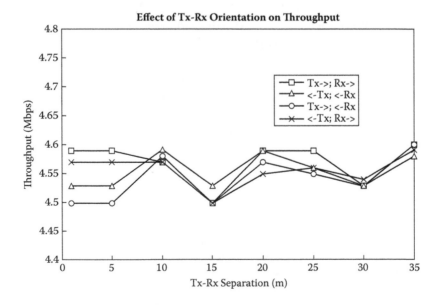

FIGURE 7.13 Effect of Tx-Rx orientation on link throughput (133.9 MB, 11 Mbps).

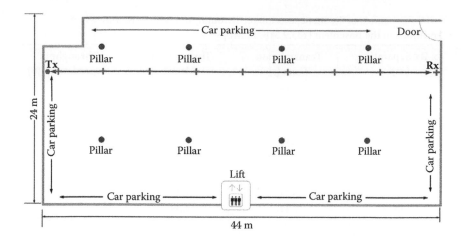

FIGURE 7.14 Floor plan of Environment A indicating the measurement locations in the basement. Positions of transmitting and receiving antennas are indicated by ● and +, respectively.

in the PCMCIA cards appear to retain their omnidirectionality when installed in the laptop computers. As the antennas' orientations did not impact throughput in this experiment, no attention was given to them in the remaining experiments.

Experiment 2: Effect of LOS Condition in the Basement
This experiment was conducted in the WY basement parking lot. The floor plan is shown in Figure 7.14. This experiment investigates the effect of LOS distance between Tx and Rx on transmission time as well as link throughput for 802.11b. The measurements were carried out in the basement, with LOS between the Tx and the Rx. The Tx was kept at a fixed point toward one end of the basement, and the Rx was moved to various locations ranging from 1 to 43 m away from the Tx.

The results are summarized in Table 7.3. The maximum throughput achieved was 4.69 Mbps for separations ≤5 m; this was chosen as the reference throughput. The throughput degradation (measured in %) is defined as the ratio of the difference between the individual link throughput and the reference throughput to the reference throughput. The throughput degradation indicates the variation of link throughput with respect to the reference throughput.

TABLE 7.3 Effect of Tx-Rx Separation on Throughput for 802.11b under LOS
Conditions in the Basement (133.9 MB, 11 Mbps)

Tx-Rx Separation (m)	Transmission Time (s)	Throughput (Mbps)	Throughput Degradation (%)
1	228	4.69	0
5	228	4.69	0
10	230	4.65	0.85
15	230	4.65	0.85
20	232	4.62	1.49
25	232	4.62	1.49
30	234	4.57	2.56
43	244	4.39	6.39

The throughput degradation is computed as follows:

$$Throughput\_Degradation = \frac{T_{ref} - T_{ind}}{T_{ref}} \times 100\% \qquad (7.1)$$

where T_{ref} is the reference throughput and T_{ind} is the individual station throughput.

Table 7.3 shows that throughput decreases slightly with increasing Tx-Rx separation, except for distances between 1 and 5 m, 10 and 15 m, and 20 and 25 m. However, this decrease in throughput is not very significant. For example, when the distance between Tx and Rx is 43 m, the throughput degradation is only 6.4%. This is mainly due to the LOS path between the Tx and Rx in the basement. The throughput measurement experiment can easily be scaled up to some 50 to 60 m of Tx-Rx separation (i.e., 100 to 120 m diameter) without serious performance degradation as long as Tx is in LOS with Rx [234].

The main conclusion is that the 802.11b WLAN can be used in large halls, such as conference rooms and lecture theaters, to provide effective wireless connectivity, as long as Tx is in LOS with Rx.

Experiment 3: Effect of Office Wall Partitions

Experiment 3 was also conducted in the Environment A office space. Figure 7.15 shows the layout of the floor before the permanent offices shown in Figure 7.12 were constructed. In Figure 7.15, a number of workspaces are located in the open-space area. These workspaces were created using temporary half-height partitions (labeled as "temporary office

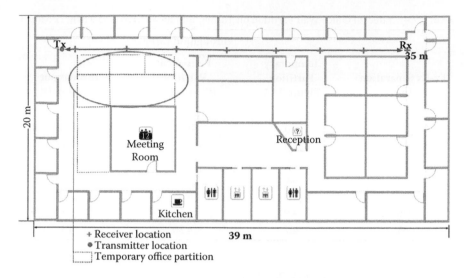

FIGURE 7.15 Floor plan of Environment A indicating the measurement locations where some offices are formed by temporary partitions.

partitions"). In this environment the effect of temporary half-height partitions was studied by measuring the throughput. Subsequently, the temporary offices were replaced by the permanent structures built from plasterboard (Figure 7.12), and the measurements were repeated. The transmission time was recorded and the link throughput was computed. The results are summarized in Table 7.4.

The results presented in Table 7.4 show that the Wi-Fi link throughput in the environment in Figure 7.12 (permanent offices) is slightly lower than that for the environment in Figure 7.15 (temporary offices). The presence of plasterboard walls with metal framing in the previously open space reduced the throughput. For example, the throughput difference is up to 10% [(5 − 4.5)/5 × 100%] at Tx-Rx separation of 5 m. The throughput difference shown in column 4 of Table 7.4 can be computed as follows:

$$Throughput\_difference = \frac{T_{TO} - T_{PO}}{T_{TO}} \times 100\% \qquad (7.2)$$

where T_{TO} is the throughput with temporary office wall partitions and T_{PO} is the throughput with permanent office wall partitions.

TABLE 7.4   Effect of Office Wall Partition on Throughput for 802.11b (133.9 MB, 11 Mbps)

Tx-Rx Separation (m)	Throughput (Mbps)		Throughput Difference (%)
	Temporary Partition (Figure 7.15)	Permanent Partition (Figure 7.12)	
1	5.0	4.50	10.0
5	5.0	4.50	10.0
10	5.0	4.63	7.4
15	5.0	4.50	10.0
20	5.0	4.57	8.6
25	5.0	4.55	9.0
30	4.9	4.53	7.5
35	4.7	4.50	4.3

Experiment 4: Effect of LOS Blockage
In this experiment the effect of LOS blockage by office walls on the transmission time, as well as throughput of the 802.11b ad hoc network, is investigated. The layout of the measurement locations is shown in Figure 7.16. As in experiment 1, the Tx was kept fixed at the leftmost end of the long narrow corridor (length 35 m), while the Rx was kept at the other end, keeping Tx in LOS with Rx. The transmission time was recorded and the link throughput was computed. Next, the Rx was placed (at a right angle) 1 m away from the first position so that the office walls blocked the LOS

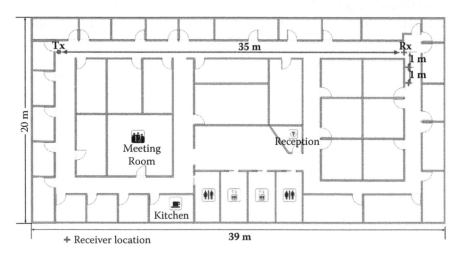

FIGURE 7.16   Floor plan of Environment A office space indicating the measurement locations for the effect of the LOS blockage experiment.

TABLE 7.5   Effect of LOS Blockage on Throughput for 802.11b (133.9 MB, 11 Mbps)

Tx-Rx Separation (m)	Throughput (Mbps)	Throughput Degradation (%)
Trial 1: 35	4.5	0
Trial 2: 35.015	0.8	82.2
Trial 3: 35.03	Connection lost	100

path between the Tx and the Rx. Finally, the Rx was placed 2 m away from the first position. The results are summarized in Table 7.5.

Table 7.5 shows that LOS blockage by office walls has a significant effect on the Wi-Fi link throughput; the increased separation was insignificant. For example, in the second trial where the Rx was placed at a position just 1 m away from the LOS path, the throughput degradation was 82.2% [(4.5 – 0.8)/4.5 × 100%]. Clearly, loss of the LOS path has a dramatic effect.

In trial 3, the Rx was placed 2 m away from the trial 1 position. The transmission failed due to the loss of the connection at RSS of –91 dBm. In this situation the LOS path was severely blocked by several office walls. Unlike in the previous trial, radio signal diffraction and reflections around the corner were not sufficient to yield an adequately strong signal to allow successful communication.

The various trials in this experiment provide some insight into the link throughput performance of an 802.11b WLAN in an obstructed office environment. These results are in agreement with the work of Geier [238] in that the dramatic effect of the loss of a LOS signal component and the subsequent reliance on multipath propagation was observed.

Experiment 5: Effect of Floors
This experiment investigated the effect of floors on the transmission time as well as link throughput for 802.11b in the peer-to-peer mode. Its layout is shown in Figure 7.17. The Tx was kept on the basement floor and the Rx was first placed on the ground floor, and subsequently on the first and second floors. The results are summarized in Table 7.6. Single-floor obstructions have a significant effect on the transmission time as well as the link throughput for 802.11b. For example, the transmission time with the ground floor obstruction (Tx in the basement and Rx on the ground floor with Tx-Rx separation of 3 m) is 1,039 s and the link throughput is 1.03 Mbps. This is approximately five times lower than the throughput obtained under the LOS condition in experiment 2 (Table 7.3).

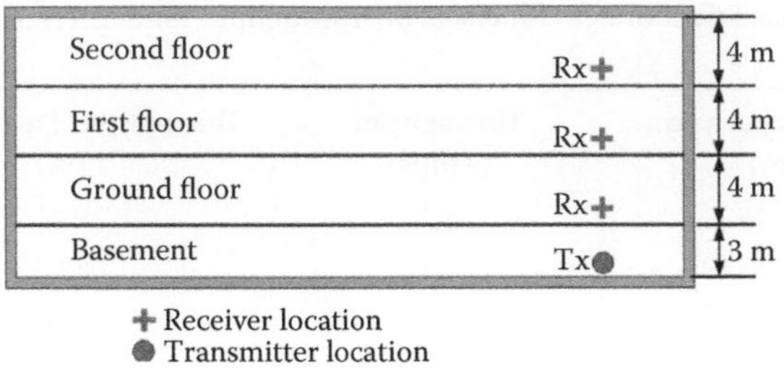

FIGURE 7.17 Layout of the effect of floors test.

TABLE 7.6 Effect of Floors on the Throughput for 802.11b in WY Building (133.9 MB, 11 Mbps, Tx in basement)

Rx Location	Transmission Time (s)	Throughput (Mbps)
Ground floor	1,039	1.03
First floor	1,504	0.71
Second floor	Connection lost	0

In the case of two-floor obstructions with a Tx-Rx separation of 7 m, the transmission time was 1,504 s and the link throughput was 0.71 Mbps. Note that two-floor obstructions have a larger effect on the link throughput degradation than single-floor obstructions. Note also that the ceiling of the basement obstructed radio frequency (RF) signals more strongly than the ground floor or the first floor of AUT's WY building. This is expected because the basement's ceiling is more strongly built, with concrete slabs and steel beams. The wireless connection was lost at RSS of –91 dBm due to the severe blockage of radio signals by three-floor obstructions with a Tx-Rx separation of 11 m.

The results presented in Table 7.6 are in accordance with the work of other network researchers [239]. The main conclusion one can draw is that 802.11 ad hoc networks are not an efficient means for providing wireless connectivity to users located on multiple floors. For better performance and coverage, an infrastructure WLAN with a wireless AP on every floor is recommended.

Experiment 6: Effect of Single-Wall Separation
This experiment was conducted, as were experiments 3 and 4, in office Environment A. The layout of the experiment is shown in Figure 7.18. Here, the effect of a single-wall separation on the transmission time, as

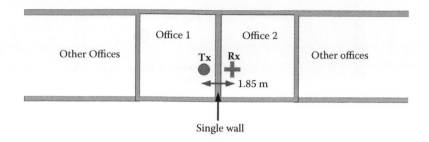

FIGURE 7.18 Floor plan of Environment A for effect of single-wall separation test. Positions of transmitting and receiving antennas are indicated by ● and +, respectively.

TABLE 7.7 Effect of a Single Wall on the Throughput for 802.11b (133.9 MB, 11 Mbps, Tx-Rx separation 1.85 m)

Obstruction	Transmission Time (s)	Throughput (Mbps)	Throughput Degradation (%)
Without wall	240	4.46	0
One wall	243	4.41	1.12

well as link throughput of 802.11b in an ad hoc mode, is investigated. The walls on this floor are plasterboard over wood and steel beam frames.

The Tx was kept in a room (door closed), while the Rx was kept in the adjacent room with Tx-Rx separation of 1.85 m. The transmission time was recorded and the link throughput was computed. In the second trial, the experiment was repeated without an obstruction (i.e., both the Tx and the Rx were placed in a room with a separation of 1.85 m). The results are summarized in Table 7.7. The decrease in the link throughput due to a single-wall separation between Tx and Rx is not very significant, being only 1.12%. An earlier study on the effect of walls on throughput shows that the performance was not degraded considerably by a separation of up to four walls [95]. This study is also in accordance with previous studies that have shown that a single plasterboard wall does not have a significant effect on the link throughput of the 802.11b network. The main conclusion is that in an obstructed office environment, adjacent rooms can be connected efficiently by using 802.11b in a peer-to-peer arrangement.

Experiment 7: Effect of Microwave Oven Interference
This experiment was conducted in a staff common room and kitchen within Environment A. This experiment investigated the effect of

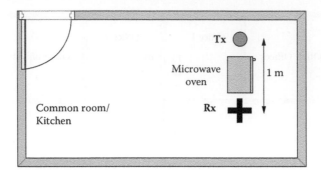

FIGURE 7.19 Effect of microwave oven test (first floor of Environment A). Positions of transmitting and receiving antennas are indicated by ● and +, respectively.

microwave oven interference on the throughput of an 802.11b ad hoc network. The layout of the experiment is shown in Figure 7.19.

A microwave oven was placed between the Tx and the Rx with a Tx-Rx separation of 1 m. As with the other experiments, a 133.9-MB file was transferred while a microwave oven was active for the duration of the transmission. The transmission time was recorded and the link throughput was computed. In the second trial, the experiment was repeated with the microwave oven inactive. The results are summarized in Table 7.8. The throughput degradation due to microwave oven interference is 29.6%. This decrease in throughput results from microwave ovens operating in the industrial, scientific, and medical (ISM) band, causing packet retransmission. An earlier study on the effect of microwave oven interference on Wi-Fi link throughput shows that the network performance degraded considerably in the presence of an active microwave oven [240].

The main conclusion to be drawn from this experiment is that a microwave oven operating in the ISM band causes performance degradation in 802.11 WLANs. The level of performance degradation will depend on the amount of interference generated by a given microwave oven. For instance,

TABLE 7.8 Effect of Microwave Oven Interference on the Throughput for 802.11b (133.9 MB, 11 Mbps, Tx-Rx separation 1 m)

Microwave Oven	Transmission Time (s)	Throughput (Mbps)	Throughput Degradation (%)
Inactive	231	4.63	0
Active	328	3.26	29.6

an old microwave oven with weaker seals generates more emissions of 2.450–2.458 GHz compared to a new microwave oven.

Environment B

In Environment B, both ad hoc and infrastructure network scenarios were used to study the impact of the radio propagation environment on WLAN performance.

Scenario 1: Ad Hoc Network

In this scenario the effect of distance between Tx and Rx on the transmission time, as well as the throughput of an 802.11b ad hoc network in a typical computer laboratory, is investigated. The measurements were carried out in the computer laboratory with LOS between the Tx and the Rx (Figure 7.20). The Tx was kept fixed at the rightmost end of the laboratory, while the Rx was moved to various locations ranging from 1 to 17.5 m away from the Tx, which covers the entire length of the computer laboratory. The location 17.5 m from the Tx is close to a metallic cabinet. For each observation, the transmission time was recorded and the link throughput was calculated. The results are summarized in Table 7.9. The maximum achieved throughput is 5 Mbps at 3 m and RSS of –60 dBm; this was chosen as the reference throughput. The throughput in the computer laboratory is more or less the same at all measured locations, except

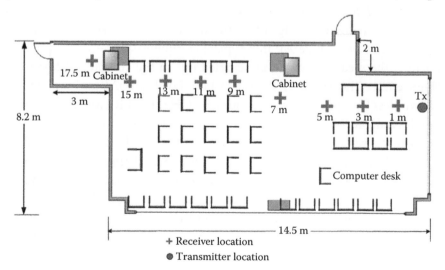

FIGURE 7.20 Floor plan of Environment B indicating the measurement locations for scenario 1 (802.11b ad hoc network).

TABLE 7.9   Effect of Tx-Rx Separation on the Throughput of an 802.11b Ad Hoc Network in Environment B (133.9 MB, 11 Mbps)

Tx-Rx Separation (m)	RSS (dBm)	Transmission Time (s)	Throughput (Mbps)	Throughput Degradation (%)
1	−66	226.8	4.95	1
3	−60	222.7	5.00	0
5	−65	227.6	4.94	1.2
7	−67	226.1	4.97	0.6
9	−70	225.6	4.98	0.4
11	−74	226.7	4.96	0.8
13	−76	229.6	4.89	2.2
15	−77	226.3	4.96	0.8
17.5	−76	235.4	4.77	4.6

at 17.5 m, where the throughput degradation was 4.6%. This throughput degradation is mainly due to the LOS blockage between the Tx and Rx signal paths by a metallic cabinet. The main conclusion to be drawn from this experiment is that the 802.11 ad hoc networks can be used in computer laboratories and lecture theaters where there is no LOS blockage between Tx and Rx to provide effective wireless connectivity. This also supports a conclusion that was made earlier.

Scenario 2: Infrastructure Network

In this scenario an 802.11g infrastructure network is used to study the performance of a single AP in a typical computer laboratory. As in scenario 1, the measurements were carried out in the computer laboratory (Figure 7.21). The wireless AP was a D-Link DWL-2100AP and two identical wireless laptops (IBM x31 Pentium 1.7 GHz, 1 GB RAM) with D-Link wireless adapters (802.11g) whose power outputs were 15 dBm. One of the laptops was set as the Tx and the other as the Rx. The AP was placed at the middle of the laboratory, and the Tx was placed approximately 1.5 m away from the AP. The Rx was placed at six locations (A, B, C, D, E, and F) to cover all the locations of workstations in the computer laboratory and measurements were conducted. The RSS values at the Rx positions ranged from −52 to −60 dBm. The Tx and Rx were positioned 1 m above the floor during the experiment by placing the laptops on trolleys. The AP was positioned 2.5 m above the floor. For each observation, a text file of 133.9 MB was sent from the Tx to the Rx through the AP. The transmission time was recorded and the link throughput was calculated. The measurement

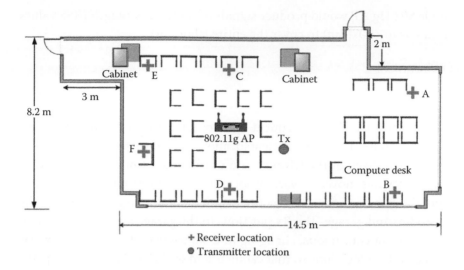

FIGURE 7.21   Floor plan of Environment B indicating the measurement locations for scenario 2 (802.11g infrastructure network).

procedure is the same as described in the "Measurement Procedure and Resources Used" section. The results are summarized in Table 7.10. The maximum achieved throughput for 802.11g is 8.85 Mbps (position C) at RSS of −52 dBm; this was chosen as the reference throughput. The throughput degradation (column 5) is computed using (7.1); it indicates the variation of AP throughput at each Rx position with respect to the reference throughput. For instance, AP throughput at location F is 22.3% lower than the reference throughput.

The decrease in throughput in the computer laboratory is mainly due to the presence of metallic cabinets in the laboratory, causing radio signal diffraction and reflection. Another observation is that the deployment of a

TABLE 7.10   Throughput for 802.11g AP in an Infrastructure Network in Environment B (133.9 MB, 54 Mbps)

Rx Position	RSS (dBm)	Transmission Time (s)	Throughput (Mbps)	Throughput Degradation (%)
A	−58	130.6	8.60	2.82
B	−57	140.5	8.00	9.60
C	−52	126.9	8.85	0
D	−54	132.5	8.48	4.18
E	−53	158.6	7.08	20
F	−60	163.2	6.88	22.26

single 802.11g AP would produce signals of sufficient strength (RSS values from −52 to −60 dBm) to cover the entire laboratory.

Environment C

The effect of LOS blockage by furniture and walls on transmission times as well as throughput of an 802.11b ad hoc WLAN is investigated in Environment C. This experiment was conducted in a residential three-bedroom house. The measurement locations are shown in Figure 7.22. The Tx was kept fixed at the leftmost end of the house (lounge/dining area), and the Rx was moved to various locations ranging from 1 to 11 m away from the Tx, which covers the entire length of the corridor and parts of the bedrooms and garage. The Rx positions in the garage and bedrooms 1, 2, and 3 are not continuous, changing in distance from the Tx. The Rx was placed at these locations so that cabinets and walls blocked the LOS path.

For each observation, the RSS and transmission times were measured and the throughput was calculated. The results are summarized in Table 7.11. The maximum achieved throughput is 4.57 Mbps, which was chosen as the reference throughput, and the throughput degradation was computed based on this reference throughput using (7.1). One can observe that throughputs are significantly lower than the reference throughput in both bedroom 3 and the garage, at Tx-Rx separations of 11.05, 11.09, and

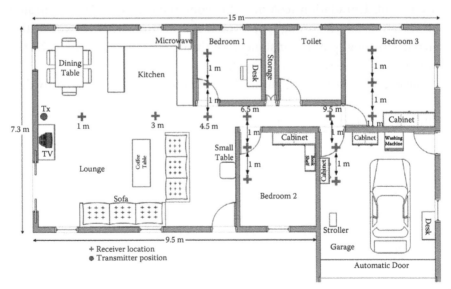

FIGURE 7.22 Floor plan of Environment C indicating the measurement locations.

TABLE 7.11   Throughput for 802.11b Ad Hoc Network in a Single-Level Three-Bedroom Suburban Residential House (133.9 MB, 11 Mbps)

Rx Location	Tx-Rx Separation (m)	RSS (dBm)	Transmission Time (s)	Throughput (Mbps)	Throughput Degradation (%)
Lounge	1	−59	250.0	4.49	1.8
Lounge	3	−63	247.1	4.55	0.4
Corridor	4.5	−65	250.1	4.49	1.8
Bedroom 1	4.61	−71	245.7	4.57	0
Bedroom 1	4.72	−72	250.6	4.48	2.0
Corridor	6.5	−74	255.2	4.40	3.7
Bedroom 2	6.58	−69	249.3	4.51	1.3
Bedroom 2	6.65	−73	246.3	4.56	0.2
Corridor	9.5	−74	246.1	4.57	0
Garage	9.55	−80	296.2	3.79	17.1
Garage	9.60	−81	254.7	4.41	3.5
Corridor	11	−72	246.1	4.57	0
Bedroom 3	11.05	−82	464.6	2.42	47.0
Bedroom 3	11.09	−84	381.8	2.94	35.7

9.55, respectively. The decreased throughput at these locations is due to the LOS blockage by furniture, cabinets, and walls. These locations had very weak RSS values in the range of −80 to −84 dBm.

The propagation measurements in Environment C provide some insight into the throughput performance of an 802.11b WLAN in a suburban residential house. It was observed that an 802.11 ad hoc network might not be effective in connecting users located in the remote bedrooms and garages. The AP would have to be carefully located to achieve better system performance.

Performance Comparison of Environments A, B, and C

Figure 7.23 plots the Tx-Rx separation between Tx and Rx against throughput of Environments A (basement and obstructed office space), B, and C. The throughput of the 802.11b ad hoc network in Environment C (suburban residential house) is very similar to the throughput obtain in the obstructed office space in Environment A. However, the 802.11b ad hoc network had a slightly lower through-put in Environment C than in the basement in Environment A and Environment B (computer laboratory).

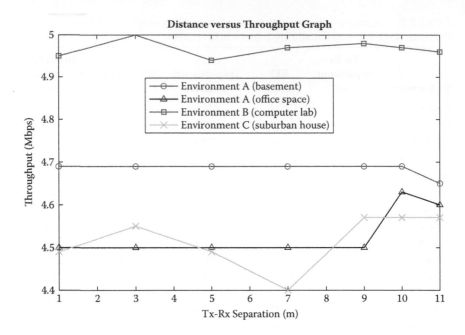

FIGURE 7.23 Tx-Rx separation versus throughput performance under Environments A, B, and C.

MEASUREMENT ACCURACY AND VALIDATION

Knowledge of the measurement system accuracy is extremely important in interpreting results. The accuracy of the propagation measurement results was improved by addressing the following issues.

- **People movement:** The measurements were conducted after hours to avoid the impact of the movement of people on system performance.

- **Co-channel interference:** During propagation measurements, a couple of neighboring WLANs were detected. To avoid co-channel interference on system performance, the AP was set to a different channel prior to data collection.

- **System configuration:** To avoid the effect of system configuration on WLAN performance, two wireless laptops with identical configurations were used in the experiments.

- **Validation:** The propagation measurements were repeated three times to obtain repeatability of results, ensuring the correctness of measurement. The measured throughputs presented in this chapter closely agree with the results obtained from the data sheet for D-Link cards and APs (Table C.4 in Appendix C). In addition, the results obtained from this study were compared with those in the works of other network researchers [25, 92, 233, 234].

FURTHER READING

For more details about subjects discussed in this chapter, we recommend the following books and references. The items in [] refer to the reference list at the end of the book.

Books

[89] Chapter 2—*Wireless Communications and Networking* by Mark and Zhuang

[27] Chapter 4—*Wireless Communications: Principles and Practice* by Rappaport

Research Papers

[98, 243, 244]

SUMMARY

The effect of indoor propagation environments on the performance of a typical 802.11 network was investigated in this chapter. Using a pair of wireless laptops and an AP, propagation measurements were conducted in various indoor environments. Through a series of experiments, the effects of orientation of transmitting and receiving antennas; pure LOS conditions; LOS blockage by office walls, office partitions, floors, and single-wall separation; microwave oven interference; and LOS blockage by walls and furniture in a suburban residential house on the 802.11b network throughput were investigated. These locations represent typical operating environments of indoor wireless systems, and RSS values ranging from strong to very weak (−43 to −83 dBm) were observed.

The propagation measurements reported in this chapter provide some insight into the link throughput for 802.11b and 802.11g WLANs. It was observed that the LOS blockage by multiple walls has a dramatic effect on the transmission time as well as the link throughput in an office space and in a suburban residential house. Propagation results showed that the data communication link between two Wi-Fi computers could be lost due to signal propagation obstruction by walls even at a relatively small separation. Consequently, although an ad hoc 802.11b network can connect adjacent rooms efficiently in a peer-to-peer manner within an obstructed office space, it might not be effective in connecting users located across the floor. Similarly, an 802.11b ad hoc network is not sufficient to connect users located in remote rooms in a suburban house. For better performance and coverage, an infrastructure network with carefully located wireless APs is required. The performance of 802.11g in an obstructed office space is investigated in Chapter 8.

KEY TERMS

Access point (AP)	Radio propagation
Antennas	Received signal strength (RSS)
Configuration	Receiver (Rx)
Direct sequence spread spectrum (DSSS)	Throughput degradation
IEEE 802.11	Transmission time
Line of sight (LOS)	Transmitter (Tx)
Link throughput	Wi-Fi computers
PCMCIA cards	Wireless local area network (WLAN)
Propagation measurements	

REVIEW QUESTIONS (SCENARIO BASED)

1. **Effect of Tx-Rx orientation:** Suppose you send a file from wireless laptop 1 (transmitter) to wireless laptop 2 (receiver) in an open-space environment. Do you think the file transmission time will be longer when you change the orientation of one of the laptops or both during the transmission period?

   Discuss the effect of transmitter-receiver orientation on the link throughput of a typical 802.11 network operating in a line-of-sight (LOS) condition (i.e., no obstruction).

2. **Effect of LOS blockage:** Consider a scenario when you send a file from wireless laptop 1 to wireless laptop 2 in an obstructed office environment. Naturally, transmitted signals will be blocked by office walls and corners. Discuss the effect of LOS blockage on link throughput of a typical 802.11g network operating in an obstructed office space.

3. **Effect of office wall partitions:** Suppose you are transmitting a file from wireless laptop 1 to wireless laptop 2 in an obstructed office environment where offices are made of temporary partitions (see Figure 7.15). Discuss the effect of office wall partitions on link throughput of a typical 802.11 network. (Hint: Do you think 802.11 link throughput will be the same with and without office wall partitions?)

4. **Effect of floors:** Consider a multistore building scenario (Figure 7.17) where you set up a wireless laptop (Tx) on the ground floor to transmit a file to another wireless laptop that you move to the first floor, second floor, third floor, and so on.

   Discuss the effect of floors on link throughput of a typical 802.11 network.

5. **Effect of microwave oven:** Suppose you are transmitting a file from one wireless laptop to another wireless laptop close to the microwave oven that you are using to cook your food. Discuss the effect of microwave oven interference on link throughput of a typical 802.11 network.

MINI-PROJECTS

The following mini-projects aim to provide a practical hands-on learning experience of the topics covered in this chapter using radio propagation measurements. Students can use Wi-Fi devices (e.g., laptops) to conduct propagation measurements.

1. The purpose of this project is to develop a sound knowledge and understanding of a radio propagation environment and its impact on WLAN performance. Conduct an in-depth literature review on the impact of propagation environments on WLAN performance. Read 15 to 20 recent relevant journal/conference papers to identify the key researchers and their main contributions. You can use Table 7.12 to record your findings.

2. **Effect of Tx-Rx orientation:** Extend the work presented in the "Environment A" section of "Measurement Results" by considering Tx and Rx to be perpendicular (90°).

TABLE 7.12   Leading Researchers and Their Contributions in WLAN Propagation Measurement

Researcher	Contribution	Year	Description/Key Concept

3. **Effect of floors test:** Extend the work presented in the "Environment A" section of "Measurement Results" (experiment 5) by placing Tx on the second floor and Rx on the first floor, ground floor, and in the basement.

4. **Analytical model:** The analytical method is a powerful tool for network modeling and performance evaluation. It is useful to be able to determine 802.11 throughput in a noisy channel analytically. Develop an analytical model for 802.11 throughput under a noisy channel.

CHAPTER 8

Performance of 802.11g in an Obstructed Office Space

LEARNING OUTCOMES

After reading and completing this chapter, you will be able to:

- Conduct propagation measurements to study the performance of 802.11g networks

- Discuss the throughput performance of 802.11g in a typical office space

- Discuss the effect of line of sight (LOS) blockage on 802.11g throughput in an obstructed office space

- Develop a simulation model for a typical 802.11g ad hoc network

- Validate 802.11g propagation measurement results

INTRODUCTION

The number of WLAN hotspots is growing significantly every year. Among the various variants of 802.11 WLANs, 802.11g is one of the most popular technologies being used in home and office networks worldwide. This popularity results from the low cost, high speed, and user mobility offered by the technology. The design of WLANs is quite different from a wired network design because of the complex and dynamic behavior of radio signal propagation characteristics. In the wireless environment, a wireless station can sense radio signals from other devices, as long as they are within the range of radio signal coverage. A radio propagation environment is one of the key factors that influences the performance of WLANs. The received signal strength (RSS) becomes weaker in a harsh propagation environment, and therefore the error rate is high, resulting in low throughput. A study of the effect of RSS on 802.11g link throughput in an obstructed office building is required to assist efficient design and deployment of such systems. To achieve this objective, a good understanding of the performance of 802.11g in an obstructed office block is required. This chapter aims to evaluate the performance of a typical 802.11g in an obstructed office block under different RSS values. In the investigation an infrastructure-based WLAN is considered. We first report on a propagation study in the "Propagation Study" section. The measurement environment, procedure, accuracy, and validation are also discussed in this section. The simulation model of a typical 802.11g network is presented, and results are discussed in the "Simulation Study" section. Finally, the system implication for 802.11g measurements is discussed in the "System Implications" section, and a brief summary ends the chapter.

PROPAGATION STUDY

Two wireless laptops with identical configurations (Intel Celeron 2.4 GHz, 512 MB RAM, MS Windows XP Professional) were used in the experiment. The 802.11g wireless adapters were D-Link DWL-G132 (54 Mbps) cards (omnidirectional) with a power output of 15 dBm [245]. The wireless AP was D-Link DWL-2100AP [233].

Measurement Environment and Procedure

An extensive measurement campaign was conducted in the School of Computing and Mathematical Sciences Building at the Auckland University of Technology (AUT) Duthie Whyte (WY) building. The measurement environment was a typical multistory, reinforced concrete building with a floor area of 39 × 20 × 4 m (Figure 8.1). We study the optimum placement of an 802.11g access point (AP) to cover the entire floor. It was observed that a single AP could not provide good coverage for the entire floor; therefore, the floor area was divided into two regions: Region 1 and Region 2. This experiment describes the measurement procedure and results, focusing on Region 1 (left-hand side of Figure 8.1), as Region 2 is identical to Region 1. The layout of the measurement locations is shown in Figure 8.1.

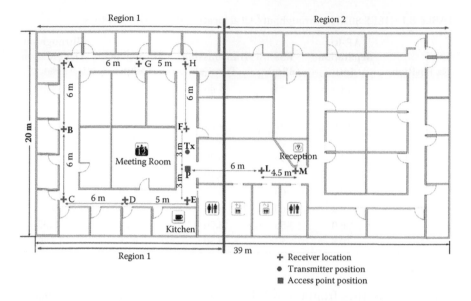

FIGURE 8.1 (SEE COLOR INSERT.) Layout of floor 1 of WY building and measurement locations.

One of the laptops was set as the transmitter (Tx) and the other as the receiver (Rx). An AP was placed at position P and the Tx was placed 2 m away from the AP. The Rx was placed at various locations and measurements were conducted. The results for 10 representative Rx positions (A, B, C, D, E, F, G, H, L, and M) are presented in Table 8.1. These Rx positions cover a range of received signal strength (RSS) values from strong to very weak (–43 to –83 dBm).

The Tx and Rx were positioned 1 m above the floor during the experiment by placing the laptops on trolleys. The AP was positioned 2 m above the floor. For each observation, a 10.9-MB file was sent from the Tx to the Rx via the AP using the "Send Files" feature of the Colligo TM Workgroup to obtain the transmission time [235]. As in other experiments, the throughput of the 802.11g AP was computed by dividing the file size (MB) with the total transmission time (seconds). The results are summarized in Table 8.1.

The Rx position and the corresponding AP-Rx separation are shown in columns 1 and 2, respectively. The RSS at each Rx location is indicated in column 3. The transmission times and the corresponding AP throughputs are shown in columns 4 and 5, respectively. As shown in Figure 8.1, Rx positions such as A, B, C, D, and G do not exactly represent continuous

TABLE 8.1 IEEE 802.11g Throughput (AP at location P, 10.9 MB, 54 Mbps)

Rx Position	AP-Rx Separation (m)	RSS (dBm)	Transmission Time (s)	Throughput (Mbps)	Throughput Degradation (%)
A	14.2	−73	12.60	6.92	36.51
B	11.4	−68	9.50	9.18	15.79
C	11.4	−62	9.60	9.08	16.67
D	5.8	−60	8.75	9.97	8.57
E	3.0	−43	8.20	10.63	2.44
F	3.0	−55	8.10	10.77	1.23
G	10.3	−63	8.50	10.26	5.88
H	9.0	−60	8.00	10.90	0
L	6.0	−55	8.70	10.02	8.05
M	10.5	−57	9.50	9.18	15.79

change in distance from the AP. Therefore, these distances are calculated by using Equation (8.1) as follows:

$$z = \sqrt{x^2 + y^2} \tag{8.1}$$

where z is the hypotenuse of a right-angled triangle with sides x and y.

Measurement Results and Discussion

Table 8.1 shows that the maximum achieved throughput is 10.9 Mbps (location H) at RSS of −60 dBm, and this was chosen as the reference throughput. Based on this reference throughput, the throughput degradation (column 6) was computed using Equation (8.2):

$$Throughput\_Degradation = \frac{T_{ref} - T_{ind}}{T_{ref}} \times 100\% \tag{8.2}$$

where T_{ref} is the reference throughput and T_{ind} is the individual station throughput.

The throughput degradation indicates the variation of AP throughput at each Rx position with respect to the reference throughput. For instance, AP throughput at location L is about 8% lower than the reference throughput.

Figure 8.2 plots RSS against 802.11g AP throughput. One can observe that although the throughput is not directly proportional to the RSS, in

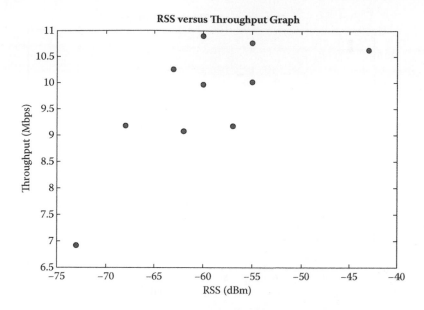

FIGURE 8.2   Effect of RSS on throughput for 802.11g in WY level 1 office space.

most cases it is better when the signal is stronger. For the RSS values ranging from –65 to –43 dBm (considered good signal strengths), the throughput of 802.11g AP is around 10 to 11 Mbps, except for the RSSs of –62 dBm
(location D) and –57 dBm (location M), where throughputs are 9.28 and
9.18 Mbps, respectively. The slightly lower throughputs in these locations
are mainly due to the wave-guiding effect in the corridors [241].

In Figure 8.3, the AP-Rx separation is plotted against 802.11g throughput; it shows that 802.11g AP throughput does not always decrease with
increasing distance between AP and Rx. However, the general trend is
that the lower throughput is achieved at high AP-Rx separation and vice
versa. For example, the maximum throughput (10.9 Mbps) is achieved at
an AP-Rx separation of 9 m, whereas the lowest throughput is obtained at
an AP-Rx separation of 14 m.

Overall Observation and Discussion

The trade-off between coverage/performance and costs is an important
issue for the deployment of WLANs in general and APs in particular. The
objective was to minimize the number of AP deployments without sacrificing network performance too much. Therefore, to find an optimum AP

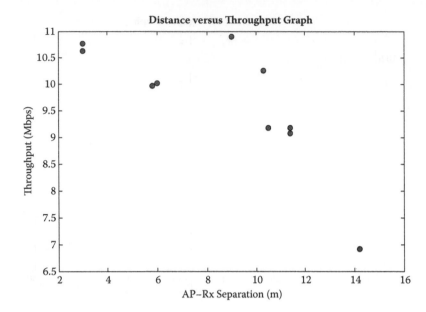

FIGURE 8.3　AP-Rx separation versus throughput for 802.11g in WY level 1 office space.

position that provides better coverage and performance, various field trials and measurements were conducted in both Regions 1 and 2 (Figure 8.1). Overall, the AP at position P provides better coverage and throughput than the APs at positions A and G in Region 1. It is observed that at least two APs are required (one for each region) to cover the entire floor.

The accuracy and validation of the measurement results are discussed next.

Measurement Accuracy and Validation

To improve the accuracy of the propagation measurement results, the following issues are considered:

- **People movement:** The measurements were conducted after hours to avoid the impact of the movement of people on system performance.

- **Co-channel interference:** To reduce the impact of the co-channel interference on system performance, all external radio sources were detected and then the experimental AP was adjusted prior to measured data collection.

- **Parameter setting:** We use default settings for wireless APs and cards to reduce possible interference for AP configurations.

- **Validation:** The propagation measurements were repeated several times to ensure the correctness of the measured data. The measured throughputs presented in the "Measurement Results and Discussion" section closely agree with the results obtained from the data sheet for D-Link cards and access points. In addition, the results obtained from this study were compared with the work of other researchers [24, 91, 241].

SIMULATION STUDY

The propagation measurement results presented in this chapter are more site specific than can be used for making decisions about the deployment of WLANs in an indoor environment; they have limitations when it comes to the generalization of the research findings. Fortunately, computer simulation can be used to predict system performance. The 802.11g infrastructure network simulation model was developed using the OPNET Modeler 14.0 [34]. The OPNET Modeler was chosen not only for its easy-to-use graphical user interface (GUI), but also for its comprehensive library of commercially available network components that helps network researchers to develop and validate network models more efficiently. This section outlines details of the simulation model, wireless station and AP configurations, and simulation results.

Modeling the Network

In the simulation model, an office network of 35 × 15 m area, similar to the obstructed office space (Figure 8.1), is used. Figure 8.4 shows a snapshot of the OPNET WLAN model with 1 AP and 20 wireless stations.

FIGURE 8.4   OPNET representation of WLAN model with 1 AP and 20 wireless stations.

Attribute	Value
⊟ Wireless LAN Parameters	[...]
⊢ BSS Identifier	Auto Assigned
⊢ Access Point Functionality	Enabled
⊢ Physical Characteristics	Extended Rate PHY (802.11g)
⊢ Data Rate (bps)	54 Mbps
⊟ Channel Settings	[...]
⊢ Bandwidth (MHz)	Physical Technology Dependent
⊢ Min Frequency (MHz)	BSS Based
⊢ Transmit Power (W)	0.032
⊢ Packet Reception-Power Threshold...	-88
⊢ Rts Threshold (bytes)	2346
⊢ Fragmentation Threshold (bytes)	2304
⊢ CTS-to-self Option	Enabled
⊢ Short Retry Limit	7
⊢ Long Retry Limit	4
⊢ AP Beacon Interval (secs)	0.1
⊢ Max Receive Lifetime (secs)	0.5
⊢ Buffer Size (bits)	2048000
⊢ Roaming Capability	Disabled
⊢ Large Packet Processing	Drop
⊞ PCF Parameters	Disabled
⊞ HCF Parameters	Not Supported

FIGURE 8.5   AP configuration and simulation parameters.

Unfortunately, the D-Link wireless cards and AP were not available in the OPNET library. Hence, a generic wireless station was configured as an 802.11g AP as well as mobile terminals (MTs).

Figure 8.5 shows AP configuration and simulation parameter setting. The transmit power of the AP was set to 32 mW, which is close to the D-Link (DWL-2100) AP that was used in the propagation measurements. Another important parameter is the packet reception power threshold (same as RSS); it was set to –88 dBm. This allows the wireless AP to communicate with wireless stations even when signals are weak, a common scenario in the obstructed office environment. Other parameters such as data rate, channel setting, and the frequency spectrum were set to the default values for 802.11g. The packet length threshold was set to 2,346 bytes (a realistic figure for wireless Ethernet networks). Each simulation run lasted for 15 min of simulated time, where the first minute was the transient period. The observations collected during the transient period are not included in the final simulation results.

The data rate, Tx power, RSS threshold, packet length threshold, and segmentation threshold are the same for the AP. All wireless stations communicate using identical half-duplex wireless radios based on the 802.11g AP. Capture effects, transmission errors due to interference and noise in the system, and hidden and exposed station problems are not considered in the simulation model. Streams of data packets arriving at stations are modeled as constant bit rate (CBR) with an aggregate mean packet generating rate of λ packets/s. The packets arriving at a wireless station are uniformly destined to $N - 1$ other stations. The stations are arbitrarily spaced within the transmission range. The WLAN performance is studied under steady-state conditions.

Simulation Results

Two important network performance metrics, mean packet delay and throughput, are used in this study. Mean packet delay is defined as the end-to-end delay of all the packets received by the medium access control (MAC) protocol from all stations, forwarded to the higher layer. This packet delay includes queuing delay and medium access delay at the source station, and packet transmission time via AP. Throughput (measured in bps) is defined as the total number of bits forwarded from the MAC layer to higher protocol layers in all the stations of the network. The simulation results report the steady-state behavior of the network and were obtained with a relative error ≤ 1%, at the 99% confidence level.

The effect of increasing the number of wireless stations (for $N = 2$, 10, 15, 20, 25, and 30 stations) on mean packet delay and throughput of the 802.11g infrastructure network is shown in Figures 8.6 and 8.7, respectively.

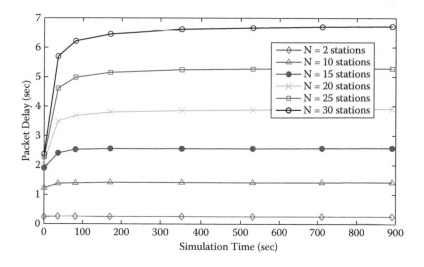

FIGURE 8.6 Effect of increasing stations on packet delay (802.11g infrastructure network).

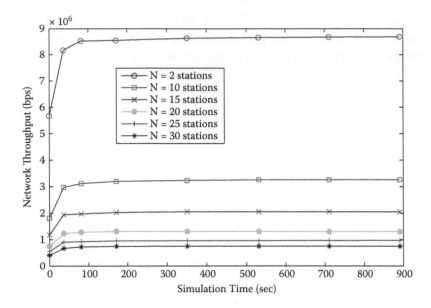

FIGURE 8.7 Effect of increasing stations on network throughput (802.11g infrastructure network).

Figure 8.6 shows that the network mean packet delay increases with N. This increase is mainly due to the channel contention and backoff delays. As N increases, users are likely to wait longer to access the channel for packet transmissions, and consequently the network mean packet delay increases. For example, the network mean delays are 0.25, 1.41, 2.54, 3.8, 5.15, and 6.48 s for $N = 2, 10, 15, 20, 25$, and 30, respectively.

Figure 8.7 shows that the 802.11g AP throughput decreases with N. For example, the network mean throughputs are 8.6, 3.2, 2.0, 1.3, 0.9, and 0.7 Mbps for $N = 2, 10, 15, 20, 25$, and 30, respectively. Because of the higher contention delays and backoff, the data being transmitted by a source station to a particular destination decreases as N increases; consequently, network mean throughput decreases.

The mean packet delay versus throughput characteristic of an 802.11g infrastructure network for $N = 2, 10, 15, 20, 25$, and 30 wireless stations is illustrated in Figure 8.8. Clearly, the network throughput decreases with N and the packet delay increases due to network traffic congestion.

The main conclusion to be drawn from Figures 8.6 to 8.8 is that the number of active stations (i.e., station density) has a significant effect on both the mean packet delay and throughput of an 802.11g infrastructure network. Both the packet delay and throughput significantly degrade (in

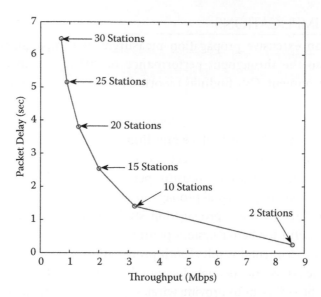

FIGURE 8.8   Packet delay versus throughput characteristic of 802.11g infrastructure network.

terms of quality of service [QoS]) for $N > 15$ stations. Therefore, for the deployment of indoor 802.11g APs in an obstructed office space, it is recommended to have fewer than 16 wireless stations per AP for wireless communication among the active stations.

Simulation Accuracy and Model Verification

OPNET Modeler is a well-known commercial network simulation package and is becoming more and more popular in academia, as the package is available to academic institutions at no cost [34]. Like ns-2, OPNET is also a credible network simulator that has been tested by numerous network engineers and researchers worldwide [83, 246–250]. OPNET Modeler 14.0 was the most recent version of the simulation package at the time of this work.

Lucio et al. [251] have tested the accuracy of network simulation and modeling using both OPNET Modeler and ns-2 by comparing the simulation results with the empirical results. Based on the modeling of CBR and File Transfer Protocol (FTP) sessions, the authors concluded that both ns-2 and OPNET Modeler perform well and provide very similar results. In addition, OPNET-based simulation models were validated through indoor propagation measurements from wireless laptops and APs for 802.11g. A good match between simulation and measurement results for $N = 2$ to 4 stations further validates the OPNET simulation models [163, 252].

SYSTEM IMPLICATIONS

Through an extensive propagation measurement campaign, we gained insight into the throughput performance of 802.11g in an obstructed office environment. Our findings reported in this chapter serve two main purposes. First, our findings may be useful in aiding managers to make informed decisions about the deployment of 802.11g networks in locations similar to AUT's WY office building. Second, this case study demonstrates, by experiment, the direct effect of RSS on system performance. The use of real hardware to measure performance avoided the complex theoretical modeling of signal propagation and system implementation.

Measured data from a propagation study in an indoor environment would be useful for better system planning and optimum placement of APs. Our experimental results (both propagation and simulation) reveal that a single AP is not adequate for signal coverage for the entire floor; it would not be sufficient to provide wireless connectivity for some 30 users located in the office block. For optimum coverage for the entire floor, multiple APs are required.

FURTHER READING

For more details about subjects discussed in this chapter, we recommend the following books and references. The items in [] refer to the reference list at the end of the book.

Books

[171] Chapter 6—*Computer Networking: A Top-Down Approach* by Kurose and Ross

Book Chapters

[253–255]

Research Papers

[163]

[256–258]

SUMMARY

In this chapter, a propagation measurement campaign for the deployment of the 802.11g AP in an obstructed office space was conducted. It was observed that a single 802.11g AP would not provide adequate coverage for the entire floor area of 780 m² in the obstructed office block. Multiple APs are required to achieve better coverage and throughput.

In addition to propagation measurements, OPNET simulation experiments were carried out to study the impact of station density on the mean packet delay and throughput of the 802.11g AP. In the OPNET model, an office network of 35 × 15 m² in area, similar to the obstructed office space in Environment A containing an 802.11g AP and 30 wireless stations, was used. The question arises as to the maximum number of wireless stations that can be supported by an 802.11g AP. Certainly, a trade-off exists between mean packet delay and throughput with a single AP. Simulation results showed that an 802.11g infrastructure WLAN can support fewer than 15 active wireless stations concurrently under high traffic loads in an obstructed office environment. WLAN performance enhancement by modifying MAC protocols is investigated in Chapter 9.

KEY TERMS

Access point (AP)
IEEE 802.11g
Infrastructure network
Obstructed office environment
OPNET Modeler
Propagation measurement

Received signal strength (RSS)
Throughput
Throughput degradation
Wireless local area network (WLAN)
Wireless stations
WLAN deployment

REVIEW QUESTIONS

1. The performance of WLANs can be affected by various factors. Identify and describe two main factors influencing the performance of a typical 802.11g network.

2. The IEEE 802.11g-based WLANs are being used in home and corporate networks worldwide. The performance of a typical 802.11g network can be degraded in obstructed office buildings. Explain why 802.11g throughput drops in an obstructed office space.

3. Suppose you want to evaluate the performance of an 802.11g network by simulation (say, OPNET or ns-2 simulator). List the important parameters that need to be considered when simulating an 802.11g ad hoc network.

4. The validation of simulation models is an important part of any simulation study. Explain how you would validate OPNET or ns-2 simulation results.

5. IEEE 802.11 throughput can be a linear function of Tx-Rx separation in an open-space environment. However, this observation may not be true for office building environments. Discuss the relationship between throughput and AP-Rx separation for a typical 802.11g network operating in an obstructed office environment.

MINI-PROJECTS

The following mini-projects aim to provide a deeper understanding of the topics covered in this chapter using literature review as well as empirical study.

1. Conduct an in-depth literature review on 802.11-based WLAN deployments in medium to large organizations. Read 15 to 20 recent relevant journal/conference papers to identify the key researchers and their main contributions. You can use Table 8.2 to record your findings.

2. **Optimization of 802.11g:** The purpose of this project is to develop a sound knowledge on WLAN optimization. In this exercise you will identify and measure the key factors optimizing the performance of a typical 802.11g network. (Hint: Identify the main two or three factors; use simulation or set up a test bed to measure them.)

3. **Simulation modeling:** Extend the simulation model presented in the "Modeling the Network" section by including a noisy channel.

TABLE 8.2   Leading Researchers and Their Contributions in the Deployment of 802.11 Networks

Researcher	Contribution	Year	Description/Key Concept

4. **Verification of OPNET results:** Verify the OPNET results presented in the "Simulation Results" section using another simulator (e.g., ns-2).

CHAPTER 9

Improving WLAN Performance by Modifying MAC Protocols

LEARNING OUTCOMES

After reading and completing this chapter, you will be able to:

- Review previous work on the enhancement of IEEE 802.11 networks

- Discuss the impact of transmission overheads on WLAN throughput

- Describe the principle of operation of the buffer unit multiple access (BUMA) protocol

- Highlight the strengths and weaknesses of the BUMA protocol

- Develop a simulation model to study the performance of BUMA

- Explain how BUMA algorithms can be implemented in Linux

INTRODUCTION

In Chapter 4, a review of the literature on wireless medium access control (MAC) protocols was presented. It is noted that previous research emphasizes the importance of MAC protocol design for optimum system performance. As an extension to this study, a method of improving WLAN performance by modifying the MAC protocol is described in this chapter.

Although there were prior investigations [77, 150] on how to modify the 802.11 MAC protocol to improve system performance, the approach taken in this work is simple and does not change the existing protocol significantly, so that the same standard-based equipment can be used without major redesign.

IEEE 802.11 has several performance limitations. One of the limitations of the 802.11 MAC protocol is its low bandwidth utilization under medium to high traffic loads, resulting in low throughput and high packet delay [20, 68, 259]. To overcome these performance problems, this chapter proposes an extension to 802.11 called buffer unit multiple access (BUMA) protocol, which was developed through minor modifications of the 802.11 distributed coordination function (DCF) [47].

In this chapter, previously related work on improvements of the original 802.11 protocol is further reviewed. The proposed BUMA protocol is described, and its performance is evaluated by simulation. The impact of protocol overhead on throughput of 802.11 and BUMA is analyzed. The implementation of BUMA is also discussed. The chapter concludes with a brief summary of the main findings.

PREVIOUS WORK ON THE ENHANCEMENT OF 802.11

Many network researchers have proposed schemes to improve the performance of the original 802.11 protocol. This section, for brevity, recapitulates only a selected set of the literature (discussed in Chapter 4) that is indicative of the range of approaches used to improve throughput, packet delay, and fairness.

Xiao [77] proposed two mechanisms, concatenation and piggybacking, in order to reduce the overhead of the 802.11 protocols and consequently improve system performance. The idea is to concatenate multiple frames in a station's queue before transmission. In the piggyback scheme, a station can piggyback a data frame onto an acknowledgment (ACK) packet.

Cali et al. [140] proposed an improvement to the 802.11 protocol called Dynamic 802.11, which is basically a distributed algorithm for dynamically altering the size of the backoff window. By observing the status of the channel, a station obtains an estimate of the network traffic and uses this estimate to tune the backoff window sizes.

Bruno et al. [260] investigated an enhancement of the 802.11 protocol called p-persistent (probability persistent) 802.11. The improvement is mainly due to the selection of a better algorithm for selecting the backoff interval. Instead of the binary exponential backoff used in the original

802.11 protocol, the backoff interval of the p-persistent 802.11 is sampled from a geometric distribution with parameter p.

Shih et al. [261] proposed a MAC protocol for wireless ad hoc networks called RTS Collisions Avoidance (RCA) to decrease the request to send (RTS) collisions and improve network throughput under high loads. The RCA protocol uses a pulse-tone exchange mechanism to decrease the chance of RTS collisions compared to the DCF RTS-CTS (clear to send) scheme. Therefore, the RCA protocol avoids wasting channel bandwidth for multiple retransmissions and has much lower control overhead than DCF.

Cesana et al. [262] investigated a new approach called IA-MAC to improve DCF's performance in environments with high interference levels. The key idea is to insert information about received power and the signal-to-interference-and-noise ratio (SINR) into the CTS header.

Lin and Liu [263] proposed a scheme called distributed cycle stealing (DCS) to improve DCF's performance. Performance improvement is achieved by power control and spatial reuse methods. In DCS, all the communications follow power-distance constraints, which guarantee that no transmission would disturb another during any communication period. In spatial reuse, a station is allowed to engage in a new communication to transmit a packet if there is no conflict between the new and the existing communication.

Ozugur et al. [264] proposed a p_{ij}-persistent carrier sense multiple access (CSMA) backoff algorithm for load balancing among the wireless links, which improves the fairness of 802.11. In this scheme, each station calculates a link access probability p_{ij} using either a connection-based (i.e., the information on the number of connections it has with its neighboring stations) or a time-based method based on the average contention period.

Jiang and Liew [62] investigated methods of improving throughput and fairness of 802.11 WLANs by reducing both the exposed and hidden station problems. They showed that the 802.11 network is not scalable due to exposed and hidden station problems, and that more access points (APs) do not yield higher total throughput. By removing these problems, it is possible to achieve scalable throughput.

Wang and Garcia-Luna-Aceves [157] proposed a hybrid channel access scheme to alleviate the fairness problem of 802.11 without sacrificing much throughput and simplicity. The scheme is based on both sender-initiated and receiver-initiated handshakes.

DESCRIPTION OF THE PROPOSED BUMA PROTOCOL

The proposed BUMA protocol described in this chapter differs from the earlier work described in the "Previous Work on the Enhancement of 802.11" section. It has different goals and capabilities. BUMA is implemented through minor modifications of DCF [46]. The design of BUMA was motivated by the key idea that a typical WLAN can increase throughput by sending a payload using fewer but longer packets [77, 224, 265]. With fewer packets used to deliver the same payload, proportionally less time is spent in the backoff state. Many network researchers have highlighted this aspect of network performance improvement [265, 266].

In BUMA, for each active connection a temporary buffer unit is created at the MAC layer where multiple packets are accumulated and combined into a single packet (with a header and a trailer) before transmission. Assuming a realistic wireless Ethernet packet length of 1,500 bytes, the optimum length of the buffer unit (Table 9.1) was empirically determined to be that of three 1,500-byte packets plus header and trailer. The optimization of buffer unit length is discussed in the "Optimization of Buffer Unit Length" section below.

The number of buffer units is determined by the number of active connections between the source and destination stations. Each link has its own buffer unit, and each buffer unit stores one or more packets where each packet appears as a MAC protocol data unit (MPDU) in the MAC layer with the same destination address. Thus, the content of a buffer unit is a large packet that appears as a MAC segment data unit (MSDU) in the

TABLE 9.1   Optimization of Buffer Unit Length (Internet Protocol [IP] datagram: 1,500 bytes)

Buffer Unit Length (packet)	Throughput (Mbps)	Mean Packet Delay (ms)
1	4.03	887
2	5.76	665
3	6.66	399
4	6.19	638
5	6.84	645
6	6.54	640
10	6.84	660
50	6.99	970
100	6.89	1,464

MAC layer with a single header and a trailer. Now the question arises about the maximum length of the combined packet (i.e., length of an MSDU).

For both wired and wireless Ethernet LANs, the maximum length of a MAC frame is 2,346 bytes, which is a fragmentation threshold. The mean packet length is about 1,500 bytes, with payload length ranges from 46 to 1,460 bytes. In the optimized BUMA scheme ($BUMA_{opt}$), the maximum length of a buffer unit is 4,534 bytes, accommodating three 1,500-byte packets plus a 34-byte envelope (MAC header and cyclic redundancy check [CRC]). In such cases, the MSDU would be fragmented into two frames before transmission since its length is greater than the fragmentation threshold.

When a station fills the buffer unit, it first schedules the packet, and then puts the next set of packets in the empty buffer unit from the same link. Under medium to high traffic loads, each station will always have packets for transmission, and the buffer unit will be filled up with packets quickly within a time interval. When traffic is low, BUMA will perform as good as DCF by reducing the buffer unit length to one packet. DCF is effectively a special case of BUMA where the buffer unit length is one packet. Therefore, in the proposed scheme, the mean packet delay will be bounded since a packet will not remain in the buffer permanently while waiting for the second and subsequent packets to arrive. The basic operation and the frame structure of the BUMA protocol are illustrated in Figures 9.1 and 9.2, respectively. The buffer unit contains multiple MPDUs (Figure 9.2). The actual number of MPDUs in a buffer unit will depend on the packet length supported by the upper protocol layers. For instance, for the transmission of a 500-byte IP datagram, a maximum of nine MPDUs would be stored in a buffer unit of 4,500 bytes.

The buffer unit mechanism described in this chapter has several benefits. First, it transmits a greater payload (by scheduling a larger packet), and consequently achieves better throughput than DCF. Second, by adopting the buffer unit mechanism, one can achieve higher bandwidth utilization and better fairness than in DCF because it wastes less potential transmission time in the backoff and channel contention processes. Referring to the example of the 500-byte IP datagram, instead of nine contention periods, only one contention period is needed to transmit nine IP datagrams. BUMA therefore dramatically reduces the average packet contention delay, especially for shorter packet lengths, while maintaining better throughput by transmitting a combined packet. Finally, the packet transmission overhead will be reduced significantly. Without the

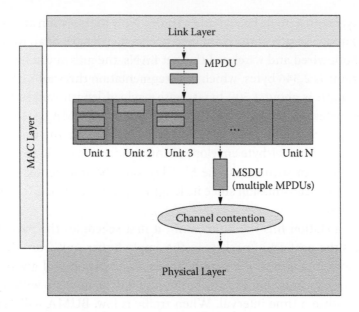

FIGURE 9.1   Basic operation of the BUMA protocol.

buffer unit mechanism, each packet transmission requires a separate set of overheads, including headers, interframe spaces, backoff time, CRC, and acknowledgments; in contrast, only one set of overheads would be used with the buffer unit mechanism. However, all these benefits come with a trade-off, a small processing delay at the stations. The transmission overheads of BUMA and DCF are analyzed in the "Protocol Overhead and Throughput Analysis" section. The processing delay at the stations is further addressed in the "Delay Performance" section.

BUMA does not require any additional control packets that might complicate protocol implementation and degrade overall system performance. The proposed scheme maintains compatibility with DCF, and does not

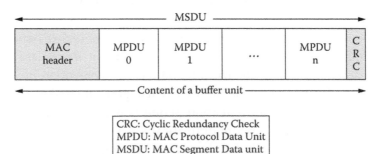

FIGURE 9.2   Frame structure of the BUMA protocol.

introduce any additional collision avoidance procedures. Thus, as with DCF, BUMA adopts the binary exponential backoff algorithm for collision resolution and avoidance. BUMA will not provide 100% fairness in channel access due to the binary exponential backoff algorithm for collision resolution. It will, however, provide better fairness than DCF.

Although BUMA is based on the concatenation mechanism proposed in [77], it differs in significant ways. BUMA does not require any additional control packets to deliver a concatenated packet, whereas [77] requires three additional control frames (i.e., a frame control type, concatenated frame count, and total length field) to deliver a super-frame. Another unique feature of BUMA is its adaptive buffer unit length, which accommodates variable-length payloads for supporting various applications, including real-time multimedia traffic. BUMA's performance is studied under heavy traffic loads, and two new performance metrics, packet drop ratio and mean deviation of throughput (MDT) fairness, are defined and used in the performance study.

Optimization of Buffer Unit Length

Yin et al. [267] investigated the packet length that optimizes DCF throughput under different channel conditions and traffic loads. A trade-off exists between a desire to reduce the overhead by adopting longer packet lengths and the need to reduce packet error rates in error-prone environments by using shorter packet lengths. For example, for an error-prone channel with $BER = 2 \times 10^{-5}$, the throughput reaches 0.6049 Mbps for a packet length of 900 bytes. However, the optimum packet length varies with changing traffic load, and the optimum packet length is longer in lighter traffic than in heavier traffic.

Both throughput and mean packet delay increase with packet length under ideal channel conditions. The mean delay and throughput of the BUMA protocol also depends on the buffer unit length. Now the question arises as to the optimum buffer unit length required to achieve the best mean packet delay and throughput. The optimal length of the buffer unit was determined empirically. In the simulation experiment, an infrastructure network was used with $N = 20$ stations, Poisson distributed packet arrivals, a packet length of 1,500 bytes (a realistic figure close to the standard wired Ethernet LANs), and User Datagram Protocol (UDP) traffic operating under uniform loads (where the packet arrival rate is the same for all stations) of 70%.

Table 9.1 summarizes the empirical results. Mean packet delay was computed based on arrival time of the first buffered packet. As shown, BUMA's throughput increases slightly with increasing buffer unit length, and then saturates at buffer unit length of 10 or more packets. The lowest mean packet delay occurs at the buffer unit length containing three packets (4,534 bytes). Considering both the throughput and mean packet delay, the maximum length of the combined packet in $BUMA_{opt}$ should be ≤4,500 bytes.

Strengths and Weaknesses

BUMA provides better bandwidth utilization than DCF because it wastes less transmission capacity in the backoff state, and consequently achieves higher throughput, lower packet delay, lower packet drop ratios, and better fairness, especially under medium to high traffic loads. In addition, BUMA requires less overhead than DCF to send the same payload. This improvement is due to BUMA's strategy where only a single header-trailer pair is required for transmitting multiple packets. Moreover, BUMA is simple and can be easily implemented within DCF without changing existing hardware. Although BUMA provides a better fairness than DCF, it does not provide 100% fairness in sharing a channel's bandwidth among the active stations. BUMA also introduces a fragmentation-defragmentation cost, as well as a small packetization delay at the stations.

PROTOCOL OVERHEAD AND THROUGHPUT ANALYSIS

Packet transmission overhead is one of the main factors in MAC inefficiency, especially for an 802.11 WLAN. In this section, the effect of transmission overhead on throughput of the BUMA and DCF protocols is analyzed.

The overhead for a successful transmission of a frame in a typical 802.11 WLAN is illustrated in Figure 9.3. Each MSDU consists of a MAC header, one or more MPDUs, and a CRC. The MAC header and CRC comprise 34 bytes, and the ACK frame is 14 bytes long. The MSDU payload (i.e., IP datagram) varies between 46 and 2,346 bytes, including IP headers.

A single user transmitting a data frame (i.e., no channel contention delay) was used to study the impact of packet transmission overhead on throughput for BUMA and DCF. If one neglects signal propagation times, then the total time (T) required for a successful frame transmission is given by

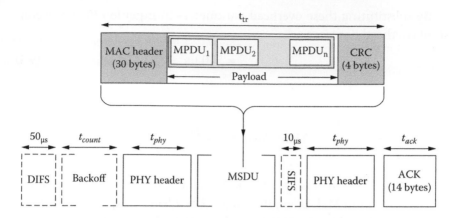

FIGURE 9.3   Overhead for a successful transmission of an MSDU.

$$T = t_{tr} + t_{overhead} \tag{9.1}$$

where t_{tr} is the data frame (i.e., an MSDU) transmission time and $t_{overhead}$ is the constant overhead.

The t_{tr} and $t_{overhead}$ can be computed by Equations (9.2) and (9.3), respectively:

$$t_{tr} = \frac{L}{R} \tag{9.2}$$

$$t_{overhead} = DIFS + t_{phy} + SIFS + t_{phy} + t_{ack} + t_{MAC} + t_{CRC} \tag{9.3}$$

where L is the frame length (i.e., the length of an MSDU), R is the data rate, DIFS is the DCF interframe space, $SIFS$ is the short interframe space, is the physical layer (PHY) t_{phy} header comprising the PHY layer convergence protocol (PLCP) preamble and header, t_{ack} is the time required for sending an ACK frame at the MAC layer, t_{MAC} is the time required for sending MAC overhead, and t_{CRC} is the time required for sending a CRC.

For 802.11b, $DIFS = 50$ μs, $SIFS = 10$ μs, t_{phy} varies according to the data rate used by the station, $t_{phy} = 192$ μs when the long PLCP header is used at 1 Mbps, and $t_{phy} = 96$ μs when the short PLCP header is used at 2, 5.5, or 11 Mbps. In the throughput calculation, the long PLCP header is used.

The combined length of the ACK, frame MAC header, and CRC is 48 bytes: 48 μs (1 Mbps) > $t_{ack} + t_{MAC} + t_{CRC}$ > 4.36 μs (at 11 Mbps). This value was rounded up to 56 μs to round up $t_{overhead}$.

By substituting these overhead parameters in Equation (9.3), the constant overhead becomes

$$t_{overhead} \cong 500 \ \mu s \qquad (9.4)$$

The proportion of the useful throughput above the MAC layer is given by [260]

$$Throughput = \frac{t_{tr}}{T} \times \frac{payload}{L} \qquad (9.5)$$

Example 9.1: Transmission of Short IP Datagrams (MPDU = 46 bytes)
The maximum MSDU length in BUMA is 4,534 bytes, this being the optimum length of the BUMA buffer unit. In this example, however, an MSDU of length <2,312 bytes is used so that it can be transmitted without fragmentation (the fragmentation threshold for wireless Ethernet networks is 2,346 bytes [39, 46]). A buffer unit of payload = 2,300 bytes (2,312/46 = 50 MPDUs after rounding down) was chosen, as illustrated in Figure 9.4b. The length of the MSDU is 2,334 bytes (2,300-byte payload and 34-byte envelope). Therefore, in the BUMA scheme the minimum overhead time required to transmit 2,300 bytes of payload is given by $Overhead_{(BUMA)} = t_{overhead}$.

For this payload, DCF's overhead is 50 times that of BUMA's. Consequently, BUMA achieves significantly better throughput than

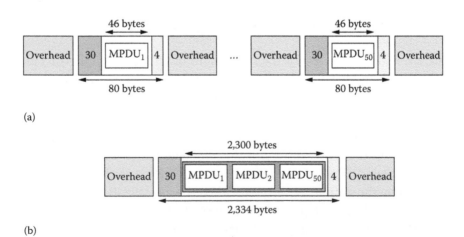

(a)

(b)

FIGURE 9.4   Protocol overheads for the transmission of short IP datagrams of 46 bytes in length for (a) 802.11b DCF and (b) BUMA$_{nonopt}$.

DCF, especially for the transmission of short IP datagrams. The effective throughput of BUMA and DCF is analyzed next.

The frame transmission time (t_{tr}) of BUMA can be calculated by using Equation (9.2) as follows:

$$t_{tr} = 2{,}334 \times 8/11 \cong 1.69 \text{ ms} \qquad (9.6)$$

By substituting the values of t_{tr} and $t_{overhead}$ in Equation (9.1), the total time (T) for a successful packet transmission is given by

$$T = 1{,}697 + 500 \cong 2.19 \text{ ms} \qquad (9.7)$$

By using Equation (9.5), the proportional nonoptimized throughput (IP layer) of BUMA (BUMA$_{nonopt}$) is

$$BUMA_{nonopt} = (1.69/2.19) \times (2{,}300/2{,}334) \cong 0.76 \qquad (9.8)$$

Similarly, the proportional throughput of the DCF is given by

$$Throughput_{802.11bDCF} = (0.058/0.558) \times (46/80) \cong 0.0599 \qquad (9.9)$$

So, if a single user sends 56-byte IP datagrams over an 11-Mbps channel, the maximum achieved throughputs using BUMA and DCF are 8.36 and 0.66 Mbps, respectively. Clearly, BUMA achieves significantly higher throughput than DCF, even though the length of the buffer unit was not optimized. The optimum length of the buffer unit is considered next.

Example 9.2: Transmission of Long IP Datagrams (MPDU = 1,500 bytes) In this example an MSDU of length 4,500 bytes (excluding MAC header and CRC) is used, which is an optimum length of the buffer unit containing three 1,500-byte MPDUs. However, this large payload is fragmented into two frames before transmission into the medium since the total length is greater than the fragmentation threshold for wireless Ethernet networks.

As shown in Figure 9.5, BUMA transmits payloads three times greater than DCF, with a marginally longer MAC overhead. In the case of long IP datagrams, BUMA achieves slightly better throughput than DCF.

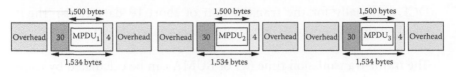

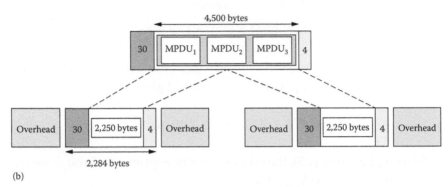

(a)

(b)

FIGURE 9.5 Protocol overheads for the transmission of large IP datagrams of 1,500 bytes in length for (a) 802.11b DCF and (b) BUMA$_{opt}$.

By using Equation (9.2), the frame transmission time (t_{tr}) of BUMA is given by

$$t_{tr} = 2 \times 2284 \times 8/11 \cong 3.32 \text{ ms} \tag{9.10}$$

The total time (T) for a successful transmission is

$$T = 3322 + 500 \cong 3.82 \text{ ms} \tag{9.11}$$

Therefore, by using Equation (9.5), the optimized IP throughput of BUMA (BUMA$_{opt}$) is

$$BUMA_{opt} = (3.32/3.82) \times (4,500/4,568) \cong 0.8562 \tag{9.12}$$

Similarly, the proportional throughput of DCF is

$$Throughput_{802.11bDCF} = (1.11/1.61) \times (1,500/1,534) \cong 0.6742 \tag{9.13}$$

If a single user transmits 1,500-byte IP datagrams over an 11-Mbps channel, the maximum achieved throughputs using BUMA and DCF are 9.4 and 7.4 Mbps, respectively.

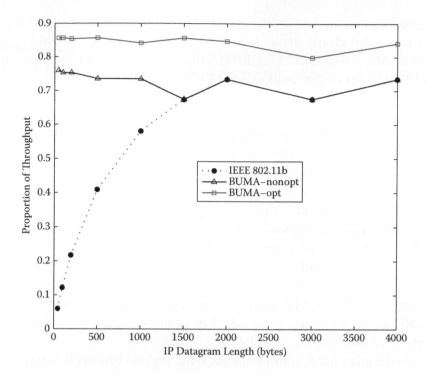

FIGURE 9.6 Throughput comparison of the 802.11b DCF, BUMA$_{nonopt}$, and BUMA$_{opt}$ protocols for a single-user network.

Figure 9.6 plots the proportional IP layer throughput versus IP datagram length for DCF, BUMA$_{nonopt}$, and BUMA$_{opt}$ for a single-user network showing that the effective throughput of DCF increases with IP datagram length (payload length) and is saturated at 2,000 bytes (close to the fragmentation threshold of 2,346 bytes). Increasing the payload length beyond 2,000 bytes does not increase the effective throughput because of the protocol's high payload fragmentation overhead.

In the case of BUMA$_{nonopt}$, the maximum allowable MSDU is set to the wireless Ethernet fragmentation threshold (so that frames can be transmitted without fragmentation). Figure 9.6 shows that BUMA$_{nonopt}$ achieves higher throughput than DCF for payload lengths ≤ 1,000 bytes; i.e., the throughput gain is more significant for short payloads (see Example 9.1). Sending a larger payload with the same set of overheads causes this improvement. However, for payloads > 1,000 bytes, BUMA$_{nonopt}$ does not improve DCF since the length of the wireless Ethernet fragmentation threshold limits the performance.

Now in the case of BUMA$_{opt}$, the optimum length of the buffer unit (4,534 bytes) becomes the maximum allowable MSDU. BUMA$_{opt}$ offers higher throughput than DCF irrespective of payload length. This is a notable result that clearly demonstrates the superiority of both $BUMA_{nonopt}$ and $BUMA_{opt}$ over DCF. Also, BUMA throughput is almost independent of IP datagram length, unlike that of DCF.

By comparing $BUMA_{nonopt}$ and $BUMA_{opt}$, one can observe that $BUMA_{opt}$ offers 10 to 18% greater throughput than $BUMA_{nonopt}$ for payload lengths smaller than 4,000 bytes. This throughput improvement is due to $BUMA_{opt}$ transmitting a slightly larger payload than $BUMA_{nonopt}$ with the same set of overheads.

Figure 9.7 compares the total packet transmission time, T, of DCF, $BUMA_{nonopt}$, and $BUMA_{opt}$ protocols for a single-user network; it shows that T increases as payload length increases. For instance, at payload length of 46 bytes, DCF requires 0.558 ms to transmit an MSDU of 80 bytes (46-byte payload and 34-byte envelope). This is because proportionally less time is required to transmit a short payload, as is illustrated in Example 9.1 (Figure 9.4a). BUMA is not as good as DCF when only a few small packets are transmitted; e.g., T is smaller for DCF when there are only three 46-byte packets, or two 500-byte packets.

On the other hand, considering the same payload length (46 bytes), the $BUMA_{nonopt}$ requires 2.13 ms to transmit an MSDU of 2,242 bytes (fifty 46-byte payloads and a 34-byte envelope). Thus, $BUMA_{nonopt}$ transmits a 50-times-larger payload than DCF in a slightly increased total packet

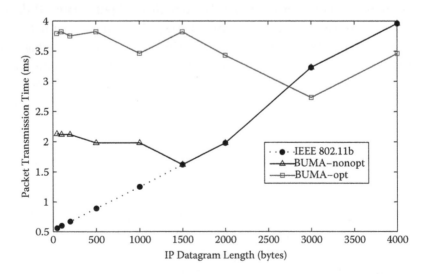

FIGURE 9.7   Packet transmission time versus IP datagram length. Comparison of the 802.11b DCF, $BUMA_{nonopt}$, and $BUMA_{opt}$ protocols.

transmission time (as illustrated in Example 9.1 [Figure 9.4b]), giving a 13-fold improvement in transmission speed. Consequently, BUMA$_{nonopt}$ achieves significantly better throughput than DCF, except in the case of very small numbers of small packets (Figure 9.6). Further, BUMA$_{opt}$ requires 3.79 ms to transmit an MSDU of 4,530 bytes (4,462-byte payload and 68-byte envelope). This payload is 97 times greater than the payload carried by DCF, giving a 14-fold improvement in transmission speed.

However, in case of larger payload length (say, ≥4,000 bytes), DCF requires 4 ms to transmit two fragmented payloads of 2,000 bytes each, and BUMA$_{nonopt}$ performs no better than DCF as a result of the fragmentation threshold. In any case, BUMA$_{opt}$ achieves slightly better performance in terms of lower packet transmission time (3.45 ms) than both DCF and BUMA$_{nonopt}$. BUMA$_{opt}$ scheme's channel access strategy of reducing overhead improves packet transmission time.

Figure 9.7 shows that the variabilities in packet transmission times (i.e., the difference between the highest and lowest transmission times) in DCF, BUMA$_{nonopt}$, and BUMA$_{opt}$ are 3.40, 2.34, and 1.09 ms, respectively. Therefore, total transmission time in BUMA$_{opt}$ is bounded since it achieves the lowest variability.

Discussion and Interpretation

The effective throughputs (obtained from analytical calculation) presented in this section are an upper bound that can be attained only for a single station passing packets to the MAC layer at the moment the previous transmission is completed. However, in real systems with multiple stations, the effective throughputs are much lower than these throughputs due to channel contention delays as well as time spent in the backoff process. From Figures 9.6 and 9.7, the conclusion can be drawn that transmission overhead has a significant effect on the throughput of DCF. Throughput degrades significantly for shorter frames due to high protocol overheads, except very small numbers of small packets. For that reason, DCF is not suitable for supporting streaming media of relatively small packets such as voice packets. BUMA$_{opt}$ achieves significantly better throughput than DCF since it transmits more payload with the same set of overheads. A performance evaluation of BUMA by simulation is presented next.

PERFORMANCE EVALUATION

In this section, the performance of BUMA is evaluated by quantitative stochastic simulation. BUMA's performance is compared with that of

DCF. The BUMA protocol was evaluated by measuring parameters such as mean packet delay, throughput, packet drop ratio, and fairness.

Simulation Environment and Parameters

There are several issues that need to be considered when selecting a network simulator for a simulation study, for example, use of reliable pseudorandom number generators, an appropriate method for analysis of simulation output data, and statistical accuracy of the simulation results (i.e., desired relative precision of errors and confidence levels). These aspects of credible simulation studies are addressed by leading simulation researchers [269–271]. The network simulation package called ns-2 [272] was used for the simulation study. The strengths and weaknesses of ns-2 are highlighted in Appendix A.

Table 9.2 lists the parameter values used in the simulation of the BUMA and DCF protocols. Each simulation run lasted for 10 min simulated time, where the first minute was the transient period. The observations collected during the transient period are not included in the final simulation results.

Modeling Assumptions

Simulation models were developed using ns-2 to study the performance of both the proposed BUMA protocol and DCF. The ad hoc (single-hop)

TABLE 9.2   Simulation Parameters

Parameter	Value
Data rate	11 Mbps
Basic rate	2 Mbps
Wireless cards	802.11b
Slot duration	20 μs
SIFS	10 μs
DIFS	50 μs
MAC header	30 bytes
CRC	4 bytes
PHY header	96 μs
Packet/traffic type	UDP
Application	Constant bit rate (CBR)
RTS-CTS	Off
PHY modulation	DSSS
Propagation model	Two-ray ground
CW_{min}	31
CW_{max}	1,023
Simulation time	10 min

and the infrastructure networks are based on 802.11b DCF with a maximum data rate of 11 Mbps. Wireless stations were simulated by setting up a grid of size 176×176 m in which the longest distance between any two stations is 250 m. This grid size is also the maximum transmission range of two simulated stations. In an infrastructure network, one central AP and several surrounding wireless stations are considered. The data traffic travels from stationary wireless stations to wired stations through an AP (i.e., uplink traffic). All stations communicate using identical half-duplex wireless radio based on DCF, with a data rate set at 11 Mbps. RTS and CTS are turned off. The Ad Hoc On-Demand Distance Vector (AODV) routing protocol and the two-ray ground propagation model are used. All sources and receivers have an omnidirectional antenna at height 1.5 m. Unless otherwise specified, all data sources are UDP traffic streams with a payload length of 1,500 bytes. Since BUMA is a modification of the DCF, the same modeling assumptions are used in simulating both protocols. To simplify the simulation model, it is assumed that each wireless station is equipped with a transceiver that has perfect power control. Further, it is assumed that capture effects, transmission errors due to interference and noise in the system, and hidden and exposed station problems do not exist. The following assumptions are made regarding the data traffic.

A1. **Packet generation:** Streams of data packets arriving at stations are modeled as independent Poisson processes with an aggregate mean packet generating rate λ packets/s.

A2. **Packet length:** Packets are of fixed length. The time axis is divided into slots of equal length, and the transmission of one packet takes one time slot.

A3. **Processing delay:** The station's latency or processing delay is negligible compared to the duration of a slot. The processing of control data contained in the header can be done in a fraction of a time slot.

A4. **Destination addresses:** The packets arriving at a station are uniformly destined to $N - 1$ other stations.

A5. **Network topology:** Both the ad hoc (single-hop) and infrastructure networks are considered in the study.

A6. **Stations spacing:** The stations can be arbitrarily spaced within the transmission range.

A7. **Analysis:** Network performance is studied under steady-state conditions.

Simulation Results and Comparison

For both individual stations and the overall network, four important network performance metrics are used: (1) throughput, (2) packet delay, (3) MDT fairness, and (4) packet drop ratio. These performance metrics were defined in Chapter 4. Recall also that the throughput (measured in Mbps) is a fraction of the total channel capacity that is used for data transmission. The mean packet delay at station $i(i = 1, 2, ..., N)$ is defined as the average time (measured in seconds) from the moment the packet is generated until the packet is fully dispatched from that station. A packet arriving at station i experiences several components of delay, including queuing delay, channel access delay (i.e., contention time), and packet transmission time. Network fairness can be achieved by providing all stations with the same grade of service, independently of the network parameters.

A new metric for packet drop ratio (P_{dr}) is defined as follows:

$$P_{dr} = \frac{N_{pd}}{N_{tp}} \tag{9.14}$$

where N_{tp} is the number of transmitted packets to the destination stations, N_{pd} is the total number of packets dropped (it is the difference between N_{tp} and successfully received packets), and P_{dr} is directly related to packet collision rates. High packet collision rates at the destination stations result in high packet drop ratios. A MAC protocol with a low packet drop ratio is desirable.

The results obtained from simulation runs for both BUMA and DCF are presented here. They demonstrate the performance of BUMA by considering both ad hoc and infrastructure networks operating under uniform loads. The traffic comprises 1,500-byte UDP packets arriving following the Poisson model. The simulation results report the steady-state behavior of the network and were obtained with a relative error ≤1%, at the 99% confidence level.

THROUGHPUT PERFORMANCE

The network throughputs versus offered load performances of BUMA and DCF with $N = 40$ stations for an ad hoc and an infrastructure network

(a)

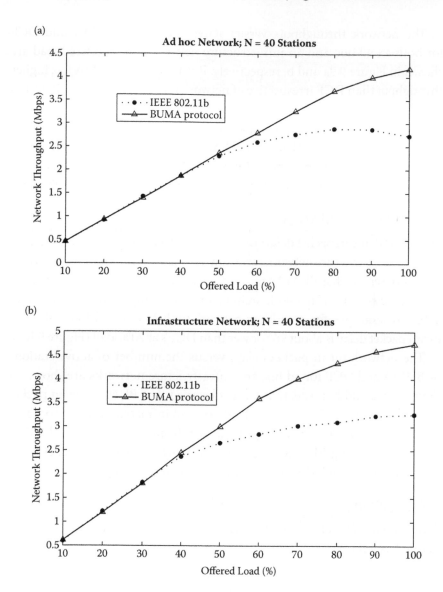

FIGURE 9.8 The effect of offered load on throughput of BUMA and 802.11b DCF: (a) ad hoc network and (b) infrastructure network.

are shown in Figure 9.8a and b, respectively. One can observe that BUMA provides higher throughput than DCF irrespective of network architecture, especially under medium to high traffic loads. For example, for an ad hoc network with $N = 40$ stations, BUMA throughput is about 45% higher than that of DCF at full loading (Figure 9.8a).

The network throughputs versus active stations of BUMA and DCF for both an ad hoc and an infrastructure network at 80% offered load are shown in Figure 9.9a and b, respectively. It is found that BUMA has higher throughput than DCF irrespective of network architecture for $N = 10$ to 100 stations. For example, for an ad hoc network with $N = 20$ stations, BUMA's throughput is about 45% higher than that of DCF at 80% load (Figure 9.9a).

The main conclusion that can be drawn from Figures 9.8 and 9.9 is that BUMA's throughput (for both individual stations and networkwide) is significantly better than that of DCF, especially under medium to high loads.

DELAY PERFORMANCE

The network mean packet delays of BUMA and DCF for $N = 40$ stations in ad hoc and infrastructure networks are shown in Figure 9.10a and b, respectively.

It is observed that BUMA's mean packet delay is better (i.e., lower) than DCF's irrespective of network architecture, especially at load greater than 40%. For example, for an ad hoc network with $N = 40$ stations, BUMA's mean packet delay is about 96% lower than DCF's at 70% load (Figure 9.10a).

The network mean packet delays versus the number of active stations of BUMA and DCF for ad hoc and infrastructure networks are shown in Figure 9.11a and b, respectively. It is observed that BUMA's mean packet delay is lower than DCF's for both ad hoc and infrastructure networks.

The main conclusion that can be drawn from Figures 9.10 and 9.11 is that stations using BUMA have a substantially lower mean packet delay than stations using DCF, especially under medium to high loads.

MDT FAIRNESS

A new metric for fairness called mean deviation of throughput (MDT) is defined as follows:

$$MDT = \frac{\sum |(T_i - \bar{T})|}{N} \tag{9.15}$$

where T_i is the throughput at station i, $\bar{T}$ is the networkwide mean throughput, and N is the number of active stations.

MDT is defined as the spread or variation of individual stations' throughput from the networkwide mean throughput. For instance, a MAC protocol is said to be 100% fair if MDT is zero (i.e., $T_i = \bar{T} \ \forall \ i$). The value of MDT indicates the level of unfairness of a MAC protocol. Hence,

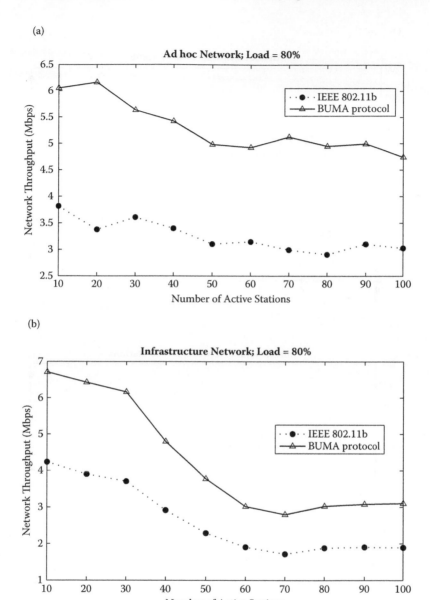

FIGURE 9.9   The effect of the number of active stations on network throughput of BUMA and 802.11b DCF: (a) ad hoc network and (b) infrastructure network.

a MAC protocol with a smaller MDT is desirable. MDT was used to compare the fairness of BUMA and DCF.

Figure 9.12 plots active links (between source and destination stations; e.g., 0→1 indicates station 0 transmits a packet to station 1) versus MDT

(a)

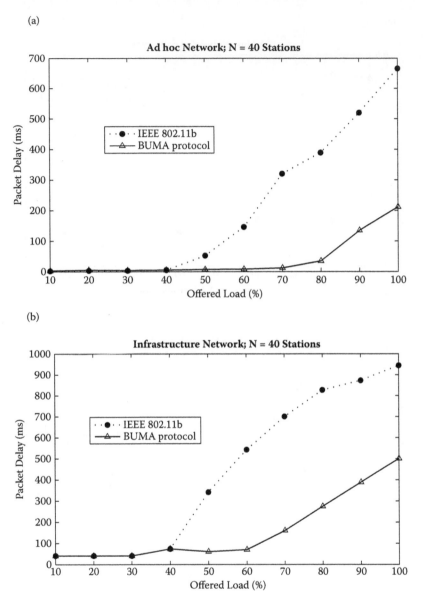

FIGURE 9.10 The effect of offered load on mean packet delay of BUMA and 802.11b DCF: (a) ad hoc network and (b) infrastructure network.

fairness for N = 20 stations for an ad hoc network (Figure 9.12a) and an infrastructure network (Figure 9.12b). It is observed that even though the proposed BUMA scheme is not 100% fair in allocating bandwidth among active stations (for example, in an ideal case the throughput of each link

(a)

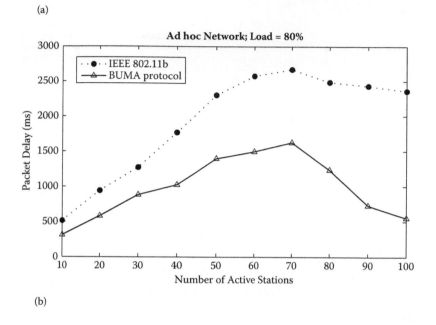

(b)

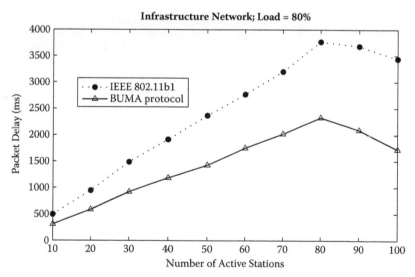

FIGURE 9.11 The effect of the number of active stations on mean packet delay of BUMA and 802.11b DCF: (a) ad hoc network and (b) infrastructure network.

should be about 5% of the total network throughput), it provides up to 50% higher MDT fairness than DCF (Figure 9.12a). The main conclusion is that at 80% load, MDT fairness (in both individual stations and network-wide) of BUMA is significantly better than that of DCF.

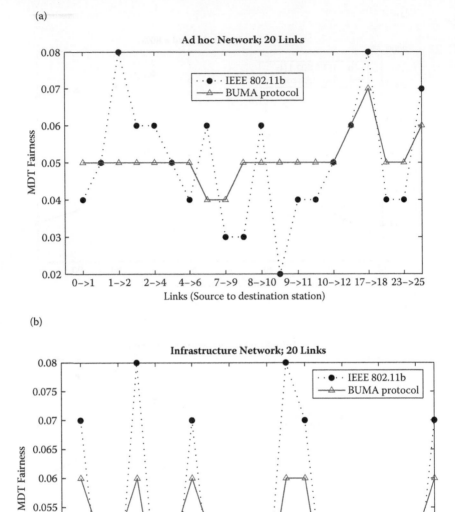

FIGURE 9.12   MDT fairness versus active links of BUMA and 802.11b DCF: (a) ad hoc network and (b) infrastructure network.

(a)

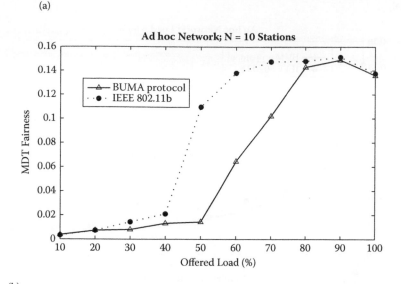

(b)

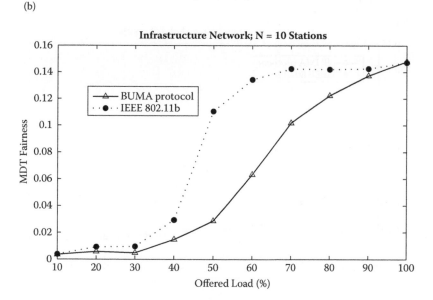

FIGURE 9.13 The effect of offered load on MDT fairness of BUMA and 802.11b DCF: (a) ad hoc network and (b) infrastructure network.

The effect of offered load on the fairness of BUMA and DCF for $N = 10$ stations for ad hoc and infrastructure networks is shown in Figure 9.13a and b, respectively. The MDT fairness of BUMA is better than that of DCF irrespective of network architecture, especially under medium to high traffic loads (50 to 80%). For example, for an infrastructure network at

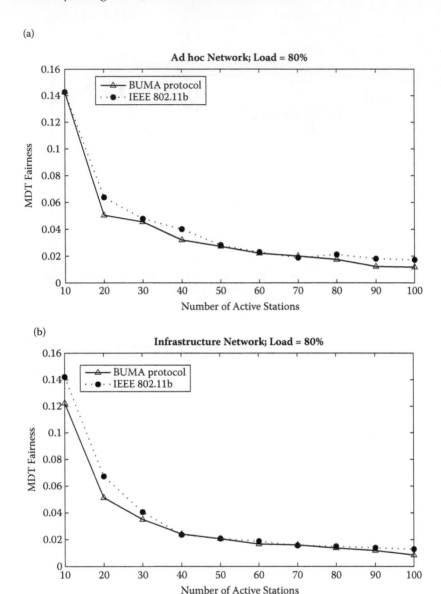

FIGURE 9.14 The effect of the number of active stations on MDT fairness of BUMA and 802.11b DCF: (a) ad hoc network and (b) infrastructure network.

50% load with $N = 10$ stations, BUMA has an MDT about 8.2% lower than that of DCF (Figure 9.13b). For offered load greater than 80%, the fairness improvement is not very significant.

The effect of active stations on the MDT fairness of BUMA and DCF in ad hoc and infrastructure networks is shown in Figure 9.14a and b, respectively. It is observed that BUMA has slightly better MDT fairness than DCF, especially for $N > 80$ stations at 80% load. However, this fairness improvement is not very significant.

The main conclusion from Figures 9.13 and 9.14 is that stations using BUMA achieve a slightly better MDT fairness than stations using DCF, especially under medium to high loads.

PACKET DROP RATIO

The packet drop ratios of BUMA and DCF for $N = 10$ to 100 stations at 80% offered load in ad hoc and infrastructure networks are shown in Figure 9.15a and b, respectively. It is observed that fewer packets are dropped in BUMA than in DCF. For example, BUMA offers about a 28.5% lower packet drop ratio than DCF for $N = 20$ stations at 80% offered load (Figure 9.15a). This improvement in packet dropping is due to BUMA's channel access strategy where relatively fewer contentions are faced by active stations (i.e., fewer packet collisions), and consequently achieves higher throughput than DCF.

SIMULATION MODEL VERIFICATION

A credible network simulator may produce invalid results if the simulation parameters are not correctly configured. Therefore, simulation model verification becomes an important part of any simulation study. The ns-2 simulation model presented in this chapter was verified in several ways. First, the detailed status information was traced throughout the simulation to verify the model. Second, the simulation model was validated through radio propagation measurements from wireless laptops and APs for 802.11b [94, 273]. A good match between simulation and real measurement results for $N = 2$ to 4 stations validates the simulation model. Third, the simulation results reported in this chapter were compared with the work of other network researchers to ensure correctness of the simulation model [24, 274]. In addition, ns-2 results were compared with the results obtained from OPNET Modeler [34], and a good match between two sets of results further validated the simulation models.

IMPLEMENTATION

The BUMA protocol described in this chapter is simple, easy to implement, and provides a low-cost solution for improving the performance of 802.11. In the BUMA scheme, the temporary link layer buffer units at each station can easily be implemented using preexisting RAM available in

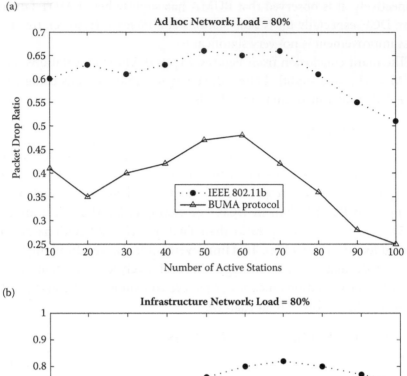

FIGURE 9.15   The effect of the number of active stations on the packet drop ratio of BUMA and 802.11b DCF: (a) ad hoc network and (b) infrastructure network.

wireless devices, including laptops and APs. These buffer units can easily be created (for storing packets) and destroyed (after successful transmissions) at runtime. Therefore, no additional hardware is required to implement the BUMA protocol.

With faster CPUs and RAM, the packetization delay at the stations will be minimal compared to the packet transmission time. The frame format of BUMA is designed in such a way that processing time for combining and decomposing frames is insignificant. The mechanisms for empty slot detection, slot synchronization, packet transmission, and packet reception can be implemented by firmware, as is used in 802.11 [37]. When the destination station receives the BUMA frame, it decomposes the combined frame into normal frames, and acknowledges the last frame only. The destination station can easily identify boundaries of the combined frames using preambles and CRC.

In heavy traffic, BUMA performs better since the buffer unit can be filled up quickly with data from the upper protocol layers (e.g., IP datagram can be encapsulated up to the maximum length of the buffer unit), and hence carries larger payload with respect to protocol overheads. In light traffic BUMA performs as well as DCF by adapting buffer unit length to just one frame.

FURTHER READING

For more details about subjects discussed in this chapter, we recommend the following books and references. The items in [] refer to the reference list at the end of the book.

Books

[171] Chapter 6—*Computer Networking: A Top-Down Approach* by Kurose and Ross

[275] *Wireless Networks* by Nicopolitidis, Obaidat, Papadimitriou, and Pomportsis

Book Chapters

[253–255]

Research Papers

[276–279]

SUMMARY

This chapter has extended the original 802.11 capabilities by including a temporary buffer unit at the MAC layer (for accumulating multiple packets for transmission) that not only eliminates bandwidth wastage in the backoff process but also significantly improves the mean packet delay, throughput, packet drop ratio, and MDT fairness.

In BUMA, the combined packet is formatted in such a way that processing time of combining and decomposing frames becomes insignificant. The optimum length of the buffer unit is found to be 4,534 bytes, which is equivalent to the combined three standard wireless Ethernet packets of 1,500 bytes each plus header and trailer. An analysis of the impact of protocol overheads on single-user throughput was presented for BUMA. BUMA has significantly better mean packet delay and throughput than DCF.

Performance comparisons of BUMA and DCF were carried out by extensive simulation experiments. Simulation results showed that BUMA's throughput is up to 45% higher, the mean packet delay is up to 96% lower, the packet drop ratio is up to 28.5% lower, and MDT fairness is up to 50% higher than DCF's in both ad hoc and infrastructure networks under medium to high traffic loads.

BUMA can be used to improve the performance of all variants of 802.11, including 802.11a/b/g, and would be a good candidate for providing time-bounded services such as wireless multimedia networks. Moreover, BUMA is simple and does not change the operation of the PHY layer. Therefore, the protocol can easily be implemented in 802.11 without changing any existing hardware.

The implementation aspect of BUMA has been discussed. RAM in wireless devices can be used to implement link layer buffer units at the stations without incurring any additional hardware costs. Fast modern processors and RAM render the station's packetization delay insignificant. Next, in Chapter 10, the effect of AP configuration and placement on WLAN performance is investigated.

KEY TERMS

Acknowledgment (ACK)
Ad Hoc On-Demand Distance Vector (AODV)
Backoff window size
Buffer unit
Buffer unit multiple access (BUMA) protocol
Carrier sense multiple access (CSMA)
Clear to send (CTS)
Concatenation
Cyclic redundancy check (CRC)
Datagram

Hidden station
IEEE 802.11
MAC protocol data unit (MPDU)
MAC segment data unit (MSDU)
Mean deviation of throughput (MDT)
Medium access control (MAC) protocol
Network topology
Packet delay
Packet drop ratio
Packet generation
Piggybacking
Payload

DCF interframe space (DIFS)
Distributed coordination function (DCF)
Ethernet LANs
Exposed station
Fairness network traffic
Frame

Poisson processes
Request to send (RTS)
Short interframe space (SIFS)
Transmission overhead
Throughput
Wireless local area network (WLAN)

REVIEW QUESTIONS

1. The traditional 802.11 networks have various limitations. List and discuss three main limitations of 802.11 networks.

2. Describe the principle of operation of the BUMA protocol.

3. Compare and contrast the frame structure of the 802.11 and BUMA protocols.

4. Discuss the potential limitations of the BUMA protocol.

5. Compare and contrast transmission overheads of the 802.11 and BUMA protocols.

6. Explain how the performance of an 802.11 can be improved by modifying a MAC protocol.

MINI-PROJECTS

The following mini-projects aim to provide a deeper understanding of the topics covered in this chapter through literature review and empirical study.

1. Conduct an in-depth literature review on wireless MAC protocols to extend the work presented in the "Previous Work on the Enhancement of 802.11" section.

2. **Optimization of buffer unit length:** Extend the work presented in the "Optimization of Buffer Unit Length" section by conducting the following simulation experiments. In all experiments consider an infrastructure network, Poisson packet arrivals, UDP traffic, and uniform loading.

Experiment	Number of Stations	Packet Length (bytes)
1	10	500, 1,000, 1,500, 2,000, 2,500, 3,000
2	20	500, 1,000, 1,500, 2,000, 2,500, 3,000
3	50	500, 1,000, 1,500, 2,000, 2,500, 3,000
4	100	500, 1,000, 1,500, 2,000, 2,500, 3,000
5	200	500, 1,000, 1,500, 2,000, 2,500, 3,000

3. **Protocol overhead and throughput analysis:** Extend the work presented in the "Protocol Overhead and Throughput Analysis" section by considering multiple users.

4. **Verification of ns-2 results:** Verify the ns-2 simulation results presented in the "Simulation Results and Comparison" section using another simulator (e.g., OPNET Modeler).

5. **Implementation of BUMA:** Implement the BUMA protocol presented in the "Description of the Proposed BUMA Protocol" section using Linux/Free BSD and test its performance. Compare the test results with simulation results presented in the "Simulation Results and Comparison" section.

6. **TCP traffic:** The results presented in the "Simulation Results and Comparison" section are based on UDP traffic. Extend the work presented in that section by considering Transmission Control Protocol (TCP) traffic.

7. **Analytical model:** Develop an analytical model for the BUMA protocol. Compare analytical results with ns-2 simulation results.

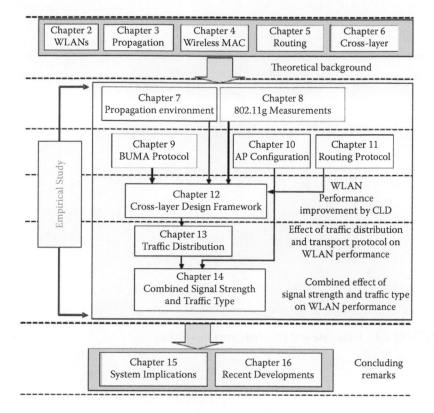

FIGURE 1.2   The structure of this book.

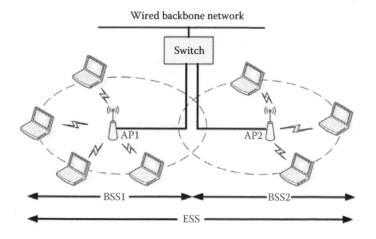

FIGURE 2.2   An infrastructure network with two BSSs.

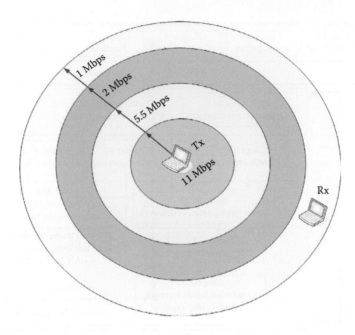

FIGURE 2.4   Data rate and coverage area in 802.11b.

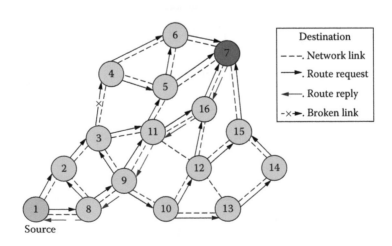

FIGURE 5.4   AODV routing mechanism.

FIGURE 7.1   External view of Environment A.

FIGURE 7.3   Internal view of Environment A office space. Offices are on both sides of the corridor.

FIGURE 7.5 Internal view of Environment A basement parking lot.

FIGURE 7.6 External view of Environment B (AUT tower).

FIGURE 7.8   The open plan computer laboratory in Environment B.

FIGURE 7.9   External view of Environment C (suburban residential house).

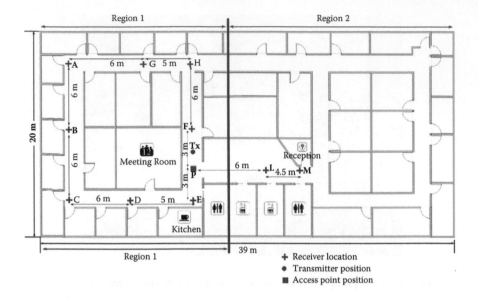

FIGURE 8.1 Layout of floor 1 of WY building and measurement locations.

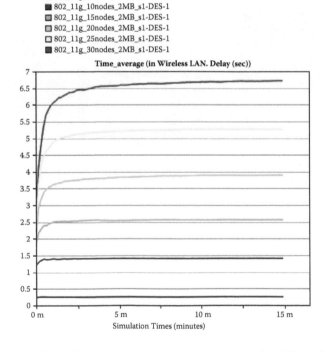

FIGURE 10.8 Effect of increasing wireless stations on packet delay of an 802.11g infrastructure network.

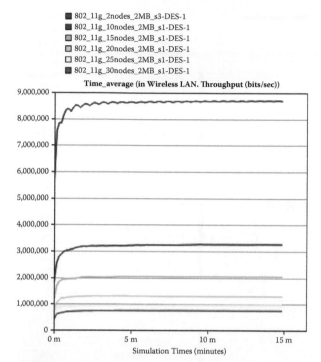

FIGURE 10.9 Effect of increasing wireless stations on throughput of an 802.11g infrastructure network.

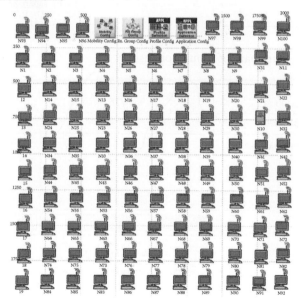

FIGURE 11.2 OPNET-based network simulation model (*N* = 100 nodes).

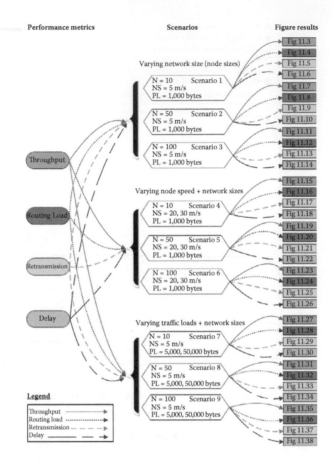

FIGURE 11.43   Summary of simulation results.

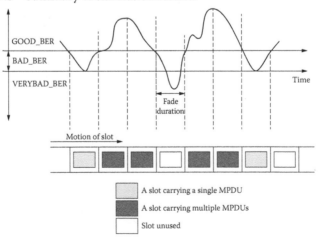

FIGURE 12.9   Illustrating the basic operation of the CLD algorithms.

Effect of AP Configuration and Placement on WLAN Performance

LEARNING OUTCOMES

After reading and completing this chapter, you will be able to:

- Describe the commonly used methods of access point configuration for WLANs

- Configure access points (APs) for setting up an infrastructure WLAN

- Position APs to optimize WLAN performance

- Conduct propagation measurements to study the effect of AP configuration and placement on WLAN performance

INTRODUCTION

In Chapter 9, the techniques for improving the performance of WLAN by redesigning wireless medium access control (MAC) protocols were outlined. This book aims to identify and measure the main factors influencing WLAN performance. To achieve this objective, a study on the effect of AP configuration and placement on the performance of an 802.11 network is required to assist an efficient planning and deployment of such systems. This chapter considers an 802.11g infrastructure network to study the effect of AP configuration and placement on system performance. To gain a better understanding of 802.11g AP configuration and to obtain unbiased results in an indoor environment, this chapter reports on the radio propagation measurements (using real hardware/software) in a controlled room at the Auckland University of Technology (AUT) within the School of Computing and Mathematical Sciences office building. The impact of AP placement on 802.11g throughput is investigated. An optimum network performance can be achieved by carefully configuring and placing APs. A detailed discussion of wireless networks, and of radio propagation in general, can be found in numerous wireless networking literature [27, 73, 171]. The network throughput with 2.4 GHz products, as well as monitoring of actual exchange of frames, has been investigated in [280]. Pelletta and Velayos [281] presented a method of measuring the maximum saturation throughput of 802.11 WLANs. They also analyzed the performance of five 802.11b APs. The AP selection strategy for the (re)association procedure in large-scale WLANs is investigated in [282]. Many previous studies in indoor WLAN deployments have adopted the engineering approach of carefully characterizing the radio propagation channel by modeling the physical environment and measuring the properties of the received signal [22, 93, 242]. In this chapter we obtain some insights into 802.11g link throughput under various AP configurations and placements in a typical indoor environment (at AUT) without using any complex mathematical modeling or radio channel characterization. Using a pair of wireless laptops and APs, we study the effect of AP configuration as well as placement on the file transmission time and the link throughput of 802.11g.

AP CONFIGURATION METHODS

The following four AP configuration scenarios are considered in this study: (1) AP mode, (2) wireless distribution system (WDS) mode, (3) WDS with AP mode, and (4) AP mode with Ethernet connection.

Most of the commercially available APs have an Ethernet port for linking them to another AP or an Ethernet switch [233]. In the experimentation, the 802.11g wireless APs (D-Link DWL-2100AP) were considered. The AP configuration is generally straightforward. The AP can be configured using the vendor-supplied software that comes with the device.

Figure 10.1 shows the main D-Link AP configuration interface. By using this interface, one can easily set up service set identifier (SSID), channel, user authentication, encryption, SSID broadcast, and quality of service (QoS). In the experimentation (described in the "Measurement

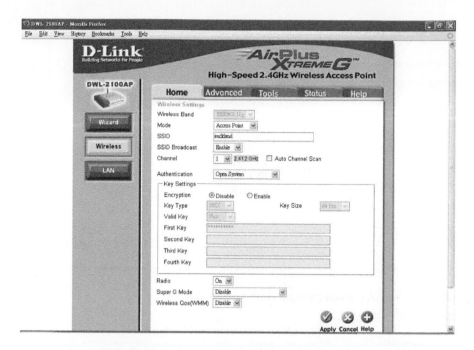

FIGURE 10.1   Screenshoot of AP configuration interface.

Procedure and Resources Used" section), both encryption and wireless QoS were disabled. The AP mode was configured using default settings for 802.11g AP. For WDS and WDS with AP modes, the remote AP MAC address was used in the remote AP selection menu. The four AP configurations are briefly described below.

- **AP mode:** The throughput measurement scenario for AP mode configuration is shown in Figure 10.2. This configuration is a popular one for use in office and home environments. In this configuration, the AP acts as a coordinator in which wireless stations (clients) are linked to the AP for communications. The AP receives data from a wireless client and forwards it to another client.

- **WDS mode:** The network scenario for WDS mode configuration is shown in Figure 10.3. In this configuration, an AP acts as a wireless bridge only, and hence the wireless clients cannot associate with the AP. In the experimentation, two Ethernet Cat 5e cables were used for linking two wireless clients to the AP. This configuration can be used for connecting two or more wireless networks located on multiple buildings, which is a common scenario for a campus network.

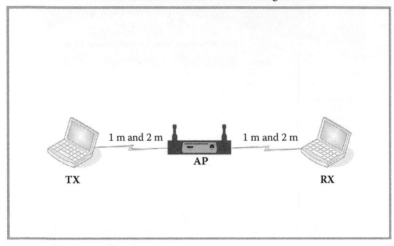

FIGURE 10.2   AP mode configuration scenario.

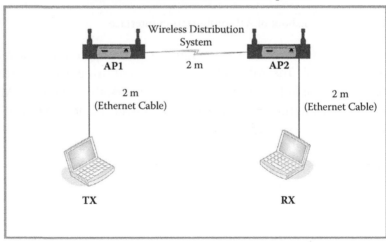

FIGURE 10.3   WDS mode configuration.

- **WDS with AP mode:** The AP configuration using the WDS with AP mode is shown in Figure 10.4. In this configuration the AP acts as both the coordinator and wireless bridge. Therefore, this configuration has the combined advantages of the AP mode and WDS mode. The radio signal coverage extension is also an advantage of using WDS with AP mode configuration.

WDS with AP Mode Measurement in the Meeting Room

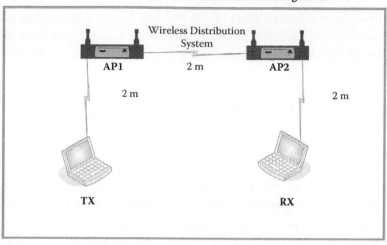

FIGURE 10.4   WDS with AP mode configuration.

AP Mode with Fast Ethernet Connection in the Meeting Room

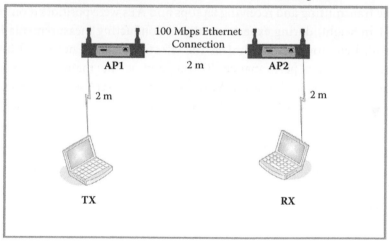

FIGURE 10.5   AP mode with Ethernet connection.

- **AP mode with Ethernet connection:** The network scenario for the AP mode with Ethernet connection is shown in Figure 10.5. In this configuration, the APs are configured as the AP mode and a Cat 5e unshielded twisted pair (UTP) cable is used for linking two APs.

MEASUREMENT PROCEDURE AND RESOURCES USED

The throughput measurements of the 802.11g AP were conducted in the staff meeting room (control environment) located on the first floor of the Duthie Whyte (WY) building at AUT (Figure 10.6). The staff meeting room is made of plasterboard with a glass door, and its dimensions are 4 × 3 m. Two wireless laptops with identical configurations (Intel Celeron 2.4 GHz, 512 MB RAM, MS Windows XP Professional) were used in the experiment. The IEEE 802.11g wireless adapters were D-Link DWL-G132 (54 Mbps) USB cards (omnidirectional) with a power output of 15 dBm [233]. The wireless APs were D-Link DWL-2100AP [233].

One of the laptops was set as the transmitting antenna (TX) and the other as the receiving antenna (RX). The transmitting and receiving laptops and APs were positioned on trolleys (1 m height) during the experimentation. The distances between TX and AP, AP and RX, and two APs were each set to 2 m, to obtain strong received signal strengths (RSSs). Conducting experiments under strong RSSs avoided retransmission and packet losses due to bit error rate (BER).

The transmitting and receiving laptops and APs were positioned on trolleys (1 m height) during experimentation. Conducting measurements in a controlled environment minimizes the effect of external noise and interference on system performance. Throughput is the main performance metric considered in this study. Various data files were sent from the TX to the RX (through APs) using the "Send File" feature of the Colligo TM

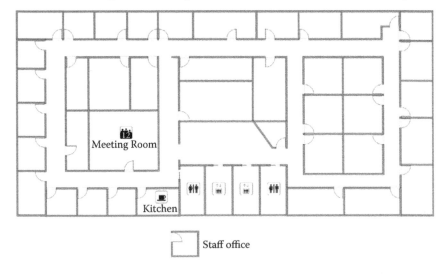

FIGURE 10.6   Location of staff meeting room in the WY office building.

Workgroup, edition 3.2 (www.colligo.com), which allows us to obtain the file transmission time. For each observation, a stopwatch was used to record the transmission time. The throughput (measured in Mbps) was computed by dividing the file size (Mbits) with the total transmission time (s).

RESULTS AND DISCUSSION FOR AP CONFIGURATION

The experimental results for the AP mode configuration are summarized in Table 10.1. The four different data files are transmitted serially from the TX to the RX as indicated in column 1. The file transmission times and the corresponding link throughputs for the TX-AP separations of 1 and 2 m are shown in columns 2, 3, 4, and 5, respectively.

As shown in Table 10.1, the effect of file size on the 802.11g link throughput is not very significant. We observe that the mean throughput for the TX-AP separation of 1 m is about 21% lower than the throughput obtained for the TX-AP separation of 2 m. This decrease in throughput is due to the fact that when two wireless stations (TX and AP) are closely located (up to 1 m), weak RSS results, and consequently low throughput is achieved. The measurement results for the WDS mode, WDS with AP, and AP mode with Ethernet connection are summarized in Tables 10.2, 10.3, and 10.4, respectively.

TABLE 10.1   Measurement Results for AP Mode

File Size (MB)	TX-AP Separation: 1 m		TX-AP Separation: 2 m	
	Time (s)	Throughput (Mbps)	Time (s)	Throughput (Mbps)
109	107.7	8.15	83.9	10.46
256	248.7	8.25	200.5	10.24
263	258.9	8.15	202.4	10.42
274	271.6	8.08	212.9	10.31
Mean throughput (Mbps)		8.16		10.36

TABLE 10.2   Measurement Results for WDS Mode

File Size (MB)	TX-AP Separation: 2 m	
	Time (s)	Throughput (Mbps)
109	46.7	18.79
256	104.7	19.60
263	108.4	19.46
274	113.9	19.26
Mean throughput (Mbps)		19.28

TABLE 10.3   Measurement Results for WDS with AP Mode

	TX-AP Separation: 2 m	
File Size (MB)	Time (s)	Throughput (Mbps)
109	151.5	5.79
256	355.2	5.78
263	369.1	5.72
274	382.7	5.73
Mean throughput (Mbps)		5.75

TABLE 10.4   Measurement Results for AP Mode with Ethernet Connection

	TX-AP Separation: 2 m	
File Size (MB)	Time (s)	Throughput (Mbps)
109	78.7	11.15
256	174.6	11.75
263	168.7	12.51
274	182.3	12.04
Mean throughput (Mbps)		11.86

For ease of comparison and interpretation, the experimental results for four AP configurations, as shown in Tables 10.1 to 10.4, are compared in Table 10.5. The effect of data file size on the 802.11g throughput performance is not very significant under all four AP configurations. We observe that among the four AP configurations, the highest (19.28 Mbps) and the lowest (5.75 Mbps) mean throughputs are obtained under the WDS mode and WDS with AP mode, respectively.

By comparing the AP mode with Ethernet connection and WDS with the AP mode configurations, one can observe that the mean throughput performance obtained under AP with Ethernet connection is more than double the mean throughput obtained under WDS with AP mode. This

TABLE 10.5   Comparison of Throughputs Obtained under Four AP Configurations

	Throughput (Mbps) of Four AP Configurations			
File Size (MB)	AP Mode	WDS with AP	AP with Ethernet	WDS Mode
109	10.46	5.79	11.15	18.79
256	10.24	5.78	11.75	19.60
263	10.43	5.72	12.51	19.46
274	10.31	5.73	12.04	19.26
Throughput (Mbps)	10.36	5.75	11.86	19.28

increase in throughput is a result of an Ethernet (100 Mbps) link between two APs that handles more traffic than the 802.11g wireless link.

By comparing the AP mode and WDS with AP mode configurations, we observe that the mean throughput obtained under the AP mode (10.357 Mbps) is significantly higher than the mean throughput obtained under the WDS with AP mode (5.755 Mbps). This increase in throughput is due to the single-hop communication between the TX and the RX.

MEASUREMENT ACCURACY AND VALIDATION

The following issues are considered to improve the accuracy of the propagation measurement results:

- **People movement:** The measurements were conducted after hours and on weekends to avoid the impact of the movement of people on system performance.

- **Co-channel interference:** To reduce the impact of co-channel interference on system performance, all external radio sources were detected and the experimental APs were adjusted accordingly prior to measured data collection.

- **Validation:** The propagation measurements were repeated several times to ensure the correctness of the measured data. The measured throughputs presented in the "Results and Discussion for AP Configuration" section closely agree with the results obtained from the data sheet for D-Link cards and access points [245]. In addition, the measurement results obtained from this study were compared with the work of other researchers [24, 91, 94, 241].

IMPLICATIONS FOR AP CONFIGURATION

Through propagation measurements in a controlled indoor environment, we obtained some insights into the impact of the AP configuration on system performance. First, this study provides useful information that will assist managers in making an informed decision about the deployment of APs in similar office locations. Second, this case study demonstrates, by experiment, the direct effect of AP configurations on system performance. The use of real hardware to measure performance avoided the complex theoretical modeling of signal propagation and system implementation. The throughput performance of an 802.11g can be optimized by carefully configuring APs during WLAN deployments.

The AP mode configuration is widely used in deploying WLANs in home and office network environments. The AP mode not only offers a platform for sharing network resources among wireless stations, but also provides a way to access wired backbone networks for all connected wireless stations. Therefore, AP capacity (i.e., throughput) will affect the number of wireless stations that can be supported by an AP. In particular, when the number of wireless stations exceeds the capacity of an AP, the deployment of multiple APs is necessary. However, the deployment of multiple APs in the same area would degrade system performance as a result of co-channel interference.

Measurement results showed that the throughput obtained under the WDS with AP mode configuration was much lower than the throughput of a wired distribution system. Although the WDS with AP configuration is a flexible solution for the deployment of WLANs, it is important to assess the traffic between two networks before implementing this configuration. On the other hand, AP with Ethernet connection would be a better solution for applications requiring high traffic handling between multiple WLAN segments. However, for linking two wired LANs through a wireless connection, the WDS configuration has the advantage of providing a wireless point-to-point link in an outdoor environment.

EXPERIMENT DETAILS FOR AP PLACEMENT

Two wireless laptops with identical configurations (Intel Celeron 2.4 GHz, 512 MB RAM, MS Windows XP Professional) were used in the experiment. The 802.11g wireless adapters were D-Link DWL-G132 (54 Mbps) cards (omnidirectional) with a power output of 15 dBm [245]. The wireless AP was D-Link DWL-2100AP [233].

A propagation measurement campaign was conducted in the School of Computing and Mathematical Sciences Building at AUT. The measurement environment was a typical multistory, reinforced concrete building with a floor area of 35 × 16 m. Measurements were performed on the first floor of the WY building, which contains concrete walls and many fixed-partitioned rooms, as shown in Figure 10.7.

One of the laptops was set as the transmitting antenna (TX) and the other as the receiving antenna (RX). Both the transmitting and receiving laptops were positioned on trolleys (55 cm in height) during the experimentation. The AP was placed at one end of the long corridor (position A). The TX was placed 2 m away from the AP (Figure 10.7). Nineteen main measurement locations (A to S) were chosen to cover the entire floor of the office block. In

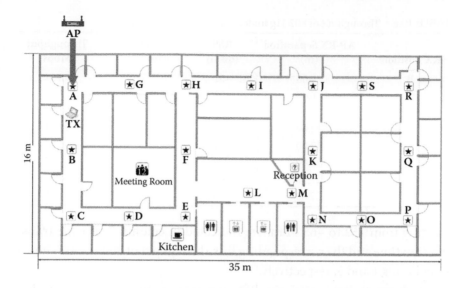

FIGURE 10.7   Layout of floor 1 of WY building and measurement locations (AP at position A).

addition, we consider measurement locations at weak RSSs, for example, the measurement location (H-3.5m)F-H, which is 3.5 m away from H (between F and H). Measurement results of these locations are included in Table 10.7.

The RX was moved to all the locations for measured data collections. A data file of 10.9 MB was sent from the TX to the RX (through AP) using the "Send Files" feature of the Colligo TM Workgroup, edition 3.2 (www.colligo.com), which allows us to obtain the file transmission time. For each observation, the transmission time and RSS were recorded. Link throughput is the main performance metric considered in this study. The throughput (measured in Mbps) is computed by dividing the file size (Mbits) by the total transmission time (s). The accuracy and validation of the measurement results are discussed next.

RESULTS AND DISCUSSION FOR AP PLACEMENT

In this section, we present propagation measurement results for (1) semi-line-of-sight (LOS) and (2) non-LOS conditions.

Semi-LOS Conditions

The experimental results for semi-LOS measured locations are summarized in Table 10.6. The RX positions and the corresponding distance from the AP are shown in columns 1 and 2, respectively. The RSS values,

TABLE 10.6 Throughput of 802.11g under Semi-LOS Conditions

RX Position	AP-RX Separation (m)	RSS (dBm)	Transmission Time (s)	Throughput (Mbps)
B	6.00	–52	9.0	9.752
G	6.00	–53	8.7	10.088
H	11.00	–59	8.7	10.088
C	12.00	–60	8.9	9.861
I	17.00	–61	8.5	10.325
J	23.00	–62	9.4	9.337
S	27.50	–63	12.1	7.253
R	32.00	–65	16.5	5.319

ranging from –52 to –65 dBm, are indicated in column 3. The file transmission time and the corresponding link throughput of 802.11g are shown in columns 4 and 5, respectively.

As shown in Table 10.6, the RSS decreases as the AP-RX separation increases. One can observe that, for RX positions J, S, and R, the link throughput decreases as RSS decreases from –62 to –65 dBm. However, this observation is not valid for RX positions B, G, H, C, and I. The maximum throughput (10.325 Mbps) is achieved at position I at RSS of –61 dBm.

By looking at the throughputs of B, G, H, and C, one can observe that the throughputs at these positions are slightly lower than the throughput obtained at I (maximum throughput), even though RSSs (–52 to –60 dBm) were stronger. The decrease in link throughputs at these locations is mainly due to the wave-guiding effect in corridors. Our findings are also in agreement with the work of other researchers surveyed in [233, 241].

Non-LOS Conditions

The experimental results for the performance evaluation of the 802.11g under non-LOS conditions are summarized in Table 10.7. Thirty-four RX positions and the corresponding AP-RX separations are shown in columns 1 and 2, respectively. The RSS values, file transmission times, and corresponding link throughputs are shown in columns 3, 4, and 5, respectively.

By looking at the AP-RX separation and RSS, one can observe that RSS either increases or decreases with increasing AP-RX separation (unlike semi-LOS conditions). For instance, the RSS at D is –71 dBm for the AP-RX separation of 13.42 m, whereas the RSS at E is –70 dBm for the 16.28 m AP-RX separation. Another observation is that the link throughput of

TABLE 10.7   Throughput of 802.11g under Non-LOS Conditions

RX Position	AP-RX Separation (m)	RSS (dBm)	Transmission Time (s)	Throughput (Mbps)
(H-1.5m)F-H	11.10	−61	9.7	9.048
(H-2.5m)F-H	11.28	−62	9.2	9.540
(H-3.5m)F-H	11.54	−68	10.8	8.126
(C-2m)C-D	12.17	−67	9.3	9.437
(C-3m)C-D	12.37	−66	9.1	9.645
F	12.53	−72	12.6	6.965
(C-4m)C-D	12.65	−67	9.6	9.142
D	13.42	−71	10	8.777
E	16.28	−70	11.8	7.438
L	19.24	−77	32	2.743
(J-1.5m)J-K	23.05	−72	24.2	3.627
(J-2.5m)J-K	23.14	−68	20.2	4.345
(J-3.5m)J-K	23.26	−76	26.4	3.324
M	23.31	−76	28	3.134
K	23.77	−79	29.3	2.995
(N-3.5m)K-N	24.52	−79	30.2	2.906
(N-2.5m)K-N	24.88	−79	34.6	2.537
(N-1.5m)K-N	25.28	−82	42.3	2.075
N	25.94	−81	50.4	1.741
(N-2m)N-O	27.73	−87	115.2	0.762
(N-3m)N-O	28.64	−87	133.2	0.659
O	30.00	−90	223.2	0.393
(P-3.5m)O-P	30.92	−90	208.2	0.422
(P-2.5m)O-P	31.85	−88	210.2	0.418
(R-1.5m)Q-R	32.04	−70	28.5	3.079
(R-2.5m)Q-R	32.10	−82	81.3	1.080
(R-3.5m)Q-R	32.19	−75	67.1	1.308
(R-4.5m)Q-R	32.31	−82	127	0.691
Q	32.56	−87	144.4	0.608
(P-1.5m)O-P	32.78	−86	193.6	0.453
(P-3.5m)P-Q	33.11	−88	185.6	0.473
(P-2.5m)P-Q	33.38	−87	156.7	0.560
(P-1.5m)P-Q	33.68	−84	102.3	0.858
P	34.18	−84	140.1	0.626

IEEE 802.11g is not always increasing with RSS. For example, the throughput (2.995 Mbps) at K is slightly higher than the throughput (1.308 Mbps) at (R-3.5m)Q-R, even though the RSS at K is weaker (−79 dBm) than the RSS (−75 dBm) at (R-3.5m)Q-R.

By comparing Tables 10.6 and 10.7, one can observe that the link throughput of 802.11g under non-LOS conditions is slightly lower than the throughput obtained under semi-LOS. This decrease in throughput is due to the LOS blockage by office walls and corners of an obstructed office block. We found that the overall throughputs are slightly higher on the left-hand side, as well as the center of the office block, than the throughputs obtained on the right-hand side (Figure 10.7).

While propagation measurements can be used for formulating an opinion about the deployment of WLANs in an indoor environment, this has limitations when it comes to the generalization of the research findings. For the prediction of system performance, a computer simulation approach was adopted in this chapter. The throughput performance study by simulation is presented next.

SIMULATION STUDY

Computer simulation is used to predict the performance of 802.11g AP in an obstructed office block. A simulation model of an 802.11g infrastructure network is developed using OPNET Modeler 14.0 [34]. OPNET Modeler was chosen not only for its easy-to-use graphic user interface (GUI), but also because it has a comprehensive library of commercially available network components that allows network researchers to develop and validate network models more efficiently.

In the simulation model an office network of 35 × 15 m area, similar to the obstructed office block discussed in the "Measurement Procedure and Resources Used" section, is considered. A generic wireless station is configured as an IEEE 802.11g AP, as well as a wireless station. The transmit power of the AP was set to 32 mW, which is close to the D-Link (DWL-2100) AP that was used in the propagation measurements. Another important parameter is the packet reception-power threshold, which was set to −88 dBm. This allows the wireless AP to communicate with wireless stations even in weak signal strengths up to −88 dBm, which is a common scenario in the obstructed office environments. Other parameters, such as data rate, channel setting, and the frequency spectrum, were set to the default values for 802.11g.

Two important network performance metrics, mean packet delay and throughput, are considered in this study. The mean packet delay (measured in seconds) is defined as the end-to-end delay of all the packets received by the MAC protocol of all wireless stations on the network and then forwarded to the higher layer. This packet delay includes queuing delay and medium access delay at the source station, and packet transmission time. The throughput (measured in bits/s) is defined as the total number of bits forwarded from the MAC layer to higher layers in all WLAN stations of the network. All simulation results report the steady-state behavior of the network and have been obtained with a relative statistical error not greater than 0.01 at the 95% confidence level. Each simulation run lasted for 15 min of simulated time, in which the first minute was the transient period. The observations collected during the transient period are not included in the final simulation results.

The effects of increasing the number of wireless stations for $N = 2, 10, 15, 20, 25,$ and 30 stations on both the network mean delay and throughput performance of the 802.11g infrastructure network are shown in Figures 10.8 and 10.9, respectively.

As shown in Figure 10.8, the mean packet delay increases with N. For example, the network mean packet delays are 0.25, 1.48, 2.52, 3.58, 5.25, and 6.75 s for $N = 2, 10, 15, 20, 25,$ and 30, respectively. The increase in packet delay for $N > 2$ stations is mainly due to the channel contention and backoff delays. As the number of active users on the network increases, users are likely to wait longer in accessing the channel for packet transmissions, and consequently, the mean packet delay increases. One can draw a conclusion from Figure 10.8 that the mean delay of 802.11g with a single AP increases significantly for $N > 15$ wireless stations.

As shown in Figure 10.9, the network mean throughput of an 802.11g infrastructure network decreases as N increases. This decrease in throughput is more significant for $N > 15$ wireless stations. For example, the mean throughputs are about 8.7, 3.25, 2.05, 1.3, 1, and 0.75 Mbps for $N = 2, 10, 15, 20, 25,$ and 30, respectively. Because of the higher contention delays and backoff, the amount of data transmitted by a source station to a particular destination decreases as N increases, and consequently the network throughput decreases.

The main conclusion one can draw from Figures 10.8 and 10.9 is that the number of active stations has a significant effect on both packet delay and throughput of a typical 802.11g network. The system performance significantly degrades for $N > 15$ stations. Therefore, for the deployment of an indoor 802.11g AP in an obstructed office block, up to 15 wireless stations per AP is recommended for communications wirelessly among the active stations on the network.

The simulation model was validated through indoor measurements from two wireless laptops and an AP for 802.11g. A good match between

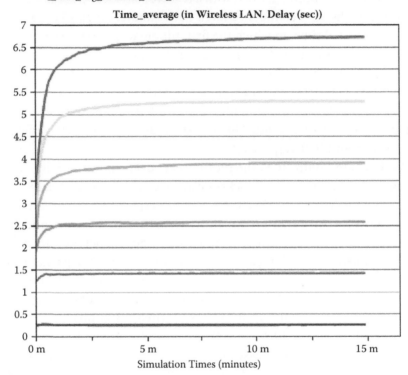

FIGURE 10.8 (SEE COLOR INSERT.) Effect of increasing wireless stations on packet delay of an 802.11g infrastructure network.

simulation and measurement results for $N = 2$ stations validates the simulation model.

IMPLICATIONS FOR AP PLACEMENT

Through extensive propagation measurement, we gained insight into the throughput performance of an 802.11g network in an obstructed office environment. The findings reported in this chapter serve two main purposes. First, they may be useful in aiding managers to make informed decisions about the deployment of 802.11g in locations similar to that of the AUT WY office building. Second, this case study demonstrates, by experiment, the direct effect of AP-RX separation and RSS on system

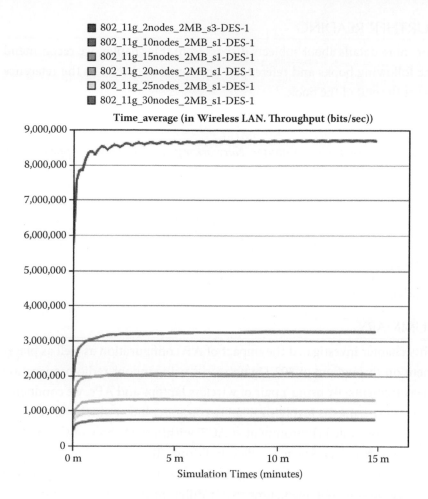

FIGURE 10.9 (SEE COLOR INSERT.) Effect of increasing wireless stations on throughput of an 802.11g infrastructure network.

performance. The use of real hardware to measure performance avoided the complex theoretical modeling of signal propagation and system implementation.

Measured data from a propagation study in an indoor environment would be useful for better system planning and optimum placement of APs. Our experimental results (both propagation and simulation) reveal that a single AP is not adequate in providing wireless connectivity for some 30 users located in the office block. For optimum coverage for the entire office floor, multiple APs are required.

FURTHER READING

For more details about subjects discussed in this chapter, we recommend the following books and references. The items in [] refer to the reference list at the end of the book.

Books

[171] Chapter 6—*Computer Networking: A Top-Down Approach* by Kurose and Ross

Research Papers

[91]

[283]

[284]

SUMMARY

This chapter investigated the impact of AP configuration as well as placement on throughput of 802.11g networks using indoor radio propagation measurements. By using a pair of wireless laptops and APs, we conducted several experiments involving 802.11g computer links, which were carried out in a controlled environment at AUT within the School of Computing and Mathematical Sciences office building. The AP configuration and placement are found to have a significant effect on the link throughput of 802.11g. Results obtained show that a different throughput performance can be achieved with a different AP configuration and placement, and the resulting throughput variation is found to be significant. By using an appropriate AP configuration and placement, an optimum system performance can be achieved. The effect of a routing protocol on WLAN performance is investigated in Chapter 11.

KEY TERMS

Access point (AP)	Received signal strength (RSS)
AP configuration	Throughput
IEEE 802.11g	WDS mode
Line of sight (LOS)	WDS with AP
Non-LOS	WLAN performance

REVIEW QUESTIONS

1. A typical WLAN performance can be tuned by proper configuration of APs. List and describe four AP configuration methods for WLANs.

2. IEEE 802.11g networks are widely used in home and office environments worldwide. Explain how you would configure an AP to set up an 802.11g infrastructure network.

3. IEEE 802.11g infrastructure networks need to be properly configured before using them. Explain how you would configure APs to optimize 802.11g networks.

4. Both AP configuration and placement play an important role in determining the performance of WLANs. Discuss the impact of AP configuration and placement on the performance of a typical 802.11 network.

5. Compare and contrast WDS mode and WDS with AP mode.

MINI-PROJECTS

The following mini-projects aim to provide a deeper understanding of the topics covered in this chapter through literature review and empirical study.

1. The purpose of this project is to develop a good knowledge and understanding of indoor WLAN deployment in terms of AP configuration and placement and their effect on system performance. Conduct an in-depth literature review on AP configuration and placement for 802.11 infrastructure networks. Read 15 to 20 recent relevant journal/conference papers to identify the key researchers and their main contributions. You can use Table 10.8 to record your findings.

2. Conduct propagation measurements to study the effect of AP configuration and placement on a typical 802.11g network to extend the work presented in the "Measurement Procedure and Resources Used" section.

3. Configure an AP to set up a typical 802.11n network. Write a short report summarizing your activities/experience.

TABLE 10.8　Leading Researchers and Their Contributions in AP Configuration and Placement

Researcher	Contribution	Year	Description/Key Concept

Effect of Routing Protocols on WLAN Performance

LEARNING OUTCOMES

After reading and completing this chapter, you will be able to:

- Develop a simulation model to study the performance of Ad Hoc On-Demand Distance Vector (AODV), Dynamic Source Routing (DSR), Temporally Ordered Routing Algorithm (TORA), and Optimized Link State Routing (OLSR)

- Validate simulation results

- Compare and contrast the performance of commonly used mobile ad hoc network (MANET) routing protocols

- Discuss the effect of node mobility on the performance of MANET routing protocols

- Discuss the effect of traffic loads on the performance of MANET routing protocols

- Discuss the effect of network size on the performance of MANET routing protocols

INTRODUCTION

In Chapter 10, the impact of access point (AP) confirmation, as well as placement on WLAN performance, was outlined. In this chapter we investigate the effect of routing protocols on WLAN performance. In MANETs, nodes often move around, join, and leave the network unexpectedly. A good understanding of the joint effect of node density and mobility for various routing protocols on a typical 802.11 is required for an efficient design and deployment of such systems. This chapter addresses the following research question: What impact do different routing protocols have on a typical 802.11 MANET for varying node density and mobility concurrently? In particular, what effect do OLSR, AODV, DSR, and TORA have on an 802.11 network for joint node density and mobility scenarios?

To answer the question posed, this chapter presents a systematic performance analysis for four typical MANET routing protocols, including one proactive routing protocol, OSLR, and three on-demand routing protocols, AODV, DSR, and TORA. These routing protocols were selected based on their popularity, published results, and interesting characteristics and features. The simulation experiments and results for four routing protocols are presented in the "Experiment's Results" section. The overall observations and interpretations are discussed in the "Overall Observation and Interpretations" section.

PERFORMANCE STUDY OF MANET ROUTING PROTOCOLS

The end-to-end packet delay, throughput, routing load, and retransmission were measured to evaluate the performance of OLSR, AODV, DSR, and TORA. The end-to-end packet delay is defined as the average time (measured in seconds) required in sending a packet from source to a destination. This includes buffering during route discovery, queuing at the interface queue, retransmission at the medium access control (MAC), propagation, and packet transmission time. The throughput (measured in bps) is the average rate of successful packet delivery. The routing load is the number of routing control packets transmitted for each data packet delivered at the destination. The retransmission is the resending attempts of packets that have been lost or damaged due to link failure.

Network Scenarios

Figure 11.1 shows the network scope and scenarios to study the performance of MANET routing protocols. The OLSR, DSR, AODV, and TORA are considered for performance modeling and comparison purposes. In the investigation, network sizes, node mobility, and data traffic loads were varied. The performance of the four selected routing protocols is studied with respect to network sizes (small, medium, and large), node mobility, and traffic loads. Table 11.1 lists the nine scenarios considered in the investigation.

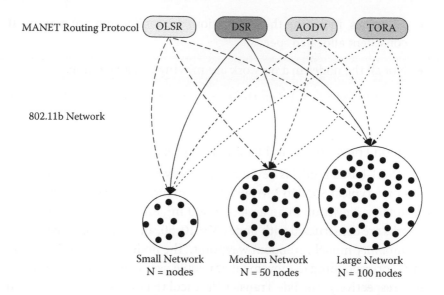

FIGURE 11.1   The network scenarios considered.

TABLE 11.1   Network Scenarios

Scenario	Description
1	Small-sized network ($N = 10$ nodes, $NS = 5$ m/s, $PL = 1,000$ bytes)
2	Medium-sized network ($N = 50$ nodes, $NS = 5$ m/s, $PL = 1,000$ bytes)
3	Large-sized network ($N = 100$ nodes, $NS = 5$ m/s, $PL = 1,000$ bytes)
4	Varying node speed in a small-sized network ($N = 10$ nodes, $NS = 20$ and 30 m/s, $PL = 1,000$ bytes)
5	Varying node speed in a medium-sized network ($N = 50$ nodes, $NS = 20$ and 30 m/s, $PL = 1,000$ bytes)
6	Varying node speed in a large-sized network ($N = 100$ nodes, $NS = 20$ and 30 m/s, $PL = 1,000$ bytes)
7	Varying traffic load in a small-sized network ($N = 10$ nodes, $NS = 30$ m/s, $PL = 5,000$ and 50,000 bytes)
8	Varying traffic load in a medium-sized network ($N = 50$ nodes, $NS = 30$ m/s, $PL = 5,000$ and 50,000 bytes)
9	Varying traffic load in a large-sized network ($N = 100$ nodes, $NS = 30$ m/s, $PL = 5,000$ and 50,000 bytes)

Modeling Assumptions

The following assumptions are made to simplify the simulation models:

- Nodes in the network are configured to generate traffic at random times.

- Multiple hops are used as required before reaching the destination.

- All nodes, including the destination, are mobile and are moving at consistent allocated speeds.

- Not all the nodes in a network are moving at a given time.

- All the nodes are using the same routing protocol (DSR, AODV, OLSR, or TORA).

Simulation Environment and Parameter Settings

An OPNET-based model is developed to study the impact of routing protocols on a typical 802.11b MANET performance. The system simulation experiments are set up in an area of 2,000 m^2. Small, medium, and large networks are constructed with nodes $N = 10$, 50, and 100, respectively. The node mobility model is random waypoint. The node speeds are 5, 20, and 30 m/s corresponding to movement of people, war machines, and slow car speed, respectively. The File Transfer Protocol (FTP) data traffic is used in the investigation. The packet lengths of data traffic are 1,000, 5,000, and 50,000 bytes, reflecting normal, medium, and high loads. Each simulation run lasted for 900 s, in which the first 10 s was the transient period. The observations collected during the transient period were not included in the final simulation results. Tables 11.2 to 11.6 list the parameter values used in the simulation.

Modeling the Network

Figure 11.2 shows the network simulation model with $N = 100$ nodes. The nodes are labeled according to the number of nodes present in the network. For example, N58 represents node number 58 in the network. N10 is a server (destination) configured to support and service FTP traffic. N58, as another

TABLE 11.2   General Parameters Used in Simulation

Parameter	Value
Simulation area	2,000 × 2,000 m
Node density	10, 50, 100 nodes
Node mobility	20, 30 (m/s)
Mobility model	Random waypoint, 0 pause time
Wireless cards/data rate	802.11b, 11 Mbps
Propagation range	250 m
Transmitter power	0.005 watt
Traffic/packet length	FTP/1,000 bytes
Simulation duration	900 s

TABLE 11.3 OLSR Parameters Used in Simulation

Parameter	Value
Willingness	Default
Hello interval	2 s
Topological control (TC) interval	5 s
Neighbor hold time	6 s
Topology hold time	15 s

TABLE 11.4 AODV Parameters Used in Simulation

Parameter	Value
Route request retries	5
Route request rate	10 (packets/s)
Hello interval (uniform)	1–1.1 s
Route error rate	10 packets/s
Node traversal time	0.04 s
Time-out buffer	2
Local repair	Enabled

TABLE 11.5 DSR Parameters Used in Simulation

Parameter	Value
Route expiry time (route cache)	300
Request table size (nodes)	64
Max request retransmission	16
Max request period (s) route discovery	10
Max buffer size for route maintenance	50 packets
Maintenance hold time	0.25 s
Maximum maintenance retransmission	2
Maintenance acknowledgment timer	0.5 s
Route replies using cached routes	Enabled
Packet salving	Enabled

TABLE 11.6 TORA Parameters Used in Simulation

Parameter	Value
Mode of operation	On demand
OPT transmission interval	300 s
IP packet discard time-out	10 s
Beacon period	20 s
Maximum beacon timer	60 s
Maximum tries (number of attempts)	3

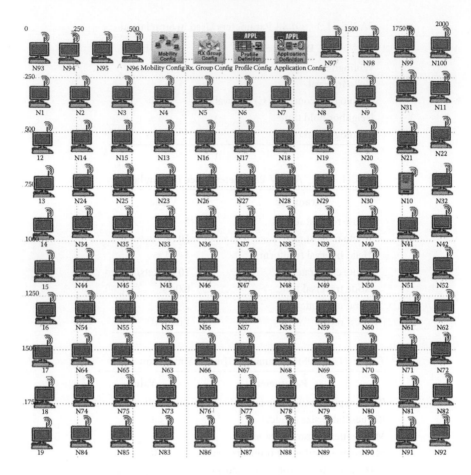

FIGURE 11.2 (SEE COLOR INSERT.)   OPNET-based network simulation model (N = 100 nodes).

node apart from N10, is configured to generate FTP traffic randomly with the ability to route received packets to their destination. All nodes, including the destination, are configured to use the same routing protocol. The mobility configuration object is used to configure the node speed.

The application definition object is used to configure both the applications and packet length. The profile definition object is used to configure applications in a profile. For example, an FTP profile is created in the profile object and configured to support FTP applications. The FTP profile is then configured in all nodes except the destination node. This will enable nodes to generate traffic. The Rx group configuration object enables nodes to move within the 2,000-m² simulated area. Traffic generated from a node that is outside the range will be discarded. The experiment is duplicated and routing protocols are changed. This is repeated for the remaining routing protocols.

EXPERIMENT'S RESULTS

All simulation results report the network steady state and were obtained with a relative statistical error ≤1%, at 99% confidence level.

Impact of Network Size (Small, Medium, and Large)

This section present the results obtained from experimental scenarios 1, 2, and 3. These scenarios outline the results of network size impact on routing protocol performance. Each scenario is presented with node sizes representing small, medium, and large networks.

Scenario 1: Small-Sized Network (N = 10, NS = 5 m/s, PL = 1,000 bytes)
Figure 11.3 compares the throughput of OLSR, DSR, AODV, and TORA for $N = 10$ nodes. The OLSR achieved the highest throughput of 3,500 bits/s. The throughputs of DSR, AODV, and TORA are 700, 400, and 600 bits/s, respectively.

Figure 11.4 compares the routing loads of OLSR, DSR, AODV, and TORA for $N = 10$ nodes. The routing load characteristics of the four routing protocols under study follow throughput behavior. For instance, OLSR maintains a routing load of 2,700 bits/s, as expected from its throughput performance. DSR, AODV, and TORA maintain the same routing loads as their throughputs, which are 700, 400, and 600 bits/s respectively.

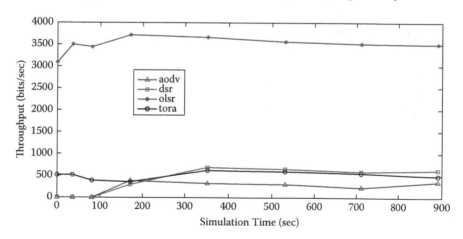

FIGURE 11.3   Throughput versus simulation time ($N = 10$, $NS = 5$ m/s, $PL = 1,000$ bytes).

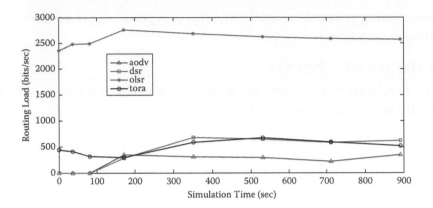

FIGURE 11.4   Routing load versus simulation time ($N = 10$, $NS = 5$ m/s, $PL = 1,000$ bytes).

Figure 11.5 compares the retransmission rates of OLSR, DSR, AODV, and TORA for $N = 10$ nodes. We observe that TORA achieved the highest average retransmission rate of 0.6 packets/s. OLSR has the second highest retransmission rate of 0.45 packets/s. AODV maintains a consistent retransmission rate of 0.15 packets/s, and the rate increases toward the end of the simulation. DSR has a lower retransmission rate.

Figure 11.6 compares the packet delays of OLSR, DSR, AODV, and TORA for $N = 10$ nodes. We observe that DSR has a slightly longer packet delay (4.5 ms) than the other three protocols. For example, the packet delays of TORA, AODV, and OLSR are 1.5, 0.5, and 0.25 ms, respectively.

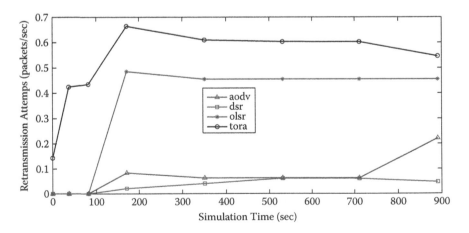

FIGURE 11.5   Retransmission versus simulation time ($N = 10$, $NS = 5$ m/s, $PL = 1,000$ bytes).

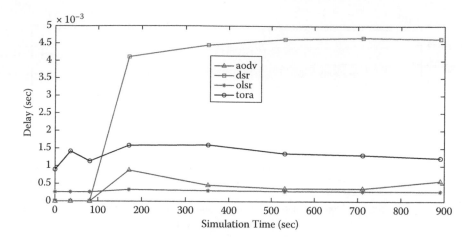

FIGURE 11.6   Packet delay versus simulation time ($N = 10$, $NS = 5$ m/s, $PL = 1,000$ bytes).

Comment: Overall, OLSR performs better in a small network scenario with $N = 10$ nodes and a node speed of 5 m/s. This is because there are fewer topological changes leading to better performance. OLSR also has the advantage of using only multipoint rely (MPR) nodes to send control messages to other nodes, and hence reduce the overhead and achieved lower delays than other protocols. DSR is better suited for a small-sized network than AODV and TORA. In a small and low-mobility network scenario, the proactive protocol (OLSR) outperformed the reactive protocols (e.g., AODV, TORA, and DSR).

Scenario 2: Medium-Sized Network (N = 50,
NS = 5 m/s, PL = 1,000 bytes)
Figure 11.7 compares throughputs of DSR, OLSR, TORA, and AODV for $N = 50$ nodes. We observe that OLSR achieved a higher throughput (44,000 bits/s), on average, than DSR, AODV, and TORA. In a small network ($N = 10$ nodes), DSR is favored over TORA and AODV. However, in the medium network scenario with $N = 50$ nodes, AODV steadily increases and outperforms TORA and DSR. AODV achieved a throughput of 12,500 bits/s, and the throughputs of TORA and DSR are 7,000 s and 5,000 bits/s, respectively. The presence of mobility enables TORA to perform better than DSR in a medium-sized network.

Figure 11.8 compares routing loads of DSR, OLSR, TORA, and AODV for $N = 50$ nodes. We observe that TORA has a higher routing load (7,500

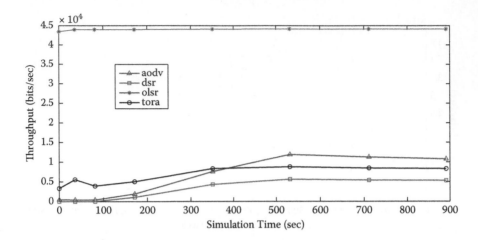

FIGURE 11.7 Throughput versus simulation time ($N = 50$, $NS = 5$ m/s, $PL = 1,000$ bytes).

bits/s) than the packets it delivers to the destination. The routing loads of OLSR, AODV, and DSR are 14,000, 6,000, and 5,000 bits/s, respectively.

Figure 11.9 compares the average retransmission rates of DSR, OLSR, TORA, and AODV for $N = 50$ nodes. OLSR had no packets for retransmissions. AODV is the second best in terms of achieving low retransmission rates (0.19 packets/s), and maintains retransmission rates lower than those of DSR (0.2 packets/s). TORA has the highest rate of packet retransmissions (1.2 packets/s).

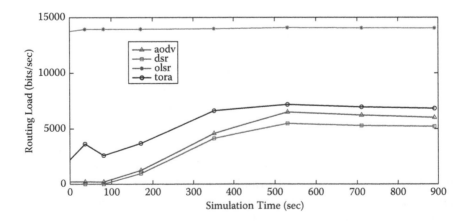

FIGURE 11.8 Routing load versus simulation time ($N = 50$, $NS = 5$ m/s, $PL = 1,000$ bytes).

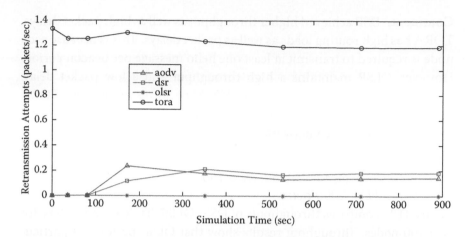

FIGURE 11.9   Retransmission versus simulation time ($N = 50$, $NS = 5$ m/s, $PL = 1,000$ bytes).

Figure 11.10 compares packet delays of DSR, OLSR, TORA, and AODV for $N = 50$ nodes. We observe that node speed and the number of intermediate nodes to the destination affected DSR performance. DSR's packet delays increased due to aggressive network flooding to establish a possible route. TORA is sensitive to packet drops, and therefore incurred a higher retransmission rate, but still maintained a lower delay than DSR. AODV has a lower delay of 0.0012 s, but OLSR achieved the lowest delay: 0.001 s.

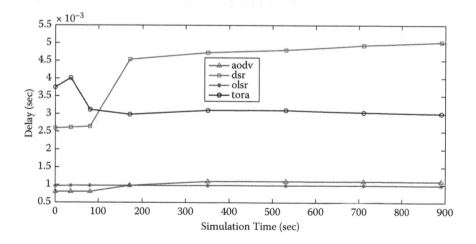

FIGURE 11.10   Packet delay versus simulation time ($N = 50$, $NS = 5$ m/s, $PL = 1,000$ bytes).

Comment: DSR achieved higher throughput as well as high packet delays. TORA has high routing loads as well as packet delays. This is because each node is required to transmit at least one hello message per beacon period. However, OLSR maintains a high throughput and a low packet delay. Among the three reactive protocols, AODV performs better than TORA and DSR. Of the four routing protocols, both OLSR and AODV perform best in a medium-sized network.

Scenario 3: Large-Sized Network (N = 100,
NS = 5 m/s, PL = 1,000 bytes)
Figure 11.11 compares throughputs of DSR, OLSR, TORA, and AODV for $N = 100$ nodes. Throughput results show that OLSR performed particularly better than the three reactive protocols studied. However, it starts to decrease after 300 s of simulation time. TORA maintains a steady increase, outperforming other reactive protocols. AODV maintains a consistent throughput, but lower than that of TORA. DSR's throughput is also lower than that of TORA and slightly increases toward the end of the simulation period. Throughputs of OLSR, TORA, AODV, and DSR are 120,000, 30,000, 25,000, and 20,000 bits/s, respectively. Of the three reactive routing protocols, TORA outperformed AODV and DSR.

Figure 11.12 compares routing loads of OLSR, AODV, DSR, and TORA for $N = 100$ nodes. DSR has a higher routing load of 22,500 bits/s compared to its throughput of 20,000 bits/s. The routing loads of TORA and AODV became consistent after 500 s of simulation time, while that of DSR

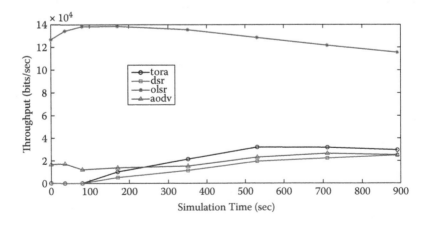

FIGURE 11.11   Throughput versus simulation time ($N = 100$, $NS = 5$ m/s, $PL = 1,000$ bytes).

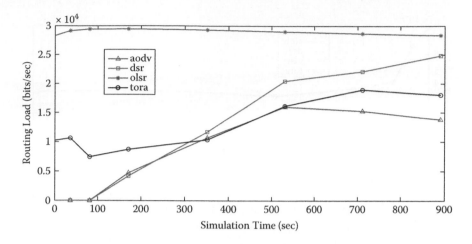

FIGURE 11.12   Routing load versus simulation time (N = 100, NS = 5 m/s, PL = 1,000 bytes).

continues to increase. This is because of the DSR characteristic of finding possible routes when a link failure has occurred.

Figure 11.13 compares retransmission of OLSR, AODV, DSR, and TORA for N = 100 nodes. We observe that TORA drops more packets than AODV and DSR. TORA has a retransmission rate of 1.4 packet/s. However, the retransmission rates of DSR and AODV are 0.6 and 0.2 packet/s, respectively. TORA and AODV maintain consistency, while DSR keeps a steady increase in retransmission to the end of the simulation time.

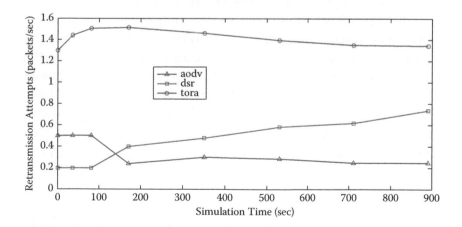

FIGURE 11.13   Retransmission versus simulation time (N = 100, NS = 5 m/s, PL = 1,000 bytes).

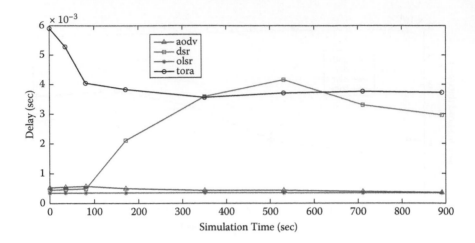

FIGURE 11.14   Packet delay versus simulation time ($N = 100$, $NS = 5$ m/s, $PL = 1,000$ bytes).

Figure 11.14 compares the packet delays of AODV, DSR, OLSR, and TORA for $N = 100$ nodes. We observe that TORA has a higher packet delay than AODV and OLSR. Both AODV and OLSR achieved smaller delays. However, DSR's delay increases and exceeds that of TORA between 400 and 600 s of simulation time. DSR uses a reactive behavior in the sense that packets wait in the buffer before a route is found, and therefore contribute to high delays. OLSR performed well in a large network for $N = 100$ nodes; however, the results are obvious that OLSR does decrease its performance as time passes. TORA, on the other hand, performs well in a large network and maintains a consistent performance. Unfortunately, it has a higher retransmission rate, which therefore leads to higher delays. OLSR and AODV maintain a good delay performance in a large network. Despite the drawbacks, the results show that OLSR and TORA are capable of running in a large network with more advantages for TORA than for OLSR.

Impact of Increasing Node Speed

This section presents results obtained from network scenarios 4, 5, and 6. We study the impact of node mobility (20 and 30 ms) on routing protocols in three different network sizes (small, medium, and large).

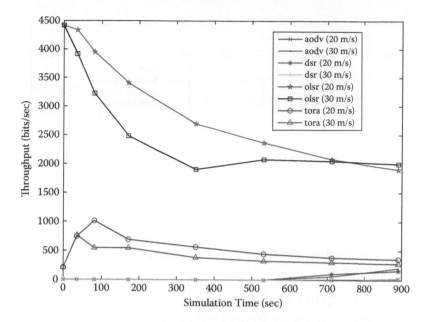

FIGURE 11.15 Throughput versus simulation time ($N = 10$, $NS = 20$ and 30 m/s, $PL = 1,000$ bytes).

Scenario 4: Varying Node Speed in a Small-Sized Network
(N = 10, NS = 20 and 30 m/s, PL = 1,000 bytes)

Figure 11.15 compares throughputs of AODV, DSR, OLSR, and TORA for varying node speeds, and the impact node mobility has in a small network. OLSR performed reasonably well; however, it has a lower throughput than the throughput obtained for scenario 1 (speed of 5 m/s). When the node speed increases from 20 to 30 m/s, the throughput of OLSR decreases and vice versa. By comparing Figures 11.3 and 11.15, one can observe that OLSR achieved throughputs of 3,500 bits/s for a node speed of 5 m/s, and decreased to 2,700 bits/s for node speed of 20 m/s. OLSR's throughput drops to 2,000 bits/s when the node speed is 30 m/s.

DSR is one of the good reactive routing protocols for a small network with $N = 10$ nodes. We observe that the throughput of DSR decreases as node speed increases from 20 and 30 m/s. For example, the throughputs of DSR for node speeds of 20 and 30 m/s are 100 and 25 bits/s, respectively.

The TORA protocol reacted favorably to node speed; throughput increases with speed. For example, TORA's throughputs for node speeds of 20 and 30 m/s are 700 and 800 bits/s, respectively. AODV reacted in

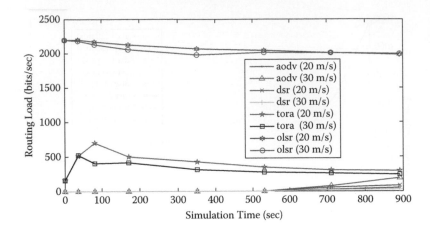

FIGURE 11.16 Routing load versus simulation time (N = 10, NS = 20 and 30 m/s, PL = 1,000 bytes).

the same way as TORA. For instance, the throughputs of AODV for node speeds of 20 and 30 m/s are 100 and 300 bits/s, respectively.

Figure 11.16 compares the routing loads of AODV, DSR, OLSR, and TORA for varying node speeds. We observe that all protocols maintain a lower and consistent routing load. OLSR differs greatly when node speed increases (i.e., routing load decreases with speed).

As node speed increases, the chances of a packet being dropped are higher. Figure 11.17 shows AODV and TORA to have higher retransmission attempts. TORA has a lower retransmission attempt when node speed

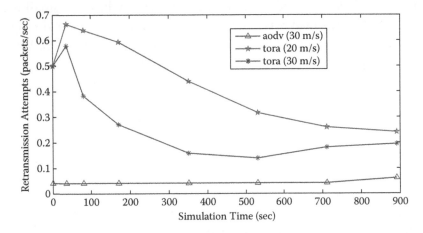

FIGURE 11.17 Retransmission versus simulation time (N = 10, NS = 20 and 30 m/s, PL = 1,000 bytes).

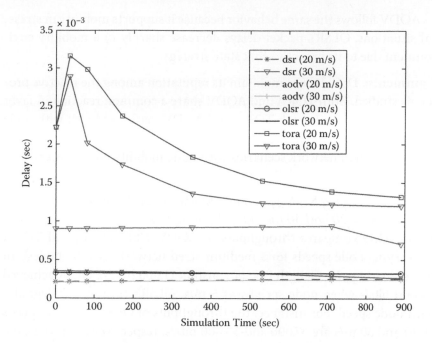

FIGURE 11.18   Packet delay versus simulation time ($N = 10$, $NS = 20$ and 30 m/s, $PL = 1,000$ bytes).

is 30 m/s than when it is 20 m/s. AODV, on the other hand, maintains lower retransmission attempts.

Figure 11.18 compares packet delays of AODV, DSR, OLSR, and TORA for varying node speeds. TORA obtained longer delays at both node speeds than other routing protocols. DSR with a node speed of 30 m/s incurred high delays. AODV and OLSR maintained consistency and achieved lower delays than DSR. When node speed increases, DSR has a high probability of having stale routes and link breakage as a result of cache routes. The aggressive broadcast messages sent for obtaining a valid route in a limited number of nodes may also contribute increased delay.

TORA reacts favorably with increasing node speed; as node speed increases, throughput increases and delay decreases. Traditionally, TORA performs well in high-density networks; it also performs well in small networks with high node mobility. TORA reacts more quickly to changing topology using multipaths, and therefore achieved higher throughput and lower delays.

AODV follows the same behavior because it supports mobility in stressful situations. OLSR's packet delays decrease sharply in a mobility environment due to its proactive link state strategy.

Comments: DSR did not maintain its reputation among the reactive protocols studied. Both TORA and AODV share a common reaction in favor of node speed. While both TORA and AODV performed well with node mobility, OLSR and DSR did not. Overall, one can recommend OLSR and TORA for small network scenarios with node mobility environment.

Scenario 5: Varying Node Speed in a Medium-Sized Network
(N = 50, NS = 20 and 30 m/s, PL = 1,000 bytes)
Figure 11.19 compares throughputs of AODV, DSR, OLSR, and TORA for varying node speeds for a medium-sized network (*N* = 50 nodes). In this scenario packet length is kept constant (1,000 bytes). OLSR achieved 44,000 bits/s when node speed was 5 m/s. OLSR's throughput degrades with node speed. For instance, the throughputs of OLSR for node speeds of 20 and 30 m/s are 37,000 and 30,000 bits/s, respectively. Similarly, the throughputs of AODV and DSR degrade with node speed. For example,

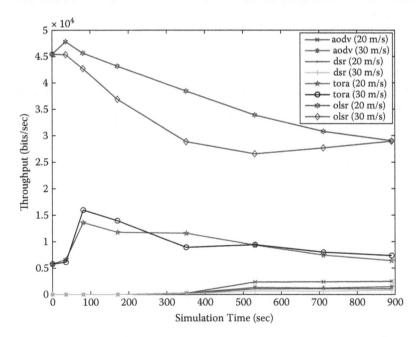

FIGURE 11.19 Throughput versus simulation time (*N* = 50, *NS* = 20 and 30 m/s, *PL* = 1,000 bytes).

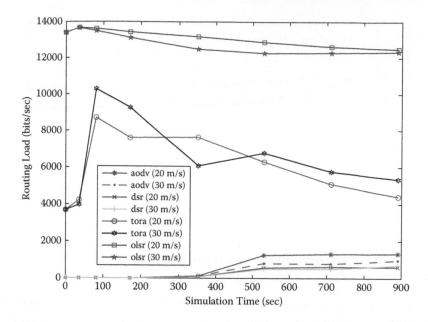

FIGURE 11.20 Routing load versus simulation time ($N = 50$, $NS = 20$ and 30 m/s, $PL = 1,000$ bytes).

the throughputs of AODV for node speeds of 5, 20, and 30 m/s are 12,500, 2,500, and 2,000 bits/s, respectively.

The throughput of DSR also degrades with node speed. We observe that the throughputs of DSR for node speeds of 5, 20, and 30 m/s are 5,000, 2,000, and 1,000 bits/s, respectively. TORA's throughput increases with node speed. For example, TORA achieved 7,000, 10,000, and 12,000 bits/s for node speeds of 5, 20, and 30 m/s, respectively. Overall, OLSR achieved the highest throughput, followed by TORA, AODV, and DSR.

Figure 11.20 compares routing loads of AODV, DSR, OLSR, and TORA for varying node speeds for a medium-sized network ($N = 50$ nodes). The routing load shows a pattern similar to those of throughput performance shown in Figure 11.19.

Figure 11.21 shows the retransmission attempts of TORA, DSR, and AODV. We observe that more data packets are dropped with node speed. TORA is rather an exception here because it has retransmission attempts even in a low-mobility environment. The pleasant behavior of TORA is that when node speed increases, retransmission rate decreases more than in networks with low node speed. DSR has a higher retransmission rate than AODV. However, AODV with a node speed of 30 m/s obtains the

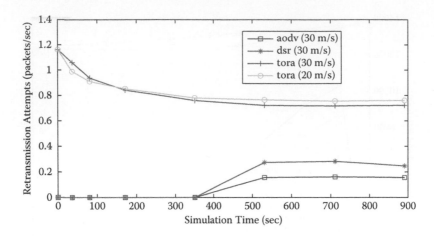

FIGURE 11.21 Retransmission versus simulation time ($N = 50$, $NS = 20$ and 30 m/s, $PL = 1,000$ bytes).

lowest retransmission rate of 0.18 packets/s, followed by DSR (30 m/s) of 0.3 packets/s. TORA has a higher retransmission of 0.8 packets/s at a node speed of 20 m/s than at 30 m/s (0.7 packets/s).

Figure 11.22 compares packet delays of AODV, DSR, OLSR, and TORA for varying node speeds for a medium-sized network ($N = 50$ nodes). We observe that OLSR maintains a lower delay regardless of node speed. While DSR's packet delay increases with node speed, AODV maintains a lower delay. TORA's delay in this scenario is different than its throughput and retransmission attempts. With node speed, both throughput and delay increase, but retransmission attempts decrease. AODV's packet delay decreases with node speed.

In summary, OLSR achieved higher throughput. It has a decreasing trend, which gives a rise to a recommendation that TORA be used in medium-sized networks in high-mobility environments. OLSR achieved lower delays than TORA. AODV may not be suitable for use in medium-sized networks with high mobility. TORA overtakes AODV as a result of its routing properties that best fit in mobility environments.

Scenario 6: Varying Node Speed in a Large-Sized Network
(N = 100, NS = 20 and 30 m/s, PL = 1,000 bytes)
Figure 11.23 compares throughputs of AODV, DSR, OLSR, and TORA for varying node speeds with network size of $N = 100$ nodes. We observe that TORA performs better among the four routing protocols considered in high node speeds. For example, TORA performed exceedingly

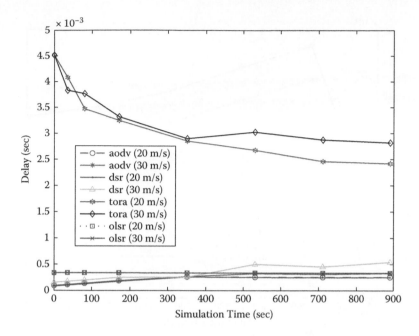

FIGURE 11.22 Packet delay versus simulation time ($N = 50$, $NS = 20$ and 30 m/s, $PL = 1,000$ bytes).

well at a node speed of 20 m/s, and past OLSR for a node speed of 30 m/s. OLSR is considered to be the next best protocol; however, the throughput of OSLR degrades as with node speed. AODV reacted differently in a large network ($N = 100$ nodes) compared to a medium-sized network ($N = 50$ nodes). The increase of node speed resulted in an increased throughput; however, in medium-sized networks, an increase in node speed resulted in reduced throughput. AODV performs well in large networks because it allows more possible routes to the destination than for a medium-sized network. The performance of DSR was unchanged regardless of network size; throughput decreases with node speed.

Let us now quantify the throughputs of all four routing protocols studied. The throughputs of TORA for node speeds of 5, 20, and 30 m/s are 30,000, 90,000, and 130,000 bits/s, respectively. The throughputs of OLSR for node speeds of 5, 20, and 30 m/s are 120,000, 37,000, and 30,000 bits/s, respectively. We observed that AODV achieved throughputs of 15,000 and 20,000 bits/s for node speeds of 5 and 20 m/s, respectively. Throughput further increases to 30,000 bits/s at a node speed of 30 m/s. The throughputs

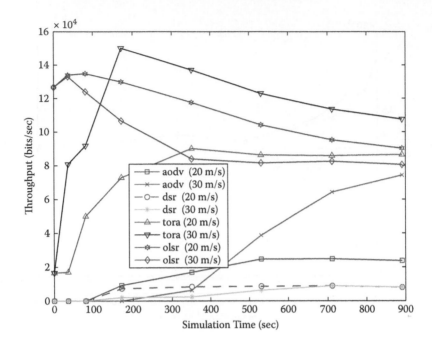

FIGURE 11.23   Throughput versus simulation time ($N = 100$, $NS = 20$ and 30 m/s, $PL = 1,000$ bytes).

of DSR are 20,000, 10,000, and 8,000 bits/s for node speeds of 5, 20, and 30 m/s, respectively.

Figure 11.24 compares routing loads of AODV, DSR, OLSR, and TORA for varying node speeds with $N = 100$ nodes. OLSR keeps a consistent routing load throughout the simulation time. However, it degrades performance with node speed. TORA's routing load shows more reaction than the other three protocols. The routing loads increase steadily at a node speed of 20 m/s. We observe that AODV obtains higher routing loads than DSR, as AODV's routing load increases with node speed and vice versa, but DSR's routing load decreases with node speed.

Figure 11.25 compares retransmission rates of AODV, DSR, OLSR, and TORA for varying node speeds with network size $N = 100$ nodes. DSR maintains low retransmissions for a node speed of 20 m/s, and the retransmission rate increases at 30 m/s. AODV maintains a low retransmission rate, and TORA has a high retransmission rate at 20 m/s.

Figure 11.26 compares packet delays of AODV, DSR, OLSR, and TORA for varying node speeds with network size $N = 100$ nodes. Both OLSR and AODV maintain lower delays than the other two protocols. DSR has

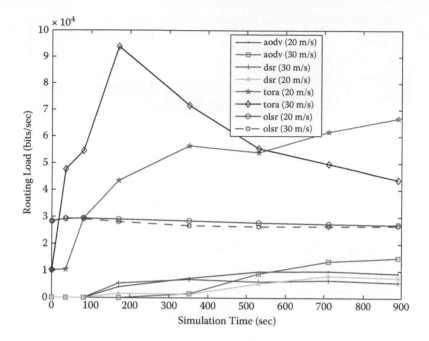

FIGURE 11.24 Routing load versus simulation time ($N = 100$, $NS = 20$ and 30 m/s, $PL = 1,000$ bytes).

a larger delay at a node speed of 30 m/s than the delays at 20 m/s. TORA has a higher delay than DSR, and follows a trend similar to that of DSR in increasing delay with node speed. OLSR maintains a lower delay than TORA. TORA is more sensitive to packet drops than OLSR and AODV. This is because OLSR uses a routing table and more MRP nodes for message control flow for flooding the network than TORA, and therefore has less impact on delays. Likewise, AODV uses a routing table with one route per destination, instead of flooding the network, resulting in lower delays.

In summary, TORA performs very well over OLSR, DSR, and AODV. OLSR's throughput decreases but maintains a lower delay than TORA. AODV has great potential to perform in such an environment, as it reacts the same way as TORA (i.e., increasing throughput with node speed). AODV behaves in this manner only in large and small networks. In medium-sized networks, AODV has the opposite reaction. Overall, TORA is considered to be the best routing protocol for increased node speed in a large network.

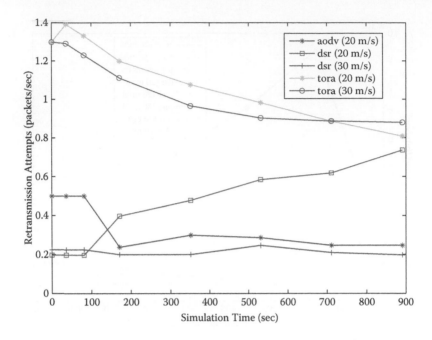

FIGURE 11.25 Retransmission versus simulation time ($N = 100$, $NS = 20$ and 30 m/s, $PL = 1,000$ bytes).

Impact of Increasing Traffic Load

This section presents simulation results obtained from scenarios 7, 8, and 9. The impact of increasing traffic loads on MANET routing protocols in three different network sizes is investigated.

Scenario 7: Varying Traffic Load in a Small-Sized Network (N = 10, NS = 30 m/s, PL = 5,000 and 50,000 bytes)

Figure 11.27 compares the throughputs of TORA, AODV, OLSR, and DSR in varying traffic loads (5,000 and 50,000 bytes) and a constant node speed of 30 m/s for a network of $N = 10$ nodes. We observe that OLSR drops packets more than 50% for low mobility and less traffic loads. OLSR did not react with packet lengths, and the throughput remains the same in packet lengths of both 5,000 and 50,000 bytes. This behavior applies to throughputs of TORA and DSR. TORA keeps a consistent throughput of 600 bits/s for both packet lengths considered.

When employing TORA in a small network ($N = 10$), both node speed and traffic load do not have a great impact on throughput performance. TORA's throughput is the same as before for a node speed of 5 m/s and a

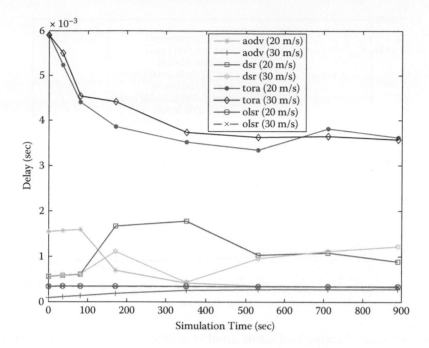

FIGURE 11.26 Packet delay versus simulation time ($N = 100$, $NS = 20$ and 30 m/s, $PL = 1,000$ bytes).

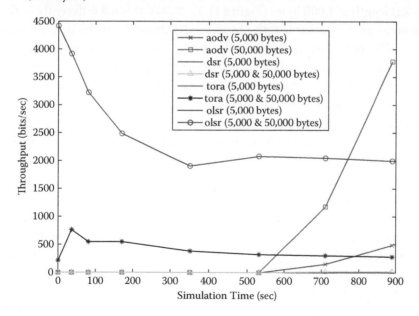

FIGURE 11.27 Throughput versus simulation time ($N = 10$, $NS = 30$ m/s, $PL = 5,000$ and 50,000 bytes).

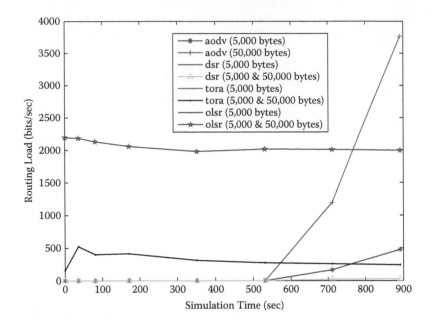

FIGURE 11.28   Routing load versus simulation time ($N = 10$, $NS = 30$ m/s, $PL =$ 5,000 and 50,000 bytes).

packet length of 1,000 bytes (Figure 11.3). AODV reacted differently in this scenario; as the packet length increases, its throughput starts to increase after 500 s of simulation time (better performance than TORA). AODV's throughput increases and passes OLSR for a packet length of 50,000 bytes.

Overall, the throughput results are as follows: OLSR achieved 2,000 bits/s for data traffic loads of 5,000 and 50,000 bytes. The throughputs of TORA and DSR are 500 and 100 bits/s, respectively. AODV achieved 600 bits/s at a packet length of 5,000 bytes and 2,500 bits/s for a packet length of 50,000 bytes.

Figure 11.28 compares routing loads of TORA, AODV, OLSR, and DSR in varying traffic loads (5,000 and 50,000 bytes) and a constant node speed of 30 m/s for $N = 10$ nodes. Most routing protocols have the same behavior as their throughput characteristics. The only routing protocol that differs in routing load is OLSR, as its routing load does not have a big drop compared to its throughput (see Figure 11.27) and maintains a load of 2,000 bits/s.

Figure 11.29 shows the packet retransmission characteristics of the four routing protocols considered. OLSR has high retransmissions of 0.2 packets/s for both packet lengths. AODV with a packet length of 50,000 bytes achieved a high throughput, but the retransmission attempt is also

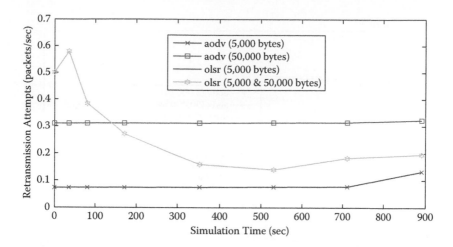

FIGURE 11.29   Retransmission versus simulation time ($N = 10$, $NS = 30$ m/s, PL = 5,000 and 50,000 bytes).

high, 0.3 packets/s. AODV with packet length of 5,000 bytes has the lowest retransmission rate of 0.1 packets/s.

Figure 11.30 compares packet delays of TORA, AODV, OLSR, and DSR in varying traffic loads (5,000 and 50,000 bytes) and a constant node speed of 30 m/s for a network of $N = 10$ nodes. DSR, in both packet lengths, maintains a low delay regardless of the increase in traffic loads. OLSR reacts in the same way as DSR. TORA has the second highest delay of 0.0015 s, and it does not vary regardless of packet length. AODV, on the other hand, attains the highest delay when packet length is 50,000 bytes. AODV has a lower delay than TORA with a packet length of 5,000 bytes.

OLSR, in most scenarios, maintains a lower packet delay. This is because of the efficient route maintenance, and there is less likelihood of packets being sent through invalid paths or in an event of link failure. We observe that AODV's packet delivery rate increased with traffic load, especially in small networks. AODV's transmission overhead is sharply increased, resulting in a much higher delay than the other three protocols studied.

In a small network with high node speed and high traffic load, OLSR degrades throughput while AODV maintains good performance. DSR, the winner in small networks, maintains a low delay by sacrificing its throughput. Results obtained have shown that both AODV and OLSR are the winners. Both the throughput and packet delay are independent of traffic load with the exception of AODV. AODV may be recommended for a network scenario with a consistent traffic load and node speed of 30

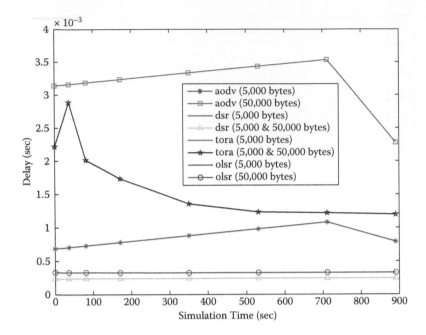

FIGURE 11.30   Packet delay versus simulation time ($N = 10$, $NS = 30$ m/s, $PL =$ 5,000 and 50,000 bytes).

m/s. However, it may not be suited for applications where high delay is not acceptable.

Scenario 8: Varying Traffic Load in a Medium-Sized Network
(N = 50, NS = 30 m/s, PL = 5,000 and 50,000 bytes)

Figure 11.31 compares throughputs of TORA, AODV, OLSR, and DSR in varying traffic loads (5,000 and 50,000 bytes) and a constant node speed of 30 m/s for a network of $N = 50$ nodes. The increase in the number of nodes causes a distinguished reaction to packet lengths. OLSR performance dropped from 36,000 bits/s to 30,000 bits/s when traffic load increased from 5,000 to 50,000 bits/s. TORA's reaction was different for both packet lengths. The throughput increases up to a simulation time of 100 s, and then decreases at a 300-s simulation time. TORA mobilizes the situation with a packet length of 50,000 bytes. TORA gains throughput of 40,000 bits/s over OLSR when the packet length is 50,000 bytes. At a packet length of 5,000 bytes, TORA maintains a throughput of 10,000 bits/s. AODV maintains the same reaction toward node mobility; as packet length increases from 5,000 to 50,000 bytes, throughput increases from 5,000 to 9,000 bits/s, respectively. DSR's performance is different in medium-sized

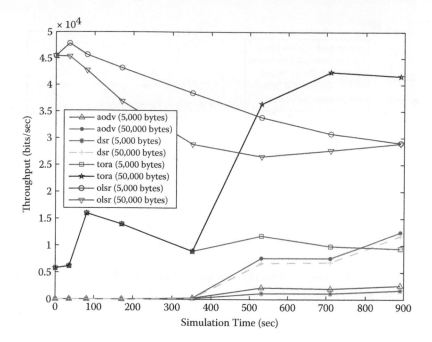

FIGURE 11.31   Throughput versus simulation time (N = 50, NS = 30 m/s, PL = 5,000 and 50,000 bytes).

networks than in small networks. DSR achieved throughputs of 4,000 and 8,000 bits/s for packet lengths of 5,000 and 50,000 bytes, respectively.

Figure 11.32 compares routing loads of TORA, AODV, OLSR, and DSR in varying traffic loads (5,000 and 50,000 bytes) with a node speed of 30 m/s for a network of N = 50 nodes. OLSR maintains a consistent network load and varies slightly when traffic load increases. The routing load characteristics of TORA, AODV, and DSR are similar to those of their throughput performance. TORA attains routing loads of 8,000 and 37,000 bits/s for packet lengths of 5,000 and 50,000 bytes, respectively. OLSR has routing loads of 14,000 and 13,900 bits/s. AODV achieved routing loads of 5,000 and 9,000 bits/s, whereas DSR has loads of 2,500 and 6,500 bits/s.

Figure 11.33 compares retransmission rates of TORA, AODV, OLSR, and DSR in varying traffic loads (5,000 and 50,000 bytes) with a node speed of 30 m/s for a network of N = 50 nodes. TORA has the highest retransmission attempts at a packet length of 5,000 bytes. DSR achieved the second highest at a packet length of 50,000 bytes. AODV has a pattern similar to that of TORA and achieved the lowest retransmission rate.

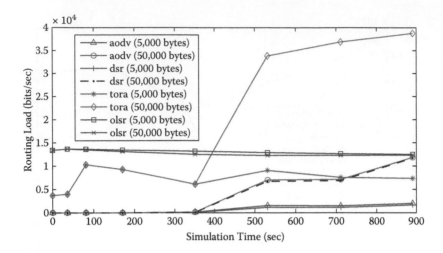

FIGURE 11.32   Routing load versus simulation time ($N = 50$, $NS = 30$ m/s, $PL = 5,000$ and $50,000$ bytes).

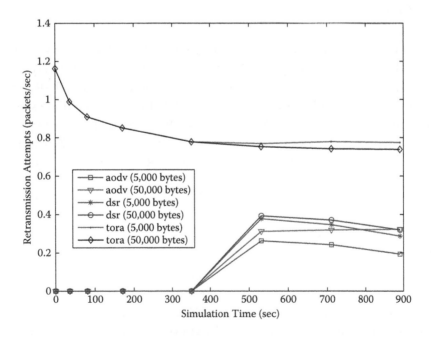

FIGURE 11.33   Retransmission versus simulation time ($N = 50$, $NS = 30$ m/s, $PL = 5,000$ and $50,000$ bytes).

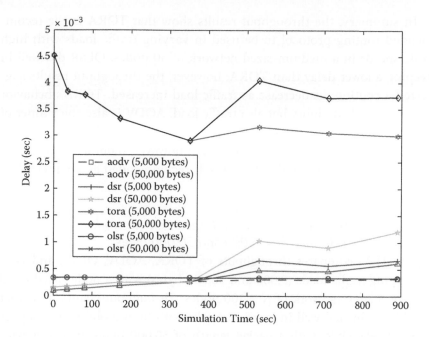

FIGURE 11.34   Packet delay versus simulation time ($N = 50$, $NS = 30$ m/s, $PL = 5,000$ and $50,000$ bytes).

Figure 11.34 compares packet delays of TORA, AODV, OLSR, and DSR in varying traffic loads (5,000 and 50,000 bytes) with a node speed of 30 m/s for $N = 50$ nodes. The results show that TORA has a lower delay with a packet length of 50,000 bytes than a packet length of 5,000 bytes. DSR with the packet length of 50,000 bytes has a higher traffic delay than it does with a packet length 5,000 bytes. OLSR and AODV maintained a lower delay. AODV has a higher delay with packet length of 50,000 bytes than a packet length of 5,000 bytes.

The number of nodes in a network plays an important role when it comes to the performance of routing protocols. The delay performances of both DSR and AODV increase with traffic load. This is because data packets can use multiple routes to a destination. AODV performs better than DSR in situations with large numbers of nodes. TORA maintains the same sensitivity to packet drop as a result of its characteristics of multiple routes to a destination. It establishes a route quickly, minimizing communication overhead by localizing the algorithmic reaction to topological changes in a high-mobility network environment. TORA has a steep rise in routing loads, which may result in increased packet drops, causing congestion.

In summary, the throughput results show that TORA is the recommended routing protocol to be used in varying traffic loads with high node speeds in a medium-sized network of 50 nodes. OLSR did well in keeping a lower delay than TORA; however, the throughput results suggested a continuous decrease as traffic load increased. TORA's behavior favors not only mobility but also traffic load. AODV is also the winner of medium-sized networks; it comes third and behaves in the same manner as TORA. Its reaction favors traffic load; however, mobility degrades its performance. AODV could also be well recommended as an alternative option in this scenario.

Scenario 9: Varying Traffic Load in a Large-Sized Network
(N = 100, NS = 30 m/s, PL = 5,000 and 50,000 bytes)
Figure 11.35 compares throughputs of TORA, AODV, OLSR, and DSR in varying traffic loads (5,000 and 50,000 bytes) with a node speed of 30 m/s for a large network of $N = 100$ nodes. Throughput results show that TORA performed well in large networks with high mobility and higher traffic loads. DSR, with a packet length of 50,000 bytes, increases pace after 350 s of simulation time and increases throughput over OLSR. The

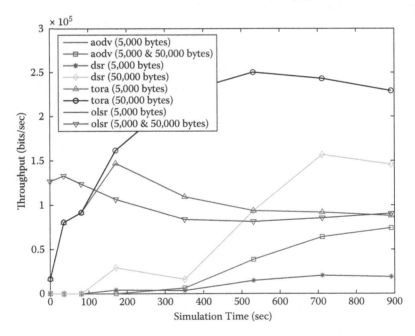

FIGURE 11.35   Average throughput versus simulation time ($N = 100$, $NS = 30$ m/s, $PL = 5,000$ and 50,000 bytes).

presence of a large node size and mobility contribute to DSR's performance improvement. In large networks, DSR is able to establish multiple routes to a destination. On the other hand, DSR has a lower throughput in low traffic loads. OLSR's throughput drops independently of packet lengths (80,000 bits/s). AODV responded with the same throughput performance to both packet lengths. It also achieves the same throughput of 70,000 bits/s regardless of traffic load. TORA achieved 100,000 bits/s for a packet length of 5,000 bytes, and throughput increased to 230,000 bits/s at a packet length of 50,000 bytes. DSR achieved a throughput of 20,000 bits/s at a packet length of 5,000 bytes and increased to 150,000 bits/s at a packet length of 50,000 bytes.

Figure 11.36 compares routing loads for all routing protocols considered. OLSR maintains a low and consistent routing load throughout simulation time.

Figure 11.37 compares retransmission rates of TORA, AODV, OLSR, and DSR in varying traffic loads (5,000 and 50,000 bytes) with a node speed of 30 m/s for a large network of $N = 100$ nodes. Overall, TORA has higher retransmission attempts than DSR. We observe that TORA has

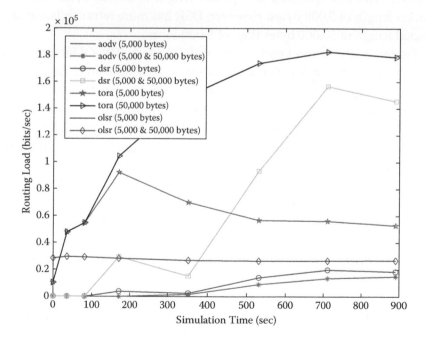

FIGURE 11.36 Average routing load versus simulation time ($N = 100$, $NS = 30$ m/s, $PL = 5,000$ and 50,000 bytes).

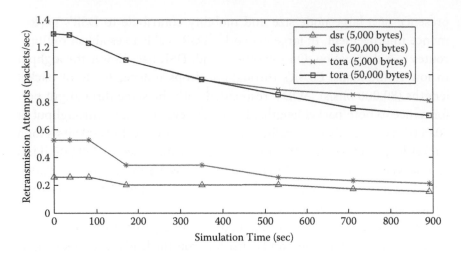

FIGURE 11.37 Average retransmission versus simulation time ($N = 100$, $NS = 30$ m/s, $PL = 5,000$ and $50,000$ bytes).

a lower retransmission rate at a packet length of 50,000 bytes than the packet length of 5,000 bytes. However, DSR has more retransmission at a packet length of 50,000 bytes than of 5,000 bytes.

Figure 11.38 compares packet delays of TORA, AODV, OLSR, and DSR in varying traffic loads (5,000 and 50,000 bytes) with a node speed of 30 m/s for a large network of $N = 100$ nodes. We observe that TORA has higher delays than the other three routing protocols studied. However, TORA's delay decreases with packet length. OLSR has a low delay and is consistent in both packet lengths. AODV shows a lower delay than OLSR and maintains the same delay for both packet lengths. DSR may have a lot of stale routes in its cache; however, results depicted a good through-put when mobility and traffic load are high in a large network. The result suggests that DSR can have a good scalability for node mobility in a large network with regards to packet overhead. This means that the control packets will not increase sharply when mobility increases, as shown in Figure 11.30.

In summary, TORA performed well in a large network and under high node mobility and traffic load conditions. DSR, on the other hand, can be used as well. TORA and DSR reacted well to traffic load and mobility in large networks; however, OLSR and AODV have no significant differences in varying traffic loads.

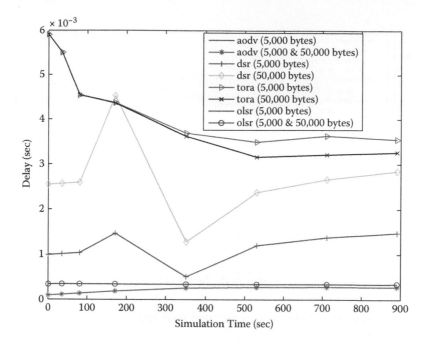

FIGURE 11.38   Average delay versus simulation time ($N = 100$, $NS = 30$ m/s, PL = 5,000 and 50,000 bytes).

COMPARATIVE ANALYSIS

To investigate the combined effect of node density and mobility for OLSR, AODV, DSR, and TORA on an 802.11 MANET, we consider three different node density scenarios, $N = 10$, 50, and 100 nodes, and two node mobility scenarios, 20 and 30 m/s.

The combined effect of node density ($N = 10$, 50, and 100 nodes) and node mobility (20 and 30 m/s) on average packet delay for OLSR, AODV, DSR, and TORA is illustrated in Figure 11.39. The average packet delay increases for all routing protocols with a number of nodes higher than 50.

Of the four routing protocols studied, TORA has high packet delays, especially for a large network with high mobility. OLSR (proactive routing protocol) achieved shorter delays because each node maintains a routing table with all possible destinations and the number of hops to each destination. When a packet arrives at a node, it is either forwarded immediately or dropped off.

AODV uses the source-initiated approach in the route discovery process, but for route maintenance it uses a table-driven mechanism. AODV performs better (in terms of packet delays) than DSR when node mobility is

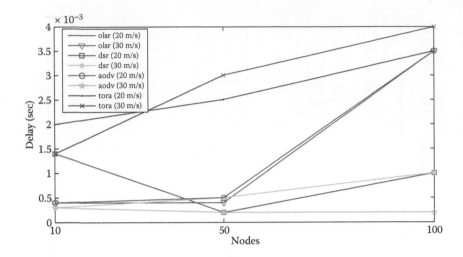

FIGURE 11.39   Packet delay versus node density (20 and 30 m/s).

high. Our findings are in close agreement with the work of other researchers [196].

The combined effect of node density and node mobility on network
throughput for OLSR, AODV, DSR, and TORA is illustrated in Figure 11.40.
The average throughput increases quickly for TORA, OLSR, and AODV
with increased node density and mobility. DSR, on the other hand, has
difficulty in finding routes when both the node density and mobility are
increased, even though throughput dropped slightly for the node density,

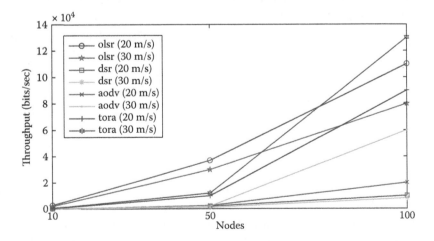

FIGURE 11.40   Throughput versus node density (20 and 30 m/s).

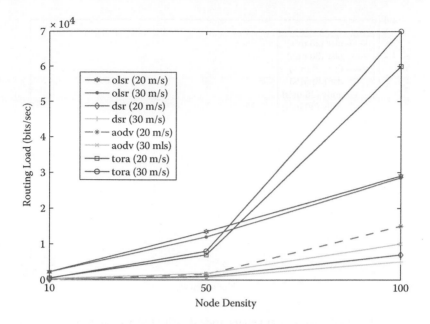

FIGURE 11.41   Routing load versus node density (20 and 30 m/s).

fewer than 50 nodes. However, OLSR achieves better throughput than the reactive protocols (TORA, AODV, and DSR) for a small- to medium-sized network. This is because OLSR senses neighboring nodes to establish a connection and finds a valid route. AODV reacted in the same way as TORA; however, the effects of mobility reduced the network throughputs. TORA offers better throughput in high mobility and a large network scenario than AODV and DSR.

The combined effect of node density and node mobility on routing load for OLSR, AODV, DSR, and TORA is illustrated in Figure 11.41. The routing load of a protocol can influence a node's efficiency of battery energy and scalability. The four routing protocols have different amounts of routing overhead. For example, OLSR has higher routing loads than AODV, DSR, and TORA for node densities smaller than 50 nodes. However, in the case of a large network (around 100 nodes), OLSR has slightly smaller routing loads than TORA. In all network scenarios, DSR has the lightest routing loads compared to the other three protocols.

The combined effect of node density and mobility on retransmission attempts for OLSR, AODV, DSR, and TORA is demonstrated in Figure 11.42. Of the four routing protocols, OLSR has the least retransmission attempts,

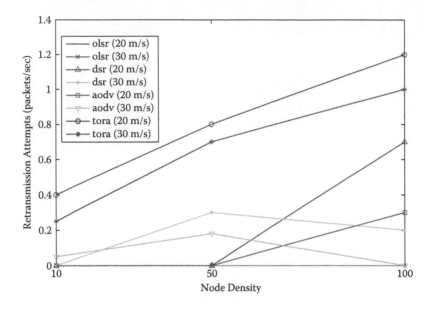

FIGURE 11.42   Retransmission versus node density (20 and 30 m/s).

whereas TORA has the highest packet retransmission rate for all network scenarios. However, AODV's packet retransmission rate is slightly lower than that of DSR, especially for a large network with more than 50 nodes and high mobility.

The summary of simulation results is presented in Figure 11.43. The well-performed routing protocol for various scenarios is shown in column 3. This might help researchers in selecting the best routing protocol for a particular network scenario.

OVERALL OBSERVATION AND INTERPRETATIONS

The simulation results presented in this chapter have provided an insight into the impact of routing protocols on WLAN performance. The presence of node mobility, network size, and traffic load implies a variety of reactions to OLSR, DSR, AODV, and TORA routing algorithms. The different properties of each routing protocol have led to a variety of differences in performance. The experimental results, discussions, and summary results (see Figure 11.43) are presented based on the effect of network size, node mobility, and packet length (i.e., traffic loads).

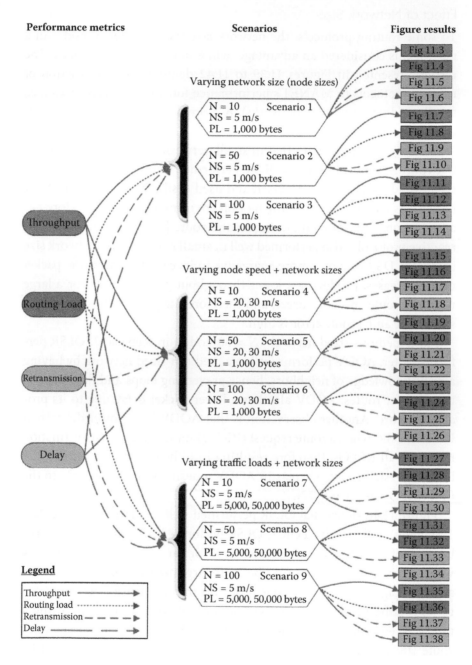

FIGURE 11.43 (SEE COLOR INSERT.)   Summary of simulation results.

Effect of Network Size

To some routing protocols, the network size (i.e., number of nodes in a network) is considered an advantage, while to others is a drawback. The results presented in Figures 11.39 to 11.42 demonstrate the reaction of routing protocols to MANET's performance for three network sizes (i.e., small, medium, and large networks). A more detailed effect on each network is presented in scenarios 1 to 3.

Scenario 1 demonstrates that in small networks ($N = 10$ nodes) proactive routing protocols, such as OLSR, performed well. By keeping a routing table, valid routes can be accessed and used easily. OLSR, by using MPR nodes, has an advantage of slow-motion environments, and therefore has a high probability of maintaining a valid route [183]. DSR, among other reactive protocols, also performed well in small networks. As network size increases, DSR becomes more aggressive in its caching; therefore, packet delay increases, producing a lower-throughput performance. For a large network, routes become larger, and therefore the probability of getting a stale route and a route error is high.

For a medium-sized network ($N = 50$ nodes) in scenario 2, OLSR performs better. AODV performs well in a medium-sized network by having a prior knowledge of neighbors, hence preventing loops and determining the freshest routes. AODV also has a lower packet delay due to its proactive nature. Another observation is that AODV has a lower delay than DSR. In DSR, when a route request (RREQ) message is sent, a destination replies to all REEQs, therefore resulting in difficulty in determining the least congested route, whereas in AODV a destination replies only to the first RREQ it receives [177].

Figure 11.40 shows that OLSR performed well in a large network ($N = 100$ nodes), followed by TORA. OLSR performs better in large networks because of proactive characteristics as it forwards requests immediately when received. OLSR also works better in large networks [285]. TORA has an advantage over other reactive protocols in high-density networks due to its routing properties by providing multiple routes and supporting a multicast environment, giving a higher probability of establishing a valid route [188]. In a large network, nodes mostly communicate to a nearby node for possible route paths and hops. If local communication predominates, the paths will remain constant as the network grows. By using the same path in a large network, nodes in the paths becomes denser; therefore, it has a higher chance of a link failure.

Effect of Node Mobility

Mobility imposes a stress to routing protocols due to link breakages and subsequent route discovery costs. Link failure is caused by invalid routes (from nodes that disappear from the network) or stale routes (nodes with expired routes). When a link failure occurs, data packet messages also increase, therefore increasing the network traffic loads. Additionally, some routing protocols may not deal well with different traffic patterns. This adds a substantial burden, which causes performance to degrade significantly during node mobility. In the presence of mobility, failure of links does happen; therefore, it requires retransmission. The accumulation of retransmission increases the network load, causing overhead, which degrades network throughput performance.

For a small network ($N = 10$ nodes), Figures 11.39 to 11.42 show that OLSR and TORA performed better than AODV and DSR. AODV's properties cause more overhead when dealing with link failures and route discoveries. DSR, on the other hand, maintains a lower route discovery due to a large cache, and therefore has less retransmission in most cases. However, due to mobility, the probability of getting a stale route in its cache is very high.

As shown in Figure 11.40, DSR achieved the lowest throughputs compared to AODV when nodes were mobile. A prior knowledge of neighboring nodes allows AODV to perform better than DSR in all network sizes when node speed increases. DSR replies heavily on the route cache to determine a valid route, which is prone to be stale with the increase in node mobility.

For a medium network ($N = 50$ nodes), OLSR and TORA performed well over AODV and DSR. Figure 11.39 shows a variation of packet delay in DSR. When mobility increases in a small network the delay is high, and in medium networks the delay decreases and further increases as the network increases. This upholds DSR to work well in low mobility and a small network size. As mobility increases, TORA did pick up momentum, even in a small network. In stressful situations, AODV performed better than DSR; however, in keeping with a route table, the mechanism may not be suitable for a medium-sized network. Figure 11.19 clearly shows that for AODV a node speed of 30 m/s may be too much to handle. TORA, on the other hand, manages well in medium- and large-sized networks, and hence increases throughput in high node mobility environments.

For a large network with $N = 100$ nodes, Figure 11.40 shows that as mobility increases, TORA outperforms OLSR. TORA can be used in a large network with high node mobility [183]. One of the factors of TORA's advance is that by providing multiple routes to destinations and supporting multicasting, it establishes routes quickly, and minimizes communication overhead by its localizing algorithm reaction to topological changes [188]. In all scenarios where node mobility is present, TORA performed well. On the other hand, TORA causes more packet drops and a higher packet delay (Figure 11.39) than any other routing protocols. TORA's high delay is believed to be from broken links to its neighbors and the neighbors' discovery mechanism, which requires each node to transmit at least one hello message per beacon period. Yet as mobility increases, the delay decreases. This supports the theory that TORA gains more throughput performance in higher-mobility networks [183].

OLSR performed well in all network sizes (Figure 11.40) and regardless of the increase in mobility. In addition, OLSR has the lowest average packet delay. This is due to the fact that OLSR is a proactive protocol, and when a packet arrives at a node, it is immediately served or dropped. Buffering enables OLSR to have a higher throughput than reactive protocols. Another obvious reason was that Transmission Control Protocol (TCP) traffic requires a route from the source to the destination and vice versa, which is demanding more from reactive protocols. Such routes are provided by OLSR [285].

Effect of Packet Length (Traffic Load)

The packet length plays an important role toward scalability of routing protocols. Figures 11.39 to 11.42 show that not all routing protocols reacted as much to varying traffic loads as to node mobility.

In a small network ($N = 10$ nodes), both AODV and OLSR have performed well (Figure 11.40). In an in-depth perspective in scenario 7, OLSR, TORA, and DSR did not react to varying packet lengths. AODV, however, does react by increasing throughputs. The reaction is favored toward mobility since AODV behaves in the same manner as TORA by increasing performance when node speed increases. AODV, being an improvement from DSR and DSDV, turns out to be a highly versatile protocol in such an environment. Furthermore, AODV outperforms other routing protocols, including DSR, in heavy traffic load situations in small networks [193]. AODV has difficulty when nodes are moving at a fast pace, as stated in [184]; however, in small networks where nodes are moving fast with a heavy traffic load, AODV performs better.

In a medium-sized network ($N = 50$ nodes), however, the performance is different; TORA and OLSR showed higher performance. Due to the impact of the number of nodes and mobility present in the network, all routing protocols reacted to data traffic. Both TORA and AODV have better performance as traffic increases, but DSR and OLSR do not. In scenarios 8 and 9, the combined node mobility and traffic load has affected the system performance. While mobility does not favor both DSR and OLSR, adding more traffic loads to the protocol decreases network performance further. On the other hand, DSR properties resulted in a higher-throughput performance for a large network ($N = 100$ nodes) and high-mobility environment.

By looking at Figure 11.40, one can observe that TORA and DSR performed well in a large network as traffic load increased. DSR responded well to higher traffic load and higher mobility than compared to those of lower traffic loads. Two subjects that would favor this reaction are (1) when connections are established, they ensure that the packets are delivered to the destination; and (2) being in a large network, and in a confined space, keeping an alternative route always pays off since there will always be a node (route) available to transfer data packets.

TORA and AODV are in favor of mobility; therefore, when the packet length increases, performance also increases. Since TORA supports multiple routes, multicasting allows TORA to perform well in high traffic loads [182]. OLSR, on the other hand, maintains a linear performance and a lower delay in all network sizes.

Figure 11.39 demonstrates the impact of joint packet length and network size on the performance of OLSR, AODV, DSR, and TORA. Packet delay in a medium-sized network for TORA is different from the delays in a large network. The reason is that in a medium-sized network, the delay increases as traffic load increases, and in a large network, delay decreases as throughput increases. AODV, however, kept a lower delay as routing load increased. This suggests that TORA may not be as good as AODV for a medium-sized network.

VALIDATION OF SIMULATION RESULTS

A credible network simulator may produce invalid results if the simulation parameters are not correctly configured. Therefore, simulation model validation becomes an important part of any simulation study. The OPNET simulation model presented in this chapter was verified in several ways. First, the detailed status information was traced throughout the simulation to verify the model. Second, the simulation model was validated by setting up a test bed using 802.11b/g wireless laptops [163]. A good match between simulation and test bed results for $N = 2$ to 4 nodes validates the simulation model. In addition, OPNET results were compared with the results obtained from ns-2 [286], and a good match between two sets of results further validated the simulation models.

FURTHER READING

For more details about subjects discussed in this chapter, we recommend the following books and references. The items in [] refer to the reference list at the end of the book.

Books

    [171] Chapter 4—*Computer Networking: A Top-Down Approach* by Kurose and Ross

Research Papers

    [80]

    [288–293]

SUMMARY

This chapter investigated the impact of routing protocols on WLAN performance by extensive simulation experiments. The effect of network size, node mobility, and traffic load on AODV, DSR, TORA, and OLSR is thoroughly examined and reported. The results obtained show that mobility is one of the contributing factors affecting the performance of all four routing protocols studied. The network size is the other factor that affects the overall system performance. In the presence of node mobility routing protocols have mixed reactions. The throughput performance of routing protocols varies from one scenario to another. The main findings are summarized in Figure 11.43, and one can select the best routing protocol that performed well in the given experimental scenarios. The performance improvement of WLAN using the cross-layer design approach is presented in Chapter 12.

KEY TERMS

Ad Hoc On-Demand Distance Vector
 (AODV)
DCF interframe space (DIFS)
Distributed coordination function (DCF)
Dynamic Source Routing (DSR)
IEEE 802.11
Mobile ad hoc network (MANET)
Node density
Node mobility
OPNET
Optimized Link State Routing (OLSR)

Packet delay
Packet length
Retransmission attempt
Routing load
Routing protocol
Simulation
Temporally Ordered Routing Algorithm
 (TORA)
Throughput
Traffic load
Wireless local area network (WLAN)

REVIEW QUESTIONS

1. The network size (i.e., number of nodes) may affect the performance of routing protocols. Discuss the effect of network size on the performance of OLSR, AODV, DSR, and TORA.

2. The node mobility affects the performance of MANET routing protocols. Discuss the effect of node mobility on the performance of OLSR, AODV, DSR, and TORA.

3. The packet length may affect the performance of MANET routing protocols. Discuss the effect of packet length on the performance of OLSR, AODV, DSR, and TORA.

4. Discuss the joint effect of network size and mobility on OLSR, AODV, DSR, and TORA.

5. Explain under what conditions OLSR performs better than AODV, DSR, and TORA.

6. Explain under what conditions AODV performs better than DSR.

MINI-PROJECTS

The following mini-projects aim to provide a deeper understanding of the topics covered in this chapter using empirical study.

1. The purpose of this project is to develop a sound knowledge of simulation modeling of MANET routing protocols. Develop a simulation model to study the performance of AODV, DSR, TORA, and OLSR.

2. Develop an algorithm (e.g., pseudocode or flowchart) for an improved routing protocol by combining the advantages of AODV, DSR, TORA, and OLSR.

3. Extend the work presented in the "Experiment's Results" section by conducting the following simulation experiments. In all experiments consider an 802.11g ad hoc network, Poisson packet arrivals, and User Datagram Protocol (UDP) traffic.

Experiment	Station	Packet Length (bytes)	Node Mobility (m/s)
1	10	1,000, 10,000, 50,000, 100,000	0
2	50	1,000, 10,000, 50,000, 100,000	5
3	100	1,000, 10,000, 50,000, 100,000	10
4	200	1,000, 10,000, 50,000, 100,000	50
5	500	1,000, 10,000, 50,000, 100,000	100

4. **Verification of OPNET results:** Verify OPNET simulation results presented in the "Experiment's Results" section using another simulator (e.g., ns-2).

CHAPTER 12

Improving WLAN Performance Using CLD Optimization

LEARNING OUTCOMES

After reading and completing this chapter, you will be able to:

- Explain the importance of channel bit error rate (BER) in 802.11 networks

- Describe the principle of operation of the channel-aware buffer unit multiple access (C-BUMA) protocol

- Describe the proposed cross-layer design (CLD) framework and algorithms

- Discuss the benefits and practical implications of the proposed CLD framework

- Develop a simulation model to study the performance of the proposed CLD

INTRODUCTION

The effect of radio propagation environments and wireless medium access control (MAC) protocols on WLAN performance was examined in Chapters 7 and 9, respectively. Traditionally, for reasons of design simplicity, the physical layer (PHY) operation was considered separately from MAC layer communications. However, in recent times it has been recognized that performance gains can be achieved by adjusting MAC protocols to suit the changing conditions of the PHY layer. This chapter proposes a joint PHY-MAC CLD framework for improving WLAN performance. The proposed CLD is based on a C-BUMA protocol. The effect of channel BER on WLAN performance is investigated in the "Effect of Channel BER on WLAN Performance" section. The implementation of BER in ns-2.31 and the performance results are also discussed in this section. The proposed CLD framework is described in the "Proposed PHY-MAC Layer Design Framework" section. The framework integrates radio propagation modeling (i.e., the PHY) and the C-BUMA protocol. The idea is to determine the status of the wireless channel and to share this knowledge with the MAC protocol, so that the network can operate efficiently even in harshly interfering environments. The performance of the proposed CLD framework is evaluated by simulation in the "Performance Evaluation" section. The validation of simulation models is outlined in the "Simulation Model Verification" section, and a brief summary concludes the chapter.

EFFECT OF CHANNEL BER ON WLAN PERFORMANCE

WLAN performance is strongly affected by channel BER. Increasing BER would result in lower throughput and higher packet delays. Although ns-2 supports various radio propagation and error models, it supports neither BER nor signal-to-noise ratio (SNR), which are important parameters that need to be considered when simulating real WLAN scenarios [294, 295].

The earlier version of ns-2 had free-space and two-ray ground reflection propagation models only. The shadowing model was added in the later version of ns-2. These propagation models are used to compute the received signal power (Pr) of each packet in WLAN simulations. The free-space model is based on the assumption of wave propagation in an environment without any obstacles (i.e., line-of-sight [LOS] path exists). The two-ray ground model is used when an LOS path exists and reflection of the ground is considered.

Ns-2 uses carrier sense threshold (CSThresh) and receive threshold (RXThresh) to determine whether a frame is received correctly. If Pr < CSThresh, the station will discard the frame. If Pr ≥ RXThresh, the frame can be received successfully provided no collision occurs; otherwise, the station will mark the frame as received. If other frames arrive at the receiver simultaneously, it compares the ratio of Pr and Pi (interfering power) to a third threshold, CPThresh (capture threshold). If Pr/Pi ≥ CPThresh, the frame will be received correctly. Otherwise, all frames are discarded because of a frame collision.

Both the free-space and two-ray ground models predict Pr as a deterministic function of distance. They both represent the communication range as an ideal circle. In reality, Pr is a random variable due to multipath propagation effects.

The shadowing model (a realistic model for simulating an office environment) consists of two parts. The first part of the model is called the path loss model. It predicts the mean received power at distance d. It uses a short distance d_0 as a reference. The second part of the shadowing model reflects the variation of the received power at a given distance, which is a lognormal random variable (i.e., Gaussian distribution if measured in dB). More details about radio propagation modeling can be found in [27]. The formulae for these propagation models can be found in Appendix A (Table A.1).

Relationship between BER and FER

The BER of distributed coordination function (DCF) channels is a function of SNR and a modulation scheme or transmission rate.

$$BER = \int (SNR, Data\ rate) \tag{12.1}$$

The curves of BER versus SNR can be derived theoretically or empirically.

Frame error rate (FER), the probability that a frame is corrupted due to transmission error, is given by [209, 211]

$$FER = 1 - (1 - BER/b)L \tag{12.2}$$

where L is the frame length (in bits) and b is the burst length (in bits). The value of b depends on the SNR; $b = 3.3$ provides a good approximation over a range of SNR values [209].

For a frame length of 1,024 bytes,

$$0.08\ FER \cong 10^{-5}\ BER \tag{12.3}$$

since $[8/100\ (errors/frame)]/[1,024\ (bytes) \times 8\ (bits)] \cong 1/100,000$ errors/ bits $= 10^{-5}$ BER.

Implementation of BER in Ns-2.31

The motivation for implementing a wireless channel BER in ns-2.31 (ns-2.31 was the most recent version of the simulation package at the time of this work) was to verify the accuracy of ns-2.31 results and to model CLD (described in the proposed "PHY-MAC Layer Design" framework section) more accurately. To implement BER in ns-2, it was necessary to compute SNR since BER is a function of SNR.

SNR for a received frame is computed in the MAC module using Equation (12.4). If more frames arrive while one is being received, the SNR is computed using Equation (12.5).

$$SNR = 10\log\frac{P_r}{TN} \tag{12.4}$$

$$SNR = 10\log\frac{P_r}{TN + \sum_{i=1}^{i-1} P_i} \tag{12.5}$$

where P_r is the received signal power, P_i is the interfering power from other frames, and TN is the receiver thermal noise.

Receiver sensitivity is the received signal power in which BER is less than 10^{-5}. To achieve this BER, SNR should be approximately 10 dB. So, one can calculate the receiver's noise from receiver sensitivity. The simulation parameters are based on the Orinoco 802.11b card [296]. The specification for this card, including receiver sensitivity, can be found in Appendix C (Table C.6).

BER is computed using empirical curves from the Intersil specification for its chipset HFA3861B [297]. Once BER is known, FER can be computed using (12.3) to determine whether a frame is received correctly. The relationship between BER, SNR, and modulation of the Intersil HFA3861B chipset can be found in Appendix C (Table C.7).

To implement SNR, BER, and FER in ns-2.31, five error models were written in Tool Command Language (TCL) scripts. The work involved rewriting the code provided by Xiuchao [298]. Table 12.1 lists the contributed error models and their brief description. A sample of the contributed code for the implementation of channel BER can be found in [299].

TABLE 12.1 Ns-2.31 Contributed Error Models and Their Description

Error Model	Description
ErrorModel80211 noise1_ -104	Used for 802.11b at 1 Mbps; BPSK
	Receiver noise floor is –104 dBm
ErrorModel80211 noise2_ -101	Used for 802.11b at 2 Mbps; QPSK
	Receiver noise floor is –101 dBm
ErrorModel80211 noise55_ -97	Used for 802.11b at 5.5 Mbps; CCK5.5
	Receiver noise floor is –97 dBm
ErrorModel80211 noise11_ -92	Used for 802.11b at 11 Mbps; CCK11
	Receiver noise floor is –92 dBm
ErrorModel80211 shortpreamble_ 1	Used for transmitting preamble of 802.11b at 1 Mbps (BPSK)

Performance Results

A simulation model was developed using ns-2.31 to study the effect of wireless channel BER on the performance of a typical DCF single-hop ad hoc network (with and without request to send–clear to send [RTS-CTS] mechanisms). The modeling assumptions are essentially the same as described in Chapter 9 (in the "Modeling Assumptions" section). Recall that all stations are stationary and communicate directly using identical half-duplex systems based on DCF. The data rate is set at 11 Mbps. Data packets of lengths 512 and 1,500 bytes are generated at the stations according to the Pareto ON-OFF (Pareto) distribution. The shadowing propagation model (a realistic model for indoor radio propagation environments) is used with $\sigma = 7$ dB. All sources and receivers have an omnidirectional antenna height of 1.5 m. Hidden and exposed station problems are not considered. Both Transmission Control Protocol (TCP) and User Datagram Protocol (UDP) streams are used as network traffic content, and the source-destination pairs for each stream are randomly chosen from the set of 10 stations. A total of nine concurrent streams are competing for MAC access.

In the simulation experiments, the offered load varies from 10 to 100% to study the impact of ns-2.31 channel BER on traffic load. All simulation results report the steady-state behavior of the network and were obtained with a relative statistical error ≤1%, at the 99% confidence level. Each simulation run lasted for 10 min of simulated time, where the first minute was the transient period. The observations collected during the transient period are not included in the final simulation results. Four important network performance metrics, network throughput, packet delay, mean deviation of throughput (MDT) fairness, and packet drop ratio, are used

TABLE 12.2 Effect of BER on Throughput of 802.11b DCF ($N = 10$ stations; Pareto packet arrivals; shadowing propagation model with $\sigma = 7$ dB)

Offered Load (%)	Traffic Type	Packet Length (bytes)	Mean Throughput (Mbps)			
			Without RTS-CTS		With RTS-CTS	
			BER	Without BER	BER	Without BER
20	UDP	512	1.161	1.161	0.966	0.966
		1,500	1.234	1.234	1.181	1.181
50	UDP	512	2.378	2.410	2.714	2.792
		1,500	2.790	2.830	2.877	2.877
60	UDP	512	2.177	2.348	3.423	3.247
		1,500	2.948	3.060	3.115	3.115
80	UDP	512	2.362	2.374	3.664	3.482
		1,500	3.114	3.202	4.003	3.836
90	UDP	512	1.760	2.363	3.687	4.208
		1,500	2.892	3.290	4.487	4.881
All loads	TCP	512	0.529	0.529	0.538	0.538
		1,500	1.427	1.561	1.157	1.157

in this study. A brief description of these metrics can be found in Chapter 4 ("MAC Protocol Performance Issues" section).

The summaries of empirical results for the effect of BER and transport protocols (TCP/UDP) on network mean throughput and packet delay are presented in Tables 12.2 and 12.3, respectively. Table 12.2 shows that network mean throughput is slightly higher for 1,500-byte packets than for 512-byte packets, for both TCP and UDP traffic. This throughput behavior is expected because proportionally larger payloads are sent through longer packets than through shorter packets. It is observed that the mean throughput for an 802.11b network without RTS-CTS is slightly higher than the throughput obtained with RTS-CTS for TCP, but not with UDP. The difference in mean throughput with and without BER is insignificant.

Table 12.3 shows that network mean packet delay is also slightly higher for 1,500-byte packets than for 512-byte packets, for TCP but not for UDP. It is also observed that the mean packet delay is better (i.e., lower packet delays) with RTS-CTS than without for both TCP and UDP. The difference in packet delays with and without BER is insignificant for TCP, but not with UDP.

The empirical results for the effect of BER and transport protocols on MDT fairness and packet drop ratios are summarized in Tables 12.4 and

TABLE 12.3   Effect of BER on Packet Delay of 802.11b DCF (N = 10 stations; Pareto packet arrivals; shadowing propagation model with σ = 7 dB)

			Mean Packet Delay (ms)			
		Packet	**Without RTS-CTS**		**With RTS-CTS**	
Offered	**Traffic**	**Length**		**Without**		**Without**
Load (%)	**Type**	**(bytes)**	**BER**	**BER**	**BER**	**BER**
20	UDP	512	2.512	2.512	1.414	1.414
		1,500	4.153	4.153	2.850	2.850
50	UDP	512	4398.603	179.364	8.450	9.259
		1,500	69.394	31.358	3.744	3.744
60	UDP	512	5105.161	208.484	709.640	50.917
		1,500	1051.899	177.764	5.800	5.800
80	UDP	512	10847.367	363.829	4757.241	114.956
		1,500	4446.027	259.308	86.728	44.081
90	UDP	512	7810.692	301.965	3441.569	155.056
		1,500	7237.782	338.616	1074.453	118.356
All loads	TCP	512	4.780	4.780	2.407	2.407
		1,500	6.559	8.662	3.215	3.215

TABLE 12.4   Effect of BER on MDT Fairness of 802.11b DCF (N = 10 stations; Pareto packet arrivals; shadowing propagation model with σ = 7 dB)

			MDT Fairness			
		Packet	**Without RTS-CTS**		**With RTS-CTS**	
Offered	**Traffic**	**Length**		**Without**		**Without**
Load (%)	**Type**	**(bytes)**	**BER**	**BER**	**BER**	**BER**
20	UDP	512	0.033	0.033	0.026	0.026
		1,500	0.022	0.022	0.020	0.020
50	UDP	512	0.042	0.046	0.034	0.053
		1,500	0.040	0.038	0.073	0.073
60	UDP	512	0.068	0.061	0.072	0.054
		1,500	0.040	0.037	0.028	0.028
80	UDP	512	0.094	0.086	0.051	0.082
		1,500	0.121	0.093	0.084	0.157
90	UDP	512	0.073	0.101	0.163	0.089
		1,500	0.106	0.081	0.099	0.097
All loads	TCP	512	0.027	0.027	0.023	0.023
		1,500	0.062	0.078	0.058	0.058

TABLE 12.5   Effect of BER on Packet Drop Ratio of 802.11b DCF ($N = 10$ stations; Pareto packet arrivals; shadowing propagation model with $\sigma = 7$ dB)

Offered Load (%)	Traffic Type	Packet Length (bytes)	Packet Drop Ratio			
			Without RTS-CTS		With RTS-CTS	
			BER	Without BER	BER	Without BER
20	UDP	512	0.012	0.012	0.017	0.017
		1,500	0.011	0.011	0.011	0.011
50	UDP	512	0.161	0.178	0.015	0.014
		1,500	0.026	0.016	0.013	0.013
60	UDP	512	0.363	0.274	0.046	0.046
		1,500	0.083	0.180	0.014	0.014
80	UDP	512	0.566	0.522	0.187	0.191
		1,500	0.290	0.317	0.096	0.121
90	UDP	512	0.570	0.514	0.169	0.274
		1,500	0.457	0.383	0.098	0.130
All loads	TCP	512	0.006	0.006	0	0
		1,500	0	0.012	0	0

12.5, respectively. Table 12.4 shows that MDT fairness is slightly better for 512-byte packets than for 1,500-byte packets, for TCP but not for UDP. It is observed that the MDT fairness is better with RTS-CTS than without for both TCP and UDP. Table 12.5 shows that the network packet drop ratio is slightly better (i.e., fewer packets are dropped) for 1,500-byte packets than for 512-byte packets, for both TCP and UDP. As with MDT fairness, the mean packet drop ratio is better with RTS-CTS than without for both TCP and UDP. This is because packets are dropped infrequently with RTS-CTS, especially under medium to high traffic loads. It is observed that the difference, both in MDT fairness and packet drop ratio, with and without BER is insignificant for TCP and UDP.

Overall, the impact of BER on system performance is found to be insignificant. This suggests that the recent versions of ns-2 (2.31 and later) are a good network simulator and provide credible results.

Comparative Analysis

For better comparison and interpretation, the empirical results presented in Tables 12.2 to 12.5 are analyzed in this section. The summary of comparative analysis is shown in Figure 12.1.

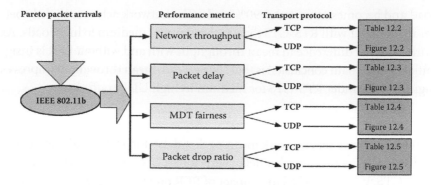

FIGURE 12.1   Effect of channel BER and transport protocols on the performance of an 802.11b ad hoc network (10 stations; packet length: 1,500 bytes; shadowing).

Impact of BER on Network Throughput

Table 12.2 shows that for TCP, network throughput is unaffected by traffic loads and that BER reduces throughput. A maximum throughput of 1.55 Mbps was achieved when neither RTS-CTS nor BER was used. Throughput using RTS-CTS fares the worst; in that case, BER's impact on the mean throughput is insignificant (see also Appendix D, Figure D.1).

The effect of BER on network mean throughput for UDP traffic is illustrated in Figure 12.2. The network mean throughput increases with traffic

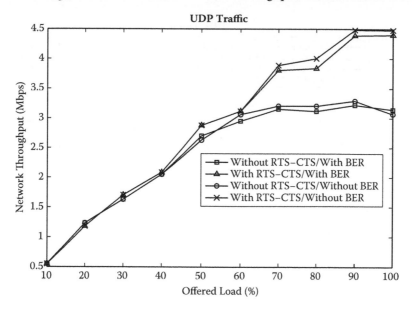

FIGURE 12.2   Network throughput versus load for UDP traffic.

load and becomes saturated at 90% loads. The network achieves slightly better throughput with RTS-CTS than without under medium to high loads. As with TCP, the difference in mean throughput with and without BER is insignificant. The main conclusion is that the network mean throughput improves significantly under RTS-CTS for medium to high UDP traffic loads.

Impact of BER on Packet Delay

Table 12.3 shows that network mean packet delay for TCP is independent of traffic load. The mean packet delay with RTS-CTS is less than that without RTS-CTS. With RTS-CTS the impact of BER on mean packet delay is insignificant. However, without RTS-CTS the mean packet delay with BER is slightly less than that without BER (see also Appendix D, Figure D.2).

The effect of BER on network mean packet delay for UDP streams is illustrated in Figure 12.3. The mean packet delay increases with traffic load, especially under medium to high loads. The packet delay increases with BER. The lowest mean packet delay is achieved with RTS-CTS but without BER. This packet delay characteristic is expected because BER causes packet retransmission and therefore increases mean packet delays.

The main conclusion to be drawn is that if UDP is used instead of TCP, the mean packet delay degrades significantly under high traffic loads. The UDP source does not adapt to network traffic congestion, and therefore it

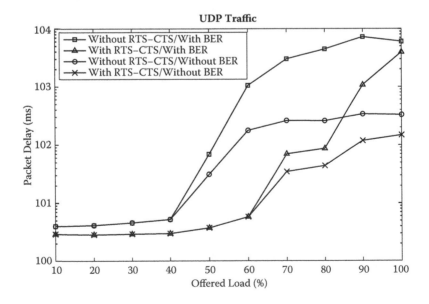

FIGURE 12.3   Network mean packet delay versus load for UDP traffic.

wastes transmission bandwidth by sending packets that will not reach the destination stations, causing packet delay degradation.

Impact of BER on Network Fairness

Table 12.4 shows that network MDT fairness is independent of traffic load. The network achieves better fairness (in terms of lower MDT) with RTS-CTS than without. The difference in MDT fairness with and without BER using RTS-CTS is insignificant, but not without RTS-CTS. Clearly, BER in the ns-2.31 with RTS-CTS improves network fairness (see also Appendix D, Figure D.3).

Figure 12.4 plots MDT fairness against traffic loads for UDP. The MDT fairness is found to be sensitive to traffic load. The network suffers severe unfairness for RTS-CTS without BER at 80% loads.

The main conclusion to be drawn is that 802.11b DCF networks with and without RTS-CTS and BER achieve slightly better MDT fairness for TCP and UDP.

Impact of BER on Packet Drop Ratio

Table 12.5 shows that mean packet drop ratios are independent of traffic load. DCF without RTS-CTS using BER achieves better packet drop ratios (in terms of less packets being dropped) than without BER. However, the

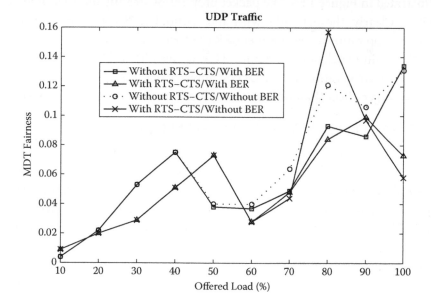

FIGURE 12.4 MDT fairness versus load for UDP traffic.

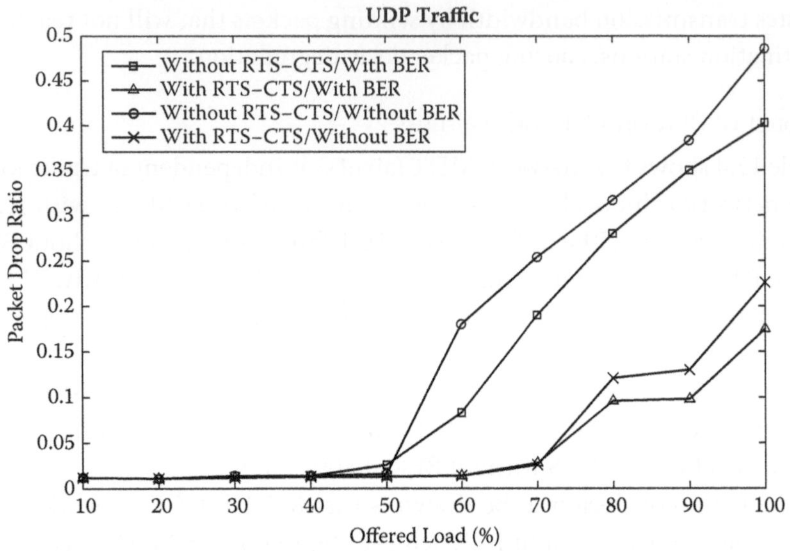

FIGURE 12.5 Network mean packet drop ratio versus load for UDP traffic.

RTS-CTS achieves the same superior performance with and without BER (see also Appendix D, Figure D.4).

The effect of BER on network mean packet drop ratios for UDP traffic is illustrated in Figure 12.5. The packet drop ratios steadily increase at loads >50%. Clearly, the networks with and without RTS-CTS achieve better packet drop ratios using channel BER than without BER.

The main conclusion is that for TCP, either RTS-CTS or BER reduces the packet drop ratio, and for UDP it appears that RTS-CTS has a significantly larger effect than BER on the reduction of the packet drop ratio.

PROPOSED PHY-MAC LAYER DESIGN FRAMEWORK

Figure 12.6 shows a block diagram of the proposed PHY-MAC-based CLD framework. The proposed CLD framework differs from the earlier work described in the "CLD Optimization: A Review of Literature" section. In the framework, radio propagation modeling (i.e., PHY layer) and the MAC protocol are integrated into one single layer. The propagation modeling predicts the wireless channel state and shares the channel status information (CSI) with the channel-aware MAC protocol (discussed later in this section), so that the MAC protocol can operate and maintain a better quality of service (QoS) even in the harsh propagation environments. Having access to the CSI before transmitting a packet, the MAC protocol

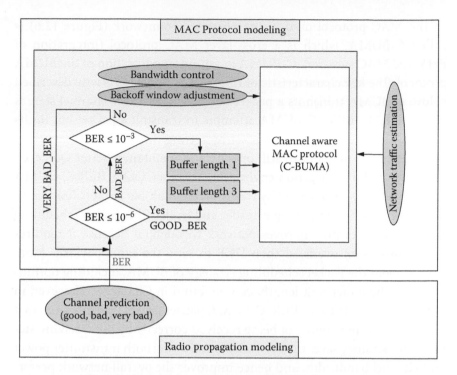

FIGURE 12.6 The proposed PHY-MAC layer design framework for WLANs.

can estimate whether the channel is good enough to guarantee a successful transmission.

The receiving station can easily determine the channel status by examining the received signal's BER. The channel's BER can be indicated in DCF by setting a special flag (i.e., control bits) in the packet trailer. However, to investigate the impact of BER on WLAN performance, it is important to classify the wireless channel state based on BER. To achieve this objective, the wireless channel states are classified into three categories: good, bad, and very bad. Table 12.6 lists the definitions of the three channel states.

TABLE 12.6   Three States of a Channel

Channel Status	Definition
Good	The wireless link is relatively "clean" and is characterized by a very small BER, which is denoted by GOOD_BER.
Bad	The wireless link is in a condition characterized by increased BER (in the order of 10^{-6} to 10^{-3}), which is denoted by BAD_BER [142].
Very bad	The BER is greater than 10^{-3}, denoted by VERYBAD_BER.

The MAC protocol used in the proposed framework (Figure 12.6) is called C-BUMA, which is a cross-layer MAC protocol (integration of PHY and MAC sublayer). C-BUMA is a minor modification of the BUMA protocol. The key characteristic of this MAC protocol is briefly described below. C-BUMA transmits a packet based on CSI. If the channel state is bad (i.e., BAD_BER), C-BUMA attempts to transmit a packet but limits the packet scheduling to one packet by setting the buffer unit length to one. Hence, the system can still operate and maintain a better QoS even in a harsh radio propagation environment. For a GOOD_BER, C-BUMA properly utilizes the channel by transmitting multiple packets (for example, three packets) with a single header and trailer. This packet scheduling strategy significantly improves network throughput because it requires less transmission overhead than DCF to send the same payload. More details about the packet scheduling strategy of BUMA, including optimization of the buffer unit length, can be found in Chapter 9. However, in the case of a VERYBAD_BER, C-BUMA pauses packet transmission, as it has a very low probability of being received correctly by the receiving station. This strategy saves the network from wasting both transmitter power and channel bandwidth, and hence improves the overall network performance. The pseudocode of the CLD algorithms is described next.

Cross-Layer Design Algorithms

For the implementation of the proposed CLD framework, two algorithms, namely, channel prediction and the MAC protocol modeling, are described below. A sample of contributed code for the implementation of CLD in ns-2.31 can be found in [299].

Channel prediction modeling: Figure 12.7 outlines the channel prediction algorithm. This algorithm estimates the channel state based on received signal strength (RSS) values. Under a slow Rayleigh-fading channel the duration of the channel being good is generally longer than the packet transmission time.

Using the prediction, the receiving station can determine whether the packet will be received correctly in the next transmission round. The accuracy of the prediction algorithm depends on how BER is interpreted at the receiving station. As shown in Figure 12.7, the proposed channel prediction algorithm is simple and does not require extensive computation. Therefore, it is easy to implement in real systems.

```
Get channel BER from the received signal;
if (BER ≤ 10⁻⁶)
  channel_state = GOOD_BER;
else if (BER ≤ 10⁻³)
  channel_state = BAD_BER;
else
  channel_state = VERYBAD_BER;
Share the channel state information with the MAC
protocol; //(Fig. 12.8)
```

FIGURE 12.7 The pseudocode of the channel prediction algorithm.

MAC protocol modeling: The 802.11 networks are slotted where a station is allowed to transmit a packet at the beginning of an empty slot and the slot length is equivalent to a packet transmission time. A slot can be either busy or empty. A single bit (B) in the header represents slot status. An empty slot has $B = 0$ and a slot carrying a packet has $B = 1$. Table 12.7 defines the two types of slot.

Figure 12.8 outlines the transmission control algorithm to be executed at each active station on the network. The proposed C-BUMA schedules a packet for transmission based on the knowledge of CSI obtained from the received packet. As mentioned earlier, this channel-aware MAC protocol improves the network performance further by scheduling three packets (optimum buffer unit length) for stations that gain network access in good channel states.

When the channel state is bad (BAD_BER), the C-BUMA transmits a single packet by setting the buffer unit length to one (as DCF). However, when the channel is in a fade (VERYBAD_BER), there would not be any viable communication between the source and the destination. Therefore, source/destination suspends the transmission for an average fade duration, which depends on the Doppler frequency and the root mean square

TABLE 12.7 Busy and Empty Slot

Slot Status	Definition
Busy	A slot is occupied carrying a packet.
Empty	A slot does not carry a packet at present; can be used for future transmission.

```
Begin
  Get CSI from the channel prediction algorithm
  (Fig. 12.7);
  Get network traffic information;
  Generate one empty slot (B = 0) during each unit
  of time;
  if (channel_state) = GOOD_BER;
    Begin
      buffer length = 3; //optimum buffer unit
       length
      slot_status = busy;
      Transmit multiple packets;
    End
  else if (channel_state) = BAD_BER;
    Begin
      buffer length = 1; //same as 802.11b DCF
      slot_status = busy;
      Transmit a single packet;
    End
  else
    Pause packet transmissions;
  Wait for the next empty slot;
End
```

FIGURE 12.8   The pseudocode of the transmission control algorithm executed at each active station.

(RMS) value of the received power [227]. The notification of the incoming fade can be implemented in DCF by setting a special flag in the header of the CTS packet or the acknowledgement (ACK) packet. Upon hearing this CTS the neighboring stations set their network allocation vectors (NAVs) to the fade duration. The channel can then be released for other transmissions. The basic operations of the CLD algorithms are illustrated in Figure 12.9.

Benefits and Practical Implications of the Proposed CLD Method

It is well known that the wireless channel state varies over time and space, and the received signal can go into deep fades [27]. If the proposed CLD is not used, the MAC sublayer is not notified about the wireless channel status. Therefore, transmitter (Tx) keeps sending packets that are discarded as a result of weak RSS values at receiver (Rx). In the worst-case scenario,

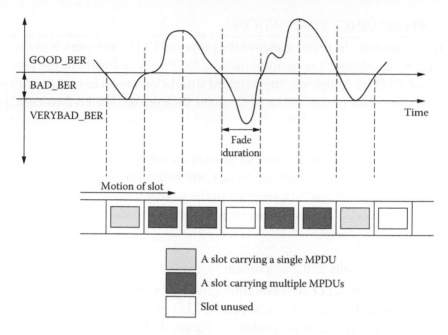

FIGURE 12.9 (SEE COLOR INSERT.) Illustrating the basic operation of the CLD algorithms. MPDU = MAC protocol data unit.

the Tx stops receiving ACKs from the Rx and eventually invokes a backoff. The Tx then starts retransmitting these packets, and if the channel state is very bad, it discards the packets permanently after the specified number of allowed retries.

Therefore, using the proposed CLD approach, one can obtain the following improvements. First, it prevents the sender from unnecessary transmissions, which leads to the reduction of power consumption for transmission. Second, it saves transmission bandwidth that can be used for transmitting payload, and hence higher network throughput can be achieved. Furthermore, the proposed CLD approach avoids packet retransmissions (having knowledge of the CSI), again reducing power consumption and saving bandwidth [107]. The channel prediction and the transmission control algorithms outlined in Figures 12.7 and 12.8, respectively, considerably improve the network performance (e.g., higher throughput and lower mean packet delay), as is evident from the simulation results presented in the "Performance Evaluation" section. The proposed CLD framework is simple and can be implemented easily without changing any existing DCF hardware.

PERFORMANCE EVALUATION

In this section, the performance of the proposed CLD framework is evaluated by simulation. The performances of DCF with and without the proposed CLD are compared. The standard simulation model in ns-2.31 with BER (described in the "Effect of Channel BER on WLAN Performance" section) is used for modeling DCF. The CLD was evaluated by measuring network mean throughput, packet delay, MDT fairness, and packet drop ratio. Recall that a wireless ad hoc network with $N = 10$ stations, Pareto packet arrivals, data packet length of 1,500 bytes, and shadowing propagation model with $\sigma = 7$ dB are used in the simulations. As previously, all simulation results were obtained with a relative statistical error ≤1%, at a 99% confidence level.

Simulation Results and Comparison

For TCP traffic, CLD increases throughput by about 13% at all loadings (Appendix D, Figure D.5). The impact of CLD on network mean throughput for UDP traffic is illustrated in Figure 12.10. The network mean throughput increases with traffic load and becomes saturated at 90% loads. Again, the CLD provides higher throughput than the network without

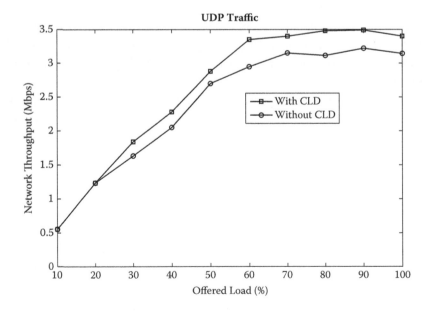

FIGURE 12.10 Network mean throughput with and without CLD for UDP traffic.

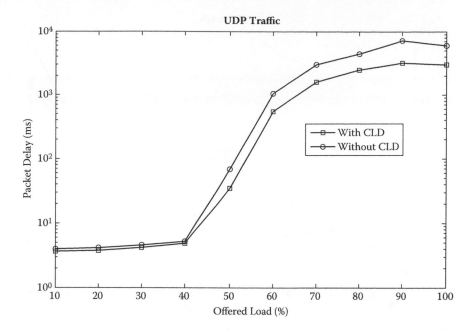

FIGURE 12.11   Network mean packet delay with and without CLD for UDP traffic.

CLD, especially under medium to high traffic loads. For example, using CLD in an ad hoc network with $N = 10$ stations, a 60% load throughput can be increased by approximately 12%. The main conclusion is that the CLD improves network mean throughput significantly in an obstructed office environment for both TCP and UDP under medium to high loads.

For TCP traffic, CLD provides about 24% lower mean packet delays at all loads (Appendix D, Figure D.6). The impact of CLD on network mean packet delay for UDP traffic is illustrated in Figure 12.11. The packet delay increases with traffic load and becomes saturated at 90% loads. The CLD approach improves network mean packet delays by 7 to 56%. The main conclusion is that stations using CLD have a substantially lower mean packet delay than stations not using CLD, especially under medium to high loads.

For TCP traffic, CLD improves MDT fairness by about 5% for all loadings (Appendix D, Figure D.7). Figure 12.12 shows that for UDP traffic, CLD improves MTD fairness by up to 40%. The main conclusion is that wireless stations using CLD achieve better MDT fairness than stations without CLD for both TCP and UDP, especially under medium to high loads.

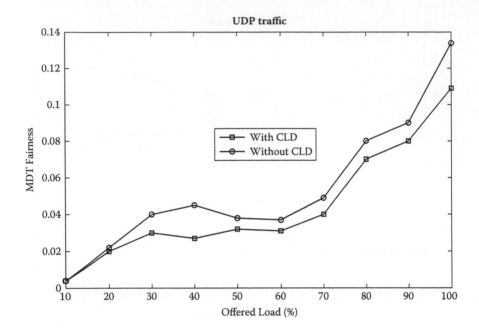

FIGURE 12.12   MDT fairness with and without CLD for UDP traffic.

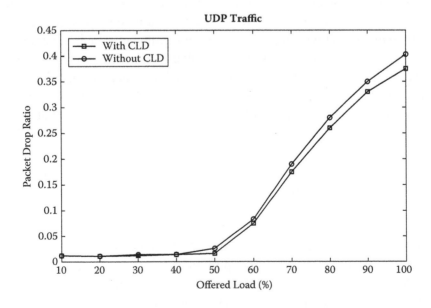

FIGURE 12.13   Packet drop ratio with and without CLD for UDP traffic.

In Figure 12.13, the packet drop ratio with and without CLD is plotted against traffic loads for UDP. About a 38.5% lower packet drop ratio is obtained under CLD at 50% offered load.

Overall Observations and Interpretations

The simulation results presented in the previous section indicate that CLD improves the network mean throughput, packet delay, MDT fairness, and packet drop ratio significantly for both TCP and UDP traffic, especially under medium to high loads. The proposed CLD significantly reduces packet drops, leading to overall network throughput improvement. It is important to note that these improvements are an all-win design because the network does not sacrifice any resources for these performance improvements (apart from the resource for performing the channel prediction).

Table 12.8 shows the impact of CLD on wireless link throughput for both TCP and UDP. The nine connections (source to destination) for a network with $N = 10$ stations are shown in column 1. It shows that CLD improves individual link throughput by 9 to 55% for TCP, and 3 to 43% for UDP. The link throughput improvement for the overall network is approximately 40 and 60% for TCP and UDP, respectively, which is significant.

TABLE 12.8   Link Throughput with and without CLD for TCP and UDP Streams (load: 80%; 9 connections; Pareto packet arrivals; shadowing model with $\sigma = 7$ dB)

| | Link Throughput (Mbps) | | | | | |
| | TCP Traffic | | | UDP Traffic | | |
Link (source to destination)	CLD (Mbps)	Without CLD (Mbps)	Improvement (%)	CLD (Mbps)	Without CLD (Mbps)	Improvement (%)
0->1	0.179	0.162	9.50	0.308	0.24	22.08
0->2	0.187	0.163	12.83	0.444	0.36	18.92
2->3	0.117	0.077	34.19	0.512	0.478	6.64
3->4	0.038	0.017	55.26	0.49	0.476	2.86
4->5	0.254	0.216	14.96	0.36	0.308	14.44
4->6	0.204	0.165	19.12	0.404	0.343	15.10
5->6	0.1	0.08	20.00	0.22	0.187	15.00
5->7	0.09	0.06	33.33	0.344	0.308	10.47
6->7	0.17	0.12	29.41	0.47	0.267	43.19
Overall network	1.7	1.3	40	3.6	3	60

SIMULATION MODEL VERIFICATION

Even though ns-2 is a credible network simulator, it will produce invalid results if the simulation parameters are not correctly configured. The ns-2 simulation model presented in this chapter was verified in several ways. First, the simulation model was validated through real measurements from wireless laptops and APs for 802.11b [94]. A good match between simulation and propagation measurement results validates the simulation model. Second, the function of individual network components and their interactions was checked. The network performance with a single user was tested first, and then the number of users was increased to test the system performance with multiple users. Third, the simulation results reported in this chapter were compared with the work of other network researchers to ensure correctness of the simulation model [220, 227]. In addition, ns-2 results were compared with the results obtained from OPNET Modeler [34], and a good match between two sets of results further validated the simulation models.

FURTHER READING

For more details about subjects discussed in this chapter, we recommend the following books and references. The items in [] refer to the reference list at the end of the book.

Books

[171] Chapter 6—*Computer Networking: A Top-Down Approach* by Kurose and Ross

[172] Chapter 4—*Computer Networks* by Tanenbaum and Wetherall

Research Papers

[208]

[213]

[300]

SUMMARY

Several characteristics pertaining to WLANs make CLD more desirable in WLANs than in wired networks. For accurate modeling of the proposed CLD, a wireless channel BER was implemented in ns-2.31. A detailed comparative analysis of the effect of BER and transport protocols on WLAN performance was presented. Empirical results showed that the wireless ns-2.31 channel BER has minor effects on system performance for both TCP and UDP traffic.

Next, the effect of a joint PHY-MAC layer CLD on the performance of a typical 802.11b network was investigated by simulation. In the simulation model, a 802.11b ad hoc network with $N = 10$ stations, Pareto packet arrivals, shadowing propagation, data packet length of 1,500 bytes, TCP and UDP streams, and offering loads from 10 to 100% were used. The network performance, such as mean throughput, packet delay, MDT fairness, and packet drop ratio, was measured. The proposed CLD integrates the radio propagation (PHY) layer and the MAC sublayer. By sharing channel information with the MAC protocol, the approach reduced unnecessary packet transmissions, and hence reduced bandwidth wastage and significantly improved system performance.

Performance comparisons of DCF with and without CLD were carried out by extensive simulation experiments. Results obtained have shown that the network achieved higher throughput (up to 13.5%), lower mean packet delay (up to 56%), better MDT fairness (up to 40%), and lower packet drop ratio (up to 38%) with CLD. This is a very promising approach considering that it is an all-win design.

The proposed CLD framework is simple and can be implemented easily in 802.11 WLANs without changing any existing hardware infrastructure. For the implementation of the proposed framework, two algorithms, channel prediction and MAC protocol modeling, were presented. The effect of traffic distribution on WLAN performance is investigated in Chapter 13.

KEY TERMS

802.11 networks	MDT fairness
Bit error rate (BER)	Medium access control (MAC)
Channel-aware buffer unit multiple access (C-BUMA)	Packet delay
	Packet dropping
Channel state information (CSI)	Short interframe space (SIFS)
Cross-layer design (CLD)	Throughput
Cyclic redundancy check (CRC)	Transmission Control Protocol (TCP)
Joint PHY-MAC layer framework	User Datagram Protocol (UDP)
MAC protocol data unit (MPDU)	Wireless local area networks (WLANs)

REVIEW QUESTIONS

1. It is well known that wireless channels have higher BER than wired networks. Discuss why the study of BER is important in wireless communication and networking.

2. Channel BER plays a key role in determining the performance of WLANs. Discuss the effect of channel BER on the performance of a typical 802.11 network.

3. C-BUMA is a channel-aware MAC protocol for WLANs. Describe the principle of operation of the C-BUMA protocol.

4. While C-BUMA provides better performance than 802.11 networks, it has some limitations as well. Discuss the strengths and weaknesses of C-BUMA.

5. C-BUMA is based on two algorithms: channel prediction and transmission control. Discuss the channel prediction and transmission control algorithms of C-BUMA.

6. The CLD framework presented in this chapter has practical implications. Discuss the benefits and practical implications of the proposed CLD framework.

MINI-PROJECTS

The following mini-projects aim to provide a deeper understanding of the topics covered in this chapter using empirical study.

1. Investigate the effect of channel BER on WLAN performance by extending the "Effect of Channel BER on WLAN Performance" section.

2. **Analytical modeling:** Develop an analytical model to optimize the proposed CLD framework introduced in the "Proposed PHY-MAC Layer Design Framework" section.

3. **Verification of ns-2 results:** Verify the ns-2 simulation results presented in the "Simulation Results and Comparison" section using another simulator (e.g., OPNET Modeler).

4. **System implementation:** Implement the CLD algorithms presented in the "Cross-Layer Design Algorithms" section in a Linux system.

Effect of Traffic Distribution on WLAN Performance

LEARNING OUTCOMES

After reading and completing this chapter, you will be able to:

- Compare and contrast exponential, Pareto, Poisson, and constant bit rate (CBR) packet arrival processes

- Discuss the impact of packet arrival distribution on 802.11 networks

- Discuss the impact of traffic arrival processes and transport protocols on WLANs

- Develop simulation models to investigate the effect of arrival processes on WLAN performance

INTRODUCTION

The effect of joint physical layer (PHY) and medium access control (MAC) layer design on WLAN performance was presented in Chapter 12. Because the distribution of traffic load strongly impacts the queuing and blocking performance of a network, the choice of the traffic distribution model and transport protocol greatly influences WLAN performance. A good understanding of the impact of traffic arrival distributions and the underlying transport protocols on system performance is required for efficient design and dimensioning of such systems. This chapter aims to analyze (by simulation) the effect of four diverse traffic models (exponential, Pareto

ON-OFF, Poisson, and CBR) on the performance of a typical 802.11b single-hop ad hoc network for Transmission Control Protocol (TCP) and User Datagram Protocol (UDP) streams.

The "Traffic Generators and Arrival Processes" section describes the traffic models used. These traffic models were chosen because of their diverse range of statistical properties and having relatively generic nature, suggesting that they can be used to model a variety of services. In the "Simulation Results and Comparative Analysis" section, empirical results obtained from simulation runs are presented. A detailed comparative analysis of the impact of packet arrival distributions on WLAN performance is also presented in this section. The "System Implications" section discusses system implications. The simulation model is verified in the "Simulation Model Verification" section, and the chapter is summarized in the last section.

TRAFFIC GENERATORS AND ARRIVAL PROCESSES

Traffic generators are needed to automate generation of packets at the stations according to desired statistics and loads. A brief description of exponential, Pareto ON-OFF, Poisson, and CBR packet arrival processes is given below. Examples of the implementation of these processes in ns-2 are also given. More details about traffic models, including packet arrival distributions and their probability density functions, can be found in many wireless communications and simulation analysis textbooks [89, 270].

> **Exponential:** The packets arrive at each station at a fixed rate during the ON periods, and no packets arrive during the OFF periods. Both ON and OFF periods are derived from an exponential distribution. The exponential distribution is very important in the queuing theory that is widely used in studying the performance of computer and data communication networks. For example, the service time of a server can often be assumed to be exponential. In ns-2, the length of packets, the average ON and OFF times, and the packet arrival rate were defined for simulation experiments using the following commands:

```
set exp0 [new Application/Traffic/Exponential]
$exp0 set packetSize_1500  (packet length)
$exp0 set burst_time_ 500ms  (average ON time for
 the generator)
$exp0 set idle_time_ 500ms  (average OFF time for
```

```
the generator)
$exp0 set rate_ 500k  (sending rate during ON times)
```

Pareto ON-OFF: The Pareto ON-OFF (Pareto) distribution is a power curve with two parameters: the shape parameter and the location parameter [301]. The packet arrival process at the stations is similar to the exponential arrival's process, except that both the ON and OFF periods are derived from a Pareto distribution. The packet interarrival times in various real-life services such as Ethernet LAN [302], TELNET, and File Transfer Protocol (FTP) [303] follow the Pareto distribution with a shape parameter ranging from 0.9 to 1.5. In ns-2, the shape of the Pareto distribution was set to 1.4 for the experiment by using the following command:

```
set p [new Application/Traffic/Pareto]
$p set shape_ 1.4  (the shape parameter used by the
 Pareto distribution)
```

Poisson: The packets arrive at each station following an independent process with independent increments, with mean λ_i packets per slot. The packet inter-arrival times are exponentially distributed with mean $1/\lambda_i$. Poisson packet arrival assumptions have been used extensively in the literature to model various telecommunication traffic; however, it has limitations for the modeling of self-similar data traffic [303]. In ns-2, the exponential ON-OFF traffic generator is configured to behave as a Poisson process by setting the variable burst time to 0 and the variable rate to a very large value.

Constant bit rate: In this process, the packets arrive at the stations at a constant rate. This is one of the most simplistic models possible, and it exactly models CBR services (e.g., voice telephony, video-on-demand). Random noise can be introduced to change packet inter-arrival times. In ns-2, the following commands were used to set the parameters, such as maximum number of packets that can be sent, packet sending rate, and a flag to specify random noise:

```
set e [new Application/Traffic/CBR]
$e set maxpkts_10,000  (the maximum number of
 packets to be sent)
```

```
$e set rate_ 64k  (packet sending rate)
$e set random_ 1  (a flag indicating random noise in
the scheduled departure times)
```

SIMULATION RESULTS AND COMPARATIVE ANALYSIS

A simulation model was developed using ns-2.31 to study the effect of packet arrival distributions on the performance of a typical 802.11b single-hop ad hoc network. The modeling assumptions are essentially the same as described in Chapter 9 (the "Modeling Assumptions" section). Recall that all stations are stationary and use half-duplex systems based on the distributed coordination function (DCF) (11 Mbps). Request to send (RTS) and clear to send (CTS) are disabled. The shadowing model with $\sigma = 7$ dB is used to model the signal propagation in the simulations. All sources and receivers have an omnidirectional antenna at height 1.5 m. Hidden and exposed station problems are not included in the simulations. Both TCP and UDP streams of packet length 512 and 1,500 bytes are used and are generated randomly from the set of 10 stations. A total of nine concurrent streams compete for network resources. The four different traffic models, exponential, Pareto, Poisson, and CBR, are used to control the traffic loads. In the simulations, network load is varied from 10 to 100%, and the impact of traffic arrival distributions on network performance is observed. The offered load is the packet arrival rate (measured in packets/s) at the stations. All simulation results report the steady-state behavior of the network and were obtained with a statistical error ≤1%, at the 99% confidence level. Each simulation runs for 10 min (simulated time), where the first minute is the transient period. The data collected during the transient period are excluded in the final results.

The four important network performance metrics, network throughput, mean packet delay, fairness, and packet drop ratio, are used. A brief description of these metrics can be found in Chapter 9. Mean deviation of throughput (MDT) fairness, defined in Equation (9.15), is used to measure the fairness of 802.11b. Recall that MDT fairness is defined as the spread or variation of an individual station's throughput from the networkwide mean throughput. A network protocol is said to be 100% fair if MDT is zero. The packet drop ratio is directly related to packet collision rates, and higher packet collisions at the destination stations result in higher packet drop ratios. A network with a low packet drop ratio is desirable.

Effect of Packet Arrival Distributions on System Performance

This section presents results obtained from simulation runs for an 802.11b network with $N = 10$ stations. The summary of empirical results for the effect of Pareto, Poisson, exponential, and CBR on network performance is presented in Tables 13.1 to 13.4, respectively.

TABLE 13.1   Impact of Pareto on 802.11b ($N = 10$ stations; shadowing model with $\sigma = 7$ dB)

Offered Load (%)	Traffic Type	Packet Length (bytes)	Network Throughput (Mbps)	Packet Delay (ms)	MDT Fairness	Packet Drop Ratio
20	UDP	512	1.161	2.512	0.033	0.012
		1,500	1.234	4.153	0.022	0.011
50	UDP	512	2.310	179.364	0.046	0.178
		1,500	2.630	31.358	0.038	0.016
60	UDP	512	2.348	208.484	0.061	0.274
		1,500	3.060	177.764	0.037	0.180
80	UDP	512	2.374	363.829	0.086	0.522
		1,500	3.202	259.308	0.093	0.317
90	UDP	512	2.363	301.965	0.101	0.514
		1,500	3.290	338.616	0.081	0.383
All loads	TCP	512	0.529	4.780	0.027	0.006
		1,500	1.561	8.662	0.078	0.012

TABLE 13.2   Impact of Poisson on 802.11b ($N = 10$ stations; shadowing model with $\sigma = 7$ dB)

Offered Load (%)	Traffic Type	Packet Length (bytes)	Network Throughput (Mbps)	Packet Delay (ms)	MDT Fairness	Packet Drop Ratio
20	UDP	512	0.072	4.707	0.001	0.011
		1,500	0.191	5.570	0.002	0.012
50	UDP	512	0.073	4.808		0.009
		1,500	0.192	4.666		0.012
60	UDP	512	0.072	4.836		0.009
		1,500	0.205	4.611	Same as 20% load	0.011
80	UDP	512	0.072	4.915		0.009
		1,500	0.195	5.733		0.010
90	UDP	512	0.071	4.938		0.009
		1,500	0.209	5.057		0.011
All loads	TCP	512	0.053	3.101	0.002	0
		1,500	0.149	3.932	0.007	0

TABLE 13.3 Impact of Exponential on 802.11b ($N = 10$ stations; shadowing model with $\sigma = 7$ dB)

Offered Load (%)	Traffic Type	Packet length (bytes)	Network Throughput (Mbps)	Packet Delay (ms)	MDT Fairness	Packet Drop Ratio
20	UDP	512	1.098	2.453	0.009	0.009
		1,500	1.140	3.887	0.011	0.011
50	UDP	512	2.129	173.012	0.036	0.183
		1,500	2.634	36.561	0.026	0.020
60	UDP	512	2.357	255.826	0.044	0.321
		1,500	2.942	143.697	0.047	0.102
80	UDP	512	2.196	327.391	0.065	0.507
		1,500	3.228	297.036	0.072	0.311
90	UDP	512	2.379	325.073	0.055	0.512
		1,500	3.244	325.840	0.066	0.398
All loads	TCP	512	0.455	4.322	0.021	0
		1,500	1.336	7.023	0.064	0.018

Table 13.1 shows that network mean throughput is slightly higher for 1,500-byte packets than for 512-byte packets, for both TCP and UDP. This throughput behavior is expected because proportionally longer payloads are achieved using longer packets, compared to shorter packets. By comparing TCP and UDP, one can observe that the network mean throughput for UDP is better than for TCP. This throughput improvement results from UDP having fewer transmission overheads than TCP (including no acknowledgment [ACK]). By looking at the network mean throughput, packet delay, MDT fairness, and packet drop ratio, one can observe that they are independent of traffic load for TCP, but not for UDP. In fact for UDP, network mean throughput increases while packet delay, MDT fairness, and packet drop ratio deteriorate with increasing traffic load.

The impact of Poisson packet arrivals on system performance is illustrated in Table 13.2. Network performance is independent of traffic load for TCP. For UDP, however, the network throughput increases with traffic load, but this increase is not very significant. Another observation is that the network experiences slightly longer packet delays for UDP than for TCP. This longer delay is expected because the network packet delay increases with throughput due to traffic congestion on the network.

TABLE 13.4   Impact of CBR on 802.11b ($N = 10$ stations; shadowing model with $\sigma = 7$ dB)

Offered Load (%)	Traffic Type	Packet Length (bytes)	Network Throughput (Mbps)	Mean Packet Delay (ms)	MDT Fairness	Packet Drop Ratio
20	TCP	512	1.165	25.040	0.082	0.073
		1,500	1.528	5.087	0.066	0
	UDP	512	2.174	33.958	0.009	0.028
		1,500	2.218	17.472	0.003	0.018
50	TCP	512	1.294	383.976	0.078	0.080
		1,500	2.720	349.797	0.173	0.065
	UDP	512	2.251	482.124	0.126	0.601
		1,500	3.234	483.517	0.166	0.452
60	TCP	512	1.285	358.420	0.082	0.084
		1,500	2.791	420.107	0.169	0.074
	UDP	512	2.356	491.381	0.132	0.655
		1,500	3.289	531.633	0.174	0.546
80	TCP	512	1.310	381.888	0.088	0.073
		1,500	2.868	404.120	0.190	0.083
	UDP	512	2.380	494.578	0.146	0.740
		1,500	3.336	553.773	0.220	0.669
90	TCP	512	1.311	366.104	0.086	0.077
		1,500	2.848	411.086	0.191	0.098
	UDP	512	2.339	492.120	0.128	0.771
		1,500	3.433	560.931	0.233	0.704

The empirical results for the effect of exponential packet arrivals on system performance are summarized in Table 13.3. As with Pareto and Poisson, the network performance for exponential arrivals is independent of traffic load for TCP. For UDP, however, the network throughput improves, while packet delay, MDT fairness, and packet drop ratio deteriorate with increasing traffic load.

The empirical results for the effect of CBR on 802.11b are summarized in Table 13.4. The mean throughput increases slightly, whereas the mean packet delay increases dramatically for both TCP and UDP streams. This dramatic increase in packet delay is due to the characteristic of CBR sources whose constant stream of packets causes traffic congestion. Another observation is that both MDT fairness and packet drop ratio deteriorate slightly for both TCP and UDP.

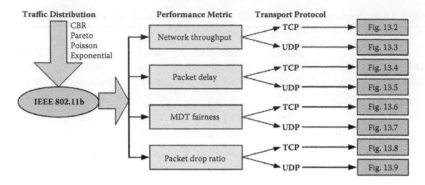

FIGURE 13.1   Effect of traffic arrival distributions and transport protocols on the performance of an 802.11b ad hoc network (10 stations; packet length: 1,500 bytes; shadowing).

Comparative Analysis

For better comparison and interpretation, the empirical results presented in Tables 13.1 to 13.4 are analyzed in this section. The summary of the comparative analyses is shown in Figure 13.1.

Impact of Traffic Arrival Distributions on Network Throughput

In Figure 13.2, the network mean throughput for TCP streams is plotted against traffic loads for exponential, Pareto, Poisson, and CBR packet

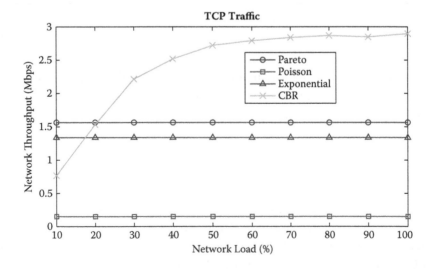

FIGURE 13.2   Mean throughput versus traffic load for TCP traffic ($N = 10$ stations; packet length: 1,500 bytes; propagation model: shadowing with $\sigma = 7$ dB).

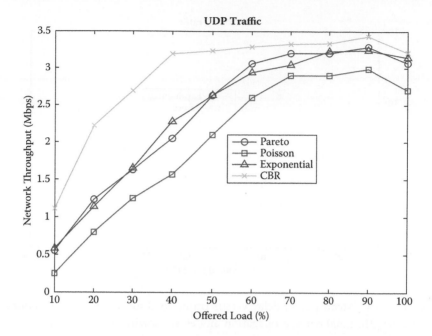

FIGURE 13.3 Mean throughput versus traffic load for UDP traffic ($N = 10$ stations; packet length: 1,500 bytes; propagation model: shadowing with $\sigma = 7$ dB).

arrivals. The network mean throughputs for exponential, Pareto, and Poisson arrivals are almost independent of traffic loads; however, the mean throughput for CBR increases with traffic load. The maximum throughput (2.89 Mbps) is achieved at full loading. One can observe the mean throughput for Pareto is slightly higher than that of exponential. Clearly, the mean throughput is reduced for Poisson arrivals.

The effect of traffic arrival distributions on network mean throughput for UDP traffic is illustrated in Figure 13.3. The network mean throughput for exponential, Pareto, and CBR increases with traffic load and becomes saturated at 90% loads. Of the four traffic arrival distributions used, the network achieves the best mean throughput performance under all loads for CBR and the worst for Poisson.

One can see in Figure 13.2 that for TCP streams, only CBR distribution loading affects throughput, whereas the loading of the others does not affect the throughput. Figures 13.2 and 13.3 show that Poisson and CBR have the largest difference and Pareto and exponential have the smallest difference in their effect. The main conclusion is that if UDP is used instead of TCP, the network mean throughput improves significantly for all traffic arrival distributions considered except Poisson. The network

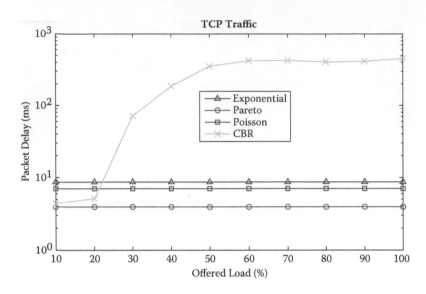

FIGURE 13.4 Mean packet delay versus traffic load for TCP ($N = 10$ stations; packet length: 1,500 bytes; propagation model: shadowing with $\sigma = 7$ dB).

achieves superior and inferior throughput performance for CBR and Poisson, respectively.

Impact of Traffic Arrival Distributions on Network Mean Packet Delay

Figure 13.4 plots network mean packet delay against traffic load for exponential, Pareto, Poisson, and CBR arrivals for TCP. The network mean packet delays for exponential, Pareto, and Poisson processes are almost independent of traffic load, as was the throughput; however, the mean packet delay for CBR increases with traffic load. By comparing the mean packet delays of all four traffic models used, one can observe that the network experiences the shortest mean delays under medium to high loads for Pareto and the longest under CBR.

Figure 13.5 compares network mean packet delays against traffic load for exponential, Pareto, Poisson, and CBR arrivals for UDP streams. The mean packet delays for both exponential and Pareto increase with traffic load, especially under medium to high loads. The network experiences longer packet delays for CBR than for exponential, Poisson, and Pareto under all loads. The mean packet delays for Poisson are significantly lower than those for exponential, Pareto, and CBR, especially under medium to high loads. This better packet delay performance is because the network is less congested in the Poisson case.

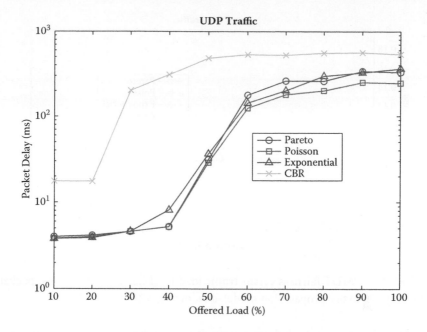

FIGURE 13.5 Mean packet delay versus traffic load for UDP (N = 10 stations; packet length: 1,500 bytes; propagation model: shadowing with σ = 7 dB).

The main conclusion is that if UDP is used instead of TCP, the mean packet delay degrades as traffic loads increase, except for Poisson arrivals. This packet delay degradation is due to the fact that a UDP source does not adapt to network traffic congestion, and therefore it wastes transmission bandwidth by sending packets that will not reach the destination stations.

Impact of Traffic Arrival Distributions on Network Fairness

In Figure 13.6, MDT fairness is plotted against traffic load for exponential, Pareto, Poisson, and CBR arrival distributions for TCP. MDT fairness for exponential, Pareto, and Poisson processes is almost independent of traffic load. By looking at the fairness graphs, one can observe that the network suffers severe unfairness for CBR arrivals, especially under medium to high loads. The network achieves slightly better fairness (lower MDT) for exponential than for Pareto. Of the four traffic models considered, Poisson arrivals result in the best fairness performance under all loads. This is an artifact of Poisson's failure to adequately model the burstiness of data traffic, which consequently generates fewer packets, thus contributing to better mean packet delay and MDT fairness [303].

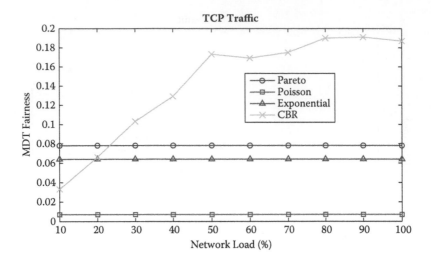

FIGURE 13.6   MDT fairness versus traffic load for TCP ($N = 10$ stations; packet length: 1,500 bytes; propagation model: shadowing with $\sigma = 7$ dB).

Figure 13.7 compares the MDT fairness for exponential, Pareto, Poisson, and CBR traffic arrival distributions for UDP. Clearly, the network suffers severe unfairness (in allocating bandwidth among active stations) for CBR, especially under medium to high loads. This unfairness performance is due to the statistical properties of CBR, in which more packets are generated at the stations, especially under high loads, contributing to worse delay and MTD fairness. However, the network achieves the best (almost 100%) MDT fairness performance for Poisson processes. These results are in accordance with the work of other network researchers [303, 304].

The main conclusions that can be drawn from Figures 13.6 and 13.7 are that when UDP is used instead of TCP, the MDT fairness degrades slightly for all traffic models used except Poisson, and that CBR arrivals fare significantly worse in both circumstances when the loads start to exceed 30%.

Impact of Traffic Arrival Distributions on Packet Drop Ratios

Figure 13.8 plots network mean packet drop ratio against traffic load for exponential, Pareto, Poisson, and CBR with TCP. Again, the mean packet drop ratios for exponential, Pareto, and Poisson processes are almost independent of traffic load; however, the packet drop ratio for CBR increases sharply at loads of 20% and tapers off starting at 40%. Of the four traffic

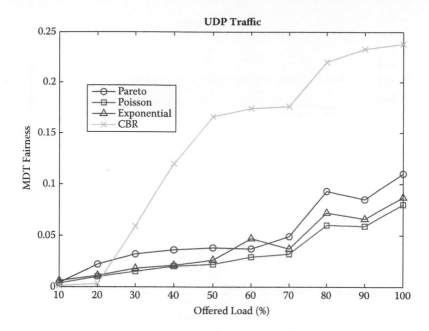

FIGURE 13.7 MDT fairness versus traffic load for UDP ($N = 10$ stations; packet length: 1,500 bytes; propagation model: shadowing with $\sigma = 7$ dB).

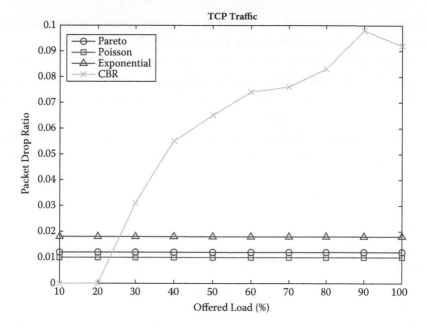

FIGURE 13.8 Network mean packet drop ratio versus load for TCP ($N = 10$ stations; packet length: 1,500 bytes; shadowing model with $\sigma = 7$ dB).

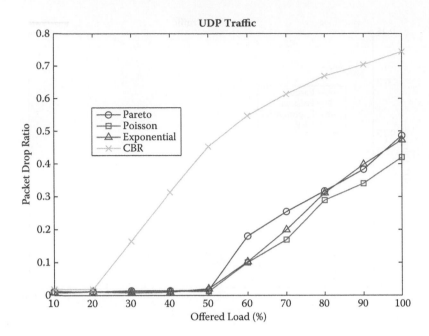

FIGURE 13.9   Network mean packet drop ratio versus load for UDP (N = 10 stations; packet length: 1,500 bytes; shadowing model with σ = 7 dB).

arrival distributions used, the packet drop ratio is better (in terms of fewer packets being dropped) for Poisson under all loads.

Figure 13.9 compares the mean packet drop ratios for exponential, Pareto, Poisson, and CBR for UDP. Again clearly, the mean packet drop ratio is best for Poisson and worst for CBR. The packet drop ratios for exponential and Pareto steadily increase at loads >50%.

The main conclusion is that if UDP is used instead of TCP, packets are dropped more frequently for all traffic models considered except Poisson. The network achieves superior packet drop ratios for Poisson for TCP and UDP because the network is less congested.

Summary of Findings

Table 13.5 summarizes the performance of an 802.11b ad hoc network for four traffic models used. The highest and lowest mean throughputs for TCP and UDP streams are obtained for CBR and Poisson, respectively.

The lowest mean packet delays for TCP and UDP are achieved for Pareto and Poisson, respectively; CBR, however, gave the greatest mean packet delays for TCP and UDP streams. The best and worst MDT fairness values and packet drop ratios for TCP and UDP are obtained for Poisson

TABLE 13.5 Summary of the 802.11b Ad Hoc Network Performance and Traffic Characteristics

Traffic Model	Throughput		Packet Delay		MDT Fairness		Packet Drop Ratio		Traffic Load-Dependent Performance
	Best	Worst	Best	Worst	Best	Worst	Best	Worst	
CBR	TCP UDP			TCP UDP	TCP UDP		TCP UDP		Yes
Poisson		TCP UDP	UDP		TCP UDP		TCP UDP		No
Pareto Exponential			TCP						With UDP

and CBR, respectively. In the case of Poisson arrivals, they appear rather at the extreme, for reasons mentioned in the "Impact of Traffic Arrival Distributions on Network Fairness" section.

The last column of Table 13.5 shows that the network performance (mean throughput, packet delay, MDT fairness, and packet drop ratio) for CBR largely depends on traffic load for both TCP and UDP. In contrast, the network performance for Poisson arrivals is almost independent of traffic load for both TCP and UDP. However, for both the Pareto and exponential the network performance is almost independent for TCP traffic, but is sensitive to UDP traffic.

SYSTEM IMPLICATIONS

The results presented in the "Simulation Results and Comparative Analysis" section provide some insight into the impact of the choice of traffic distribution model and transport protocols on assessing WLAN performance. Results obtained show that the traffic arrival distribution has a significant effect on the network mean throughput, packet delay, MDT fairness, and packet drop ratio of a typical 802.11b ad hoc network for TCP and UDP.

From a real application point of view a question may arise about the choice of the right traffic distribution model for a particular application. Figure 13.10 illustrates the best model to use for an application to meet a certain quality of service (QoS) requirement (in terms of data rate and packet delays). For instance, if an application requires high bandwidth (data rate), then CBR is the best model to use for TCP and UDP. For another application requiring low mean packet delay for TCP traffic, Pareto is the best model to use for this application.

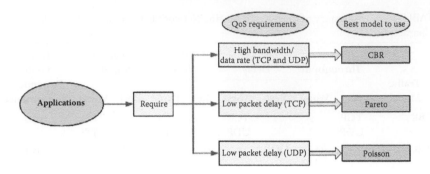

FIGURE 13.10 The best traffic distribution model to use for a particular application.

SIMULATION MODEL VERIFICATION

Before evaluating system performance it was necessary to verify that the simulation models represent reality. The method for verifying the ns-2 simulation models presented in this chapter is essentially the same as described in Chapters 4 and 6. First, the function of individual network components and their interactions was checked. Second, the network performance with a single user was tested, and then the number of users was increased to 10 to test the system performance with multiple users. The results presented in this chapter are closely matched with the results presented in Chapter 6 for ns-2.31 without BER. Third, the network was tested for both TCP and UDP traffic, and the corresponding results were checked for validity. Fourth, ns-2 results were compared with the results obtained from OPNET Modeler [34], and a close match between two sets of results further validated the simulation models. The simulation results reported in this chapter were also compared with the work of other network researchers to ensure the correctness of the simulation results [32, 305, 306].

FURTHER READING

For more details about subjects discussed in this chapter, we recommend the following books and references. The items in [] refer to the reference list at the end of the book.

Books

[37] Chapters 25 and 26—*Computer Networks and Internets with Internet Applications* by Comer

Research Papers

[293]

[307]

SUMMARY

In this chapter, the impact of traffic arrival distributions and transport protocols on the performance of a typical 802.11b ad hoc network was investigated by extensive simulation experiments. In the investigation, exponential, Pareto, Poisson, and CBR models were used. In the simulation model, an 802.11b ad hoc network with $N = 10$ stations, a shadowing propagation model, data packet lengths of 512 and 1,500 bytes, TCP and UDP traffic, and network loadings from 10 to 100% were used. The network performance was measured in terms of mean throughput, packet delay, MDT fairness, and packet drop ratio.

A detailed comparative analysis of the effect of packet arrival distributions and transport protocols on system performance was presented. Empirical results have shown that the network achieved a slightly higher mean throughput for 1,500-byte packets than for 512-byte packets for both TCP and UDP traffic. The network mean throughput for UDP traffic is better than that for TCP under all loads.

The network performance for exponential, Pareto, and Poisson arrivals was found to be almost independent of traffic loads. On the other hand, the network performance for CBR was sensitive to traffic loads. Of the four traffic models used, the network achieved best and worst mean throughputs with CBR and Poisson, respectively. The mean throughput of Pareto was found to be slightly better than that of exponential for TCP under all loads. Overall, the best and worst packet delays, MDT fairness values, and packet drop ratios were for Poisson and CBR, respectively. It was observed that Poisson and CBR had the largest effect on system performance, whereas Pareto and exponential had the smallest effect.

When UDP is used instead of TCP, the network mean throughput improves significantly for all traffic models used except Poisson. However, when UDP is used instead of TCP, both the mean packet delays and packet drop ratios degrade slightly for all four traffic models types. The combined effect of signal strength and traffic type on WLAN performance is investigated in Chapter 14.

KEY TERMS

Constant bit rate (CBR)
DCF interframe space (DIFS)
Distributed coordination function (DCF)
Exponential
IEEE 802.11
Network allocation vector (NAV)
Packet arrival processes
Pareto ON-OFF

Point coordination function (PCF)
Poisson
Rayleigh fading channel
Request to send (RTS)
Signal collision
Throughput
Traffic arrival distribution
Wireless local area network (WLAN)

REVIEW QUESTIONS

1. The traffic arrival distributions play a key role in determining the performance of WLANs. List and describe four commonly used traffic arrival distributions in WLANs.

2. Discuss the importance of traffic arrival processes in WLANs.

3. Discuss the effect of packet arrival distributions on 802.11 throughput and packet delay.

4. Discuss the impact of traffic arrival distributions and transport protocols on the performance of a typical 802.11 network.

5. Explain how you would select the best traffic distribution model to meet the requirements of a particular application.

MINI-PROJECTS

The following mini-projects aim to provide a deeper understanding of the topics covered in this chapter through literature review and empirical study.

1. **Literature review:** Conduct an in-depth literature review on traffic generation and arrival processes. Read 15 to 20 recent relevant journal/conference papers to identify the key researchers and their main contributions on traffic generation processes. You can use Table 13.6 to record your findings.

TABLE 13.6   Leading Researchers and Their Contributions in Traffic Generation and Arrival Processes

Researcher	Contribution	Year	Description/Key Concept

2. **Simulation study:** Repeat the work presented in the "Simulation Results and Comparative Analysis" section by conducting the following simulation experiments. In all experiments consider an 802.11g network, TCP and UDP traffic, and uniform loading, with a shadowing model with $\sigma = 7$ dB.

Experiment	Station	Packet Length (bytes)
1	10	500, 1,000, 1,500, 2,000, 2,500, 3,000
2	20	500, 1,000, 1,500, 2,000, 2,500, 3,000
3	50	500, 1,000, 1,500, 2,000, 2,500, 3,000
4	100	500, 1,000, 1,500, 2,000, 2,500, 3,000
5	200	500, 1,000, 1,500, 2,000, 2,500, 3,000

3. **Verification of ns-2 results:** Verify the ns-2 simulation results presented in the "Simulation Results and Comparative Analysis" section using another simulator (e.g., OPNET Modeler).

Combined Effect of Signal Strength and Traffic Type on WLAN Performance

LEARNING OUTCOMES

After reading and completing this chapter, you will be able to:

- Discuss the impact of received signal strength (RSS) values on video traffic over WLANs

- Discuss the combined effect of signal strength and traffic type on WLAN performance

- Develop a simulation model of voice over IP (VoIP) traffic using OPNET Modeler

- Discuss the impact of increasing the number of VoIP clients on packet delay and jitter

- Discuss the impact of increasing the number of video clients on delay and throughput

- Validate simulation results using appropriate methods

INTRODUCTION

In Chapter 13, the effect of traffic arrival distributions and transport protocols on WLAN performance was examined. One of the main objectives of this book is to quantify the key influencing factors on WLAN performance. With the growing popularity of multimedia streaming applications over WLANs, it is important to study the impact of real-time audio and video streaming on WLAN performance for different RSS values. This study is useful for the design, deployment, and capacity planning of larger WLANs. This chapter addresses the following research question: *What impact do the different RSS values of voice and video traffic have on WLAN performance?*

In particular, how sensitive are voice and video quality of service (QoS) parameters (e.g., playback delay) to changes in the channel conditions? These questions are evaluated by comparing playback delays of voice and video traffic for a typical 802.11g network for different RSS values.

The purpose of this chapter is threefold. First, the combined effect of RSS and traffic type on WLAN performance is studied to answer the above research question. In the investigation, both ad hoc and infrastructure network scenarios are used. It was observed that RSS has a significant effect on the playback delays of voice and video traffic, especially at higher bit rates. Second, this study seeks to understand the relationship between wireless channel conditions and user-perceived quality of audio and video streams. Third, this study seeks to determine the number of wireless voice and video applications an 802.11g access point (AP) can support. This is evaluated by simulation experiments.

The network configuration and methodology used is described in the "Experiment's Details" section, as are the scenarios for the performance study of audio and video streaming over a WLAN for different RSS values. The propagation measurement results are presented in the "Empirical Results" section, and they are validated in the "Measurement Accuracy and Validation" section. A simulation study for the performance evaluation of voice and video traffic over an 802.11g AP is presented in the "Simulation Study" section. The details of network modeling, simulation results, and model validation are also included in this section. Finally, the chapter is summarized in the last section.

EXPERIMENT'S DETAILS

Methodology and Scenarios

A network was set up to study the impact of different RSS values of audio and video streaming on the performance of a typical 802.11 WLAN. In this investigation, a radio propagation measurement was used for system performance evaluation. This measurement approach is exploratory in the sense that there was very limited prior research in performance estimation of multimedia traffic over a WLAN under different channel conditions to guide this research endeavor. Therefore, an empirical study through propagation measurements was adopted in this study. In addition, OPNET simulation models were used for system performance prediction. Table 14.1 lists the three scenarios that were used in the investigation.

As mentioned earlier, there were very limited empirical studies evaluating the performance of media streaming over WLANs reported in the networking literature. Kuang and Williamson [308] investigated the performance of real audio and real video streaming over an 802.11b network under different channel error conditions. It was observed that the subjective streaming quality is good for excellent and good channel conditions, while the fair and poor channel conditions produce jerky and blurred pictures. Mena and Heidemann [309] studied real audio traffic characteristics from an audio server and found that real audio traffic was non-Transmission Control Protocol (TCP) friendly. Shimakawa et al. [310] investigated the performance of video-conferencing and data traffic over an 802.11g network for both the distributed coordination function (DCF) and enhanced distributed channel access (EDCA) protocols.

> **Scenario 1:** In this scenario an ad hoc network (Figure 14.1) with two identical wireless laptops (IBM x31 Pentium 1.7 GHz, 1 GB RAM, MS Windows XP Professional) was used. Each laptop had a D-Link DWL-650 (802.11b) network adapter with a power output of 14 dBm [234]. One of the laptops was set as transmitter (Tx) and the other as receiver (Rx).

TABLE 14.1   Experiment's Scenarios

Scenario	Description
1	Audio and video traffic over an ad hoc network
2	Audio and video traffic over an infrastructure network *without* contention
3	Audio and video traffic over an infrastructure network *with* contention

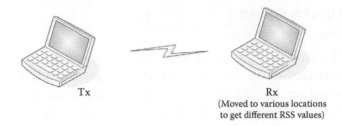

Tx

Rx
(Moved to various locations
to get different RSS values)

FIGURE 14.1   Setup for scenario 1 (802.11b ad hoc network).

For the experiment both laptops were placed on chairs (45 cm in height) simulating lap height. The Tx location was fixed and the Rx was moved to various locations in an obstructed office space (Auckland University of Technology [AUT] tower; described in the "Environment B: AUT Tower" section in Chapter 7) to get the different RSS values ranging from −44 to −89 dBm. The Tx was configured (using the "File Share" feature of the Colligo TM Workgroup [235]) to share the audio and video files with the Rx. In the experiments, audio MPEG audio layer 3 (MP3) formatted files and video Windows media video (WMV) formatted files were used. For each observation, the shared file was played at the Rx by using RealPlayer 11.0 (media client software), and its playback time was measured. The playback delays were calculated using the time difference between recording and playback times. The results for various audio and video bit rates and file formats are presented in the "Empirical Results" section.

Scenario 2: This scenario used an infrastructure network with a mobile wireless laptop (media client) running RealPlayer 11.0, using a D-Link DWL-G132 (802.11g) network adapter, a media server (Helix Server Unlimited Edition) running Linux on a 3.0-GHz Intel Pentium 4, 2 GB RAM, and a D-Link DWL-2100AP (802.11g) AP connected to

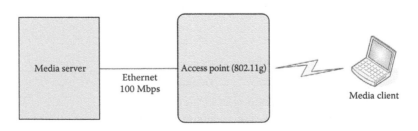

Media server

Ethernet
100 Mbps

Access point (802.11g)

Media client

FIGURE 14.2   Setup for scenario 2 (802.11g AP with a media client).

the media server via a 100-Mbps Ethernet card. The setup is shown in Figure 14.2.

In the experiment, audio files (MP3 format) with bit rates of 64, 96, 112, 128, 160, 192, 256, and 320 kbps were used. For video traffic, real media (RM) (450 kbps) and real media variable bit rate (RMVB) (750 and 1,000 kbps) formats were used. The media client was configured and associated to the AP. The Real-Time Streaming Protocol (RTSP) was used for delivering audio and video traffic over the 802.11g network. For each observation, the media client played audio and video files using RealPlayer, the playback times were measured, and playback delays were calculated. The empirical results for various audio and video bit rates, RSS values, and network configurations are presented in the "Empirical Results" section.

Scenario 3: This scenario is an extension to scenario 2 where four fixed wireless clients were added to generate channel contention (Figure 14.3). In all other respects, this scenario was identical to scenario 2. The results for scenario 3 are presented in the "Empirical Results" section.

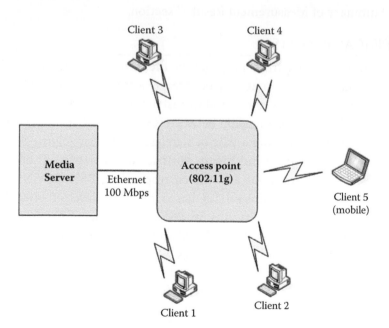

FIGURE 14.3   Setup for scenario 3 (802.11g AP with four fixed wireless clients and one mobile client).

TABLE 14.2   Qualitative Characterization of Wireless Channel

Channel State	RSS Range (dBm)	SNR (dB)
Excellent	≥ −60	≥40
Good	−61 to −75	39 to 25
Fair	−76 to −80	24 to 20
Bad	−81 to −89	19 to 11
Very bad	≤ −90	≤10

Experiment's Design

To investigate the impact of wireless channel conditions on streamed voice and video quality, one should classify the wireless channel states. To this end, wireless channel conditions were classified into five categories: excellent, good, fair, bad, and very bad. These signal strength categories are based on the link status meter on the D-Link cards [234], and the work of other network researchers [308, 311]. Table 14.2 lists these categories together with their RSS and signal-to-noise ratio (SNR) values. The transport protocol layer, User Datagram Protocol (UDP), and streaming control protocol, RTSP, were used. The summary of results for the impact of channel conditions on streamed audio and video quality is presented in the "Summary of Measurement Results" section.

EMPIRICAL RESULTS

The results obtained from propagation measurements are reported in this section. The preliminary results are presented first, followed by the detailed results for both ad hoc and infrastructure networks.

To investigate the relationship between RSS and SNR, a simple experiment was conducted using a pair of wireless laptops, involving wireless fidelity (Wi-Fi) computer links in an obstructed office space. The Rx was placed at different locations and the corresponding RSS and SNR were measured using Netstumbler [312] based on noise level at −100 dBm. Table 14.3 summarizes the results for RSS values ranging from excellent (−40 dBm) to very bad (−91 dBm). Based on these results, a linear relationship between SNR and RSS is derived as follows:

$$SNR = RSS - (Noise\ level) \tag{14.1}$$

TABLE 14.3   Measured RSS and SNR Using Netstumbler (noise level: −100 dBm)

RSS (dBm)	−40	−41	−42	−59	−60	−61	−69	−70	−71	−79	−80	−81	−89	−90	−91
SNR (dB)	60	59	58	41	40	39	31	30	29	21	20	19	11	10	9

TABLE 14.4   Audio Playback Delay for Different RSS Values and Bit Rates with an Ad Hoc Network (audio recording time: 2 min 26 s, MP3 format)

RSS (dBm)	Audio Playback Delay (s) at Seven Selected Audio Bit Rates						
	64 kbps	96 kbps	112 kbps	128 kbps	160 kbps	256 kbps	320 kbps
−44	0	0	0	0	0	0	0
−56	0	0	0	0	0	0	0
−66	0	0	0	0	0	0	0
−76	0	0	0	0	0	0	0
−82	0	0	0	0	0	0	0
−84	0	0	0	0	0	0	37.8
−86	0	0	0	0	0	7.3	62.7
−88	0	0	0	0	23.6	47.8	72.1
−89	Wireless connection lost						

Scenario 1: Ad Hoc Network

Scenario 1's results are summarized in Tables 14.4 and 14.5, respectively. Table 14.4 shows that playback delay first becomes apparent at −84 dBm; it increases with higher bit rates and becomes more significant for weaker RSS values, when at a very weak RSS of −89 dBm the wireless link between the Tx and Rx is lost irrespective of bit rate. There is no playback delay at 64, 96, 112, and 128 kbps at RSS of −88 dBm. The playback delay starts at 160 kbps, and at 160, 256, and 320 kbps it is 23.6, 47.8, and 72.1 s, respectively.

Table 14.5 shows that the video playback delay starts at −82 dBm and increases with rising bit rates and weakening RSS. For instance, at RSS of

TABLE 14.5   Video Playback Delay for Different RSS Values and Bit Rates with an 802.11b Ad Hoc Network (video recording time: 3 min 23 s, WMV format)

RSS (dBm)	Video Playback Delay (s) at Five Selected Video Bit Rates				
	384 kbps	512 kbps	768 kbps	1,000 kbps	1,500 kbps
−42	0	0	0	0	0
−53	0	0	0	0	0
−64	0	0	0	0	0
−73	0	0	0	0	0
−82	10.3	20.4	66.1	89.8	122.5
−84	133.8	193.4	157.2	238.6	306.4
−86	153.2	212.6	261.5	354.3	363.7
−88	188.1	237.5	288.7	433.4	472.5
−89	Wireless connection lost				

TABLE 14.6   Audio Playback Delay for Different RSS Values and Bit Rates with an Infrastructure Network without Contention (audio recording time: 2 min 26 s)

RSS (dBm)	Audio Playback Delay (s) at Seven Selected Audio Bit Rates						
	64 kbps	96 kbps	112 kbps	128 kbps	160 kbps	256 kbps	320 kbps
−45	0	0	0	0	0	0	0
−56	0	0	0	0	0	0	0
−64	0	0	0	0	0	0	0
−75	0	0	0	0	0	0	0
−80	0	0	0	0	0	0	0
−82	0	0	0	0	0	0	0
−84	0	0	0	0	0	0	0
−86	0	0	0	0	0	0	0
−88	0	0	0	0	0	0	6.6
−90	0	0	0	0	0	3.7	49.4
−91	Wireless connection lost						

−88 dBm, the video playback delays at 384, 512, 768, 1,000, and 1,500 kbps are 188.1, 237.5, 288.7, 433.4, and 472.5 s, respectively. For both audio and video traffic, the wireless link between the Tx and Rx was lost at RSS of −89 dBm.

Scenario 2: Infrastructure Network without Contention

Scenario 2's results are summarized in Tables 14.6 and 14.7, respectively.

Table 14.6 shows that there is no audio playback delay at 64, 96, 112, 128, and 160 kbps at RSS of −90 dBm. The playback delay starts at 256 kbps, and increases with bit rates at RSS of −90 dBm. However, at −91 dBm, the wireless link between the Tx and Rx was lost irrespective of bit rate. By comparing scenarios 1 and 2, one can observe that an 802.11g infrastructure network performs better (in terms of lower audio playback delays) than that of an 802.11b ad hoc network.

Table 14.7 shows there are no video playback delays at 450 and 750 kbps for RSS of −82 dBm. The video playback delay increases with increasing bit rates and decreasing RSS values becoming more significant for very weak RSS. For instance, at RSS of −88 dBm, the playback delays at 450, 750, and 1,000 kbps are 152.7, 180.7, and 272.5 s, respectively. The wireless link between the Tx and Rx was lost at RSS of −91 dBm.

Scenario 3: Infrastructure Network with Contention

Scenario 3's results are summarized in Tables 14.8 and 14.9, respectively.

TABLE 14.7   Video Playback Delay for Different RSS Values and Bit Rates with an Infrastructure Network without Contention (video recording time: 1 min 23 s)

RSS (dBm)	Video Playback Delay (s) at Three Selected Video Bit Rates		
	450 kbps	750 kbps	1,000 kbps
−46	0	0	0
−55	0	0	0
−65	0	0	0
−71	0	0	0
−75	0	0	0
−80	0	0	0
−82	0	0	36.4
−84	0	13.8	62.4
−86	57.8	104.2	186.0
−88	152.7	180.7	272.5
−90	168.7	223.1	421.3
−91	Wireless connection lost		

Table 14.8 shows there are no audio playback delays for 64, 96, 112, and 128 kbps at RSS of −88 dBm. Playback delay starts at 160 kbps and increases with increasing bit rates and decreasing RSS values. However, the wireless link between the Tx and Rx was lost irrespective of bit rate at RSS of −91 dBm. By comparing scenarios 2 and 3, one can conclude

TABLE 14.8   Audio Playback Delay for Different RSS Values and Audio Bit Rates with an Infrastructure Network with Contention (audio recording time: 2 min 26 s)

RSS (dBm)	Audio Playback Delay (s) at Seven Selected Audio Bit Rates						
	64 kbps	96 kbps	112 kbps	128 kbps	160 kbps	256 kbps	320 kbps
−44	0	0	0	0	0	0	0
−56	0	0	0	0	0	0	0
−66	0	0	0	0	0	0	0
−74	0	0	0	0	0	0	0
−80	0	0	0	0	0	0	0
−82	0	0	0	0	0	0	0
−84	0	0	0	0	0	0	0
−86	0	0	0	0	0	0	0
−88	0	0	0	0	1.4	7.3	24.1
−90	0	0	0	0	3.4	17.4	82.7
−91	Wireless connection lost						

TABLE 14.9 Video Playback Delay for Different RSS Values and Video Bit Rates with an Infrastructure Network with Contention (video recording time: 1 min 23 s)

RSS (dBm)	Video Playback Delay (s) at Three Selected Video Bit Rates		
	450 kbps	**750 kbps**	**1,000 kbps**
−45	0	0	0
−56	0	0	0
−66	0	0	0
−70	0	0	0
−76	0	0	0
−80	4	7.2	16.2
−82	6.2	23.2	58.8
−84	7.6	35.5	96.9
−86	26.8	76.7	156.3
−88	78.6	141.5	223.6
−90	123.1	246.7	313.6
−91	Wireless connection lost		

that for audio playback, an infrastructure network without contention performs slightly better than an infrastructure network with contention.

Table 14.9 shows there is no video playback delays at RSS ≥ −76 dBm irrespective of bit rate. The video playback delay increases with bit rates and becomes more significant for very weak RSS. For instance, at RSS of −90 dBm, the video playback delays at 450, 750, and 1,000 kbps are 123.1, 246.7, and 313.6 s, respectively. This increase in playback delay is due to high retransmission of video frames. The wireless link between the Tx and Rx was lost at RSS of −91 dBm.

Summary of Measurement Results

The playback of the audio and video streams was very smooth for excellent and good channel conditions. For the fair channel condition, the playback of the audio sound quality was good; however, the video playback was jerky, indicating loss of video frames, though the visual quality of displayed video frames was good. For the bad channel condition, the audio quality deteriorated and the video playback was jerky (and in some cases appeared to freeze), and some individual pictures were blurry or truncated due to significant frame losses. In the case of a very bad channel, attempts to set up the streaming connections failed due to the high frame loss rate. Table 14.10 summarizes the results obtained from subjective assessment of streaming quality.

TABLE 14.10   Impact of Channel Conditions on Audio and Video Quality

Channel Condition	Audio Quality	Video Quality
Excellent	Very smooth	Very smooth
Good	Smooth	Smooth
Fair	Good	Playback was jerky, though the visual quality of displayed video was good
Bad	Deteriorated	Playback was jerky, some individual pictures were blurry or truncated
Very bad	Streaming connection failed	

For fair comparison and interpretation, the main results presented in Tables 14.4 to 14.9 are summarized in Table 14.11. The three network topologies are identified in the first column. For each scenario, the traffic type (audio and video) and the corresponding two selected bit rates are shown in columns 2 and 3, respectively. Playback delays at RSS of –80, –82, –88, –90, and –91 dBm are shown in columns 4 to 8, respectively.

The ad hoc network introduces slightly higher audio and video playback delays than the infrastructure network with and without contention at RSS greater than –82 dBm, irrespective of bit rate. Greater video playback delay was expected because their higher bit rates increased their retransmission rates.

TABLE 14.11   Combined Effect of RSS and Traffic Type on Playback Delay for 802.11 (WCL = wireless connection lost)

Topology	Traffic Type	Bit Rate (kbps)	Playback Delay (s) at Five Selected RSS Values				
			–80 dBm	–82 dBm	–88 dBm	–90 dBm	–91 dBm
Scenario 1	Audio	64	0	0	0	WCL	WCL
(ad hoc network		320	0	0	72.1	WCL	WCL
802.11b)	Video	384	0	10.3	188.1	WCL	WCL
		1,000	0	89.8	433.4	WCL	WCL
Scenario 2	Audio	64	0	0	0	0	WCL
(infrastructure		320	0	0	6.6	49.4	WCL
network without	Video	450	0	0	152.7	168.7	WCL
contention 802.11g)		1,000	0	36.4	272.5	421.3	WCL
Scenario 3	Audio	64	0	0	0	0	WCL
(infrastructure		320	0	0	24.1	82.7	WCL
network with	Video	450	4	6.2	78.6	123.1	WCL
contention 802.11g)		1,000	16.2	58.8	223.6	313.6	WCL

By comparing scenarios 2 and 3, one can observe that the 802.11g infrastructure network performs better overall without contention than with contention. For example, the network without contention does not incur any video playback delays, hereas the network with contention introduces video playback delays beginning at RSS of –80 dBm, irrespective of bit rate. The network without contention also achieves lower audio playback delays than with contention at RSS of –88 to –90 dBm, at 320 kbps. Unexpectedly, the network without contention incurs slightly longer video playback delays than with contention at RSS of –88 to –90 dBm, irrespective of bit rate. The reason for this anomaly is assumed to be the variability of noise floor (background noise) as a result of the propagation measurements being conducted at different times [313, 314]. Nonetheless, the audio and video streaming connection failed at –91 dBm for all three network scenarios.

MEASUREMENT ACCURACY AND VALIDATION

The method of obtaining measurement accuracy and validation of results is essentially the same as described in Chapter 7 (the "Measurement Accuracy and Validation" section). Recall that the accuracy of the measurements was improved by (1) avoiding the impact of the movement of people on system performance and (2) reducing the impact of the co-channel interference. Conducting propagation measurements after hours in a controlled environment avoided the impact of moving people on system performance. During propagation measurements, a couple of neighboring WLANs were detected. The AP was set to a different frequency channel prior to data collection, to avoid the impact of possible co-channel interference on system performance.

The measured playback delays presented in this chapter closely agree with the results obtained from D-Link cards and APs [233, 245]. These results were compared with the work of other network researchers for correctness [308, 315].

SIMULATION STUDY

The propagation study focused on measuring the playback delays of audio and video traffic under different channel states, whereas the simulation study explores end-to-end packet delay, jitter, and throughput of voice and video traffic for an 802.11g network with varying device densities (e.g., N = 2, 5, 10, and 15 clients). The characteristic of simulated voice and video traffic at the packet level is investigated.

For modeling voice and video traffic, VoIP and video-conferencing applications were chosen. The 802.11g infrastructure network is modeled in OPNET Modeler 15.0 [34] to study the impact of voice and video traffic on WLAN performance with varying device densities. The effect of RSS on network performance is also examined for VoIP traffic. This section describes in detail the simulation models, parameter settings, and results.

Modeling the Network

In the simulation model an office network of 15 × 10 m floor area is used, similar to the computer laboratory in Environment B (Chapter 7, Figure 7.21).

Figure 14.4 shows the OPNET representation of a VoIP simulation model, comprising one wireless VoIP server, one 802.11g AP, and 15 wireless VoIP clients. The VoIP server is used to generate voice packets for a

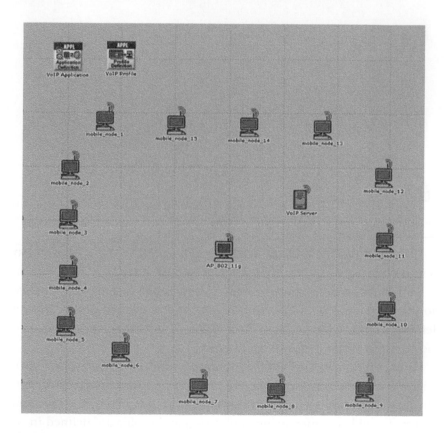

FIGURE 14.4 OPNET representation of an 802.11g network with a VoIP server, 1 AP, and 15 clients.

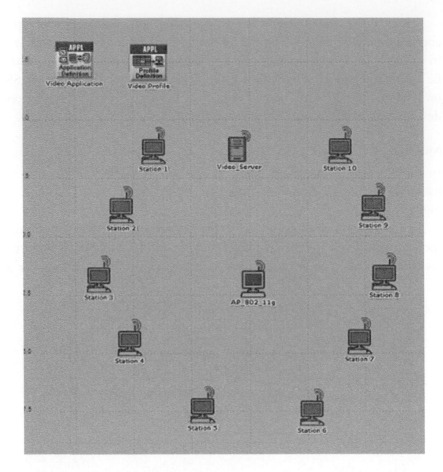

FIGURE 14.5   OPNET representation of an 802.11g infrastructure network with a wireless video server, 1 AP, and 15 clients.

VoIP application. The VoIP application is defined in the "VoIP Application" definition object as shown in Figure 14.4 (top left box).

VoIP clients are essentially wireless stations accessing the VoIP application through an 802.11g AP. The client profile is defined in the "Profile" definition object shown next to the application definition object; it enables the clients to access the VoIP application.

Figure 14.5 shows the OPNET simulation model for video traffic, comprising 1 wireless video server, 1 802.11g AP, and 15 wireless video clients. The video server generates video packets for the video-conferencing application. The video-conferencing application and profile are defined in the same way as VoIP, was described earlier. Each video client can therefore access the video-conferencing application through an 802.11g AP. Both

TABLE 14.12   Parameters in the Simulation

Parameter	Value
Data rate	54 Mbps
Access point (AP)	802.11g
Wireless cards (clients and servers)	802.11g
Transmit power (AP, client, and server)	32 mW
RSS threshold (receiver sensitivity)	−88, −77, −66 dBm
Traffic type	Voice, video
Application	VoIP, video-conferencing
VoIP encoder	VoIP quality
VoIP packet payload	160 bytes
Video-conferencing encoder	VCR quality video
Video encoding rate (frame rate)	30 frames/s
Request to send–clear to send (RTS-CTS)	Off
Frame fragmentation	Off
Buffer length (AP and clients)	2,048,000 bits
Simulation time	1 h

VoIP and video-conferencing applications are included in their respective profiles to enable the proper operation of the simulation models.

Table 14.12 lists the parameter values that were used in the performance study simulation of voice and video traffic over an 802.11g network. Each simulation is run for 1 h of simulated time to obtain steady-state results. The observations collected during the initial 20-min transient period are not included in the final simulation results. It should be noted that there was no traffic on the network for the first 105 s to allow for the networking hardware to settle.

In the simulation of VoIP, the voice encoder was set to VoIP quality, which is very similar to G.711 with a VoIP payload length of 160 bytes. For video-conferencing, a videocassette recorder (VCR) quality video is used with a rate of 30 frames/s.

Simulation Results

The results obtained from simulation runs for voice and video traffic are presented in this section.

Performance of VoIP Traffic

The effect of increasing VoIP wireless clients on end-to-end packet delay is illustrated in Figure 14.6. The end-to-end packet delay increases slightly with client numbers. The maximum end-to-end packet delay is about 65 ms for $N = 15$ clients, which is acceptable for VoIP QoS requirements.

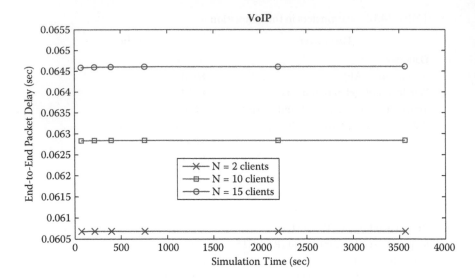

FIGURE 14.6 Effect of increasing the number of VoIP wireless clients on end-to-end packet delay.

For more than 15 VoIP clients (not shown in Figure 14.6), the network experiences delays exceeding 80 ms, resulting in unacceptable VoIP QoS. Therefore, for the deployment of 802.11g infrastructure networks in an obstructed office block, fewer than 16 wireless clients per AP are recommended for VoIP communications.

Jitter (measured in seconds) is another important metric for performance evaluation of VoIP traffic. Jitter is defined as follows: if two consecutive voice packets leave a source station at times t_1 and t_2 and are played back at a destination station at times t_3 and t_4, then jitter $= (t_4 - t_3) - (t_2 - t_1)$. Negative jitter indicates that the delay variance at the destination station is smaller than that of the source station. Ideally, a VoIP network should be jitter-free.

The effect on jitter of increasing the number of VoIP clients is shown in Figure 14.7. The network experiences small jitter at the start of the simulation for $N = 10$ and 15 clients and becomes almost zero at the end of 1 h of simulated time. This confirms that the VoIP network performance is acceptable for up to 15 concurrent clients.

The effect of increasing the number of VoIP wireless clients ($N = 2$, 10, and 15 clients) on network mean throughput is demonstrated in Figure 14.8. Clearly, the mean throughput increases with N. This throughput characteristic is expected; proportionally more voice packets are transferred per second over the network, resulting in higher throughput.

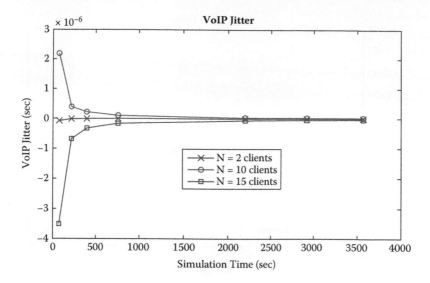

FIGURE 14.7   Effect of increasing the number of VoIP wireless clients on jitter.

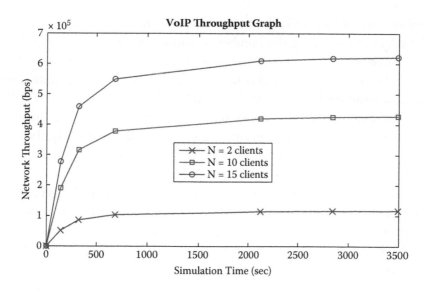

FIGURE 14.8   Effect of increasing the number of VoIP wireless clients on network mean throughput.

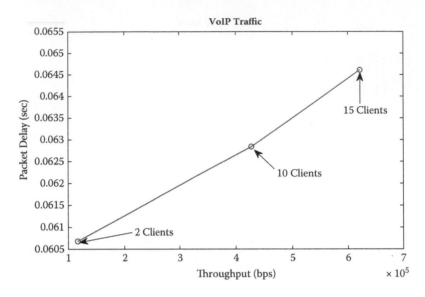

FIGURE 14.9   Packet delay versus throughput characteristics of VoIP traffic.

The mean packet delay versus throughput characteristics of VoIP traffic for N = 2, 10, and 15 clients is illustrated in Figure 14.9. The network throughput increases with N, and the packet delay increases due to network congestion.

Performance of Video-Conferencing (Video) Traffic
The effect of increasing the number of wireless video clients on end-to-end packet delay for an 802.11g infrastructure network is illustrated in Figure 14.10. End-to-end packet delay increases with N. For example, the network mean packet delays are 0.55, 1.07, 2.05, and 2.9 s for N = 2, 5, 10, and 15 clients, respectively. The increase in packet delay for $N \geq 2$ clients is mainly due to the channel contention and backoff delays. Clearly, the network experiences longer packet delays as the number of active video clients increases.

It was observed that the network experiences significantly longer packet delays for N > 15 video clients (not shown in Figure 14.10 because the y-axis is out of range), resulting in unacceptable video QoS. Therefore, for the deployment of 802.11g APs in an obstructed office space, fewer than 16 video clients per AP are recommended.

Figure 14.11 shows the effect on channel access delay of increasing the number of video clients for an 802.11g infrastructure network. Channel access delay increases with N, as expected. For example, the channel access

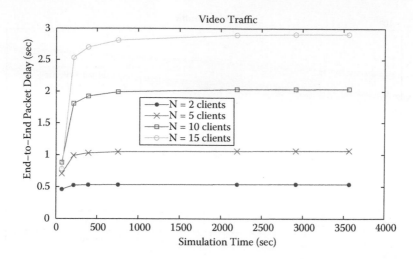

FIGURE 14.10   Effect of increasing the number of wireless video clients on end-to-end packet delay.

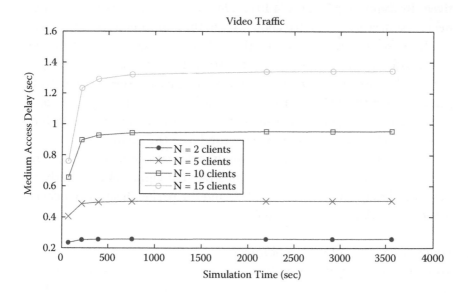

FIGURE 14.11   Effect of increasing the number of wireless video clients on channel access delay.

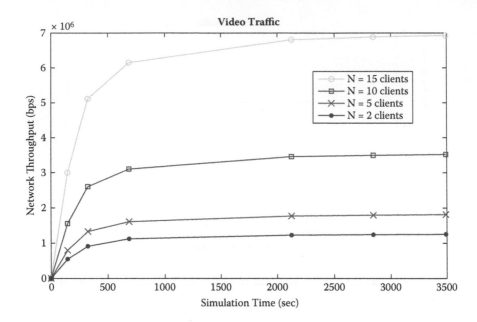

FIGURE 14.12   Effect of increasing the number of wireless video clients on network mean throughput.

delays are 0.26, 0.5, 0.96, and 1.35 s for $N = 2$, 5, 10, and 15 clients, respectively. By comparing Figures 14.10 and 14.11, one can observe that the channel access delays contributed about 47% to the end-to-end packet delays.

The effect on network mean throughput of increasing the number of video clients for an 802.11g infrastructure network is illustrated in Figure 14.12. Mean throughput increases with N, as expected. For example, the mean throughputs are 1.25, 1.8, 3.5, and 7 Mbps for $N = 2$, 5, 10, and 15 clients, respectively. This increase in throughput is due to more video packets being transferred per second over the network.

The mean packet delay versus throughput characteristic of video traffic for $N = 2$, 5, 10, and 15 clients is illustrated in Figure 14.13. Clearly, the network throughput increases with N and the packet delay also increases due to network traffic congestion.

Effect of RSS on Network Performance

To study the effect of RSS on the performance of a typical 802.11g infrastructure network, the VoIP simulation model shown in Figure 14.4 was used with $N = 15$ VoIP clients in an office network of 15×10 m area. The 802.11g network was simulated for each of the three different RSS values:

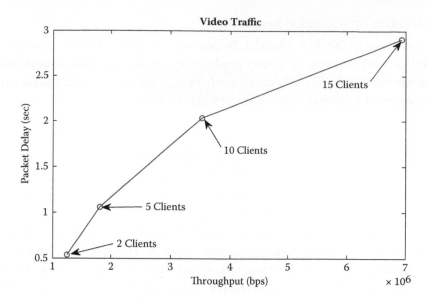

FIGURE 14.13   Mean packet delay versus throughput characteristics of video traffic.

−66, −77, and −88 dBm. The parameters used in the simulation are listed in Table 14.12.

Results obtained show that RSS does not have any significant impact on end-to-end packet delay, jitter, and throughput (Figures D.1 to D.3 in Appendix D). The reason for this is that the area covered by the simulated office network is relatively small, where all wireless clients operate with reasonably good signal strengths anyway; thus, OPNET produces identical results for all three RSS values used.

Overall Observation and Interpretation

The simulation results reveal that for voice and video transmission over an 802.11g network all major characteristics (jitter, end-to-end packet delay, channel access delay, and throughput) are heavily dependant on client numbers and become unacceptably poor for $N > 15$. Therefore, for the deployment of an 802.11g AP in an obstructed office block, it is recommended that for effective communications there be fewer than 16 wireless clients per AP. However, RSS has an insignificant impact on VoIP mean packet delay, jitter, and throughput for a 15×10 m WLAN in an obstructed office space.

Validation of Simulation Results

Even though OPNET Modeler is one of the most credible commercial network simulators, it may produce invalid results if the simulation parameters are incorrectly configured. Thus, simulation model validation becomes an important part of any simulation study. Before evaluating the system performance, it was necessary to verify that the simulation models represent reality. The OPNET models presented in this chapter were verified essentially the same way as described in Chapter 7. First, OPNET simulation models were validated through indoor propagation measurements from wireless laptops and APs for an 802.11g network. A good match between simulation and measurement results for $N = 2$ to 4 stations validates the OPNET models. Second, the function of individual network components and their interactions was checked. Third, the network performance with a single user was tested, and then the number of users was increased to 2, 5, 10, and 15 to test the system performance with multiple users. Finally, simulation time was recorded for all events to further assist in the debugging and model validation.

FURTHER READING

For more details about subjects discussed in this chapter, we recommend the following books and references. The items in [] refer to the reference list at the end of the book.

Books

   [36] Chapter 9–*Wireless Personal and Local Area Networks* by Sikora

Research Papers

   [293]

   [316]

SUMMARY

The combined effect of RSS and traffic type on WLAN performance was investigated through indoor propagation measurements. In the investigation, infrastructure networks with and without channel contention as well as ad hoc networks were studied. Measurement results have shown that an 802.11g infrastructure network without contention achieved lower video playback delays than with contention at RSS of –82 dBm and stronger. Unexpectedly, however, it was found that an 802.11g infrastructure network without contention achieved slightly higher video playback delays than with contention at RSS of −88 to −90 dBm, irrespective of bit rate; it is presumed that it was caused by an unidentified noise source. Further, the audio and video streaming connection failed at −91 dBm in both ad hoc and infrastructure network scenarios. It was observed that the video playback delays are slightly higher than the corresponding audio playback delays, especially for weak RSS values with higher bit rates.

The subjective streaming quality is good for excellent and good channel conditions, while fair and bad channel conditions produce jerky and blurred pictures and the overall audio quality deteriorates. The streaming service did not work (i.e., connection failed) for very bad channel conditions.

The simulation showed that the end-to-end packet delay and jitter for an 802.11g infrastructure network deteriorated significantly for $N > 15$ clients. Therefore, to achieve effective communication in an 802.11g network deployed in an obstructed office space, fewer than 16 wireless clients per AP are recommended. To accommodate more users, multiple carefully configured APs are required. Simulation results obtained show that the effect of RSS on VoIP end-to-end packet delay, jitter, and throughput is insignificant for an office network of 15×10 m dimension. The implication for system planning and deployment is discussed in Chapter 15.

KEY TERMS

Access point (AP)	Real-Time Streaming Protocol (RTSP)
Ad hoc network	Received signal strength (RSS)
Bit rate	Signal-to-noise ratio (SNR)
Channel condition	Throughput
Channel contention	Topology
Enhanced distributed channel access (EDCA)	User Datagram Protocol (UDP)
IEEE 802.11g	Video playback delay
Media client	Voice and video traffic
Media server	Voice over IP (VoIP)
Playback time	Wireless local area network (WLAN)

REVIEW QUESTIONS

1. RSS has a significant effect on multimedia transmission over WLANs. Discuss the impact of RSS values on voice and video traffic over a typical 802.11 network.

2. The wireless channel state plays a key role in determining the performance of WLANs. Discuss the relationship between video playback delays and wireless channel state.

3. To understand the performance of VoIP traffic over WLANs, it is useful to be able to model VoIP using a credible simulation tool, such as OPNET or ns-2. Explain how VoIP traffic can be modeled using OPNET Modeler.

4. The number of VoIP clients on a WLAN system has implications on system performance. Discuss the effect of increasing the number of VoIP clients on end-to-end delay and jitter of a typical WLAN.

5. As VoIP clients, the number of video clients has implications on system performance. Discuss the effect of increasing the number of video clients on packet delay and throughput.

6. Discuss the delay versus throughput characteristics of video traffic.

MINI-PROJECTS

The following mini-projects aim to provide a deeper understanding of the topics covered in this chapter through literature review and empirical study.

1. Conduct an in-depth literature review on multimedia traffic over wireless networks. Read 15 to 20 recent relevant journal/conference papers to identify the key researchers and their main contributions on multimedia traffic over wireless networks. You can use Table 14.13 to record your findings.

TABLE 14.13   Leading Researchers and Their Contributions in Multimedia Traffic over Wireless Networks

Researcher	Contribution	Year	Description/Key Concept

2. **Audio playback delay measurement:** Extend the work presented in the "Scenario 2: Infrastructure Network without Contention" section by considering the following bit rates: 256, 512, 1,000, 1,500, and 2,000 kbps.

3. **Video playback delay measurement:** Extend the work presented in the "Scenario 2: Infrastructure Network without Contention" section by considering the following bit rates: 1,000, 1,500, 2,000, 2,500, and 3,000 kbps.

4. **Simulation modeling:** Develop a simulation model to generalize the measurement results presented in the "Scenario 2: Infrastructure Network without Contention" section.

III

Concluding Remarks

III

Implications for System Planning and Deployment

LEARNING OUTCOMES

After reading and completing this chapter, you will be able to:

- Outline an evolutionary path of various 802.11 networks

- Draw guidelines for system planners to design and deploy indoor WLAN systems

- Discuss the issues in the deployment of WLANs in single- and multifloor office buildings

- Discuss various approaches in achieving high-performance in WLANs using cross-layer design

INTRODUCTION

The key factors influencing WLAN performance were studied in Chapters 7 to 14. One of the objectives of this book is to develop guidelines for optimum system design, planning, and deployment. To achieve this objective, the following key question is answered: *What sort of guidelines can be drawn from the analysis of results that enable system planners to design and deploy better indoor WLAN systems?* This chapter draws conclusions from the analysis of results outlined in Chapters 7 to 14 from a system planning perspective. A set of guidelines for planning and deploying indoor WLANs is also presented in this chapter.

In the "An Evolutionary Path for Adopting WLAN Technology" section, an evolutionary path for deploying indoor WLANs is suggested. The "Deployment of WLANs" section discusses practical issues in the deployment of WLANs in single-floor and multifloor office buildings, a computer laboratory, and a residential house environment. A summary of major findings in this book with respect to system planning and deployment is also presented in this section. The "Deploying High-Performance WLANs" section discusses approaches in achieving high performance in WLANs using cross-layer design (CLD). Recommendations for future research are presented in the "Recommendation for Future Development" section, and a brief summary concludes the chapter.

AN EVOLUTIONARY PATH FOR ADOPTING WLAN TECHNOLOGY

Figure 15.1 shows an evolutionary path for adopting and deploying indoor WLAN systems. At the bottom left (low-cost and low-performance) region of the system upgrade path, 802.11b technology offers a relatively low level of system performance at relatively low deployment costs. At the top right, the 802.11ac network offers a significant performance advantage (>1 Gbps) at relatively high unit costs compared to the conventional 802.11b/g/n systems [317–319]. The cost per unit of 802.11ac cards and access points (APs)/routers will come down as the 802.11ac working committee ratifies

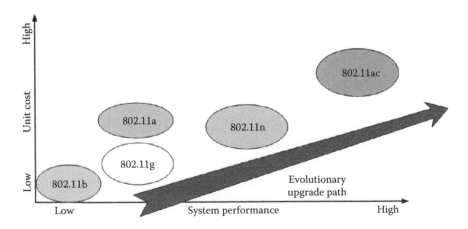

FIGURE 15.1 An evolutionary path of various 802.11 WLANs.

the technology. The 802.11ac standard uses orthogonal frequency division multiplexing (OFDM) and multiuser multiple-input multiple-output (MU-MIMO) technologies to boost the system performance.

Both 802.11g and 802.11a offer moderate system performance and are commonly used in homes, offices, and hotspots for Internet access. However, many organizations have deployed 802.11g networks over 802.11a because 802.11g cards and APs are cheaper and are compatible with 802.11b. These technologies provide a smooth transition to high-performance 802.11n networks as demand dictates.

DEPLOYMENT OF WLANS

Deploying an enterprise WLAN is a new challenge even for experienced system planners. Planning for both performance (i.e., capacity) and radio frequency (RF) coverage is one of the key design issues. Generally, carefully locating and configuring the APs can meet these requirements. Research has shown that the layout must be based on propagation measurements, not just on "rule of thumb" calculations [4, 22, 320, 321]. These measurements involve extensive testing and careful consideration of radio propagation issues when the service area is large, such as an entire office building. This book has investigated these WLAN design issues and challenges empirically. A notable contribution of this book is the quantification of the impact of radio propagation environments on WLAN performance in several deployment scenarios. When deploying a WLAN, system planners are often given flexibility in choosing various networking devices within the limited budget to satisfy current and future needs. This section provides some practical guidelines for deploying WLANs in a typical office building, computer laboratory, and residential house environment.

Single-Floor Office Scenario
Deployment of Ad Hoc Networks
When planning for deployment of an ad hoc WLAN in an obstructed office space (single-floor), system planners need to quantify the effect of line-of-sight (LOS) blockage by office walls on system performance. Appropriate deployment strategies (e.g., proper placement of APs) can then be implemented to maintain the desired level of performance. This book has examined the effect of LOS blockage on throughput for 802.11b ad hoc networks. Analysis results from the "Environment A" section in Chapter 7 (experiment 4) show that the LOS blockage has a significant effect on the wireless fidelity (Wi-Fi) link throughput. It is interesting to

note that throughput degraded by about 82% from the reference (LOS) throughput when the receiver (Rx) was placed just 1 m away from the LOS path between transmitter (Tx) and Rx. In one trial, the Rx was placed 2 m away from the LOS path and the data communication link failed at RSS $\geq$ –91 dBm. The propagation measurement results presented in Chapter 7 confirm that loss of the LOS path in an obstructed office environment has a dramatic effect on system performance.

Deployment of Infrastructure Networks

When planning for deployment of an infrastructure WLAN (which is a more realistic scenario for campus and corporate networks) in an obstructed office space, system planners need to determine the optimum number and locations of APs to achieve the desired performance and coverage. An extensive measurement campaign was used to evaluate both the optimum number and locations of 802.11g APs for adequate performance and coverage of the target office space for this book. Potential external interferences and their impact on system performance have not been investigated in this book. However, wireless APs have been configured to reduce co-channel interference, and hence improve the system performance. The objective of these field trials and measurements was to minimize the number of APs deployed without sacrificing network performance. Analysis results from the "Propagation Study" in Chapter 8 show that a minimum of two 802.11g APs are required to cover the entire floor area of 780 m^2 (Environment A). The location of an AP in the target office space is found to be very significant as far as throughput and coverage are concerned. For example, AP at location P provides better throughput and coverage than the other eight locations, A to H (Figure 8.1). RSS values in the range from –45 to –80 dBm were observed during measurement. System planners must determine the optimum number and locations of APs. When assigning APs channel frequencies, system planners need to ensure that adjacent APs use nonoverlapping channels. For example, both the 802.11b and 802.11g provide three nonoverlapping channels, whereas 802.11a offers eight or more, depending on the country in which the wireless equipment is used. When deploying WLANs in a multistory building, system planners should consider the channel overlap (i.e., frequency reuse) between floors of the building to improve system capacity.

Multifloor Office Scenario

When deploying a WLAN for an office that is spread over multiple floors of a building, system planners need to quantify the effect of floors on system performance. This book has investigated the impact of floors on throughput for an 802.11b WLAN. Analysis results from the "Environment A" section in Chapter 7 show that floor obstructions (Tx in the basement and Rx on the ground floor with a Tx-Rx separation of 3 m) have a significant effect on the throughput for the 802.11b network. For example, the Wi-Fi link throughput with the ground floor obstruction is 1.03 Mbps, which is approximately five times lower than the throughput obtained under LOS conditions in the basement parking lot (Table 7.3). As could be expected, two-floor obstructions (Tx was placed on the floor of the basement while the Rx was placed on the first floor with a Tx-Rx separation of 7 m) degrade the throughput more than single-floor obstructions. For three-floor obstructions (Tx was placed on the floor of the basement while the Rx was placed on the second floor with a Tx-Rx separation of 11 m), the wireless link was lost at RSS of –91 dBm due to the severe blockage of radio signals. It was shown that 802.11 ad hoc networks are not suitable for providing wireless connectivity to users located on multiple floors of an office building. For good performance and coverage, infrastructure WLANs with carefully located wireless APs on every floor are required.

Computer Laboratory

When planning the deployment of a WLAN in a typical computer laboratory, system planners need to quantify the effect of computers and furniture in the laboratory on system performance, and to determine the optimum number of APs for good performance. The optimum locations for APs can then be determined to achieve a desired level of performance. This book has investigated the effect of the presence of computers, furniture, and metallic cabinets in a computer laboratory (floor area of 144 m², Environment B) on 802.11g AP throughput. Analysis results from the "Environment B" section in Chapter 7 show that the presence of metallic cabinets in the laboratory significantly degrades 802.11g AP throughput. For example, AP throughput at a location behind the metallic cabinets is about 22% lower than the reference throughput, which is the maximum achieved throughput in the laboratory. It has been shown that one 802.11g AP produced signals of sufficient strength (–52 to –60 dBm) to cover the entire laboratory.

Residential House Environment

When planning a WLAN in a typical suburban residential house, system planners need to quantify the effect of LOS blockage (between the Tx and

Rx) by walls and furniture on system performance. This book has investigated the effect of LOS blockage in a three-bedroom wood-framed suburban residential house on throughput for an 802.11b ad hoc network. Analysis results from the "Environment C" section in Chapter 7 show that the LOS blockage by house walls, furniture, and cabinets has a significant effect on throughput for an 802.11b network, as in an office environment. For example, throughputs are significantly lower than the reference throughput in both the bedrooms and the garage, where the LOS path (between the Tx and the Rx) is severely blocked by house furniture, cabinets, and walls. It has been shown that an 802.11 ad hoc network is unsuitable for providing wireless connectivity to users located in the bedrooms and garage of Environment C. Good performance would require a carefully located AP. Figure 15.2 shows the throughput measurement results in the form of a map for the WY level 1 office block. Overall the better throughput is achieved closer to the access point (AP).

Summary of Findings

Table 15.1 summarizes the empirical results obtained, for the impact of propagation environments on WLAN performance, from studies in this book. The throughput of an 802.11b ad hoc network in the suburban residential house is very similar to the throughput obtained in the obstructed office space and computer laboratory. Clearly, throughputs are significantly lower in non-LOS conditions for all three propagation environments.

TABLE 15.1   Impact of Propagation Environments on WLAN Performance Examined in This Book (802.11b ad hoc networks)

Tx-Rx Separation (m)	LOS/ Non-LOS	Link Throughput in Three Selected Environments		
		Obstructed Office Space (Mbps)	Laboratory (Mbps)	Residential House (Mbps)
1	LOS	4.5	4.95	4.49 (lounge)
9.5	LOS	4.63	4.98	4.57 (corridor)
9.55	Non-LOS	—	—	3.79 (garage)
11	LOS	4.64	4.96	4.57 (corridor)
11.05	Non-LOS	—	—	2.42 (bedroom)
11.09	Non-LOS	—	—	2.94 (bedroom)
17.5	Non-LOS	—	4.77	—
35	LOS	4.5	—	—
35.01	Non-LOS	0.8	—	—
35.03	Non-LOS	Connection lost	—	—

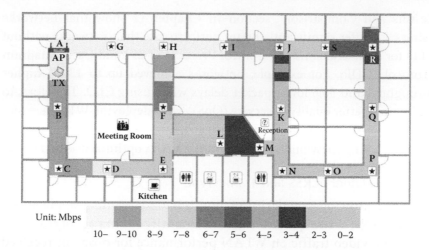

FIGURE 15.2   Layout of floor 1 of the Duthie Whyte (WY) building and measurement locations. Measurement results in a throughput map.

DEPLOYING HIGH-PERFORMANCE WLANS

Although physical layer (PHY), medium access control (MAC), and upper protocol layers individually play an important role in determining WLAN performance, research has shown that WLANs optimized on a single-layered protocol architecture do not provide high performance, especially for multimedia applications [209, 224, 300, 322]. To overcome network performance problems, CLD approaches (sharing information between two or more protocol layers) have been shown to be very promising and have attracted a lot of attention in recent years. When deploying high-performance WLANs, system designers and planners need to adopt a CLD framework to improve network performance. A CLD framework for estimating as well as improving WLAN performance was developed in this book (Chapter 12). This section presents guidelines for improving WLAN performance using CLD optimization.

Joint PHY-MAC Layer Design

CLD approaches are needed to optimize WLAN system performance. This book has developed a joint PHY-MAC CLD framework to improve WLAN performance. The MAC protocol developed in the proposed framework is channel-aware buffer unit multiple access (C-BUMA), which is a cross-layer MAC protocol developed as a minor modification of the BUMA protocol (Chapter 12). Analysis results from the "Simulation

Results and Comparison" section in Chapter 12 show that networks using CLD offer significantly better performance than networks without CLD for both Transmission Control Protocol (TCP) and User Datagram Protocol (UDP). For example, networks achieved up to 13.5% higher throughput and 56% lower packet delays when using CLD. Therefore, to maintain a better quality of service (QoS), when deploying WLANs, especially in harsh propagation environments, system planners should consider deploying these high-performance WLANs optimized with a CLD.

Combined Effect of RSS and Traffic Type

With the growing popularity of multimedia streaming applications over WLANs, system planners need to quantify the impact of real-time audio and video traffic on WLAN performance for different received signal strength (RSS) values and bit rates. This book has investigated the combined effect of RSS and traffic type on 802.11g WLANs using a variety of propagation measurements (Chapter 14). In particular, this book has examined the sensitivity of voice and video QoS parameters (e.g., playback delay) to changes in channel conditions. Analysis results in the "Empirical Results" section in Chapter 14 confirm that RSS has an effect on the playback delays of voice and video traffic, especially for higher bit rates. It was also shown that an 802.11g AP performs better without contention than with contention at RSS ≥ −82 dBm, irrespective of bit rate. It was also observed that the video transmission failed at RSS of −91 dBm in both ad hoc and infrastructure networks. Therefore, when planning for multimedia WLANs, system planners need to consider deploying high-performance WLANs optimized with CLD to achieve a better QoS.

RECOMMENDATION FOR FUTURE DEVELOPMENT

This book provides a significant contribution in answering the research question: What are the key factors influencing WLAN performance, and how can these performance-limiting factors be quantified? This section outlines a number of possible future researches that could help further understanding of the problem.

WLAN Performance Evaluation in the Presence of Hidden and Exposed Stations

This book has focused on the performance estimation of WLANs by assuming no hidden and exposed station problems in the network. This assumption basically simplifies simulation models for performance analysis. However, wireless networks in real environments may have both hidden and exposed stations that limit the performance of WLANs. Although there have been some attempts to address both the hidden and exposed station problems in WLANs in the networking literature [58, 62, 323], an in-depth study (both analytical and simulation) on the impact of hidden and exposed stations on WLAN performance under realistic scenarios would be a useful contribution.

Performance Study of 802.11a Networks

In this book, the key WLAN performance-limiting factors were quantified, including MAC protocols, radio propagation environments, and traffic type and their distributions using 802.11b/g equipment. Both 802.11b and 802.11g operate at 2.4 GHz, and they support up to 11 and 54 Mbps, respectively. However, 802.11a operates at 5 GHz and has different radio propagation characteristics than 802.11b/g. The impact of using 5-GHz signals on WLAN performance, especially in obstructed office spaces and residential houses, has not been investigated in this book because of the unavailability of 802.11a cards and APs. As an extension to the work presented in this book, the impact of key performance-limiting factors on WLAN performance needs to be quantified, focusing on noise and co-channel interference using 802.11a equipment.

Rate Adaptation QoS-Aware MAC Protocol for Multimedia WLANs

In this book, a particular emphasis was to improve WLAN performance by modifying wireless MAC protocols. A new MAC protocol called BUMA was developed as a minor modification of the existing 802.11 distributed coordination function (DCF) and showed promising results (Chapter 9). C-BUMA, a second MAC protocol, was developed by extending the BUMA protocol for CLD optimization (Chapter 12). A robust rate-adaptive QoS-aware MAC protocol is required to assist efficient design and deployment of WLAN systems to support multimedia applications. The design and performance evaluation of such a rate-adaptive multimedia MAC protocol would be an important extension to this research.

Cross-Layer Design with Adaptive Payload and Rate Adaptation for Multimedia WLANs

In this book, a joint PHY-MAC CLD framework was developed and presented in Chapter 12. The channel prediction and transmission control algorithms included in the proposed framework considerably improve system performance. However, this channel-aware CLD assumes fixed payload length and data rate. Research has shown that payload length has a significant effect on WLAN throughput [20, 224, 264]. Using a higher payload length (e.g., 2,000 bytes) for video transmission can significantly improve the throughput in good channel conditions. However, in environments where the packet error rate is high (low signal-to-noise ratio [SNR] regions), a lower payload length (e.g., 200 bytes) might be preferable. It would be useful to provide link adaptation by varying the data rate and payload length as a function of channel conditions. The development of a robust CLD scheme where the payload length and data rate are jointly optimized for better system performance is a logical extension to the work presented in Chapter 12.

Development of an Adapting Routing Protocol for WLANs

Research has shown that routing protocols play an important role in discovering routes between mobile wireless stations, and hence improve system performance [44, 324, 325]. This book has investigated the impact of routing protocols on WLAN performance (Chapter 11). Various ways of improving WLAN performance by quantifying key performance-limiting factors using a traditional mobile ad hoc network (MANET) routing protocol such as an Ad Hoc On-Demand Distance Vector (AODV) have also been investigated. This allows quantification of key WLAN performance-limiting factors such as MAC protocols, radio propagation environments, traffic type, and their distributions without diverting from the main focus.

While network researchers and designers have developed a variety of routing protocols to improve system performance for MANETs, the fact remains that each protocol is optimized for a particular application or scenario. For example, the Destination Sequenced Distance Vector (DSDV) and ADOV protocols are good for small networks, whereas Dynamic Source Routing (DSR) and Temporally Ordered Routing Algorithm (TORA) are designed for large networks (more than 200 nodes) with high mobility. A channel-aware adaptive routing protocol that can support high mobility, varying node densities, and better bandwidth is required to assist efficient design and deployment of such systems. The design and performance evaluation of such an adaptive routing protocol would be a useful contribution.

Development of Antenna-Aware Propagation Models

In this book both radio propagation measurements and computer simulation are being used for the estimation of WLAN performance without the use of propagation modeling. The propagation measurement is inevitably site specific, which is partially mitigated in this study by conducting various experiments in two office buildings and a suburban residential house, as well as using simulation study. In WLANs, the types of transmitting and receiving antennas being used can have a significant impact on system performance [23, 25]. This is because they determine radio signal propagation in wireless channels. The development of accurate and computationally efficient propagation models that incorporate the effects of different types of antennas is a logical extension to the study presented in this book.

FURTHER READING

For more details about subjects discussed in this chapter, we recommend the following books and references. The items in [] refer to the reference list at the end of the book.

Books

[171] Chapter 6—*Computer Networking: A Top-Down Approach* by Kurose and Ross

[172] Chapter 4—*Computer Networks* by Tanenbaum and Wetherall

Research Papers

[326]

SUMMARY

This chapter has presented guidelines for deploying WLANs in office buildings and residential houses from the perspective of system planning. These guidelines have been derived from the analysis of results presented in Chapters 7 to 14 and provide useful information to assist managers and house occupants to make informed decisions in the deployment of WLANs in similar office and house situations. A number of possible extensions to this research have also been suggested.

The currently available WLAN deployment technologies are graphically summarized. Large-scale deployment of WLANs in office buildings and residential houses and their performance issues were examined. Regardless of technology, system planners need to determine the key factors influencing system performance. Data from a propagation study in an indoor environment would be useful for better system planning, including configuring and optimizing locations of APs.

Recommendations for future developments of this research are outlined. They include system performance evaluation in the presence of hidden and exposed stations, performance studies of 802.11a WLANs, QoS-aware MAC protocol development for multimedia networking, development of a robust CLD scheme where payload and rate adaptation are jointly optimized, and design of an adaptive routing protocol for WLANs. An investigation into propagation models that incorporate the effect of antennas is also suggested as future work. Next, the recent developments in WLANs are discussed in Chapter 16.

KEY TERMS

Access point (AP)
Cross-layer design (CLD)
IEEE 802.11a/b/g/n
Line of sight (LOS)
Multiple-input multiple-output (MIMO)
Obstructed office block

Orthogonal frequency division
  multiplexing (OFDM)
Radio frequency (RF)
Transmission overhead
Throughput
WLAN deployment

REVIEW QUESTIONS

1. WLANs are emerging technologies that are deployed worldwide. Discuss the trends in the deployment of 802.11 WLANs.

2. It is useful to have clear guidelines for indoor WLAN system design and deployment. Outline the guidelines for system planners in the design and deployment of indoor WLAN systems.

3. WLANs have various issues when it comes to deployment in office buildings. Identify and discuss two main issues in the deployment of WLANs in a single-floor office building.

4. The deployment of WLANs in multifloor office buildings can be very challenging. Identify and discuss two main issues/challenges in the deployment of WLANs in multifloor office buildings.

5. Discuss various approaches of achieving high-speed WLANs using cross-layer design.

MINI-PROJECTS

The following mini-projects aim to provide a deeper understanding of the topics covered in this chapter through literature review.

1. Write an in-depth review report on the guidelines for system planners in the design and deployment of indoor WLAN systems. (Hint: Read 10 to 15 recent relevant journal/conference papers on indoor WLAN design and deployment and summarize your findings; discuss the performance issues/challenges.)

2. Write an in-depth review report on the deployment of WLANs in multifloor office buildings. (Hint: Read 10 to 15 recent relevant journal/conference papers on multifloor indoor WLAN deployment and summarize your findings; discuss the performance issues, AP location, and placement issues.)

Recent Developments in WLANs

LEARNING OUTCOMES

After reading and completing this chapter, you will be able to:

- Discuss the recent developments in high-performance gigabit capacity WLANs

- Discuss the recent developments in supporting emergency traffic in WLANs

- Discuss the recent developments in wireless mesh and cognitive radio networks

- Discuss the recent developments in vehicle-to-vehicle communications

- Discuss the recent developments in green communication and networking

- Discuss new developments in WLAN security protocols

INTRODUCTION

In Chapter 15, the implications for WLAN system design and deployment were discussed. A set of guidelines for planning and deploying of indoor WLANs was also presented. It is interesting to note how rapidly WLAN technologies have been evolving, from 802.11 in 1997, to 802.11a/b in 1999,

802.11g in 2003, and 802.11n in 2009. This chapter provides an overview of the recent developments in WLAN technologies and standardization. The high-performance WLAN technologies such as 802.11n, 802.11ac, and 802.11ad are introduced in the "IEEE 802.11n: High-Performance Wi-Fi," "IEEE 802.11ac: Next-Generation Wi-Fi," and "IEEE 802.11ad: Very High Throughput Wi-Fi" sections, respectively. The WLAN supporting emergency traffic (802.11u) and vehicle-to-vehicle communication (802.11p) are discussed in the "IEEE 802.11u: Emergency QoS" and "IEEE 802.11p: Vehicle-to-Vehicle Communication" sections, respectively. While wireless mesh networking (WMN) is an attractive solution for low-cost broadband Internet access, cognitive radio networks (CRNs) play an important role in improving spectrum usage and efficiency. Overviews of WMN and CRN are presented in the "IEEE 802.11s: Wireless Mesh Networking" and "IEEE 802.22 Cognitive Radio Network" sections, respectively. Green communication and networking has attracted a lot of attention in recent years as far as an energy-efficient network is concerned. The "Green Networking" section provides an overview of green communication and networking. Finally, we discuss possible solutions for WLAN security in the "802.11i: Secure Wireless Network" section, and a brief summary concludes the chapter.

IEEE 802.11N: HIGH-PERFORMANCE WI-FI

To meet the increasing demands for high-performance WLANs, 802.11n was standardized by IEEE in 2009. The 802.11n working group has focused on increasing network throughput and the overall system capacity. However, increasing effective throughput involves improvement in signal encoding techniques, multiple-input multiple-output (MIMO) antenna design, and the medium access control (MAC) layer frame structure. The 802.11n standard operates in both the 2.4- and 5-GHz bands, and can therefore be backward compatible with 802.11a/b/g [232].

IEEE 802.11n was designed to improve on 802.11g in the amount of bandwidth supported by using multiple data streams provided by MIMO technology (discussed in the "MIMO" section). In MIMO system, receivers use complex algorithms to separate the out-of-phase signals and recombine multiple streams together, resulting in a much higher aggregate data rate than 802.11a/b/g. For example, using a 40-MHz channel, four streams, and the optional short guard interval, the maximum data rate of 600 Mbps can be achieved by an 802.11n. In summary, 802.11n achieves high performance as a result of changes in three main areas: use of MIMO, enhancements in physical layer (PHY) transmission, and MAC enhancements. The MIMO technology is described next.

MIMO

MIMO uses multiple transmitters and receivers to transfer more data at the same time. Wireless cards and access points (APs) with 802.11n support MIMO. This is part of the technology that allows 802.11n to reach much higher speeds than products without 802.11n. MIMO is a major enhancement provided by 802.11n (as opposed to 802.11g). In a MIMO scheme, the source data stream is divided into n substreams, one for each of the n transmitting antennas. The individual substreams are the input to the transmitting antennas (multiple input). At the receiving end, m antennas receive the transmissions from the n source antennas via a combination of line-of-sight transmissions and multipaths. The outputs from the m receiving antennas (multiple output) are combined with the signals from the other receiver radios. With a lot of complex mathematics, the result is a much better received signal than can be achieved with either a single antenna or multiple frequency channels. IEEE 802.11n defines a number of different combinations for the number of transmitters and the number of receivers, from 2×1 to 4×4. Each additional transmitter or receiver in the system increases the signal-to-noise ratio (SNR). However, the incremental gains from each additional transmitter or receiver diminish rapidly. The gain in SNR is large for each step from 2×1 to 2×2 and to 3×2, but the improvement with 3×3 and beyond is relatively small [327].

PHY Enhancement

In addition to MIMO, 802.11n makes a number of changes in the radio transmission scheme to increase system capacity. The most significant of these techniques, known as channel bonding, combines two 20-MHz channels to create a 40-MHz channel. Using orthogonal frequency division multiplexing (OFDM), this allows for twice as many subchannels, doubling the transmission rate.

MAC Enhancement

The 802.11n aggregates multiple MAC frames into a single block (single header and tailor) for transmissions. Frame aggregation is a process of packing multiple MAC segment data units (MSDUs) or MAC protocol data units (MPDUs) together to reduce the overheads and averaging them over multiple frames, thereby increasing effective throughput. There are two types of frame aggregation in 802.11n: (1) aggregation of MPDUs at the bottom of the MAC (A-MPDU) and (2) aggregation of MSDUs at the top of the MAC (A-MSDU). A-MPDU aggregation requires the use of block acknowledgment, which was introduced in 802.11e and optimized in 802.11n. This is a major MAC layer enhancement provided by 802.11n. Once a station acquires the channel for transmission, it can transmit long packets without significant delays between transmissions. The receiver sends a single block acknowledgment. Frame aggregation can result in significantly improved efficiency in the use of the transmission capacity. IEEE 802.11n provides a significant performance gain, especially for networks in which a small number of users are actively competing for transmission time [232].

IEEE 802.11AC: NEXT-GENERATION WI-FI

IEEE 802.11ac is the next-generation WLAN standard that can offer Gigabit Ethernet capacity (speed) using wireless fidelity (Wi-Fi) technology. IEEE 802.11ac is an evolutionary improvement to 802.11n, which will be approved by the Wi-Fi Alliance in early 2014. The idea was to improve on 802.11n in the amount of bandwidth supported by utilizing multiuser MIMO technology. It provides high throughput by operating in the 5-GHz band and is backward compatible with 802.11n's 5-GHz band.

Theoretically, 802.11ac enables multistation WLAN throughput of at least 1 Gbps and a single link throughput of at least 500 Mbps. The first generation of 802.11ac products are built around 80 MHz, delivering up to 433 Mbps (low end), 867 Mbps, (mid-tier), or 1,300 Mbps (high end) at the PHY. The second-generation products promise more channel bonding and spatial streams and will provide data rates of up to 3.47 Gbps. While 802.11n can be thought of as an Ethernet hub that can only transfer a single frame at a time to all its ports, 802.11ac would allow an AP to send multiple frames to multiple clients at the same time over the same frequency spectrum. With multiple smart antennas, an AP can behave like a wireless switch. More details about 802.11ac can be found in the IEEE standards and white papers [287, 328].

In summary, the enhanced performance of 802.11ac can be achieved by extending the air interface of 802.11n in the following areas:

- **More channel bonding:** Mandatory 80-MHz channel bandwidth for stations (40 MHz maximum in 802.11n) and 160 MHz available optionally.

- **More MIMO spatial streams:** Support for up to eight spatial streams (four in 802.11n).

- **Multiuser MIMO (MU-MIMO):** Multiple stations, each with one or more antennas, transmit or receive independent data streams simultaneously.

- **Denser modulation:** 256 QAM, rate 3/4 and 5/6, added as optional modes (64 QAM, rate 5/6 maximum in 802.11n).

- **MAC modifications:** Mostly to support above changes.

IEEE 802.11AD: VERY HIGH THROUGHPUT WI-FI

While 802.11ac is an extension of the existing 802.11n specification, 802.11ad is a completely new generation very high throughput Wi-Fi that was standardized by IEEE at the end of 2012. It operates in the 60-GHz band, as opposed to the 2.4- or 5-GHz band. An IEEE working group (TGad) and the Wireless Gigabit Alliance (WiGig) jointly proposed 802.11ad, which aims to provide an alternative solution for ad hoc short-range connectivity (e.g., between a Blu-ray player and the TV, eliminating the need for the high-definition multimedia interface (HDMI) cable) in support of extremely high data rates (up to 7 Gbps). Use of 60 GHz can be realized by the fact that both the 2.4- and 5-GHz bands for the traditional 802.11 standards are heavily congested and lack the capacity to deliver the very high throughput needed for emerging business and consumer applications. For example, the multi-gigabit data rates required for high-definition multimedia transmissions, including 4k and 8k digital cinema and three-dimensional video streaming between devices in the same room, must be accommodated in the new-generation Wi-Fi, such as 802.11ad. The global unlicensed band at around 60 GHz meets that requirement. The unlicensed frequency allocations at around 60 GHz in each country/region do not match exactly, but there is substantial overlap. At least 3.5 GHz of contiguous spectrum is available in all regions that have allocated spectrum. The International Telecommunication Union (ITU)-R-recommended channelization comprises four channels that are each 2.16 GHz wide. They are centered on 58.32, 60.48, 62.64, and 64.80

GHz. Channel 2, which is globally available, is therefore the default channel for equipment operating in this frequency band [329].

The design goal of 802.11ad was to be backward compatible with IEEE 802.11 standards for WLANs and for 802.11ac and 802.11ad to be compatible at the MAC layer, able to differ only in PHY layer characteristics. The 802.11ad also defines procedures to enable WiGig-compliant devices to hand over sessions to operate in the 2.4- or 5-GHz bands. Devices could then have three radios: 2.4 GHz for general use (may suffer from interference), 5 GHz for more robust and higher-speed applications, and 60 GHz for ultra-high-speed operation within a room [330].

IEEE 802.11U: EMERGENCY QOS

IEEE 802.11u-2011 is an amendment to the IEEE 802.11-2007 standard to add features that improve interworking with external networks and to support emergency traffic services over infrastructure-based WLANs. The key features of 802.11u are briefly describe below:

- **Interworking with external networks:** IEEE 802.11u allows 802.11 devices to interwork with external networks, such as public hotspots or other public networks, irrespective of whether the service is subscription based or free.

- **802.11u enables higher-layer functionalities to provide overall end-to-end quality of service (QoS):** The 802.11u standard allows network discovery and selection, enabling of information transfer from external networks, emergency services, and interfacing of subscription service provider networks to 802.11 that support interworking with external networks. The network discovery and selection can be achieved in the following ways:

  1. 802.11u discovers available networks (i.e., preassociation) through the advertisement of access network type (e.g., private network, free public network, fee public network).

  2. Using Generic Advertisement Service (GAS) layer 2 transport of an advertisement protocol's frames between a mobile device and a server in the network prior to authentication. The access point is responsible for the relay of a mobile device's query to a server in the carrier's network and for delivering the server's response back to the mobile.

3. 802.11u provides Access Network Query Protocol (ANQP), which is a query and response protocol used by a mobile device to discover a range of information, including the hotspot operator's domain name (a globally unique, machine-searchable data element); roaming partners accessible via the hotspot, along with their credential type and extensible authentication protocol (EAP) method supported for authentication; IP address type availability (for example, IPv4, IPv6); and other metadata useful in a mobile device's network selection process.

More details about this standard can be found in the 802.11u documents and white papers [86, 212].

IEEE 802.11P: VEHICLE-TO-VEHICLE COMMUNICATION

IEEE 802.11p is an amendment to the IEEE 802.11 standard (approved on July 15, 2010), which includes wireless access in vehicular environments (WAVE). The 802.11p specification describes the functions and services required by WAVE stations to operate in a rapidly varying environment and exchange messages either without having to join a basic service set (BSS) or within a WAVE BSS. It also defines the WAVE signaling technique and interface functions that are controlled by the 802.11 MAC [331].

Basically, 802.11p provides an enhancement to 802.11 to support Intelligent Transportation Systems (ITS) applications. This includes data exchange between high-speed intervehicles and the roadside infrastructure in the licensed ITS band of 5.9 GHz (5.85–5.925 GHz). IEEE 1609 is a higher-layer standard based on the 802.11p. The ultimate vision is a nationwide network that enables communication between vehicles and roadside access points or other vehicles. In Europe, 802.11p is used as a basis for the ITS-G5 standard, supporting the GeoNetworking protocol for vehicle-to-vehicle and vehicle-to-infrastructure communication. ITS-G5 and GeoNetworking are being standardized by European Telecommunication Standards Institute (ETSI) ITS.

The 802.11p standard was developed as a result of the following amendments to the 802.11 standard:

- **Transmissions outside the context of a BSS:** As the communication link between the vehicles and the roadside infrastructure might exist for only a short period, the 802.11p amendment defines a way to exchange data through that link without the need to establish a BSS (i.e., without the need to wait for the association and authentication procedures to complete before exchanging data). The 802.11p-enabled stations use the wildcard BSSID (a value of all 1s) in the frame header and start sending and receiving data frames as soon as they arrive on the communication channel. Because such stations are neither associated nor authenticated, the authentication and data confidentiality mechanisms provided by the 802.11 standard cannot be used. These kinds of functionality must then be provided by higher network layers.

- **Timing advertisement:** This amendment adds a new management frame for timing advertisement, which allows 802.11p-enabled stations to synchronize themselves with a common time reference. The only time reference defined in the 802.11p amendment is Coordinated Universal Time (UTC).

- **Enhanced receiver performance:** Some optional enhanced channel rejection requirements (for both adjacent and nonadjacent channels) are specified in this amendment to improve the immunity of the communication system to out-of-channel interference. They only apply to OFDM transmissions in the 5-GHz band (i.e., 802.11a PHY layer).

- **Use of the 5.9-GHz band:** The 802.11p amendment allows the use of the 5.9-GHz band (5.850–5.925 GHz) with 5, 10, and 20 MHz channel spacings, and specifies the requirements for using this band in the United States and Europe.

More details about this standard can be found in 802.11p documents and white papers [332].

IEEE 802.11S: WIRELESS MESH NETWORKING

Wireless mesh networking has gained immense research interest in the past few years due to high recognition in the wireless industry as a simple-to-install, cost-effective, scalable, and wider coverage and capacity-capable wireless technology. It has great potential to provide low-cost high-speed Internet access citywide in metropolitan areas and support high bandwidth consumer services such as streaming video that can profoundly impact our lives in a positive way. Many current mesh network deployments are based on Wi-Fi technology, the common term for wireless services meeting the IEEE 802.11 standards [333].

Despite the potential benefits of WMNs, mesh itself does not stand alone but is a component of a total Wi-Fi networking solution where many research challenges remain, especially when concurrent users are served with multimedia traffic. The primary intention of mesh networking at the early stage of development was to address two issues that are critical in rendering Wi-Fi deployments. One was improving coverage with meshed access points, and the other one was to provide cost-effective backhaul using the wireless meshing techniques. However, recent advances in Wi-Fi last-mile access and high growth in online videos on web-based streaming services have created other major challenges for network researchers to increase the per user data rate of a typical WMN supporting a large number of concurrent and content-rich multimedia applications. Traditional approaches of WMN optimization in individual layers of the Open Systems Interconnection (OSI) reference model [334] using policy-based traffic prioritization are no longer effective when it comes to multiple users transmitting multimedia traffic simultaneously.

Further supporting QoS at the MAC layer, network layer, or transport layer, even with application layer resource demand intelligence, is fairly difficult in multihop WMNs where dynamic behavior results in high packet loss ratios, causing an adverse impact on the quality of multimedia. Performance modeling and optimization of cross-layers of these networks with the visibility of radio channel behavior and demand for resource consumption from media-rich applications are required for efficient design and deployment of such systems.

WMN is in the process of standardization by the IEEE 802.11s task group (Draft 12.0 in June 2011). The Internet Engineering Task Force (IETF) had also set up a wireless mesh network known as the mobile ad hoc network (MANET), with a separate set of standards. Both MANET and WMN nodes exploit the redundancy of connected nodes and have the ability of self-organize, self-discover, self-heal, and self-configure. However, in real-world applications MANETs are implemented with mobile and more power constrained nodes, and the infrastructure is less self-organized. In contrast, WMNs are typically a collection of more organized stationary nodes and may use multiple radios for the purpose of wireless mesh backhauling for WLAN with one radio, and the other radio for AP functionality [335].

The primary objective of 802.11s standardization was to define the 802.11 PHY and MAC layers to create a wireless distribution system (DS) that is capable of automating topology learning and wireless path configuration for self-learning, self-forming, and self-healing wireless paths. The standard defines a dynamic and radio-aware path selection mechanism for delivery of data on both single-hop and multihop networks. Any wireless node complying with these functionalities is said to be a wireless mesh-capable node that forms a WMN or a mesh cloud. One of the key issues in WMN standardization is the adaptation of legacy distributed medium access schemes to share the medium that has inherent unfairness in achieving concurrent transmissions between mesh nodes in a multihop mesh network. However, it is important that WMN standards address these challenging issues without compromising the compatibilities of WMN to continue to evolve as a cost-effective backhauling technology for WLANs [293, 336].

IEEE 802.22 COGNITIVE RADIO NETWORK

Cognitive radio (CR) is an emerging radio technology that enables a network to use spectrum in a dynamic manner (i.e., spectrum allocation on demand). The most significant characteristic of a CR is the capability to sense the surrounding radio environment (e.g., transmission frequency, bandwidth, power, and modulation) to make a decision to adapt the parameters in achieving a better QoS. It coordinates the spectrum usage to identify the unused spectrum [337].

The main elements of a CRN are the licensed or primary users (PUs) and the CR or secondary (unlicensed) users (SUs). To maintain the priority in accessing the spectrum, the operations of PUs must not be affected by SUs. The main idea is that a CRN monitors radio spectrum bands and uses the spectrum holes opportunistically with the least possible interference to PUs caused by SUs. These capabilities can be realized through efficient spectrum management functions in four main areas: spectrum sensing, spectrum decision, spectrum sharing, and spectrum mobility. CRs should decide on the best spectrum band to use from all the available bands to meet QoS requirements. Therefore, spectrum management functions play an important role in such systems [338].

The IEEE 802.22 standard (approved on July 1, 2011) for wireless regional area networks (WRANs) specifies a cognitive air interface for fixed, point-to-multipoint WRANs that operate on unused TV bands in the VHF/UHF (54–862 MHz). The signals at these frequencies can travel up to 40 km from a base station (BS) [339]. The 802.22 network is responsible for ensuring that it creates no undue interference to other users of the relevant spectrum. The overall network comprises the BS and a number of user equipments, known as customer premises equipment (CPE). The CPEs scan the various channels that are open for their use and send back information about signals and strengths on the channels to the BS equipment. The BS makes the decision about which channels are occupied and whether they can be used for the 802.22 transmissions. In this way, the 802.22 WRAN performs spectrum sensing across the whole network and adjusts itself accordingly. This means that the 802.22 system is a true CRN, rather than an individual CR operating in isolation.

GREEN NETWORKING

Green communication and networking is one of the hot topics in computer networking today. It focuses on efficient networking with respect to design, operation, and management. The aim is to design energy-efficient (green network) telecommunication networks. This includes designing energy-efficient MAC and routing protocols, and networking devices such as switches, routers, and servers. This is in line with the trend toward "greening" just about everything, from cars to coffee cups. This trend has encompassed Information and Communication Technology (ICT) in general, including the data center and the network. The idea is to avoid wasting channel bandwidth and power.

From the network management point of view, upgrading older networking devices to greener, more energy-efficient equipment can cut down costs in the long run. More details on green networking and the reasons for going green can be found in networking textbooks and papers [340–343].

802.11I: SECURE WIRELESS NETWORK

The Wi-Fi Alliance introduced the second generation of Wi-Fi Protected Access (WPA) security known as Wi-Fi Protected Access 2 (WPA2), which is based on the final 802.11i amendment to the 802.11 standard ratified in June 2004. IEEE 802.11i makes use of the Advanced Encryption Standard (AES) block cipher, whereas wired equivalent privacy (WEP) and WPA use the RC4 stream cipher. The 802.11i is a new standard that provides an enhanced security that includes the use of the 802.1X authentication protocol, improved key distribution and management, and stronger encryption using AES. More features, including methods to secure an ad hoc network, secure deauthentication and disassociation procedures, secure fast handoff between access points, and implement enhanced encryption protocols, are also supported by 802.11i. More details about the deployment of WPA and WPA2 can be found in [344]. In summary, organizations can use WPA in conjunction with 802.1X authentication as a short-term solution to WLAN security. For a long-term solution, companies can adopt the new 802.11i standard [345, 346].

FURTHER READING

For more details about subjects discussed in this chapter, we recommend the following books and references. The items in [] refer to the reference list at the end of the book.

Books

[368] *Wireless Mesh Networking* by Zhang, Luo, and Hu

[347] *Green Communications and Networking* edited by Yu, Zhang, and Leung

[172] Chapter 4—*Computer Networks* by Tanenbaum and Wetherall

Research Papers

[279]

[330]

[338]

[347–349]

SUMMARY

The latest developments in WLAN technologies have been outlined and discussed. We first introduced 802.11n, a high-performance WLAN that is a major enhancement to its predecessors, 802.11g and 802.11a. The higher data rate is achieved by using MIMO technology, high channel bandwidth, and MAC layer frame aggregation. We then introduced 802.11ac, the next-generation Wi-Fi technology for gigabit capacity. The 802.11ac standard is a major enhancement to 802.11n, and the high data rate is achieved by using wider radio frequency (RF) bandwidth, more MIMO spatial streams, and high-density modulation. We also introduced a new Wi-Fi standard for very high throughput called 802.11ad, operating in the 60-GHz band, suitable for HD video streaming between devices in the same room.

The 802.11u-2011 working group introduced a new standard called 802.11u for interworking with external networks and supporting emergency traffic over infrastructure WLANs. The 802.11u specification contains requirements in the areas of enrollment, network selection, emergency call support, emergency alert notification, user traffic segmentation, and service advertisement.

An overview of 802.11p for vehicle-to-vehicle and vehicle-to-infrastructure communication is presented. IEEE 802.11s is an amendment to 802.11 for mesh networking, defining how wireless devices can interconnect to create a WLAN mesh network. We introduced IEEE 802.22 WRAN, a cognitive radio network that performs spectrum sensing across the whole network. Green communication and networking is the practice of consolidating devices and designing energy-efficient protocols. Finally, 802.11i is introduced, which is a new standard for secure WLANs.

KEY TERMS

802.11ac	Cognitive ratio (CR)
802.11ad	Emergency QoS
802.11i	Emerging networking technology
802.11n	Green networking
802.11p	Multiple-input multiple-output (MIMO)
802.11s	Vehicle-to-vehicle communication
802.11u	Wireless mesh network

REVIEW QUESTIONS

1. Identify and describe four emerging network technologies for WLANs.

2. List and describe three main features of 802.11ac.

3. Discuss the differences between 802.11ac and 802.11ad.

4. Discuss the IEEE standard in supporting emergency traffic in WLANs. Include in your discussion the need for such a standard.

5. Discuss the potential features of an IEEE standard for vehicle-to-vehicle (V2V) communication.

6. Discuss the main purpose of designing wireless mesh networks.

7. Discuss why cognitive radio networks are needed.

8. Discuss the main motivation for designing green networking.

9. Discuss the recent development in WLAN security protocols.

MINI-PROJECTS

The following mini-projects aim to provide a deeper understanding of the topics covered in this chapter through literature review.

1. **Emergency QoS:** Read 10 to 15 recent journal/conference papers on supporting emergency traffic in WLANs and identify the key researchers and their main contributions. Use Table 16.1 to record your findings.

2. **V2V communication:** Read 10 to 15 recent journal/conference papers on V2V communications and identify the key researchers and their main contributions. Use Table 16.2 to record your findings.

3. **Mesh networking:** Read 10 to 15 recent journal/conference papers on WMN MAC and routing protocols and identify the key researchers and their main contributions. Use Table 16.3 to record your findings.

4. **Cognitive radio network:** Read 10 to 15 recent journal/conference papers on cognitive radio MAC and routing protocols and identify the key researchers and their main contributions. Use Table 16.4 to record your findings.

5. **Green networking:** Read 10 to 15 recent journal/conference papers on green communication and networking. Identify the key researchers and their main contributions on green communication and networking. Use Table 16.5 to record your findings.

6. **Wireless security:** Read 10 to 15 recent journal/conference papers on wireless network security and identify the key researchers and their main contributions. Use Table 16.6 to record your findings.

TABLE 16.1   Leading Researchers and Their Contributions in Supporting Emergency Traffic in WLANs

Researcher	Contribution	Year	Description/Key Concept

TABLE 16.2   Leading Researchers and Their Contributions in V2V Communications

Researcher	Contribution	Year	Description/Key Concept

TABLE 16.3   Leading Researchers and Their Contributions in WMN MAC and Routing Protocols

Researcher	Contribution	Year	Description/Key Concept

TABLE 16.4   Leading Researchers and Their Contributions in Cognitive Radio MAC and Routing Protocols

Researcher	Contribution	Year	Description/Key Concept

TABLE 16.5   Leading Researchers and Their Contributions in Green Communication and Networking

Researcher	Contribution	Year	Description/Key Concept

TABLE 16.6   Leading Researchers and Their Contributions in Wireless Network Security

Researcher	Contribution	Year	Description/Key Concept

Glossary

Access method: This term generally refers to a scheme by which stations may access a network via a shared medium. *See also* channel access protocol.

Access point (AP): Typically, infrastructure-based wireless networks provide access to the wired backbone network via an AP. The AP may act as a repeater, bridge, router, or even as gateway to regenerate, forward, filter, or translate messages. All communication between mobile devices has to take place via the AP.

ACK: Generally refers to the acknowledgment of the receipt of the last transmission.

Ad hoc network: A class of wireless network architecture in which there is no fixed infrastructure or wireless access points. In ad hoc networks, each mobile station acts as router to communicate with other stations. Such a network can exist on a temporary basis to share some resources among the mobile stations.

Animation: The abstract execution of a system model. Two terms are barely distinguished; *animation* has the sense of symbolic execution, while *simulation* has a more general sense and may deal with performance.

ARP: Address Resolution Protocol is used to translate between IP addresses and hardware addresses. There is an ARP utility found on both Microsoft and UNIX operating systems that can be used to view and modify the ARP cache.

Attenuation: The continuous loss of the signal's strength as it travels through a medium.

Backbone: A network of high-speed communication lines that carries the bulk of the traffic between major segments of the networks.

Backoff: The retransmission delay (usually random) enforced by contention media access control protocols after a station that wanted to transmit sensed a carrier on the physical medium.

Bandwidth: In general, the theoretical capacity (measured in bits per second or slots per second) of a data communication channel. For example, the bandwidth of a Fast Ethernet network is 100 Mbps. The greater the bandwidth is, the higher the possible data transmission rate. However, the technical definition of bandwidth is as follows: "The bandwidth of a channel is the difference between the highest and the lowest frequency of a communication channel that can be transmitted over a medium." For example, the public telephone network has a voice channel bandwidth of 3.1 KHz. Each channel can pass frequencies in the range of 300 to 3,400 Hz. Therefore, the bandwidth is 3,100 Hz, or 3.1 KHz.

Baseband: This term refers to the characteristic of a networking technology in which the entire channel capacity of the medium is used by one data signal. Thus, only one node transmits at a time. Ethernet LAN is an example of a baseband network.

Bit rate: The speed at which bits are transmitted, usually expressed in bits per second (bps). *See also* bps.

bps: Bits per second. Represents the rate at which data can be transmitted across a network. The number of bits per second may differ from the baud rate because more than one bit can be encoded in a single baud.

Broadband: A broadband transmission employs several transmission channels on a single physical medium. Thus, more than one node can transmit at a time. In New Zealand, Telecom's Jetstream is an example of a broadband technology.

Broadcast domain: It refers to a network segment where each node receives a broadcast packet sent from any of these devices are said to be in a broadcast domain.

Channel: A single communication path (e.g., cable media or wireless) over which a message flows.

Channel access protocol: Also known as media access control (MAC) protocol. A protocol (i.e., set of rules) that is used to access the shared channel on the network. Examples of access protocols are Ethernet CSMA/CD and token passing.

Collision: When two or more packets are simultaneously sent on a common network medium that only can transmit a single packet at a time. The packets collide and are corrupted and need to be re-sent.

Collision: An event that occurs on a CSMA/CD network when two stations attempt to transmit simultaneously. The signals interfere with each other, forcing the two stations to back off and try again.

Collision detection: A network management technique that allows each computer to transmit whenever it chooses. If a collision is detected, the messages are retransmitted.

Collision domain: A single physical or logical network segment using Ethernet technology through which collisions will be propagated. Devices in a collision domain communicate directly with each other and share the network medium.

CRC: Cyclic redundancy check. This is a method for checking for errors in a data stream. It uses a polynomial (a pattern of ones and zeros) as a divisor in a modified division of the entire data stream. The remainder of the division is appended to the message along with the data used as a verification by the receiver of the data stream.

Cross-development: The process of using software development tools like compilers, linkers, and debuggers, which are resident on a reprogrammable computer, to produce executable programs for an embedded computer system. The executable programs must then be transferred from the reprogrammable computer (called the development system) to the embedded computer (called the target system) for testing.

CSMA: Carrier sense multiple access. This is a channel access method in which a station senses the channel (e.g., listens to the channel) before sending a packet into the network—trying to find out whether another station is attempting to send a signal at the same time.

CSMA/CA: Carrier sense multiple access with collision avoidance. This is a popular access method used by wireless LAN. Before transmission, a station senses the channel. If the channel is idle, the packet is transmitted right away. If the channel is busy, the stations keep sensing the channel until it is idle, and then waits a uniformly distributed random backoff period before sensing the channel again. If the channel is still idle, it transmits its packet; otherwise, it backs off again. The backoff mechanism results in the avoidance of the collision of packets from multiple transmitters that all sense a clear channel at about the same time. All directed traffic receives a positive acknowledgment. Packets are retransmitted if an acknowledgment is not received.

CSMA/CD: Carrier sense multiple access with collision detection. This is a popular access method used by Ethernet LAN based on carrier sensing. Under this scheme, a computer senses the channel and transmits data if the channel is found to be idle (i.e., free). If the channel is busy, the station continues to sense (i.e., listen to) the channel until the channel is idle, and then transmits immediately. If a collision is detected during transmission, the station ceases transmission immediately. After a collision, a station waits a randomly determined amount of time, and then attempts to transmit again.

Cycle accurate: A simulator that models the operation of a processor on a cycle-by-cycle basis so that the state of the processor at the end of each cycle is correct.

Data link layer: This is the second layer of the OSI model, and it defines the pattern or purpose of the bits of a frame. Except for the physical layer, which defines the electronics behind a computer interface, it is the lowest level of the OSI model.

Datagram: A datagram is a block of data meant to be treated as a unit. If the datagram is too large to be handled by a network, it is possible to fragment it for transmission into smaller packets.

DHCP: Dynamic Host Control Protocol. Used to issue and obtain IP addresses, on both local area networks and wide area networks.

Direct sequence spread spectrum (DSSS): A transmission technique used to avoid interference and achieve a higher throughput. Instead of a single carrier frequency, a sender and receiver agree to use a set of frequencies concurrently. The practical application of DSSS is in wireless LAN.

Dynamic loading: The ability of a system to load additional software components (e.g., Java classes) as it executes.

Dynamic routing: A form of routing in which the routes that packets take in a network are able to change as a function of time. The routes can change as a result of node or link failures, or as a result of node or link characteristics (speed, cost, etc.), including the volume of traffic that is currently being serviced.

Ethereal: An open-source implementation of a packet sniffer. Available freely at http://www.ethereal.com.

Ethernet: A popular LAN technology that uses a shared channel and the CSMA/CD access method. Basic Ethernet operates at 10 Mbps,

Fast Ethernet operates at 100 Mbps, and Gigabit Ethernet operates at 1,000 Mbps.

Extended service set (ESS): In a large-scale, campus-wide WLAN, a wired backbone network would connect several BSSs via APs to form a single network, and thereby extend the wireless coverage area. Such a single network is called an extended service set (ESS) and has its own identifier, the ESSID, which is the name of that network and is used to distinguish it from different networks.

Firewalls: A software application running on a device that is responsible for filtering incoming and outgoing traffic.

Frame: The formatted packet that the underlying hardware accepts and delivers.

Frequency hopping spread spectrum (FHSS): A technology normally used in wireless LANs. FHSS operates by transmitting short bursts of data on different frequencies. One burst is transmitted on one frequency, a second burst is transmitted on a second and different frequency, and so forth.

Gbps: Gigabits per second. It is a unit of data transfer equal to 1,000 Mbps or 10^9 bps.

GUI: Graphical user interface. Most of the modern operating systems provide a GUI, which enables a user to use a pointing device, such as a computer mouse, to provide the computer with information about the user's intentions.

Hub: A networking device that interconnects two or more workstations in a star-wired local area network and broadcasts incoming data onto all outgoing connections. To avoid signal collision, only one user can transmit data through the hub at a time.

IBSS: Independent basic service set. A wireless LAN configuration without access points. IBSS is also referred to as ad hoc mode wireless network.

IEEE: Institute of Electrical and Electronic Engineers. It is one of the largest professional nonprofit organizations in the world. IEEE defines network standards (e.g., IEEE 802.11).

IEEE 802.11ac/ad: The 802.11ac is the next-generation Wi-Fi technology; it is a major enhancement to 802.11n to achieve a high data rate by using wider RF bandwidth, more MIMO spatial streams, and high-density modulation. IEEE 802.11ad is a new standard for very high throughput multigigabit Wi-Fi operating in the 60 GHz band. This is suitable for short-range communications such as HD video streaming between devices in the same room.

IEEE 802.11b/a/g/e/i/n: Generally refers to WLAN standards. The IEEE 802.11b is the wireless LAN standard with a maximum bandwidth of 11 Mbps operating in the 2.4-GHz band. The 802.11a standard is the high-speed WLAN with a maximum bandwidth of 54 Mbps operating in the 5-GHz band. The 802.11g standard is backward compatible with 802.11b with a maximum bandwidth of 54 Mbps operating in the 2.4-GHz band. IEEE 802.11e is a standard for quality of service in 802.11 WLANs. IEEE 802.11i is an 802.11 WLAN security standard. IEEE 802.11n is a high-speed WLAN standard that uses MIMO. It supports both 2.4 and 5 GHz and is backward compatible with 802.11b/g and 802.11a.

Infrared: Electromagnetic waves whose frequency range is above that of microwave but below the visible spectrum. The applications of infrared technology include TV remote control and WLAN systems.

Infrastructure network: A class of wireless network architecture in which mobile stations communicate with each other via access points, which are usually linked to a wired backbone. Such a network has a fixed infrastructure and a centralized control.

IP address: A 32-bit-long address assigned to hosts using TCP/IP. In dotted decimal format the address is written as four octets separated with periods that are made up of a network ID section, an optional subnet ID section, and a host ID section.

LAN: Local area network. A class of computer networks covering a relatively small geographic area, e.g., a room, a building, or a campus. A LAN is owned by a single organization and physically located within the organization's premises. Ethernet is the most popular LAN architecture.

Local loop: A term that telephone companies use to refer to the wiring between the central office and a subscriber (e.g., an individual business or residence). A variety of technologies have been developed to provide high-speed digital services over existing local loop wiring.

Logical topology: The way data are sent internally from one computer (or device) to another connected computer or device.

MAC address: Also known as physical address. Each MAC address is a 48-bit binary address (normally written in hexadecimal notation). If the unique MAC address that exists on the NIC of the receiving computer is identical to the destination MAC address defined in a packet, the computer will attempt to receive the packet and process the data. All other computers on the network that have different physical addresses will not attempt to accept the packet for processing.

MAN: Metropolitan area network. A MAN is a backbone network that links multiple LANs in a large city or a metropolitan region.

Medium access control protocol: *See* channel access protocol.

Mesh topology: A network architecture in which a node has a point-to-point connection to other nodes. Since every node has a dedicated point-to-point link to every other device, mesh topology offers the highest throughput (i.e., faster speed) as well as better fault tolerance than any other topology. Mesh topologies are not very popular for LANs because they are very expensive and difficult to change. For example, to connect n devices on a network, you will need $n(n - 1)/2$ connections and $(n - 1)$ ports per device. Thus, for a network of 10 workstations, there will be 45 physical links (interfaces) between them.

MHz: Megahertz—a measure of frequency equivalent to 1 million cycles per second.

Network interface card (NIC): A hardware device (i.e., card) that plugs into a workstation, file server, printer, or other device to connect it to a network and communicate with other network nodes. A NIC can be thought of as both a transmitter and a receiver (i.e., it is a transceiver).

Network layer: This is the third layer of the OSI model, and it defines the means for host-to-host logical addressing across a network. In the OSI model, it is immediately above the data link layer.

Network simulator: A computer program that simulates the layout and behavior of a network and enables network activity to be initiated and observed.

Network traffic: The network traffic denotes the number, size, and frequency of packets transmitted across a network at a given amount of time.

Node: Any device connected to a network such as a personal computer (PC), a mainframe computer, a router, a printer, or other network equipment.

Noise: Unwanted electrical or electromagnetic energy that degrades the quality of signals and data.

NOS: Network operating system. A complex program that can manage the common resources of a local area network. In addition, an NOS performs the standard operating system services. Examples of NOS include NetWare, Linux, and MS Windows 2003.

OFDM: Orthogonal frequency division multiplexing.

OSI model: Open Systems Interconnection. A network architecture for developing network protocol standards. The OSI model formally defines and codifies the concept of layered network architecture. The OSI model consists of the following seven layers: (1) physical, (2) data link, (3) network, (4) transport, (5) session, (6) presentation, and (7) application.

Packet: A generic term used to define a unit of data, including routing and other information that is sent through an Internet.

Packet forwarding: The process by which protocol data units in a packet-based network are sent from their source to their destination.

Packet switching: A transmission method in which packets are transmitted over a networking medium that maintains several paths between the sender and the receiver.

Peer-to-peer network: A class of network in which a computer can communicate with any other networked computers on an equal or peer-like basis without going through an intermediary, such as a server or a dedicated host.

Physical topology: This refers to the way computers and other devices are connected on the network physically.

Protocol: A protocol is a collection of rules for formatting, ordering, and error-checking data sent across a network.

Router: A computer or a device that connects networks having the same or a different access method, such as Ethernet network to a token ring network. A router can forward packets to networks by using a decision-making process based on data stored in a routing table. The router discovers the most efficient route based on both the table data and information supplied by the e-network manager.

Routing: A process that occurs on a network when a packet is shunted from router to router along the path to the target destination.

Routing is based on identifying the destination network from the IP address of the target machine.

Static routing: A form of routing in which the routes that packets take in a network do not change as a function of time once they are configured.

WAN: Wide area network. A WAN covers a large geographical area (e.g., a country or a continent). Telephone networks and the Internet are examples of WANs.

Wi-Fi antenna: Generally refers to an antenna used with Wi-Fi equipment to enhance the transmission and reception of the wireless signals used in the transfer of data between the sending equipment and the intended receiving equipment.

Wireless channel: Generally refers to a communication medium in which signals travel through space instead of through a physical cable. Electromagnetic radio waves are used as a wireless channel.

Wireless LAN: Refers to a LAN that uses infrared or radio frequencies rather than physical cable as the transmission medium.

Wireless link: Generally refers to a pathway for the transmission of information via a modulated unconstrained electromagnetic wave.

Workstation: An end user computer that has its own CPU and is used as a client to access another computer, such as a file server.

References

1. D. Watson. IT vital part of new Auckland Hospital. *ComputerWorld New Zealand*, 2003, p. 1. Retrieved from www.computerworld.co.nz.
2. R. Evans and N. I. Sarkar. Mobile commerce implementation in the hospital environment: issues, challenges and future trends. *The New Zealand Bulletin of Applied Computing and Information Technology*, 2(1), 2004. Retrieved March 2004 from http://www.naccq.ac.nz/bacit/0201/2004Evans_SarkarMC_health.html.
3. B. Brewin. Wireless moves into the enterprise. *ComputerWorld New Zealand*, 2004, p. 10. Retrieved from www.computerworld.co.nz.
4. A. Hills. Large-scale wireless LAN design. *IEEE Communications Magazine*, 39(11), 98–107, 2001.
5. A. Hills. Wireless Andrew [mobile computing for university campus]. *IEEE Spectrum*, 36(6), 49–53, 1999.
6. C. Keall. Hotspot for teacher. *NZ PC World*, 2003, p. 45.
7. P. Brislen. Telecom gets serious about wireless. *ComputerWorld New Zealand*, 2005. Retrieved October 30, 2005, from www.computerworld.co.nz.
8. B. J. Bennington and C. R. Bartel. Wireless Andrew: building a high speed, campus-wide wireless data network. *Mobile Networks and Applications*, 6(1), 9–22, 2001.
9. Avantikumar. Malaysian university rolls out new wireless WAN. *ComputerWorld New Zealand*, 2008, p. 20. Retrieved from www.computerworld.co.nz.
10. P. Brislen. Why go wireless? *CIO*, 51, 53, 2004.
11. AUT library facilities. Retrieved February 20, 2012, from www.aut.ac.nz.
12. Wireless Internet service launched in city. In *CityScene*. Auckland, New Zealand: Auckland City Council, 2009, p. 1.
13. S. Lawson. Nokia to sponsor free Wi-Fi in New York parks. *ComputerWorld New Zealand*, July 17, 2006, p. 23. Retrieved from www.computerworld.co.nz.
14. P. Sayer. Paris plans 400 free Wi-Fi hotspots and laptop seats around city. *ComputerWorld New Zealand*, July 17, 2006, p. 23.
15. S. Lawson. Dual-mode smartphones help boost Wi-Fi. *ComputerWorld New Zealand*, January 19, 2009, p. 13. Retrieved from www.computerworld.co.nz.

16. A. Tufail, M. Fraser, A. Hammad, K. K. Hyung, and S.-W. Yoo. An empirical study to analyze the feasibility of WiFi for VANETs. Presented at the 12th Conference on Computer Supported Cooperative Work in Design (CSCWD), April 16–18, 2008, pp. 553–558.

17. A. P. Subramanian, P. Deshpande, J. Gao, and S. R. Das. Drive-by localization of roadside WiFi networks. Presented at the 27th IEEE INFOCOM '08, April 13–18, 2008, pp. 1391–1399.

18. N. Prasad and A. Prasad. *WLAN systems and wireless IP for Next generation communications*. Boston: Artech House, 2002.

19. What is a wireless LAN? Retrieved September 1, 2013, from http://sss-mag.com/pdf/proximwhatwlan.pdf.

20. N. I. Sarkar and K. W. Sowerby. Buffer unit multiple access (BUMA) protocol: an enhancement to IEEE 802.11b DCF. Presented at the IEEE Global Telecommunications Conference (GLOBECOM '05), St. Louis, MO, November 28–December 2, 2005, pp. 2584–2588.

21. J. Fitzgerald and A. Dennis. *Business data communications and networking*. 10th ed. New York: John Wiley & Sons, 2009.

22. D. C. K. Lee, M. J. Neve, and K. W. Sowerby. The impact of structural shielding on the performance of wireless systems in a single-floor office building. *IEEE Transactions on Wireless Communications*, 6(5), 1787–1695, 2007.

23. A. H. Wong, M. J. Neve, and K. W. Sowerby. Performance analysis for indoor wireless systems employing directional antennas. *IEE Proceedings Communications*, 152(6), 890–896, 2005.

24. P. C. Ng and S. C. Liew. Throughput analysis of IEEE 802.11 multi-hop ad hoc networks." *IEEE/ACM Transactions on Networking*, 15(2), 309–322, 2007.

25. A. H. C. Wong. Antenna selection and deployment strategies for indoor wireless communication systems. PhD thesis, Department of Electrical and Computer Engineering, University of Auckland, Auckland, New Zealand, 2007.

26. D. C. K. Lee. Indoor wireless communication system performance enhancement via environmental modification. PhD thesis, Department of Electrical and Computer Engineering, University of Auckland, Auckland, New Zealand, 2007.

27. T. S. Rappaport. *Wireless communications: principles and practice*. 2nd ed. Englewood Cliffs, NJ: Prentice-Hall, 2002.

28. S. Y. Seidel and T. S. Rappaport. 914 MHz path loss prediction models for indoor wireless communications in multifloored buildings. *IEEE Transactions on Antennas and Propagation*, 40(2), 207–217, 1992.

29. S. Grace Hui-Hsia, K. W. Sowerby, M. J. Neve, and A. G. Williamson. A frequency-selective wall for interference reduction in wireless indoor environments. *IEEE Antennas and Propagation Magazine*, 48(5), 29–37, 2006.

30. J. Cao and C. Williamson. Towards stadium-scale wireless media streaming. Presented at the 14th IEEE International Symposium on Modeling, Analysis, and Simulation of Computer and Telecommunication Systems (MASCOTS '06), September 11–14, 2006, pp. 33–42.

31. S. Gupta and C. L. Williamson. An experimental study of video traffic on an Ethernet local area network. Presented at the IEEE Global Telecommunications Conference (GLOBECOM '94), November 28–December 2, 1994, pp. 558–562.

32. T. Kuang and C. Williamson. A measurement study of realmedia audio/video streaming traffic. Presented at the SPIE ITCOM, Boston, July 30–31, 2002, pp. 68–79.

33. ns-2 contributed code. 2011. Retrieved January 10, 2013, from www.isi.edu/nsnam/ns/ns-contributed.html.

34. OPNET Modeler. Retrieved April 10, 2013, from www.opnet.com.

35. S. Ivanov, A. Herms, and G. Lukas. Experimental validation of the ns-2 wireless model using simulation, emulation, and real network. Presented at the 4th Workshop on Mobile Ad-Hoc Networks (WMAN '07), Bern, Switzerland, February 26–March 2, 2007, pp. 433–444.

36. A. Sikora. *Wireless personal and local area networks.* New York: Wiley, 2003.

37. D. E. Comer. *Computer networks and internets with Internet applications.* 5th ed. Englewood Cliffs, NJ: Prentice Hall, 2009.

38. R. Bruno, M. Conti, and E. Gregori. A simple protocol for the dynamic tuning of the backoff mechanism in IEEE 802.11 networks. *Computer Networks,* 37(1), 33–44, 2001.

39. IEEE. IEEE standard for wireless LAN: medium access control (MAC) and physical layer (PHY) specifications. IEEE 802.11 WG. New York: IEEE, 1997.

40. J. Wu and I. Stojmenovic. Ad hoc networks. *IEEE Computer,* 37(2), 29–31, 2004.

41. C.-C. Yang and L.-P. Tseng. Fisheye zone routing protocol: a multi-level zone routing protocol for mobile ad hoc networks. *Computer Communications,* 30(2), 261–268, 2007.

42. L. Layuan and L. Chunlin. A QoS multicast routing protocol for clustering mobile ad hoc networks. *Computer Communications,* 30(7), 1641–1654, 2007.

43. T. Jian, X. Guoliang, C. Chandler, and Z. Weiyi. Link scheduling with power control for throughput enhancement in multihop wireless networks. *IEEE Transactions on Vehicular Technology,* 55(3), 733–742, 2006.

44. H. D. Trung, W. Benjapolakul, and P. M. Duc. Performance evaluation and comparison of different ad hoc routing protocols. *Computer Communications,* 30(1), 2478–2496, 2007.

45. M. S. Gast. *802.11 wireless networks—the definitive guide.* 2nd ed. Sebastopol, CA: O'Reilly Media, 2005.

46. IEEE. *Part II: wireless LAN medium access control (MAC) and physical layer (PHY) specifications: high-speed physical layer extension in the 2.4 GHz band.* IEEE 802.11b WG. New York: IEEE, 1999.

47. D. Qiao, S. Choi, and K. G. Shin. Interference analysis and transmit power control in IEEE 802.11a/h wireless LANs. *IEEE/ACM Transactions on Networking,* 15(5), 1007–1020, 2007.

48. Broadcom. IEEE 802.11g: the new mainstream wireless LAN standard. 2003. Retrieved May 23 2007, from http://www.54g.org/pdf/802.11g-WP104-RDS1.

49. IEEE. Part II: wireless LAN medium access control (MAC) and physical layer (PHY) specifications: high-speed physical layer in the 5 GHz band. IEEE 802.11a WG/D5.0. New York: IEEE, 1999.

50. C. Bemmoussat, F. Didi, and M. Feham. On the support of multimedia applications over wireless mesh networks. *International Journal of Wireless and Mobile Networks (IJWMN)*, 5(2), 157–173, 2013.

51. D. J. Goodman and A. Saleh. The near/far effect in local ALOHA radio communications. *IEEE Transactions on Vehicular Technology*, 36(1), 19–27, 1987.

52. Z. Hadzi-Velkov and B. Spasenovski. Capture effect with diversity in IEEE 802.11b DCF. Presented at the Eighth IEEE International Symposium on Computers and Communication (ISCC '03), June 30–July 3, 2003, pp. 699–704.

53. K. Jae Hyun and L. Jong Kyu. Capture effects of wireless CSMA/CA protocols in Rayleigh and shadow fading channels. *IEEE Transactions on Vehicular Technology*, 48(4), 1277–1286, 1999.

54. V. Bharghavan. Performance evaluation of algorithms for wireless medium access. Presented at the IEEE Computer Performance and Dependability Symposium (IPDS '98), Durham, NC, September 7–9, 1998, pp. 86–95.

55. S. Khurana, A. Kahol, and A. P. Jayasumana. Effect of hidden terminals on the performance of IEEE 802.11 MAC protocol. Presented at the IEEE 23rd Annual Conference on Local Computer Networks (LCN), October 11–14, 1998, pp. 12–20.

56. Z. J. Haas and J. Deng. Dual busy tone multiple access (DBTMA): a new medium access control for packet radio networks. Presented at the IEEE International Conference on Universal Personal Communications (ICUPC), October 5–9, 1998, pp. 973–977.

57. W. M. Moh, D. Yao, and K. Makki. Analyzing the hidden-terminal effects and multimedia support for wireless LAN. *Computer Communications*, 23(1), 998–1013, 2000.

58. S. Ray, D. Starobinski, and J. B. Carruthers. Performance of wireless networks with hidden nodes: a queuing-theoretic analysis. *Computer Communications*, 28(14), 1179–1192, 2005.

59. T. You, C.-H. Yeh, and H. Hassanein. CSMA/IC: a new class of collision-free MAC protocols for ad hoc wireless networks. Presented at the Eighth IEEE International Symposium on Computers and Communication (ISCC '03), June 30–July 3, 2003, pp. 843–848.

60. C. L. Fullmer and J. J. Garcia-Luna-Aceves. Complete single-channel solutions to hidden terminal problems in wireless LANs. Presented at the IEEE International Conference on Communications, Montreal, June 8–12, 1997, pp. 575–579.

61. P. Karn. MACA—a new channel access method for packet radio. Presented at the 9th ARRL/CRRL Amateur Radio Computer Networking Conference, Ontario, Canada, September 22, 1990, pp. 134–140.

62. L. B. Jiang and S. C. Liew. Improving throughput and fairness by reducing exposed and hidden nodes in 802.11 networks. *IEEE Transactions on Mobile Computing*, 7(1), 34–49, 2008.

63. V. Bharghavan. MACAW: a media access protocol for wireless LANs. Presented at the ACM Annual Conference on Applications, Technologies, Architectures, and Protocols for Computer Communications (SIGCOMM '94), London, August 31–September 2, 1994, pp. 212–225.

64. T. You, C.-H. Yeh, and H. Hassanein. A new class of collision prevention MAC protocols for wireless ad hoc networks. Presented at the IEEE International Conference on Communications (ICC '03), Anchorage, AK, May 11–15, 2003, pp. 1135–1140.

65. C. L. Fullmer and J. J. Garcia-Luna-Aceves. Solutions to hidden terminal problems in wireless networks. *ACM SIGCOMM Computer Communication Review*, 27(4), 39–49, 1997.

66. N. Jain, S. R. Das, and A. Nasipuri. A multichannel CSMA MAC protocol with receiver-based channel selection for multihop wireless networks. Presented at the 10th IEEE International Conference on Computer Communications and Networks, October 15–17, 2001, pp. 432–439.

67. J. Mo, H.-S. Wilson So, and J. Walrand. Comparison of multichannel MAC protocols. *IEEE Transactions on Mobile Computing*, 7(1), 50–65, 2008.

68. L. Yun, L. Ke-Ping, Z. Wei-Liang, and C. Qian-Bin. A novel random back-off algorithm to enhance the performance of IEEE 802.11 DCF. *Wireless Personal Communications*, 36(1), 29–44, 2006.

69. R. Oliveira, L. Bernardo, and P. Pinto. The influence of broadcast traffic on IEEE 802.11 DCF networks. *Computer Communications*, 32(2), 439–452, 2009.

70. B. Alawieh, C. M. Assi, and H. Mouftah. Investigating the performance of power-aware IEEE 802.11 in multihop wireless networks. *IEEE Transactions on Vehicular Technology*, 58(1), 287–300, 2009.

71. IEEE. *Part II: wireless LAN medium access control (MAC) and physical layer (PHY specifications): MAC enhancements for QoS*. IEEE 802.11e/D6.0, draft supplement to IEEE 802.11. New York: IEEE.

72. C. Sunghyun. IEEE 802.11e MAC-level FEC performance evaluation and enhancement. Presented at the IEEE Global Telecommunications Conference (GLOBECOM '02), November 17–21, 2002, pp. 773–777.

73. W. Stallings. *Data and computer communications*. 9th ed. NJ: Pearson Higher Education, 2010.

74. H. Hassanein, T. You, and H. T. Mouftah. Infrastructure-based MAC in wireless mobile ad-hoc networks. *Ad Hoc Networks*, 3(6), 717–743, 2005.

75. IEEE. *Amendment to IEEE Std 802.11, as amended by IEEE stds 802.11a-1999, 802.11b-1999, 802.11b-1999/Cor 1-2001, and 802.11d-2001*. IEEE 802.11g WG. New York: IEEE, 2003.

76. T. Joshi, A. Mukherjee, Y. Younghwan, and D. P. Agrawal. Airtime fairness for IEEE 802.11 multirate networks. *IEEE Transactions on Mobile Computing*, 7(4), 513–527, 2008.

77. Y. Xiao. Concatenation and piggyback mechanisms for the IEEE 802.11 MAC. Presented at the IEEE Wireless Communications and Networking Conference, March 21–25, 2004, pp. 1642–1647.

78. C. Chaudet, D. Dhoutaut, and I. G. Lassous. Performance issues with IEEE 802.11 in ad hoc networking. *IEEE Communications Magazine*, 43(7), 110–116, 2005.

79. M. K. Denko and T. Jun. Cross-layer design for cooperative caching in mobile ad hoc networks. Presented at the 5th IEEE Consumer Communications and Networking Conference (CCNC '08), January 10–12, 2008, pp. 375–380.

80. F. Kargl and E. Schoch. Simulation of MANETs: a qualitative comparison between JiST/SWANS and ns-2. Presented at the International Conference on Mobile Systems, Applications and Services, San Juan, Puerto Rico, June 11–14, 2007, pp. 41–46.

81. B. Han, W. Jia, and L. Lin. Performance evaluation of scheduling in IEEE 802.16 based wireless mesh networks. *Computer Communications*, 30(4), 782–792, 2007.

82. M. David, D. Ken, and L. Doug. Modeling the 802.11 distributed coordination function in nonsaturated heterogeneous conditions. *IEEE/ACM Transactions on Networking*, 15(1), 159–172, 2007.

83. K. Salah and A. Alkhoraidly. An OPNET-based simulation approach for deploying VoIP. *International Journal of Network Management*, 16(1), 159–183, 2006.

84. S. S. Kolahi. Traffic dimensioning of CDMA systems using simulation and modelling. PhD thesis, Department of Electrical and Computer Engineering, University of Auckland, Auckland, New Zealand, 2008.

85. K. S. Butterworth. Performance, planning and deployment of DS-CDMA in-building wireless communication systems. PhD thesis, Electrical and Computer Engineering, University of Auckland, Auckland, New Zealand, 2000.

86. IEEE. *IEEE standard for information technology—telecommunications and information exchange between systems—local and metropolitan area networks—specific requirements—part 11: wireless medium access control (MAC) and physical layer (PHY) specifications: amendment 9: interworking with external networks.* IEEE 802.11u-2011. New York: IEEE, 2011.

87. D. P. Agrawal and Q.-A. Zeng. *Introduction to wireless and mobile systems.* 2nd ed. Toronto: Thomson, 2006.

88. P. M. Shankar. *Introduction to wireless systems.* New York: John Wiley & Sons, 2002.

89. J. W. Mark and W. Zhuang. *Wireless communications and networking.* Englewood Cliffs, NJ: Prentice-Hall, 2003.

90. R. J. Punnoose, R. S. Tseng, and D. D. Stancil. Experimental results for interference between Bluetooth and IEEE 802.11b DSSS systems. Presented at the 54th IEEE Vehicular Technology Conference (VTC '01—Fall), October 7–11, 2001, pp. 67–71.

91. T. M. Schafer, J. Maurer, and W. Wiesbeck. Measurement and simulation of radio wave propagation in hospitals. Presented at IEEE 56th Vehicular Technology Conference (VTC '02—Fall), September 24–28, 2002, pp. 792–796.

92. N. Moraitis and P. Constantinou. Indoor channel measurements and characterization at 60 GHz for wireless local area network applications. *IEEE Transactions on Antennas and Propagation*, 52(12), 3180–3189, 2004.

93. D. Pena, R. Feick, H. Hristov, and W. Grote. Measurement and modeling of propagation losses in brick and concrete walls for the 900-MHz band. *IEEE Transactions on Antennas and Propagation*, 51(1), 31–39, 2003.

94. N. I. Sarkar and K. W. Sowerby. Wi-Fi performance measurements in the crowded office environment: a case study. Presented at the 10th IEEE International Conference on Communication Technology (ICCT '06), Guilin, China, November 27–30, 2006, pp. 37–40.

95. A. Messier, J. Robinson, and K. Pahlavan. Performance monitoring of a wireless campus area network. Presented at the 22nd Annual Conference on Local Computer Networks, November 2–5, 1997, pp. 232–238.

96. C. R. Anderson and T. S. Rappaport. In-building wideband multipath measurements at 2.5 and 60 GHz. *IEEE Transactions on Wireless Communications*, 3(3), 922–928, 2004.

97. H. Y. D. Yang. Analysis of RF radiation interference on wireless communication systems. *IEEE Antennas and Wireless Propagation Letters*, 2, 126–129, 2003.

98. T. Murakami, Y. Matsumoto, K. Fujii, and Y. Yamanaka. Effects of multi-path propagation on microwave oven interference in wireless systems. Presented at the IEEE International Symposium on Electromagnetic Compatibility, May 11–16, 2003, pp. 749–752.

99. T. Murakami, Y. Matsumoto, K. Fujii, A. Sugiura, and Y. Yamanaka. Propagation characteristics of the microwave oven noise interfering with wireless systems in the 2.4 GHz band. Presented at the 14th IEEE Conference on Personal, Indoor and Mobile Radio Communications (PIMRC '03), September 7–10, 2003, pp. 2726–2729.

100. I. Howitt. Bluetooth performance in the presence of 802.11b WLAN. *IEEE Transactions on Vehicular Technology*, 51(6), 1640–1651, 2002.

101. L. He and W. Yin. Interference evaluation of Bluetooth and IEEE 802.11b systems. Presented at the 4th International Conference on Microwave and Millimeter Wave Technology (ICMMT), August 18–21, 2004, pp. 931–934.

102. J. H. Jo and N. Jayant. Performance evaluation of multiple IEEE 802.11b WLAN stations in the presence of Bluetooth radio interference. Presented at IEEE International Conference on Communications, 2003, pp. 1163–1168.

103. J. A. Park, S. K. Park, P. D. Cho, and K. R. Cho. Analysis of spectrum channel assignment for IEEE 802.11b wireless LAN. Presented at the 5th International Symposium on Wireless Personal Multimedia Communications, October 27–30, 2002, pp. 1073–1077.

104. X. Xu, C. Zhang, and X. Lin. Using different orthogonal code sets for CCK modulation to mitigate co-channel interference among WLANs. Presented at the IEEE International Symposium on Communications and Information Technology, October 12–14, 2005, pp. 885–888.

105. D. T. S. Yoong. Performance of IEEE 802.11b wireless LANs suffering mutual interference. ME thesis, Department of Electrical and Computer Engineering, University of Auckland, Auckland, New Zealand, 2004.

106. A. V. Pais. The deployment and performance of indoor/outdoor DS-CDMA systems with multiuser detection. PhD thesis, Department of Electrical and Computer Engineering, University of Auckland, Auckland, New Zealand, 2007.

107. V. Sridhara, H. Shin, and S. Bohacek. Performance of 802.11 b/g in the interference limited regime. *Computer Communications*, 31(8), 1579–1587, 2008.

108. S. Kawade, T. G. Hodgkinson, and V. Abhayawardhana. Interference analysis of 802.11b and 802.11g wireless systems. Presented at the 66th IEEE Vehicular Technology Conference (VTC '07), September 30–October 3, 2007, pp. 787–791.

109. A. Prasad and N. Prasad. *802.11 WLANs and IP networking: security, QoS, and mobility*. Boston: Artech House, 2005.

110. R. Olexa. *Implementing 802.11, 802.16 and 802.20 wireless networks: planning, troubleshooting, and maintenance*. Boston: Elsevier, 2004.

111. J. Bardwell. You believe you understand what you think I said.... The truth about 802.11 signal and noise metrics: a discussion clarifying often-misused 802.11 WLAN terminology. December 10, 2007. Retrieved from http://madwifi.org/attachment/wiki/UserDocs/RSSI/you_believe_D100201.pdf?format=raw.

112. Introduction to signal processing: signals and noise. Retrieved March 5, 2011, from http://www.wam.umd.edu/~toh/spectrum/SignalsAndNoise.html.

113. C. Steger, P. Radosavljevic, and J. P. Frantz. Performance of IEEE 802.11b wireless LAN in an emulated mobile channel. Presented at the 57th IEEE Semiannual Vehicular Technology Conference (VTC '03—Spring), April 22–25, 2003, pp. 1479–1483.

114. P. Chatzimisios, A. C. Boucouvalas, and V. Vitsas. Influence of channel BER on IEEE 802.11 DCF. *IEE Electronics Letters*, 39(23), 1687–1689, 2003.

115. G. H.-H. Sung, K. W. Sowerby, M. J. Neve, and A. G. Williamson. A frequency-selective wall for interference reduction in wireless indoor environments. *IEEE Antennas and Propagation Magazine*, 48(5), 29–37, 2006.

116. Y. Kwon, Y. Fang, and H. Latchman. A novel MAC protocol with fast collision resolution for wireless LANs. Presented at the IEEE INFOCOM '03, March 30–April 3, 2003, pp. 853–862.

117. M. S. Obaidat and D. G. Green. An adaptive protocol model for IEEE 802.11 wireless LANs. *Computer Communications*, 27(12), 1131–1136, 2004.

118. Z. Yin and V. C. M. Leung. Performance improvements of integrating ad hoc operations into infrastructure IEEE 802.11 wireless local area networks. *Computer Communications*, 28(10), 1123–1137, 2005.

119. I. Aad, Q. Ni, C. Barakat, and T. Turletti. Enhancing IEEE 802.11 MAC in congested environments. *Computer Communications*, 28(14), 1605–1617, 2005.

120. A. Firag and H. Sirisena. Wireless MAC scheme for service differentiation. Presented at the IFIP TC6/WG6.8 Working Group Conference on Personal Wireless Communications (PWC '02), Singapore, October 23–25, 2002, pp. 209–216.

121. B. Hamdaoui and K. G. Shin. OS-MAC: an efficient MAC protocol for spectrum-agile wireless networks. *IEEE Transactions on Mobile Computing*, 7(8), 915–930, 2008.

122. K. Anna and M. Bassiouni. A new framework for QoS provisioning in WLANS using p-persistent 802.11 MAC. *Computer Communications*, 31(17), 4035–4048, 2008.

123. M. Natkaniec and A. R. Pach. PUMA—a new channel access protocol for wireless LANs. Presented at the 5th International Symposium on Wireless Personal Multimedia Communications, October 27–30, 2002, pp. 1351–1355.

124. H. Zhu and G. Cao. On improving the performance of IEEE 802.11 with multihop concepts. Presented at the 12th International Conference on Computer Communications and Networks (ICCCN '03), October 20–22, 2003, pp. 151–156.

125. E. C. Kao. A dynamic random channel reservation for MAC protocols in multimedia wireless networks. MSc thesis, Department of Computer Science, University of Canterbury, Christchurch, New Zealand, 2001.

126. A. Chandra, V. Gummalla, and J. Limb. Wireless medium access control protocols. *IEEE Communications Surveys and Tutorials*, 3(2), 2–15, 2000.

127. Z. Haas and J. Deng. Dual busy tone multiple access (DBTMA)—a multiple access control scheme for ad hoc networks communication. *IEEE Transactions on Communications*, 50(6), 975–985, 2002.

128. A. Gummalla and J. Limb. Wireless collision detection (WCD): multiple access with receiver initiated feedback and carrier detect signal. Presented at the IEEE International Conference on Communications, New Orleans, June 18–22, 2000, pp. 397–401.

129. C. L. Fullmer and J. J. Garcia-Luna-Aceves. Floor acquisition multiple access (FAMA) for packet-radio networks. Presented at the ACM Annual Conference on Applications, Technologies, Architectures, and Protocols for Computer Communications (SIGCOMM '95), Cambridge, MA, August 28–September 1, 1995, pp. 262–273.

130. N. Amitay and S. Nanda. Resource auction multiple access (RAMA) for statistical multiplexing of speech in wireless PCS. Presented at the IEEE International Conference on Communications (ICC '93), Geneva, May 23–26, 1993, pp. 605–609.

131. G. Bianchi, F. Borgonovo, L. Fratta, L. Musumeci, and M. Zorzi. C-PRMA: a centralized packet reservation multiple access for local wireless communications. *IEEE Transactions on Vehicular Technology*, 46(2), 422–436, 1997.

132. J. M. Wong and K. Chua. Access and control in a cellular wireless ATM network. Presented at the IEEE International Conference on Communications, New Orleans, June 18–22, 2000, pp. 1524–1529.

133. N. Erasala and D. C. Yen. Bluetooth technology: a strategic analysis of its role in global 3G wireless communication era. *Computer Standards and Interfaces*, 24(3), 193–206, 2002.

134. L. Kleinrock and F. Tobagi. Packet switching in radio channels: part I—carrier sense multiple-access modes and their throughput-delay characteristics. *IEEE Transactions on Communications*, 23(12), 1400–1416, 1975.

135. N. Abramson. The ALOHA system—another alternative for computer communications. Presented at Fall Joint Computer Conference, 1970, pp. 281–285.

136. M. Gerla and J. T. Tsai. Multicluster, mobile, multimedia radio network. *Wireless Networks*, 1(3), 255–265, 1995.

137. R. Garces and J. J. Garcia-Luna-Aceves. Collision avoidance and resolution multiple access: first-success protocols. Presented at the IEEE International Conference on Communications (ICC '97), June 8–12, 1997, pp. 699–703.

138. G. Bianchi, L. Fratta, and M. Oliveri. Performance evaluation and enhancement of the CSMA/CA MAC protocol for 802.11 wireless LANs. Presented at the 7th IEEE International Symposium on Personal, Indoor and Mobile Radio Communications (PIMRC '96), Taipei, Taiwan, October 15–18, 1996, pp. 392–396.

139. A. Muir and J. J. Garcia-Luna-Aceves. An efficient packet sensing MAC protocol for wireless networks. *Mobile Networks and Applications*, 3(2), 221–234, 1998.

140. F. Cali, M. Conti, and E. Gregori. IEEE 802.11 protocol: design and performance evaluation of an adaptive backoff mechanism. *IEEE Journal on Selected Areas in Communications*, 18(9), 1774–1786, 2000.

141. F. Cali and M. Conti. Dynamic tuning of the IEEE 802.11 protocol to achieve a theoretical throughput limit. *IEEE/ACM Transactions on Networking*, 8(6), 785–799, 2000.

142. P. Nicopolitidis, G. I. Papadimitriou, M. S. Obaidat, and A. S. Pomportsis. TRAP: a high performance protocol for wireless local area networks. *Computer Communications*, 25(11), 1058–1065, 2002.

143. M. Natkaniec and A. R. Pach. An analysis of backoff mechanism used in IEEE 802.11 networks. Presented at the IEEE ISCC, Antibes, Juans les Pins, France, July 3–6, 2000, pp. 444–449.

144. Z. Fang, B. Bensaou, and J. Yuan. Collision-free MAC scheduling algorithms for wireless ad hoc networks. Presented at the IEEE Global Telecommunications Conference (GLOBECOM '04), Dallas, TX, November 29–December 3, 2004, pp. 2770–2774.

145. Z. Y. Fang and B. Bensaou. A novel topology-blind fair medium access control for wireless LAN and ad hoc networks. Presented at the IEEE International Conference on Communications (ICC '03), Anchorage, AK, May 11–15, 2003, pp. 1129–1134.

146. Z. Fang, B. Bensaou, and Y. Wang. Performance evaluation of a fair backoff algorithm for IEEE 802.11 DFWMAC. Presented at the 3rd ACM International Symposium on Mobile Ad Hoc Networking and Computing, EPFL Lausanne, Switzerland, June 9–11, 2002, pp. 48–57.

147. Y. Wang and B. Bensaou. Achieving fairness in IEEE 802.11 DFWMAC with variable packet lengths. Presented at the IEEE Global Telecommunications Conference (GLOBECOM '01), San Antonio, TX, November 25–29, 2001, pp. 3588–3593.

148. S. Jagadeesan, B. S. Manoj, and C. S. R. Murthy. Interleaved carrier sense multiple access: an efficient MAC protocol for ad hoc wireless networks. Presented at the IEEE International Conference on Communications (ICC '03), Anchorage, AK, May 11–15, 2003, pp. 1124–1128.

149. J. Peng, L. Cheng, and B. Sikdar. A wireless MAC protocol with collision detection. *IEEE Transactions on Mobile Computing*, 6(12), 1357–1369, 2007.

150. H. Minooei and H. Nojumi. Performance evaluation of a new backoff method for IEEE 802.11. *Computer Communications*, 30(18), 3698–3704, 2007.

151. G. Bianchi. Performance analysis of the IEEE 802.11 distributed coordination function. *IEEE Journal on Selected Areas in Communications*, 18(3), 535–547, 2000.

152. K.-C. Chen and C.-H. Lee. RAP—a novel medium access control protocol for wireless data networks. Presented at the IEEE Global Telecommunications Conference (GLOBECOM '93), Houston, TX, November 29–December 2, 1993, pp. 1713–1717.

153. M. M. Carvalho and J. J. Garcia-Luna-Aceves. Delay analysis of IEEE 802.11 in single-hop networks. Presented at the 11th IEEE International Conference on Network Protocols, November 4–7, 2003, pp. 146–155.

154. P. Ferre, A. Doufexi, A. Nix, and D. Bull. Throughput analysis of IEEE 802.11 and IEEE 802.11e MAC. Presented at the IEEE Wireless Communications and Networking Conference (WCNC '04), March 21–25, 2004, pp. 783–788.

155. W. Kim, W. Kim, and D. C. Cox. Throughput enhancement for IEEE 802.11a wireless LANs. Presented at the 66th IEEE Vehicular Technology Conference (VTC '07—Fall), September 30–October 3, 2007, pp. 1341–1345.

156. A. Kamerman and G. Aben. Net throughput with IEEE 802.11 wireless LANs. Presented at the IEEE Wireless Communications and Networking Conference (WCNC '00), September 23–28, 2000, pp. 747–752.

157. Y. Wang and J. J. Garcia-Luna-Aceves. Throughput and fairness in a hybrid channel access scheme for ad hoc networks. Presented at the IEEE Wireless Communications and Networking (WCNC '03), March 16–20, 2003, pp. 988–993.

158. T. Pagtzis, P. Kirstein, and S. Hailes. Operational and fairness issues with connection-less traffic over IEEE 802.11b. Presented at the IEEE International Conference on Communications (ICC '01), June 11–14, 2001, pp. 1905–1913.

159. N. I. Sarkar. Fairness studies of IEEE 802.11b DCF under heavy traffic conditions. Presented at the First IEEE International Conference on Next-Generation Wireless Systems (ICNEWS '06), Bangladesh, January 2–4, 2006, pp. 11–16.

160. M. H. Ye, C. T. Lau, and A. B. Premkumar. A modified power saving mode in IEEE 802.11 distributed coordinator function. *Computer Communications*, 28(10), 1214–1224, 2005.

161. H.-P. Lin, S.-C. Huang, and R.-H. Jan. A power-saving scheduling for infrastructure-mode 802.11 wireless LANs. *Computer Communications*, 29(17), 3483–3492, 2006.

162. S. Jayashree, B. S. Manoj, and C. S. R. Murthy. A battery aware medium access control (BAMAC) protocol for ad hoc wireless networks. Presented at the 5th IEEE International Symposium on Personal, Indoor and Mobile Radio Communications, September 5–8, 2004, pp. 995–999.

163. N. I. Sarkar and E. Lo. Indoor propagation measurements for performance evaluation of IEEE 802.11g. Presented at the IEEE Australasian Telecommunications Networks and Applications Conference (ATNAC '08), Adelaide, Australia, December 7–10, 2008, pp. 163–168.

164. W.-Y. Lin and J.-S. Wu. Modified EDCF to improve the performance of IEEE 802.11e WLAN. *Computer Communications*, 30(4), 841–848, 2007.

165. D. Chie, C. Yang-Jie, and W. Jia-Yuan. The performance study of contention-based differentiation mechanisms in IEEE 802.11e MAC layer. Presented at the 14th IEEE Conference on Personal, Indoor and Mobile Radio Communications, September 7–10, 2003, pp. 1415–1419.

166. W. Stallings. *Wireless communications and networks*. Englewood Cliffs, NJ: Prentice Hall, 2002.

167. A. Doran. *The essential guide to wireless communications applications—from cellular systems to Wi-Fi*. 2nd ed. Englewood Cliffs, NJ: Prentice-Hall, 2002.

168. E. R. Berlekamp, E. E. Peile, and S. P. Pope. The application of error control to communications. *IEEE Communications Magazine*, 25, 44–57, 1987.

169. G. Bianchi. IEEE 802.11-saturation throughput analysis. *IEEE Communications Letters*, 2(12), 318–320, 1998.

170. A. Banchs and L. Vollero. Throughput analysis and optimal configuration of 802.11e EDCA. *Computer Networks*, 50(11), 1749–1768, 2006.

171. J. F. Kurose and K. W. Ross. *Computer networking: a top-down approach*. 6th ed. NY: Pearson, 2013.

172. A. S. Tanenbaum and D. J. Wetherall. *Computer Networks*. 5th ed. Englewood Cliffs, NJ: Prentice Hall, 2011.

173. E. Alotaibi and B. Mukherjee. A survey on routing algorithms for wireless ad-hoc and mesh networks. *Computer Networks*, 56(2), 940–965, 2012.

174. X. Hong, K. Xu, M. Gerla, and C. A. Los Angeles. Scalable routing protocols for mobile ad hoc networks. *Network, IEEE*, 16(4), 11–21, 2002.

175. A. K. Pandey and H. Fujinoki. Study of MANET routing protocols by GloMoSim simulator. *International Journal of Network Management*, 15(6), 393–410, 2005.

176. S. H. Amer and J. A. Hamilton Jr. Performance evaluation: running DSR and TORA routing protocols concurrently. Presented at the 2007 Summer Computer Simulation Conference, 2007, pp. 1–5.

177. C. Mbarushimana and A. Shahrabi. Comparative study of reactive and proactive routing protocols performance in mobile ad hoc networks. Presented at the 21st International Conference on Advanced Information Networking and Applications Workshops (AINAW '07), 2007, pp. 679–684.

178. M. Abolhasan, T. Wysocki, and E. Dutkiewicz. A review of routing protocols for mobile ad hoc networks. *Ad Hoc Networks*, 2(1), 1–22, 2004.

179. A. Kumar, L. C. Reddy, and P. S. Hiremath. Performance comparsion of wireless mobile ad hoc network routing protocols. *International Journal of Computer Science and Network Security (IJCSNS)*, 8(6), 337–343, 2008.

180. S. Bali, J. Steuer, and K. Jobmann. Capacity of ad hoc networks with line topology based on UWB and WLAN technologies. Presented at the Wireless Telecommunications Symposium (WTS '08), 2008, pp. 17–24.

181. C. S. R. Murthy and B. S. Manoj. Ad hoc wireless networks: architectures and protocols. Upper Saddle River, NJ: Prentice Hall, 2004.

182. E. M. Royer and C. K. Toh. A review of current routing protocols for ad hoc mobile wireless networks. *IEEE Personal Communications*, 6(2), 46–55, 1999.

183. A. Zaballos, A. Vallejo, G. Corral, and J. Abella. Adhoc routing performance study using OPNET Modeler. Presented at the OPNETWORK, Washington, DC, August 2006.

184. A. Boukerche. Performance evaluation of routing protocols for ad hoc wireless networks. *Mobile Networks and Applications*, 9(4), 333–342, 2004.

185. E. M. Royer and C. E. Perkins. An implementation study of the AODV routing protocol. Presented at the Wireless Communications and Networking Conference, IEEE (WCNC '02), 2000, pp. 1003–1008.

186. A. Quintero, S. Pierre, and B. Macabéo. A routing protocol based on node density for ad hoc networks. *Ad Hoc Networks*, 2(3), 335–349, 2004.

187. S. Gupta. Performance evaluation of ad hoc routing protocols using ns2 simulations. Retrieved July 23, 2008, from http://www.cs.utk.edu/~gupta/Adhoc.doc.

188. S. R. Chaudhry, A. Al-Khwildi, Y. Casey, H. Aldelou, and H. S. Al-Raweshidy. A performance comparison of multi on demand routing in wireless ad hoc networks. Presented at the IEEE International Conference on Wireless and Mobile Computing, Networking and Communications (WiMob '05), 2005, pp. 1–8.

189. S. R. Das, R. Castaneda, J. Yan, and R. Sengupta. Comparative performance evaluation of routing protocols for mobile, ad hoc networks. Presented at the 7th International Conference on Computer Communications and Networks (IC3N '98), 1998, pp. 153–161.

190. S. Giannoulis, C. Antonopoulos, E. Topalis, and S. Koubias. ZRP versus DSR and TORA: a comprehensive survey on ZRP performance. Presented at the 10th IEEE Conference on Emerging Technologies and Factory Automation (ETFA '05), 2005, pp. 1–8.

191. C. R. Dow, P. J. Lin, S. C. Chen, J. H. Lin, and S. F. Hwang. A study of recent research trends and experimental guidelines in mobile ad-hoc network. Presented at the 19th International Conference on Advanced Information Networking and Applications (AINA '05), 2005, pp. 1–6.

192. K. U. R. Khan, R. U. Zaman, and A. V. Reddy. Performance comparison of on-demand and table driven ad hoc routing protocols using NCTUns. Presented at the Tenth International Conference on Computer Modeling and Simulation (UKSIM '08), 2008, pp. 336–341.

193. G. Jayakumar and G. Gopinath. Performance comparison of two on-demand routing protocols for ad-hoc networks based on random way point mobility model. *American Journal of Applied Sciences*, 5(6), 659–664, 2008.

194. Q. Biao, H. Jianhua, and Y. Zongkai. Simulation of wireless ad hoc routing protocols and its evaluation. *Journal—Huazhong University of Science and Technology Nature Science*, 32(8), 66–69, 2004.

195. L. Layuan, L. Chunlin, and Y. Peiyan. Performance evaluation and simulations of routing protocols in ad hoc networks. *Computer Communications*, 30(8), 1890–1898, 2007.

196. S. R. Das, C. E. Perkins, and E. M. Royer. Performance comparison of two on-demand routing protocols for ad hoc networks. Presented at the Nineteenth Annual Joint Conference of the IEEE Computer and Communications Societies (INFOCOM '00), Tel Aviv, Israel, March 2000, pp. 3–12.

197. H. Pucha, S. M. Das, and Y. C. Hu. The performance impact of traffic patterns on routing protocols in mobile ad hoc networks. *Computer Networks*, 51(12), 3595–3616, 2007.

198. S. A. Hussein, K. Mahmood, and Z. E. Garcia. Factors affecting performance of AODV. *Information Technology Journal*, 6(2), 237–241, 2007.

199. B. Divecha, A. Abraham, C. Grosan, and S. Sanyal. Impact of node mobility on MANET routing protocols models. *Journal of Digital Information Management*, 5(1), 1–19, 2007.

200. F. D. Rango, J. C. Cano, M. Fotino, C. Calafate, P. Manzoni, and S. Marano. OLSR vs DSR: a comparative analysis of proactive and reactive mechanisms from an energetic point of view in wireless ad hoc networks. *Computer Communications*, 31(16), 3843–3854, 2008.

201. D. D. Perkins, H. D. Hughes, and C. B. Owen. Factors affecting the performance of ad hoc networks. Presented at the IEEE International Conference on Communications (ICC '02), 2002, pp. 2048–2052.

202. C. E. Perkins, E. M. Royer, S. R. Das, and M. K. Marina. Performance comparison of two on-demand routing protocols for adhoc networks. *IEEE Personal Communications*, 8(1), 16–28, 2001.

203. J. Zhang, J. Zou, and Q. Zhao. MANET routing protocol for improving routing discovery based on AODV. Presented at the International Conference on Networks Security, Wireless Communications and Trusted Computing, April 25–26, 2009, pp. 197–200.

204. S. A. Obeidat, A. N. Aldaco, and V. R. Syrotiuk. Cross-layer opportunistic adaptation for voice over ad hoc networks. *Computer Networks*, 56(2), 762–779, 2012.

205. Z. Ning, L. Guo, Y. Peng, and X. Wang. Joint scheduling and routing algorithm with load balancing in wireless mesh network. *Computers and Electrical Engineering*, 38(3), 533–550, 2012.

206. L. Dong. Opportunistic media access control and routing for delay-tolerant mobile ad hoc networks. *Wireless Networks*, 18(8), 949–965, 2012.

207. V. Srivastava and M. Motani. Cross-layer design: a survey and road ahead. *IEEE Communications Magazine*, 43, 112–119, 2005.

208. L. Chen, S. H. Low, and J. C. Doyle. Cross-layer design in multihop wireless networks. *Computer Networks*, 55(2), 480–496, 2011.

209. X. Zhang, J. Tang, H.-H. Chen, S. Ci, and M. Guizani. Cross-layer-based modeling for quality of service guarantees in mobile wireless networks. *IEEE Communications Magazine*, 44, 100–106, 2006.

210. M. Madueno and J. Vidal. Joint physical-MAC layer design of the broadcast protocol in ad hoc networks. *IEEE Journal on Selected Areas in Communications*, 23(1), 65–75, 2005.

211. S. Lee and K. Chung. Joint quality and rate adaptation scheme for wireless video streaming. Presented at the 22nd International Conference on Advanced Information Networking and Applications (AINA '08), March 25–28, 2008, pp. 311–318.

212. K. Wierenga. IEEE 802.11u overview. Retrieved June 8, 2013, from http://www.terena.org/activities/tf-mobility/meetings/19/wierenga-802.11u.pdf.

213. N. I. Sarkar, K. Nisar, and H. Chieng. Modelling and performance studies of ATM networks over email, FTP, voice and video. *International Journal of Information Communication Technologies and Human Development (IJICTHD)*, 5(4), 2013.

214. M. S. Hasan, H. Yu, A. Griffiths, and T. C. Yang. Simulation of distributed wireless networked control systems over MANET using OPNET. Presented at the 2007 IEEE International Conference on Networking, Sensing and Control, London, 2007, pp. 699–704.

215. Y. A. Alqudah and Y. Huiqin. On handover performance analysis in mobile WiMAX networks. Presented at the Mobile WiMAX Symposium, July 9–10, 2009, pp. 20–23.

216. I. F. Akyildiz and X. Wang. Cross-layer design in wireless mesh networks. *IEEE Transactions on Vehicular Technology*, 57(2), 1061–1076, 2008.

217. I. Al-wazedi and A. K. Elhakeem. Cross layer design using adaptive spatial TDMA and optimum routing for wireless mesh networks. *AEU—International Journal of Electronics and Communications*, 65(1), 44–52, 2011.

218. F. Foukalas, V. Gazis, and N. Alonistioti. Cross-layer design proposals for wireless mobile networks: a survey and taxonomy. *IEEE Communications Surveys and Tutorials*, 10(1), 70–85, 2008.

219. M. Lee, M. Kang, M. Kim, and J. Mo. A cross-layer approach for TCP optimization over wireless and mobile networks. *Computer Communications*, 31(11), 2669–2675, 2008.

220. P. Cheng, Z. Zhang, H.-H. Chen, and P. Qiu. A framework of cross-layer design for multiple video streams in wireless mesh networks. *Computer Communications*, 31(8), 1529–1539, 2008.

221. Y. Yuan, Z. Baoyu, L. Wentao, and D. Chentuo. An opportunistic cooperative MAC protocol based on cross-layer design. Presented at the 2007 International Symposium on Intelligent Signal Processing and Communication Systems (ISPACS '07), November 28–December 01, 2007, pp. 714–717.

222. Q. Xia, X. Jin, and M. Hamdi. Cross layer design for the IEEE 802.11 WLANs: joint rate control and packet scheduling. *IEEE Transactions on Wireless Communications*, 6(7), 2732–2740, 2007.

223. W. Ge, J. Zhang, and S. Shen. A cross-layer design approach to multicast in wireless networks. *IEEE Transactions on Wireless Communications*, 6(3), 1063–1071, 2007.

224. S. Choudhury and J. D. Gibson. Payload length and rate adaptation for multimedia communications in wireless LANs. *IEEE Journal on Selected Areas in Communications*, 25(4), 796–807, 2007.

225. D. Moltchanov, Y. Koucheryavy, and J. Harju. Cross-layer modeling of wireless channels for data-link and IP layer performance evaluation. *Computer Communications*, 29(7), 827–841, 2006.

226. J. Dunn, M. Neufeld, D. Sheth, D. Grunwald, and J. Bennett. A practical cross-layer mechanism for fairness in 802.11 networks. *Mobile Networks and Applications*, 11(1), 37–45, 2006.

227. P. P. Pham, S. Perreau, and A. Jayasuriya. New cross-layer design approach to ad hoc networks under Rayleigh fading. *IEEE Journal on Selected Areas in Communications*, 23(1), 28–39, 2005.

228. R. Zhang and M. K. Tsatsanis. Network-assisted diversity multiple access in dispersive channels. *IEEE Transactions on Communications*, 50(4), 623–632, 2002.

229. S. Shakkottai, T. S. Rappaport, and P. C. Karlsson. Cross-layer design for wireless networks. *IEEE Communications Magazine*, 41(10), 74–80, 2003.

230. M. Conti, G. Maselli, G. Turi, and S. Giordano. Cross-layering in mobile ad hoc network design. *Computer*, 37(2), 48–51, 2004.

231. M. Dirani, C. Tarhini, and T. Chahed. Cross-layer modeling of capacity in wireless networks: application of UMTS/HSDPA, IEEE 802.11 WLAN and IEEE 802.16 WiMax. *Computer Communications*, 30(17), 3384–3391, 2007.

232. IEEE 802.11n-2009: amendment 5: enhancements for higher throughput. Retrieved June 6, 2013, from http://en.wikipedia.org/wiki/IEEE_802.11n.

233. D-Link wireless access point (802.11 b/g) DWL-2100AP. Retrieved January 10, 2013, from http://www.dlink.com/products/.

234. *D-Link DWL-650 PCMCIA wireless adapter user's manual.* Retrieved April 10, 2013, from ftp://ftp2.dlink.com/Wireless/DWL650/Manual/.

235. Colligo Workgroup. Edition 3.2. Retrieved January 20, 2013, from www.colligo.com/.

236. WirelessMon: Wi-Fi monitoring software. Retrieved February 5, 2012, from www.passmark.com/products/wirelessmonitor.html.

237. D. T. S. Yoong. Performance of IEEE 802.11b wireless LANs suffering mutual interference. ME thesis, Department of Electrical and Computer Engineering, University of Auckland, Auckland, New Zealand, April 2004.

238. J. Geier. Multipath a potential WLAN problem. Retrieved August 15, 2006, from http://www.wifiplanet.com/tutorials/article.php/1121691.

239. B. Bing. *Broadband wireless access.* Boston: Kluwer Academic Publishers, 2000.

240. A. R. Prasad, N. R. Prasad, A. Kamerman, H. Moelard, and A. Eikelenboom. Performance evaluation, system design and network deployment of IEEE 802.11. *Wireless Personal Communications,* 19, 57–79, 2001.

241. M. K. Awad, K. T. Wong, and Z.-B. Li. An integrated overview of the open literature's empirical data on the indoor radiowave channel's delay properties. *IEEE Transactions on Antenna and Propagation,* 56(5), 1451–1468, 2008.

242. D. Xu, J. Zhang, X. Gao, P. A. Zhang, and Y. A. Wu. Indoor office propagation measurements and path loss models at 5.25 GHz. Presented at the IEEE 66th Vehicular Technology Conference (VTC '07—Fall), September 30–October 3, 2007, pp. 844–848.

243. A. R. Prasad, N. R. Prasad, A. Kamerman, H. Moelard, and A. Eikelenboom. Indoor wireless LANs deployment. Presented at the 51st IEEE Vehicular Technology Conference (VTC '00), May 15–18, 2000, pp. 1562–1566.

244. S. P. T. Kumar, B. Farhang-Boroujeny, S. Uysal, and C. S. Ng. Microwave indoor radio propagation measurements and modeling at 5 GHz for future wireless LAN systems. Presented at IEEE Asia Pacific Microwave Conference, November 30–December 3, 1999, pp. 606–609.

245. D-Link wireless USB adapter (802.11g) DWL-G132. Retrieved April 10, 2013, from http://www.dlink.com/products/.

246. J. Chow. Development of channel models for simulation of wireless systems in OPNET. *Transactions of the Society for Computer Simulation International,* 16(3), 86–92, 1999.

247. K. A. Banitsas, Y. H. Song, and T. J. Owens. OFDM over IEEE 802.11b hardware for telemedical applications. *International Journal of Mobile Communications,* 2(3), 310–327, 2004.

248. D. B. Green and M. S. Obaidat. Modeling and simulation of IEEE 802.11 WLAN mobile ad hoc networks using topology broadcast reverse-path forwarding (TBRPF). *Computer Communications,* 26(15), 1741–1746, 2003.

249. C. Zhu, O. W. W. Wang, J. Aweya, M. Oullette, and D. Y. Montuno. A comparison of active queue management algorithms using the OPNET Modeler. *IEEE Communications Magazine,* 40(6), 158–167, 2002.

250. X. Chang. Network simulations with Opnet. Presented at the 31st Conference on Winter Simulation, Phoenix, AZ, December 5–8, 1999, pp. 307–314.

251. G. F. Lucio, M. Paredes-Farrera, E. Jammeh, M. Fleury, and M. J. Reed. OPNET Modeler and Ns-2: comparing the accuracy of network simulators for packet-level analysis using a network testbed. Retrieved June 15, 2010, from http://privatewww.essex.ac.uk/~gflore/.

252. N. I. Sarkar and K. W. Sowerby. The combined effect of signal strength and traffic type on WLAN performance. Presented at the IEEE Wireless Communication and Networking Conference (WCNC '09), Budapest, Hungary, April 4–8, 2009, pp. 1–5.

253. B. O'Hara and A. Petrick. *The IEEE 802.11 handbook: a designer's companion.* 2nd ed. New York: IEEE Press, 2005.

254. N. I. Sarkar. Performance modeling of IEEE 802.11 WLAN using OPNET: a tutorial. In *Handbook of research on discrete event simulation environments: technologies and applications*, ed. E. Abu-Taieh and E. Sheikh. Hershey, PA: IGI Global, 2010, pp. 398–417.

255. N. I. Sarkar and R. Membarth. Modeling and simulation of IEEE 802.11g using OMNeT++. *In Handbook of research on discrete event simulation environments: technologies and applications*, ed. E. Abu-Taieh and E. Sheikh. Hershey, PA: IGI Global, 2010, pp. 379–397.

256. N. I. Sarkar and E. Lo. Performance studies of 802.11g for various AP configuration and placement. Presented at the 2011 IEEE Symposium on Computers and Informatics (ISCI 2011), Kuala Lumpur, Malaysia, March 20–22, 2011, pp. 29–34.

257. G. Bianchi, F. Formisano, and D. Giustiniano. 802.11b/g link level measurements for an outdoor wireless campus network. Presented at the International Symposium on a World of Wireless, Mobile and Multimedia Networks, June 26–29, 2006, pp. 1–6.

258. C. Sunghyun and J. del Prado Pavon. 802.11g CP: a solution for IEEE 802.11g and 802.11b inter-working. Presented at the 57th IEEE Semiannual Vehicular Technology Conference (VTC '03—Spring), April 22–25, 2003, pp. 690–694.

259. J. He and H. K. Pung. Performance modelling and evaluation of IEEE 802.11 distributed coordination function in multihop wireless networks. *Computer Communications*, 29(13–14), 1300–1308, 2006.

260. R. Bruno, M. Conti, and E. Gregori. Optimization of efficiency and energy consumption in p-persistent CSMA-based wireless LANs. *IEEE Transactions on Mobile Computing*, 1(1), 10–31, 2002.

261. K.-P. Shih, W.-H. Liao, H.-C. Chen, and C.-M. Chou. On avoiding RTS collisions for IEEE 802.11-based wireless ad hoc networks. *Computer Communications*, 32(1), 69–77, 2009.

262. M. Cesana, D. Maniezzo, P. Bergamo, and M. Gerla. Interference aware (IA) MAC: an enhancement to IEEE 802.11b DCF. Presented at the 58th IEEE Vehicular Technology Conference (VTC '03—Fall), Orlando, FL, October 4–9, 2003, pp. 2799–2803.

263. R. C. Lin and C.-Y. Liu. Enhancing the performance of IEEE 802.11 wireless LAN by using a distributed cycle stealing mechanism. Presented at the 4th IEEE International Workshop on Mobile and Wireless Communications Network, September 9–11, 2002, pp. 564–568.

264. T. Ozugur, M. Naghshineh, P. Kermani, and J. A. Copeland. Fair media access for wireless LANs. Presented at the IEEE Global Telecommunications Conference (GLOBECOM '99), Rio de Janeiro, Brazil, December 5–9, 1999, pp. 570–579.

265. M. Ergen and P. Varaiya. Formulation of distributed coordination function of IEEE 802.11 for asynchronous networks: mixed data rate and packet size. *IEEE Transactions on Vehicular Technology*, 57(1), 436–447, 2008.

266. S. Ganguly, V. Navda, K. Kim, A. Kashyap, D. Niculescu, R. Izmailov, S. Hong, and S. R. Das. Performance optimizations for deploying VoIP services in mesh networks. *IEEE Journal on Selected Areas in Communications*, 24(11), 2147–2158, 2006.

267. J. Yin, X. Wang, and D. P. Agrawal. Modeling and optimization of wireless local area network. *Computer Communications*, 28(10), 1204–1213, 2005.

268. M. Heusse, F. Rousseau, G. Berger-Sabbatel, and A. Duda. Performance anomaly of 802.11b. Presented at the IEEE INFOCOM, March 30–April 3, 2003, pp. 836–843.

269. K. Pawlikowski, H.-D. J. Jeong, and J.-S. R. Lee. On credibility of simulation studies of telecommunication networks. *IEEE Communications Magazine*, 40(1), 132–139, 2002.

270. A. M. Law and W. D. Kelton. *Simulation modelling and analysis*. 3rd ed. New York: McGraw-Hill, 2000.

271. B. Schmeiser. Simulation output analysis: a tutorial based on one research thread. Presented at the 2004 Winter Simulation Conference, December 5–8, 2004, pp. 162–170.

272. K. Fall and K. Varadhan. *The ns manual. The VINT project*. Retrieved January 10, 2013, from http://www.isi.edu/nsnam/ns/doc/.

273. W. Siringoringo and N. I. Sarkar. Teaching and learning Wi-Fi networking fundamentals using limited resources. In *Selected readings on telecommunications and networking*, ed. J. Gutierrez. Hershey, PA: IGI Global, 2009, pp. 22–40.

274. P. Nicopoliditis, G. I. Papadimitriou, and A. S. Pomportsis. *Wireless networks*. New York: John Wiley & Sons, 2003.

275. P. Nicopolitidis, M. S. Obaidat, G. I. Papadimitriou, and A. S. Pomportsis. *Wireless networks*. New York: John Wiley & Sons, 2003.

276. G. Tian and Y.-C. Tian. Modelling and performance evaluation of the IEEE 802.11 DCF for real-time control. *Computer Networks*, 56(1), 435–447, 2012.

277. P. Nicopolitidis, G. Papadimitriou, and A. Pomportsis. A MAC protocol for bursty traffic ad-hoc wireless LANs with energy efficiency. *Wireless Personal Communications*, 67(2), 165–173, 2012.

278. K.-S. Katarzyna. A survey of MAC layer solutions to the hidden node problem in ad-hoc networks. *Ad Hoc Networks*, 10(3), 635–660, 2012.

279. Y. Cao, D. Qu, and T. Jiang. Throughput maximization in cognitive radio system with transmission probability scheduling and traffic pattern prediction. *Mobile Networks and Applications*, 17(5), 604–617, 2012.

280. A. Kamerman and G. Aben. Throughput performance of wireless LANs operating at 2.4 and 5 GHz. Presented at 11th IEEE International Symposium on Personal, Indoor and Mobile Radio Communications (PIMRC), September 18–21, 2000, pp. 190–195.

281. E. Pelletta and H. Velayos. Performance measurements of the saturation throughput in IEEE 802.11 access points. Presented at Third International Symposium on Modeling and Optimization in Mobile, Ad Hoc, and Wireless Networks, 2005, pp. 129–138.

282. D. Lei, B. Yong, and C. Lan. Access point selection strategy for large-scale wireless local area networks. Presented at the IEEE Wireless Communications and Networking Conference (WCNC '07), March 11–15, 2007, pp. 2161–2166.

283. Y. Lee, K. Kim, and Y. Choi. Optimization of AP placement and channel assignment in wireless LANs. Presented at 27th Annual IEEE Conference on Local Computer Networks, November 6–8, 2002, pp. 831–836.

284. J. Choi and K. G. Shin. QoS provisioning for large-scale multi-ap WLANs. *Ad Hoc Networks*, 10(2), 174–185, 2012.

285. T. Clausen, P. Jacquet, and L. Viennot. Comparative study of routing protocols for mobile ad-hoc networks. *INRIA Research Report*, 5135, 1–25, 2004.

286. M. Greis. Ns-2 tutorial. Retrieved January 10, 2013, from http://www.isi.edu/nsnam/ns/tutorial/index.html.

287. *802.11ac: the fifth generation of Wi-Fi.* Technical White Paper. Retrieved August 29, 2013, from http://www.cisco.com/en/US/prod/collateral/wireless/ps5678/ps11983/white_paper_c11-713103.html.

288. N. Costagliola, P. López, F. Oliviero, and S. Romano. Energy- and delay-efficient routing in mobile ad hoc networks. *Mobile Networks and Applications*, 17(2), 281–297, 2012.

289. J. Chen, R. Boreli, and V. Sivaraman. Improving the efficiency of anonymous routing for MANETs. *Computer Communications*, 35(5), 619–627, 2012.

290. L. Hogie, P. Bouvry, and F. Guinand. An overview of MANETs simulation. *Electronic Notes in Theoretical Computer Science*, 150(1), 81–101, 2006.

291. R. S. Al-Qassas, M. Ould-Khaoua, and L. M. Mackenzie. Performance evaluation of a new end-to-end traffic-aware routing in MANETs. Presented at the 12th International Conference on Parallel and Distributed Systems (ICPADS '06) 2006, pp. 1–6.

292. E. Papapetrou, P. Vassiliadis, E. Rova, and A. Zarras. Cross-layer routing for peer database querying over mobile ad hoc networks. *Computer Networks*, 56(2), 504–520, 2012.

293. G. Hiertz, D. Denteneer, L. Stibor, Y. Zang, X. P. Costa, and B. Walke. The IEEE 802.11 universe. *IEEE Communications Magazine*, 48(1), 62–70, 2010.

294. P. Chevillat, J. Jelitto, A. N. Barreto, and H. L. Truong. A dynamic link adaptation algorithm for IEEE 802.11a wireless LANs. Presented at the IEEE International Conference on Communications (ICC '03), Anchorage, AK, May 11–15, 2003, pp. 1141–1145.

295. P. Chatzimisios, A. C. Boucouvalas, and V. Vitsas. Performance analysis of IEEE 802.11 DCF in presence of transmission errors. Presented at the IEEE International Conference on Communications (ICC '04), Paris, France, June 20–24, 2004, pp. 3854–3858.

296. ORiNOCO 11b client PC card specification. Retrieved August 29, 2013, from http://www.proxim.com/products/wifi.

297. HFA3861B—direct sequence spread spectrum baseband processor. Retrieved August 29, 2013, from http://www.datasheetdir.com/HFA3861B+Wireless.

298. W. Xiuchao. Simulate 802.11b channel within ns-2. Retrieved January 5, 2013, from http://www.comp.nus.edu.sg/~wuxiucha/research/reactive/report/80211ChannelinNS2_new.pdf.

299. N. I. Sarkar. Implementation of channel BER in ns-2.31. Retrieved April 10, 2013, from http://elena.aut.ac.nz/homepages/staff/Nurul-Sarkar/ns-2.

300. Z. Qian and Z. Ya-Qin. Cross-layer design for QoS support in multihop wireless networks. *Proceedings of the IEEE*, 96(1), 64–76, 2008.

301. J. Gordon. Pareto process as a model of self-similar packet traffic. Presented at the IEEE Global Telecommunications Conference (GLOBECOM '95), November 13–17, 1995, pp. 2232–2236.

302. W. E. Leland, M. S. Taqqu, W. Willinger, and D. V. Wilson. On the self-similar nature of Ethernet traffic (extended version). *IEEE/ACM Transactions on Networking*, 2(1), 1–15, 1994.

303. S. Floyd and V. Paxson. Wide area traffic: the failure of Poisson modeling. *IEEE/ACM Transactions on Networking*, 3(3), 226–244, 1995.

304. S.-G. Liu, P.-J. Wang, and L.-J. Qu. Modeling and simulation of self-similar data traffic. Presented at the 4th IEEE International Conference on Machine Learning and Cybernetics, Guangzhou, August 18–21, 2005, pp. 3921–3925.

305. B. C. Sowden and K. W. Sowerby. The impact of traffic type on the propagation dependent performance of a CDMA system. Presented at the IEEE International Conference on Communications (ICC '03), Anchorage, AK, May 11–15, 2003, pp. 377–381.

306. O. Tickoo and B. Sikdar. On the impact of IEEE 802.11 MAC on traffic characteristics. *IEEE Journal on Selected Areas in Communications*, 21(2), 189–203, 2003.

307. G. I. Ivascu, S. Pierre, and A. Quintero. QoS routing with traffic distribution in mobile ad hoc networks. *Computer Communications*, 32(2), 305–316, 2009.

308. T. Kuang and C. Williamson. Realmedia streaming performance on an IEEE 802.11b wireless LAN. Presented at the IASTED Wireless and Optical Communications, Banff, Alberta, Canada, June 27–29, 2001, pp. 306–311.

309. A. Mena and H. Heidemann. An empirical study of real audio traffic. Presented at the IEEE INFOCOM, Tel Aviv, Israel, March 26–30, 2000, pp. 101–110.

310. M. Shimakawa, D. P. Hole, and F. A. Tobagi. Video-conferencing and data traffic over an IEEE 802.11g WLAN using DCF and EDCA. Presented at the IEEE International Conference on Communications (ICC '05), Seoul, Korea, May 16–20, 2005, pp. 1324–1330.

311. D. Eckhardt and P. Steenkiste. Measurement and analysis of the error characteristics of an in-building wireless network. *Computer Communications Review*, 26(4), 243–254, 1996.

312. Netstumbler 0.4.0. Retrieved January 15, 2011, from www.netstumbler.com.

313. J. Alberola, I. H. Flindell, and A. J. Bullmore. Variability in road traffic noise levels. *Applied Acoustics*, 66(10), 1180–1195, 2005.

314. J. Hasty. Origins of extrinsic variability in eukaryotic gene expression. Presented at the Bio Micro and Nanosystems Conference (BMN '06), January 15–18, 2006, pp. 31–31.

315. N. Cranley and M. Davis. Performance evaluation of video streaming with background traffic over IEEE 802.11 WLAN networks. Presented at the 1st ACM Workshop on Wireless Multimedia Networking and Performance Modeling (WMuNeP '05), Montreal, Quebec, Canada, October 13, 2005, pp. 131–139.

316. Z. Haifeng, C. Guotai, and Y. Lun. Video transmission over IEEE 802.11n WLAN with adaptive aggregation scheme. Presented at the IEEE International Symposium on Broadband Multimedia Systems and Broadcasting (BMSB), March 24–26, 2010, pp. 1–5.

317. J. Winters. 802.11n throttles up WLAN throughput. *ComputerWorld New Zealand*, 2004, p. 20.

318. E. Perahia. IEEE 802.11n development: history, process, and technology. *IEEE Communications Magazine,* 46(7), 48–55, 2008.

319. D. T. C. Wong, M. R. Shajan, Y.-C. Liang, and F. P. S. A. Chin. Performance analysis of cooperative MAC in IEEE 802.11n for multiclass traffic. Presented at the IEEE 66th Vehicular Technology Conference (VTC '07—Fall), September 30–October 3, 2007, pp. 205–209.

320. E. Lo. An investigation of the impact of signal strength on Wi-Fi link throughput through propagation measurement. Master of Computer and Information Sciences (MCIS) thesis, School of Computing and Mathematical Sciences, Auckland University of Technology, Auckland, 2007.

321. R. Hutchins and E. W. Zegura. Measurements from a campus wireless network. Presented at the IEEE International Conference on Communications (ICC '02), New York, April 28–May 2, 2002, pp. 3161–3167.

322. Z. Peng, Z. Wenjun, and L. Chunwen. Joint design of source rate control and QoS-aware congestion control for video streaming over the Internet. *IEEE Transactions on Multimedia*, 9(2), 366–376, 2007.

323. F.-Y. Hung and I. Marsic. Analysis of non-saturation and saturation performance of IEEE 802.11 DCF in the presence of hidden stations. Presented at the IEEE 66th Vehicular Technology Conference (VTC '07—Fall), September 30–October 3, 2007, pp. 230–234.

324. F. D. Rango, J.-C. Cano, M. Fotino, C. Calafate, P. Manzoni, and S. Marano. OLSR vs DSR: a comparative analysis of proactive and reactive mechanisms from an energetic point of view in wireless ad hoc networks. *Computer Communications*, 31(16), 3843–3854, 2008.

325. A. Dana, A. Yadegari, M. Hajhosseini, and T. A. Mirfakhraie. A robust cross-layer design of clustering-based routing protocol for MANET. Presented at the 10th International Conference on Advanced Communication Technology (ICACT '08), February 17–20, 2008, pp. 1055–1059.

326. W. Tianlin and H. H. Refai. Network performance analysis on IEEE 802.11g with different protocols and signal to noise ratio values. Presented at the Second IFIP International Conference on Wireless and Optical Communications Networks (WOCN '05), March 6–8, 2005, pp. 29–33.

327. M. Collados and A. Gorokhov. Antenna selection for MIMO OFDM WLAN systems. *International Journal of Wireless Information Networks*, 12(4), 205–213, 2005.

328. IEEE 802.11ac. Retrieved May 23, 2013, from http://en.wikipedia.org/wiki/IEEE_802.11ac.

329. L. Ruetsch. What's the difference between IEEE 802.11ac and 802.11ad? Retrieved June 18, 2013, from http://mwrf.com/test-amp-measurement/what-s-difference-between-ieee-80211ac-and-80211ad.

330. D. Ngo. Wi-Fi to cultivate speedy 60GHz band. Retrieved June 18, 2013, from http://news.cnet.com/8301-17938_105-20004689-1.html?part=rss&subj=news&tag=2547-1_3-0-20/.

331. M. Amadeo, C. Campolo, and A. Molinaro. Enhancing IEEE 802.11p/WAVE to provide infotainment applications in VANETs. *Ad Hoc Networks*, 10(2), 253–269, 2012.

332. IEEE. Part 11: wireless LAN medium access control (MAC) and physical layer (PHY) specifications: amendment 6: wireless access in vehicular environments. IEEE 802.11p. New York: IEEE, 2010.

333. IEEE 802.11s: wireless LAN medium access control (MAC) and physical layer (PHY) specifications: simple efficient extensible mesh (SEE-Mesh) proposal. Retrieved August 29, 2013, from https://mentor.ieee.org/802.11/dcn/05/11-05-0562-00-000....

334. The OSI reference model. Retrieved May 10, 2013, from http://www.thecertificationhub.com/networkplus/the_osi_ref_model.htm.

335. G. R. Hiertz, Z. Yunpeng, S. Max, T. Junge, E. Weiss, and B. Wolz. IEEE 802.11s: WLAN mesh standardization and high performance extensions. *IEEE Network*, 22(3), 12–19, 2008.

336. G. R. Hiertz, D. Denteneer, S. Max, R. Taori, J. Cardona, L. Berlemann, and B. Walke. IEEE 802.11s: the WLAN mesh standard. *IEEE Wireless Communications*, 17(1), 104–111, 2010.

337. Z. Li, F. R. Yu, and M. Huang. A distributed consensus-based cooperative spectrum sensing in cognitive radios. *IEEE Transactions on Vehicular Technology*, 59(1), 383–393, 2010.

338. I. F. Akyildiz, W.-Y. Lee, M. C. Vuran, and S. Mohanty. Next generation/dynamic spectrum access cognitive radio wireless networks: a survey. *Computer Networks*, 50(13), 2127–2159, 2006.

339. IEEE 802.22 spectrum sensing and cognitive network. Retrieved June 8, 2013, from http://www.radio-electronics.com/info/wireless/ieee-802-22/cognitive-network-spectrum-sensing.php.

340. X. Wang, A. Vasilakos, M. Chen, Y. Liu, and T. Kwon. A survey of green mobile networks: opportunities and challenges. *Mobile Networks and Applications*, 17(1), 4–20, 2012.

341. Y. Liu, S. Xie, Y. Zhang, R. Yu, and V. Leung. Energy-efficient spectrum discovery for cognitive radio green networks. *Mobile Networks and Applications*, 17(1), 64–74, 2012.

342. M. Chen, A. Vasilakos, and D. Grace. Advances in green mobile networks. *Mobile Networks and Applications*, 17(1), 1–3, 2012.

343. Z. Hasan, H. Boostanimehr, and V. K. Bhargava. Green cellular networks: a survey, some research issues and challenges. *IEEE Communications Surveys and Tutorials*, 13(4), 2011.

344. Anonymous. Deploying Wi-Fi protected access (WPA) and WPA2 in the enterprise. March 2005. Retrieved August 15, 2005, from http://www.wi-fi. org/membersonly/getfile.asp?f=WFA_02_27_05_WPA_WPA2_White_ Paper.pdf.

345. IEEE 802.11-2007: wireless LAN medium access control (MAC) and physical layer (PHY) specifications. Retrieved June 6, 2013, from http://standards. ieee.org/about/get/802/802.11.html.

346. IEEE 802.11i-2004: amendment 6: medium access control (MAC) security enhancements (pdf). Retrieved June 6, 2013, from http://standards.ieee.org/ getieee802/download/802.11i-2004.pdf.

347. F. R. Yu, X. Zhang, and V. C. M. Leung. *Green communications and networking*. Boca Raton, FL: CRC Press, 2012.

348. Y. Du, H. Li, W. Lin, L. Liu, X. Wang, S. Khan, and S. Wu. A new cooperative spectrum sensing scheme for cognitive ad-hoc networks. *Mobile Networks and Applications*, 17(6), 746–757, 2012.

349. C. Passiatore, P. Camarda, C. Sacchi, B. Bellalta, A. Vinel, C. Schlegel, F. Granelli, and Y. Zhang. A MAC protocol for cognitive radio wireless ad hoc networks. In *Multiple access communications*. Vol. 6886, Lecture Notes in Computer Science. Berlin: Springer, 2011, pp. 1–12.

350. W. J. Garrison. NETWORK II.5, LANNET II.5 and COMNET II.5. Presented at 1991 Winter Simulation Conference, Phoenix, AZ, December 8–11, 1991, pp. 72–76.

351. C. McDonald. The CNET network simulator (v2.0.9). Retrieved February 10, 2012, from www.csse.uwa.edu.au/cnet/.

352. X. Zeng, R. Bagrodia, and M. Gerla. GloMoSim: a library for parallel simulation of large-scale wireless networks. Presented at the 12th Workshop on Parallel and Distributed Simulation (PADS '98), Banff, Alberta, Canada, May 26–29, 1998, pp. 154–161.

353. CMU Monarch Project. Retrieved February 10, 2012, from http://www. monarch.cs.cmu.edu.

354. L. Breslau, D. Estrin, K. Fall, S. Floyd, J. Heimann, A. Helmy, P. Huang, S. McCanne, K. Varadhan, Y. Xu, and H. Yu. Advances in network simulation. *Computer*, 33(5), pp. 59–67, 2000.

355. P. L'Ecuyer. Software for uniform random number generation: distinguishing the good and the bad. Presented at the 2001 Winter Simulation Conference, Arlington, VA, December 9–12, 2001, pp. 95–105.

356. S. K. Park and R. W. Miller. Random number generators: good ones are hard to find. *Communications of the ACM*, 31(10), 1192–1201, 1988.

357. P. L'Ecuyer, S. Richard, E. J. Chen, and W. D. Kelton. An object-oriented random number package with many long streams and substreams. *Operations Research*, 1(1), 2001.

358. M. Matsumoto and T. Nishimura. Mersenne Twister: A623-dimensionally equidistributed uniform pseudorandom number generator. *ACM Transactions on Modeling and Computer Simulation*, 7(1), 3–30, 1999.

359. B. Hechenleitner and K. Entacher. On shortcomings of the ns-2 random number generator. In *Communication networks and distributed systems modeling and simulation*, ed. T. Znati and B. McDonald. Vista, CA: Society for Modeling and Simulation International, 2002, pp. 71–77.

360. N. I. Sarkar and R. McHaney. Modeling and simulation of IEEE 802.11 WLANs: a case study of a network simulator. Presented at 2006 Information Resources Management Association International Conference, Washington, DC, May 21–24, 2006, pp. 715–718.

361. A. Hegedus, G. M. Maggio, and L. Kocarev. A ns-2 simulator utilizing chaotic maps for network-on-chip traffic analysis. Presented at the IEEE International Conference on Circuits and Systems (ISCAS '05), May 23–26, 2005, pp. 3375–3378.

362. M. Wellens, M. Petrova, J. Riihijarvi, and P. Mahonen. Building a better wireless mousetrap: need for more realism in simulations. Presented at the Second Annual Conference on Wireless On-Demand Network Systems and Services (WONS '05), January 19–21, 2005, pp. 150–157.

363. J. M. Seppälä, T. Bräysy, and P. Lilja. Simulating devices with adaptive antenna arrays using OPNET integrated with MATLAB. Presented at the 4th ACM Workshop on Performance Monitoring and Measurement of Heterogeneous Wireless and Wired Networks, Tenerife, Canary Islands, Spain, April 15, 2009, pp. 159–166.

364. K. Salah and A. Alkhoraidly. An OPNET based simulation approach for deploying VoIP. *International Journal of Network Management*, 16(3), 159–183, 2006.

365. P. P. Garrido, M. P. Malumbres, and C. T. Calafate. ns-2 vs. OPNET: a comparative study of the IEEE 802.11 e technology on MANET environments. Presented at the 1st International Conference on Simulation Tools and Techniques for Communications, Networks and Systems and Workshops, Marseille, France, 2008, pp. 1–10.

366. J. Fitzgerald and A. Dennis. *Business data communications and networking*. 9th ed. New York: John Wiley & Sons, 2007.

367. S. Khan, S. A. Mahmud, K. K. Loo, and H. S. Al-Raweshidy. A cross-layer rate adaptation solution for IEEE 802.11 networks. *Computer Communications*, 31(8), 1638–1652, 2008.

368. Y. Zhang, J. Luo, and H. Hu. *Wireless mesh networking*. Boston: Auerbach Publications, 2006.

Appendix A: Network Simulator 2 (Ns-2)

NS-2 SIMULATION ENVIRONMENT

While various simulators exist for building a variety of WLAN models [34, 350–352], ns-2 is one of the most widely used simulators today. Ns-2 is an object-oriented discrete-event network simulator originally developed at Lawrence Berkeley Laboratory at the University of California, Berkeley, as part of the Virtual InterNetwork Testbed (VINT) project. Berkeley released the initial code that made WLAN simulation possible in ns-2. The Monarch project at Carnegie Mellon University has extended the ns-2 with support for node mobility, a realistic physical (PHY) layer model, and an implementation of distributed coordination function (DCF) [353].

Ns-2 is an open-source software package and has improved significantly over time through various contributions made by network researchers worldwide. It has three substantial changes from ns version 1: (1) the more complex objects in ns v1 have been decomposed into simpler components for greater flexibility, (2) the configuration interface is now an object-oriented version of TCL (OTCL), and (3) the interface code to the OTCL interpreter is separate from the main simulator [272].

STRENGTHS AND WEAKNESSES

Ns-2 is available for download on a variety of operating systems at no cost, including Red Hat Linux, FreeBSD, and MS Windows XP. Another strength of ns-2 is that many network researchers are contributing toward further extension of ns-2 since it is an open-source software package [33]. Authors of research papers often publish ns-2 code that they used, allowing other researchers to build upon their work using the original code. This is particularly useful to academia, specifically master's and doctoral students who are looking for a tool for network modeling and performance comparison.

Ns-2 has a rich library of network and protocol objects, including nodes, links, and queues. In ns-2, there are two class hierarchies, namely, the compiled C++ hierarchy and interpreted OTCL, with one-to-one correspondence between them. The compiled C++ hierarchy provides a greater efficiency in simulation runs in terms of faster simulation execution, which is particularly useful for detailed analysis of a network protocol's behavior.

Ns-2 is a multiprotocol simulator that supports a wide range of network protocols, including unicast and multicast routing algorithms, network and transport layer protocols, transmission control protocol (TCP) congestion control, router queuing policies, reservation and integrated services, and application layer protocols such as Hypertext Transfer Protocol (HTTP) [272]. In addition, ns-2 incorporates a range of link layer protocols and scheduling algorithms, including wireless and mobile networks [354]. Ns-2's in-built network animation tool allows graphical display of links, packet streams, network node positions, and movement that is very useful for debugging and testing network models. Ns-2 also supports several traffic generators, including Poisson, Pareto, exponential, constant bit rate (CBR), and hyperexponential.

In stochastic discrete-event simulation, the pseudorandom number generators (PRNGs) are used in generating various random variables, including traffic generators, random movement of wireless nodes, and link error models. Therefore, it is important for network researchers to select a network simulator that has a good PRNG. However, ns-2 (versions 2.1b9 and later) implements a combined multiple recursive generator (MRG32k3a) proposed by L'Ecuyer [355], which is one of the well-established generators that has been tested thoroughly for its robustness. This generator replaces the previous implementation of PRNG, which was a rather weak generator based on the minimal standard multiplicative linear congruential generator of Park and Miller [356]. More details about PRNGs and their strengths and weaknesses can be found in the computer simulation and modeling literature [269, 270, 355–359].

The implementation of MRG32k3a in ns-2 provides 1.8×10^{19} independent streams of random numbers, each of which consists of 2.3×10^{15} substreams, and each substream has a period (i.e., the number of random numbers before overlap) of 7.6×10^{22}, with a total period for the entire generator of 3.1×10^{57}. With these features of PRNG, ns-2 can produce acceptable (unbiased) results, and consequently users of ns-2 do not need to worry about the credibility of their simulation results as long as they use valid simulation models. The source code for ns-2 PRNG can be found in the ns-2 package under tools/rng.h and tools/rng.cc [272].

In spite of possessing strengths, ns-2 has several limitations. First, it does not provide any support for creating sophisticated graphical presentations of simulation output data. The raw data must be processed using scripting languages such as awk or perl to produce data in a suitable format for tools like Xgraph or Gnuplot [272, 360]. Another disadvantage of ns-2 is that it is not a user-friendly package because of its text-based interface, and many student researchers point out that ns-2 has a steep learning curve. A tutorial contributed by Marc Greis [286] and the continuing evolution of ns documentation have improved the situation, but ns-2's split-programming model remains a barrier to many developers. Ns-2 does not support simulation of co-channel interference, which is one of the major limitations of ns-2's WLAN simulation engine. These limitations of ns-2 are also highlighted by leading network simulation researchers [361, 362].

TABLE A.1   Radio Propagation Models in Ns-2

Model	Formula	Description
Free space	$$P_r(d) = \frac{P_t G_t G_r^2}{(4\pi)^2 d^2 L}$$	$P_r(d)$ is the received signal power at distance d and Pt is the transmitted signal power. Gt and Gr are the antenna gains of the transmitter and receiver, respectively. L $(L \geq 1)$ is the system loss factor, and λ is the wavelength. It is common to select $Gt = Gr = 1$ and $L = 1$ in ns-2 simulation.
Two-ray ground	$$P_r(d) = \frac{P_t G_t G_r h_t^2 h_r^2}{(4\pi)^2 d^2 L}$$	h_t and h_r are the heights of the transmit and receive antennas, respectively.
Shadowing	(i) The path loss model: $$\left.\frac{\overline{P_r(d)}}{P_r(d_0)}\right|_{dB} = -10\beta \log \frac{d}{d_0}$$ (ii) The overall shadowing model: $$\left.\frac{P_r(d)}{P_r(d_0)}\right|_{dB} = -10\beta \log \frac{d}{d_0} + X_{dB}$$	β is called the path loss exponent and is usually empirically determined by field measurement. $\beta = 2$ for free-space propagation. X_{dB} is a Gaussian random variable with zero mean and standard deviation σdB. σdB is shadowing deviation and can be obtained by measurement.

RADIO PROPAGATION AND ERROR MODELS IN NS-2

Table A.1 lists the three propagation models with their brief description. The source code for free-space, two-ray ground, and shadowing models can be found in the ns-2 simulation package in ~ns/propagation, ~ns/tworayground, and ~ns/shadowing, respectively.

Appendix B: OPNET Modeler

OPNET is an object-oriented, discrete-event, and general purpose network simulator. It provides a comprehensive modeling library for simulating and analyzing network performance [34]. Moreover, it has distinct functions for creating a network environment, such as comprehensive library of network protocols, a graphic user interface (GUI) analysis tool, OPNET Modeler, modifiable source codes, graphical results, and autogenerated statistical results [363]. By its typical functions, OPNET is one of the widely used simulation tools in network design, testing, and performance evaluation.

OPNET has gained considerable popularity in both academia and industry by providing a number of sample network models that are commercially available network components [364]. Interestingly, one major reason for the wide use of OPNET is that it provides more than just basic features to academic institutions free of charge. Thus, OPNET is the preferred tool in the academic arena [364].

OPNET requires high specifications for PC and consumes a large amount of memory [365]. OPNET provides four hierarchical editors (Network, Node, Process, and Parameter) that allow the development of a network model in detail. A model developed at one layer can be used by another model at a higher layer, and a detailed setting can be added at each editor's stage. Consequently, these hierarchical editors play a significant role in the modeling and later operations of the network. In addition, OPNET provides open interfaces to the C language, so the user can easily modify operation rules or add his or her own restrictions by using the Probe editor. Therefore, the user can collect numerical results and capture every single moment of the simulation process. Interestingly, data can be collected as both animation type and graphical type by its analysis tool, which makes the data analysis easier [350]. The main advantages of using OPNET are its (1) simulation of real-life network scenarios by using commercially available network components, (2) reusable and modifying network scenarios, and (3) facilities to insert real-time data from other compatible software.

Appendix C: The IEEE 802.11 Standard

IEEE 802.11 STANDARDS FAMILY

TABLE C.1   Relative Advantages and Disadvantages of 802.11 Technologies

Standard	Year	Comments
802.11	Ratified 1997	Too slow for most applications and therefore 802.11 products are no longer manufactured
802.11b	Ratified 1999	Low cost; low throughput; signal range is good and not easily obstructed; home appliances may interfere on the unregulated frequency band
802.11a	Ratified 1999	High speed; high cost; regulated frequencies prevent signal interference from other devices; shorter-range signal that is more easily obstructed
802.11g	Ratified 2003	High speed; costs more than 802.11b; signal range is good and not easily obstructed; backward compatible; appliances may interfere on the unregulated signal frequency
802.11i	Ratified 2004	Security improvements for the 802.11 family
802.11e	Ratified 2005	Quality of service (QoS) support; voice over wireless Internet Protocol (IP) and streaming multimedia
802.11n	Ratified 2009	Boost data rate using multiple-input multiple-output (MIMO) technology and medium access control (MAC) layer frame aggregation; more resistant to signal interference from outside sources
802.11p	Ratified 2010	Wireless access in vehicular environments (WAVE)
802.11u	Ratified 2011	New standard for interworking with external networks that support emergency traffic over infrastructure-based wireless local area networks (WLANs)
802.11s	Not yet ratified	Wireless mesh networks

IEEE 802.11 FRAME AND OVERHEAD

Table C.2 shows the frame structure and overhead-related parameters of 802.11.

TABLE C.2   Comparison of 802.11 and 802.3 Frame and Header Parameters

Parameter	802.11a (54 Mbps)	802.11g (54 Mbps)	802.11b (11 Mbps)	802.3 (Ethernet LAN)
DIFS	34 μs	28 μs	50 μs	IFS 9.6 μs
SIFS	16 μs	10 μs	10 μs	Not applicable
Slot time	9 μs	9 μs	20 μs	51.2 μs
Preamble and PHY header	20 μs	20 μs	Short: 96 μs Long: 192 μs	6.4 μs
MAC header and CRC	34 bytes	34 bytes	34 bytes	18 bytes
Payload data	46–1,500 bytes	46–1,500 bytes	46–1,500 bytes	46–1,500 bytes
MAC overhead per ACK	14 bytes	14 bytes	14 bytes	Not applicable

Source: IEEE, *IEEE Standard for Wireless LAN: Medium Access Control (MAC) and Physical Layer (PHY) Specifications*, IEEE 802.11 WG, New York: IEEE, 1997; IEEE, *Part II: Wireless LAN Medium Access Control (MAC) and Physical Layer (PHY) Specifications: High-Speed Physical Layer Extension in the 2.4 GHz Band*, IEEE 802.11b WG, New York: IEEE, 1999; IEEE, *Part II: Wireless LAN Medium Access Control (MAC) and Physical Layer (PHY) Specifications: High-Speed Physical Layer in the 5 GHz Band*, IEEE 802.11a WG/D5.0, New York: IEEE, 1999; IEEE, *Amendment to IEEE Std 802.11, as Amended by IEEE Stds 802.11a-1999, 802.11b-1999, 802.11b-1999/Cor 1-2001, and 802.11d-2001*, IEEE 802.11g WG, New York: IEEE, 2003.

Note: DIFS = distributed coordination function (DCF) interframe space; SIFS = short interframe space; PHY = physical layer; MAC = medium access control; CRC = cyclic redundancy check; ACK = acknowledgment.

IEEE 802.11 AND HYPERLAN2

Table C.3 gives a brief overview of 802.11 and hyperLAN2 in terms of frequency range, air access scheme, and data rate.

TABLE C.3 Comparison of 802.11 and HyperLAN2

Technology	Frequency Range	Air Access Scheme	Data Rate (Mbps)
802.11	2.4 GHz	FHSS, DSSS, Infrared (Ir)	1, 2
802.11a	5.15–5.25 GHz (50 mW) 5.25–5.35 GHz (250 mW) 5.725 to 5.825 GHz (1W)	OFDM	6, 9, 12, 18, 24, 36, 48, 54
802.11b	2.4–2.4835 GHz	DSSS using CCK	1, 2, 5.5, 11
802.11g	2.4–2.4835 GHz	CCK and OFDM	6, 9, 12, 18, 24, 36, 48, 54
HyperLAN2	5.15–5.35 GHz 5.470–5.725 GHz	OFDM	6, 9, 12, 18, 24, 36, 48, 54

Source: IEEE, *IEEE Standard for Wireless LAN: Medium Access Control (MAC) and Physical Layer (PHY) Specifications*, IEEE 802.11 WG, New York: IEEE, 1997; IEEE, *Part II: Wireless LAN Medium Access Control (MAC) and Physical Layer (PHY) Specifications: High-Speed Physical Layer Extension in the 2.4 GHz Band*, IEEE 802.11b WG, New York: IEEE, 1999; IEEE, *Part II: Wireless LAN Medium Access Control (MAC) and Physical Layer (PHY) Specifications: High-Speed Physical Layer in the 5 GHz Band*, IEEE 802.11a WG/D5.0, New York: IEEE, 1999; IEEE, *Amendment to IEEE Std 802.11, as Amended by IEEE Stds 802.11a-1999, 802.11b-1999, 802.11b-1999/Cor 1-2001, and 802.11d-2001*, IEEE 802.11g WG, New York: IEEE, 2003.

Note: FHSS = frequency-hopping spread spectrum; DSSS = direct sequence spread spectrum; Ir = infrared; OFDM = orthogonal frequency division multiplexing; CCK = complementary code keying.

RELATIONSHIP BETWEEN RECEIVER SENSITIVITY AND THROUGHPUT

Table C.4 shows receiver sensitivity, data rate, and estimated throughput of 802.11b and 802.11g. The receiver sensitivity and data rate are shown in columns 2 and 3, respectively. These figures are from D-Link wireless card specifications [245].

The throughputs of 802.11b and 802.11g under the low load and normal conditions are 3 Mbps (27.3% of 11 Mbps) and 11 Mbps (20.4% of 54 Mbps), respectively [253, 366]. The actual throughput, as indicated in column 4, is computed as follows:

$$\text{Throughput of 802.11b} = \text{Data rate} \times 27.3\% \qquad (C.1)$$

$$\text{Throughput of 802.11g} = \text{Data rate} \times 20.4\% \qquad (C.2)$$

TABLE C.4   Data Rate and Estimated Throughput for Different Receiver Sensitivity

Technology	Receiver Sensitivity (dBm)	Data Rate (Mbps)	Actual Throughput (Mbps)
802.11b	−82	11	3.0
802.11b	−87	2	0.5
802.11g	−88	6	1.2
802.11g	−86	9	1.8
802.11g	−84	12	2.5
802.11g	−82	18	3.7
802.11g	−78	24	4.9
802.11g	−74	36	7.3
802.11g	−69	48	9.8
802.11g	−66	54	11.0

Source: D-Link Wireless USB Adapter (802.11g) DWL-G132, retrieved April 10, 2013, from http://www.dlink.com/products/.

DATA RATE VERSUS TRANSMISSION RANGES OF 802.11B

TABLE C.5   Data Rate versus Transmission Ranges According to Path Loss Models

Transmission Range	1 Mbps	2 Mbps	5.5 Mbps	11 Mbps
Receiver sensitivity for 10^{-5} BER (transmit power: 15 dBm)	−93 dBm	−90 dBm	−87 dBm	−84 dBm
Open plan building (range factor per dB: 1.110)	485 m	354 m	259 m	189 m
Semiopen office (range factor per dB: 1.072)	105 m	85 m	69 m	56 m
Closed office (range factor per dB: 1.053)	46 m	40 m	34 m	29 m

Source: A. R. Prasad et al., *Wireless Personal Communications*, 19, 57–79, 2001.
Note: BER = bit error rate.

ORINOCO 802.11B CARD SPECIFICATION

TABLE C.6   Orinoco 802.11b Card Specification

	BPSK	QPSK	CCK5.5	CCK11
Receiver sensitivity	−94 dBm	−91 dBm	−87 dBm	−82 dBm
Range—open (m)	550	400	270	160
Range—semiopen (m)	115	90	70	50
Range—closed (m)	50	40	35	25
Transmit power	15 dBm or 32 mW			
Frequency	2.472 GHz			

Source: Proxim, http://www.proxim.com/products/wifi.

INTERSIL HFA3861B DATA SHEET: BER, SNR, AND MODULATION

TABLE C.7   Intersil HFA3861B: Relationship between BER, SNR, and Modulation

SNR (dB)	BPSK (1 Mbps)	QPSK (2 Mbps)	CCK5.5 (5.5 Mbps)	CCK11 (11 Mbps)
5	5×10^{-2}	6×10^{-2}	4×10^{-2}	1.2×10^{-2}
6	5×10^{-2}	6×10^{-2}	1.3×10^{-2}	6×10^{-3}
7	1.2×10^{-2}	1.7×10^{-2}	4.1×10^{-3}	2×10^{-3}
8	4.1×10^{-3}	6×10^{-3}	1.3×10^{-3}	7×10^{-4}
9	1.1×10^{-3}	1.7×10^{-3}	3.3×10^{-4}	2.5×10^{-4}
10	2.2×10^{-4}	4×10^{-4}	8×10^{-5}	8×10^{-5}
11	4×10^{-5}	6.3×10^{-5}	1.5×10^{-5}	2.7×10^{-5}
12	2.9×10^{-6}	8.9×10^{-6}	2.7×10^{-6}	8×10^{-6}
13	3.6×10^{-7}	1.3×10^{-6}	5×10^{-7}	1.9×10^{-6}
14	4×10^{-8}	2.7×10^{-7}	5×10^{-8}	3.9×10^{-7}
15	3×10^{-9}	4×10^{-8}	1×10^{-8}	1.02×10^{-7}
16	1.8×10^{-10}	4×10^{-9}	1.1×10^{-9}	3×10^{-8}
17	1.8×10^{-10}	4×10^{-9}	1.1×10^{-9}	4×10^{-9}

Source: http://www.datasheetdir.com/HFA3861B+Wirelen.
Note: BER = bit error rate; SNR = signal-to-noise ratio.

Appendix D: Additional Results for Chapter 12

The simulation results presented in this appendix are obtained with $N = 10$ stations, packet length of 1,500 bytes, Pareto arrivals, and the shadowing propagation model (Figures D.1–D.7). (Note: BER = bit error rate; WLAN = wireless local area network; TCP = Transmission Control Protocol; DCF = distributed coordination function; RTS–CTS = request to send–clear to send; MDT = mean deviation of throughput; CLD = cross-layer design.

IMPACT OF NS-2.31 CHANNEL BER ON WLAN PERFORMANCE

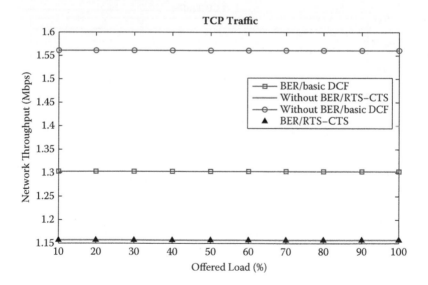

FIGURE D.1   Network throughput versus load for TCP traffic.

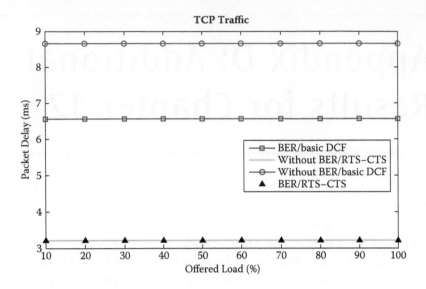

FIGURE D.2   Network packet delay versus load for TCP traffic.

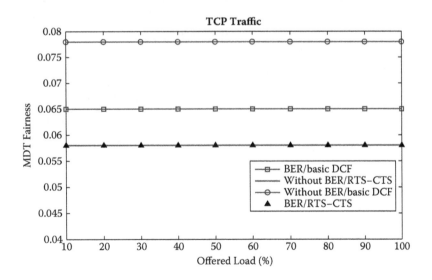

FIGURE D.3   MDT fairness versus load for TCP traffic.

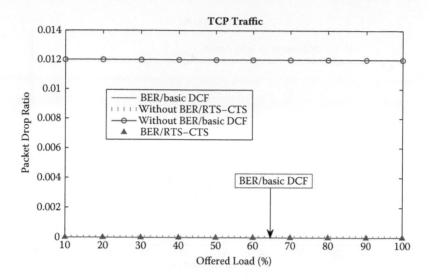

FIGURE D.4   Network packet drop ratio versus load for TCP traffic.

CROSS-LAYER WLAN DESIGN

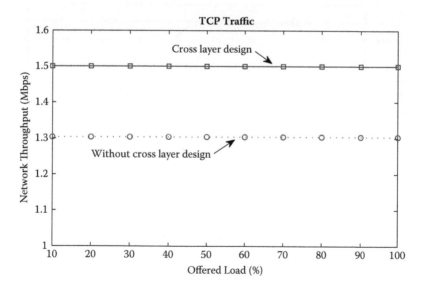

FIGURE D.5   Network throughput with and without CLD for TCP traffic.

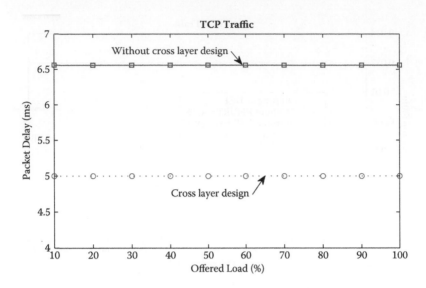

FIGURE D.6 Network packet delay with and without CLD for TCP traffic.

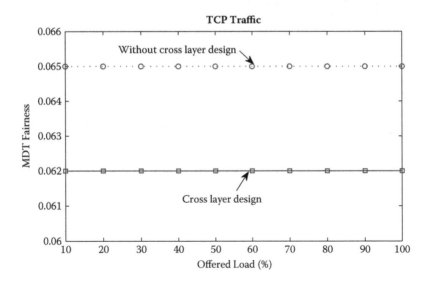

FIGURE D.7 MDT fairness with and without CLD for TCP traffic.

Index

Printed and bound by CPI Group (UK) Ltd, Croydon, CR0 4YY

23/10/2024

01777693-0010